Eunice C
#94 Corey Colonial
Agawam Mass
01001
# 7868686

Eunice C
#94 Corey Colonial
Agawam Mass

# THE WHOLE LAY MINISTRY CATALOG

# THE WHOLE
# LAY MINISTRY CATALOG

## Barbara Kuhn

A Crossroad Book
THE SEABURY PRESS · NEW YORK

1979
The Seabury Press
815 Second Avenue
New York, N.Y.  10017

Printed in the United States of America


Library of Congress Cataloging in Publication Data

Kuhn, Barbara, 1937-
    The whole lay ministry catalog.

    "A Crossroad book."
    1.  Lay ministry.  I.  Title.
BV677.K83              253          78-13046
ISBN 0-8164-2187-0

To Harry Griffith,
whose encouragement, counsel, and
assistance will always be remembered

# Contents

# Why This Book Was Written

Readers are entitled to know why a book was written, for whom it was written, and by whom it was written. Therefore I would like to take this opportunity to explain how this work came about and how I came to write it. Because of the increasing awareness of the importance of lay ministry, the Episcopal Diocese of Central Florida first commissioned me to prepare a book that would do the following:

1. Aid in an understanding of the laity's role in the ministry of the church.

2. Assist people in discovering their unique spiritual gifts and natural talents.

3. Help people discover their "calling" to particular ministries.

4. Offer scripturally sound descriptions, guidelines, training helps, and practical suggestions for implementing lay ministries of various kinds.

5. Provide resources and other aids in evaluating, improving, and expanding the laity's involvement in the work of Christ's Kingdom on earth.

This book - based on the first work - is an attempt to meet these objectives, and it is offered to clergy and laity alike - for any ministry of the church or the community, to be effective, must be acknowledged and shared by those both ordained and nonordained.

Much of this work came as an outgrowth of my involvement as teacher, counselor, consultant, and lay leader in my own parish and community. Although most of this book reflects personal experience, I cannot say that I have actively participated in all the ministries described; I have, however, researched them, observed them, and interviewed those who have been involved in them. It is my prayer that this book will offer a comprehensive and practical guide to fulfilling Christ's command to follow his example of loving service. Perhaps the most important reason it had to be written is expressed by Jesus in the second verse of Luke 10: "The harvest truly is great, but the laborers are few . . . . "

Barbara Kuhn

# Preface

> I am the vine, ye are the branches.  He
> that abideth in me and I in him, the same
> bringeth forth much fruit; for without me
> ye can do nothing . . . .Herein is my Fa-
> ther glorified that ye bear much fruit; so
> shall ye be my disciples (John 15:5,8).

In Jesus' beautiful analogy of the vine and the branches, he reminds us of several things.  First, that we can accomplish nothing
apart from him.  Just as a branch can bear no fruit if it is cut off
from the life-source of the vine, so Christians can produce no fruits
of spiritual good works without complete dependence upon Jesus Christ.
Second, the illustration clearly demonstrates that being fruitful is
expected.  Dead branches are cut off and cast away.  Conversely, the
fruitful branches become a source of delight to the Father, who is
the husbandman or gardener.  Third, we learn that fruitfulness will
be rewarded, that the Father will be glorified by fruit-bearing, and
that fruitfulness is the sign of being a true disciple.

While all Christians may agree with the truths expressed in this
illustration, not all Christians know how to go about becoming the
fruit-bearers they should be.  This book is offered as an aid in understanding the various lay ministries available to Christians of all
walks of life and as an aid in finding the particular ministries to
which individuals are called.  It is dedicated to all Christian laypersons with the hope that they will "go forth and bear much fruit."

Sincere appreciation is expressed to the Episcopal Diocese of
Central Florida who commissioned the writing of this work, to Harry
Griffith who gave support and editorial assistance, and to the Ad Hoc
Committee on Lay Ministry which provided assistance and encouragement.
Unless otherwise specified, all Scripture quotations are from the
King James Version of the Bible.

# 1 · Lay Ministry Defined and Refined

### What?

Lay ministry means different things to different people.  It is
a paradox, being at the same time both a simple and a complex term.
While it is generally understood that a layperson is any nonordained
person, and the word ministry refers to offering help or aid, nevertheless, there is still confusion as to the breadth and scope of a
lay minister's role.  In some churches the layperson's duties may be
limited to specified, selected, and traditional church functions such
as singing in the choir or teaching a church school class.  In other
churches, lay people assist with duties requiring more specialized
training and responsibility such as hospital calling, evangelism, and
counseling.  Although the role may vary from church to church, the
intent is the same universally:  lay ministers are people in the body
of Christ following the scriptural admonition to "serve one another"
(Gal. 5:13).

### Why?

The reason for having the laity share responsibilities of ministry with the clergy is obvious.  One minister alone, even if assisted
by deacons or other clergy, simply cannot be all things to all people.
There are not enough hours in a day or enough physical and spiritual
energies in one body for a single minister to meet the total demands
of an entire congregation.  A more important reason is that it is
scriptural.  When Moses was attempting to do his job alone, the Lord
sent his father-in-law to counsel him otherwise, saying, "It is not
good.  You will surely wear away.  You are not able to perform alone.
Provide out of the people able men such as fear God to help you"
(Ex. 18:17-23).

The New Testament teaching on "body ministry" (I Cor. 12) likewise exhorts the entire congregation to share in ministering one to
another.  Christianity was never meant to be a passive religion with
its adherents sitting by, watching a selected few do all the Kingdom's
work.  The book of Acts describes the first-century church as a bee-
hive of activity where everyone was involved in praying, sharing,
loving, teaching, and giving.  The Great Commission of Matthew 28:19
admonishes Christ's followers to "go . . . make disciples . . . teach
. . . baptize" (action words).  If each Christian would seek and find
his or her individual calling and then faithfully perform that ministry, there would be fewer overworked clergy and more vibrant and effective churches!

## Who?

Many Christians believe that only clergy, missionaries, and a few, select laypersons receive a "call" to serve God. The fact is that everyone has a place of ministry. Those who argue that they have no talent or that they are unskilled or that they are inadequate in one or more ways have only to look to Moses as an example. Moses used every excuse he could think of to escape his calling. He thought he had a good out when he reminded God that he was slow of speech and would, therefore, make a poor speaker or leader. To Moses, God replied, "Who made man's mouth?" It was a reminder that God promises to equip his servants for whatever calling he gives them. Often, the more inadequate and incapable people feel, the more likely they will be usable, for they will depend upon God's ability, not their own. The Lord frequently uses unlikely prospects in his service, so that no one can say a servant did anything through human strength. All the glory goes to the Lord. I Corinthians 1:26-27 says it this way: "You see your calling, brethren, how that not many mighty, not many noble are called. But God chooses the foolish things of the world to confound the wise, and God chooses the weak to confound the mighty."

When the Scriptures tell us that many are called but few are chosen, it becomes evident that we can remove ourselves from being chosen if we do not respond to the call when it is given. There are numerous biblical examples of simple, uneducated, and seemingly inadequate people being used in mighty ways when they gave the proper responses. When God called a humble peasant girl named Mary to be the mother of the Saviour, she responded, "Be it unto me according to thy word." When the call came to a little lad named Samuel, the response was, "Thy servant heareth." Fishermen dropped their nets to follow Jesus' call; a tax collector quit his job to answer the call. Shepherds said, "Let us go!" St. Paul said, "What will you have me to do?" And Isaiah said, "Here am I. Send me." The Lord has not stopped issuing calls. In his infinite wisdom, he has set apart a place of service for each of his children. Some are called to visible ministries, recognized and applauded by many; others are called to unseen, unlauded ministries known only to God; all are called to be available to perform the ministry that is tailor-made for the individual: "God has called us with an holy calling, not according to our works, but according to his own purpose and grace, which was given us in Christ Jesus before the world began" (II Tim. 1:9).

## Where?

For some people there is a distinct division between their spiritual life (which includes church attendance and performing religious duties) and their secular life (which includes home life, work, recreation, and social relationships). Such a distinction should not exist. Jesus was the same wherever he was - whether he was reading the Scriptures in the synagogue, enjoying the party at the wedding in Cana, healing the sick, or relaxing at the home of his friends in Bethany. With his life as our example, we must, likewise, consider our ministry as a way of life, an attitude that should pervade every action in every life situation. Although the church is the first place that comes to mind as the logical locality for Christian ministry, it is by no means the only place for service. Jesus took great care to explain to his followers that whenever and wherever they fed the hungry, clothed the naked, visited the sick, showed hospitality to a stranger, or counseled those in prison, they were, in reality, ministering to him: "Inasmuch as ye have done it unto the least of these, ye have done it unto me" (Matt. 25:40). One who takes such an attitude will find that life takes on new meaning. Whether it is a mother preparing meals and ironing shirts, a business-man closing a deal, students preparing themselves for their life's work, a consumer dealing with an unpleasant store clerk, or anyone else in any sort of life activity, there is a choice - either seeing the activity as a dutiful chore that must be reluctantly contended with, or seeing it as an opportunity to minister love to others in the name of Jesus. The first step in all forms of ministry is be-ginning with the premise that Christians exist in the world to be like Jesus, One who came not to be ministered unto, but to minister. If all Christians adopted such an attitude, think of the changes that could occur in homes, schools, businesses, communities, govern-ments, and the world!

### How?

Once a Christian is convinced that God does, after all, have a special calling for him or her beyond the basic attitude of seeing each life activity as a form of ministry, what then? How does one go about discovering one's particular gifts and ministries? Does one wait for an angel to appear or expect to hear God's call from a burning bush? Such would be the exception, not the rule. There are some practical steps that can be taken in seeking to find God's will in an individual's life. First, read and understand what the Scrip-tures have to say about gifts and ministries. Second, do some in-trospection and self-analysis to determine where one's own unique attributes fit into the overall scope of body ministry. And third, take appropriate action.

### Gifts and Ministries of the Holy Spirit

The Scriptures have much to say about spiritual gifts (the equip-ment or "tools" necessary for service) and ministries (the tasks that need to be performed by the body of Christ). Part of the problem of determining one's calling is difficulty in properly interpreting these Scriptures and correctly deciding which gifts and ministries are one's own. The following is an attempt to define and explain gifts and ministries, which are described in such passages as I Cor-inthians 12, Romans 12, and Ephesians 4.

Spiritual Gifts (I Cor. 12): The supernatural gifts of the Holy Spir-it are the Lord's divine aids to assist believers beyond their own natural, human abilities and strengths. Human intellect and action are subject to error; therefore, Christ's followers need divine intervention and help - the Infinite supplementing and directing the finite's feeble efforts. The nine spiritual gifts described in I Corinthians 12 are not one's natural talents or abilities, but rather, supernatural gifts bestowed by the Almighty for his own purposes and intents. Natural abilities are also used by the Lord, but they are supplemented from time to time with these supernatural abilities. These nine gifts may be categorized into three groups: mental gifts (wisdom, knowledge, discernment), action gifts (faith, miracles, healing), and vocal gifts (prophecy, tongues, interpretation of tongues). Because all the gifts are in Jesus, they may be more clearly explained as those things which Jesus thinks, those things which Jesus does, and those things which Jesus speaks. Because Jesus is the ultimate example, the manifestation of spiritual gifts becomes nothing more than thinking, acting and speaking like Jesus, or "letting this mind be in you which is also in Christ Jesus."

The Gift of Wisdom: This gift is divine guidance or a revelation of truth that comes supernaturally rather than from the human intellect. It is frequently given to those who are offering counsel or advice to others or to those who need supernatural wisdom in a moment of crisis or stress. An example of Jesus manifesting the Holy Spirit's gift of wisdom occurred at the time his accusers tried to entrap him about paying tribute to the Roman government, and Jesus replied, "Render to Caesar the things that are Caesar's and unto God the things that are God's." The Sermon on the Mount is an entire message of divine wisdom, for "turning the other cheek, going the extra mile, returning good for evil, and praying for enemies" are not natural, human responses, but rather, supernatural and divine responses which only the wisdom of the Almighty could conceive. Another example of spiritual wisdom occurred when Peter and John appeared before the council of high priests, who "took knowledge of them and marveled because they perceived that they were unlearned and ignorant men." Ignorant fishermen could match wits with the scholars because the supernatural gift of God's wisdom was in operation. Practical applications of the gift of wisdom in Christian ministry may be observed whenever a counselor, teacher, or spiritual director speaks an inspired message or whenever anyone thinks thoughts or says words that are not one's own, but are divinely inspired. Such a word of wisdom will witness in the spirits of believers who are open to them as being God's truth revealed to humankind.

The Gift of Knowledge: This gift is the manifestation of supernatural understanding of past circumstances or divine insight about people or problems transcending human experience, as when Jesus "knew" that the woman of Samaria had had five husbands and then told her "all things that ever she did." Because the Holy Spirit's knowledge was in operation, Jesus could do this, even though he had never met the woman before. Peter "knew" that Ananias and Sapphira had lied about the price of the land they had sold, even though Peter was not there when the transaction occurred. A word of knowledge may be given prior to a healing or other supernatural moving of the Holy Spirit in human affairs. A minister may "know" who is to be healed or what the cause of the illness is or what a person's deepest needs are without prior instruction or experience about the matter. Other examples of the gift of knowledge in operation in daily life may include such things as guidance (knowing what to do without question); counseling (knowing the cause of a problem or knowing the proper solution); intercession (knowing about a person or a situation in order to pray about it correctly); and signs to an unbeliever (supernatural knowledge witnessing to the person that God's power is at work).

The Gift of Discernment: Because Satan can counterfeit the gifts of the Holy Spirit (he can give a false prophecy through someone, bring about a healing through a medium or cultist, and do seemingly miraculous works in order to deceive the faithful), a Christian needs the ability to see through the disguises when Satan it appearing as "an angel of light" (II Cor. 11:14). Discernment is knowing that which is of the Holy Spirit and that which is of an evil spirit. Jesus exercised the gift of discernment when he rebuked Peter's seemingly encouraging words and said, "Get behind me, Satan . . . .Thou savorest not the things that be of God but those that be of men" (Matt. 16:22-23). Likewise, Paul discerned that the "truths" that came from the lips of the possessed damsel of Acts 16:16-18 were influenced by the power of divination, so he rebuked the spirit and commanded it to come out of her. This faculty for accurately discriminating in a questionable situation and recognizing that which is of the flesh or the devil (however camouflaged these works may be) is certainly needed in today's world where appearances are often deceiving. A discerning Christian - even without having read the pertinent Scriptures or without having received prior teaching - can receive an inner witness that something is amiss. This "alarm clock," which signals the detection of the difference between good and evil, is a powerful and necessary gift of the Spirit. Those involved in the ministry of deliverance (exorcism) certainly need such a gift, as do all those who become involved in any service for the Lord. Prayer group leaders must be conscious of the possibility of false prophets or disruptive influences, which can confuse or thwart the moving of the Spirit at a group gathering. Discernment is also necessary in counseling and healing ministries in order to ascertain the root causes of problems - whether they be of physical, mental, spiritual, or demonic origin. It is also an aid in examining one's motives for what may appear to be worthwhile actions but which, in reality, are not God's will in the matter. For reasons too numerous to mention, all Christians need the gift of discernment at work in their lives.

The Gift of Faith: The supernatural gift of faith is given in what appears to be impossible situations and enables one to "go out on a limb" to trust God rather than circumstances or human inclinations. When aged Abraham believed God for a son, when Noah built the ark under a cloudless sky, when Peter got out of the boat to walk on water, and when the Virgin Mary believed that the Holy Spirit would father her child without a natural husband, these were people acting under "supernatural" faith. The _fruit_ of faith (Gal. 5:22) is to be produced in the Christian's life by one's own actions of piety and devotion, but the _gift_ of faith is given and received supernaturally. Both, however, require action on the part of the believer, for "faith without works is dead." There are innumerable times in the life of a Christian when the gift of faith is needed, for without faith it is impossible to please God or do his works. Whenever one receives a call to service, whenever a program or ministry is lacking in funds or support, whenever doctors give up in their efforts to effect a cure for a patient, whenever evangelistic efforts seem to be ignored, or whenever protection from difficulties or "impossible" situations is nowhere to be found, these are the times when the gift of faith is often put into operation to remove the mountains of doubt and to allow God's mighty hand to move. This kind of faith cannot be "worked up" emotionally or counterfeited. It is a gift from God to be _received_ and then acted upon.

The Gift of Healing: Jesus, the Great Physician, said that the works he did his followers would do also, and this statement certainly includes the manifestation of healing gifts. Just as Jesus used various means for exhibiting healing power (touching, praying, speaking, casting out demons, utilizing the faith of others), Christians become channels of the gifts of healing through various ways - prayers of intercession, the laying on of hands, anointing with oil, confession, receiving Communion, appropriating the promises of Scriptures, claiming recovery by affirmations of faith, and various other acts under the direction and anointing of the Holy Spirit. Because wholeness of mind, body, and spirit is God's highest will for his children, his healing power is ever at work to cleanse, renew, revive, and cure all that prevents wholeness, and he works in cooperation with the faithful who are praying and ministering to that end. Although Jesus alone has the power to heal, he ministers the gifts of healing through those he calls to such a ministry. Every Christian can and should evidence gifts of healing in one way or another - either by speaking words of healing and consolation to those who may be suffering, or by interceding in prayer for the sick, or by holding a gift of faith for the recovery of those who are as yet unhealed. Certainly, those with a definite call to the healing ministry (hospital callers, doctors, inner healing counselors, etc.) should manifest these healing gifts, but even those without such a ministry can be prayer channels and a source of encouragement to those who are needy and suffering.

The Gift of Miracles: A close companion to the gift of faith, the gift of miracles is the supernatural intervention of the Lord in the affairs of human beings in unexplainable ways that may deviate from known laws of nature or human abilities. Miracles should not be thought of as some form of magic or superhuman power that can be produced by humanistic efforts such as through transcendental meditation or mind control over matter. A believer cannot "conjure up" a miracle at will. Like all other gifts, miracles come from the Holy Spirit and are, therefore, under his control. The believer is only the instrument through which miraculous works are manifested as the Spirit operates and directs. The parting of the Red Sea and the raising of Lazarus from the dead were the miraculous responses of the Holy Spirit to the prayers of Moses and Jesus for divine intervention. Some mistakenly believe that the "age of miracles" is past, but signs, wonders, and miraculous happenings occur every day, often going unnoticed by those who do not believe they can happen or who explain away God's marvelous works. Although quite common occurrences, the miracles of natural and supernatural birth (being born and "born again" into God's family) are events that humans cannot duplicate or accomplish apart from the Creator of all life. More dramatic evidences of the gift of miracles at work may be observed in healing services or whenever one has a vision, has a visitation from an angel or other heavenly presence, or has received an interpretation of a dream with spiritual significance as a message from God. There have also been numerous reports of divine intervention in rescues from death or danger and even cases of the dead being raised again to life. Because even Jesus himself did not do many mighty acts in places of unbelief, an atmosphere of faith is best for God's power to become most fully operational. Many people never experience a miracle because they expect none. However, this should never be true of those who minister for the Lord in any form of service, because to do God's work, miracles are often necessary to overcome Satan's opposition, humanity's limitations, and the world's skepticism.

The Gift of Prophecy: Prophecy is God communicating with human beings through the words of another person. Just as the Holy Spirit spoke through the prophets of the Old Testament and through the apostles of the New Testament (see Acts 21:10-11 and Acts 23:3 for examples of New Testament prophecy), he continues to speak through his servants today. Although everyone may not be involved full-time in a prophet's ministry, any Spirit-led Christian may evidence the gift of prophecy from time to time. Prophecy may take the form of guidance, exhortation, revelation, or loving reproof, and may be spoken through whomever the Spirit chooses. Included in the prophecy may be a word of wisdom or a word of knowledge. A person does not prophesy at will, but with a special anointing given at a selected moment by the sovereign Spirit for a definite purpose. Prophecy may be given for one person or for a group gathering. Holy Spirit prophecy is not fortune-telling (although a word of knowledge about future events may be brought forth at times), but it is more usually for the edification and encouragement of others (more "forth-telling" than "fore-telling"). Although Paul encouraged prophecy, he also warned that prophecy should be tested ("the spirits of the prophets are subject to the prophets"). One of the tests for determining true prophecy is the test of fulfillment (God does not lie, so his prophecies always are true or come true). A second test is the agreement of prophecy with Scriptures (Spirit-anointed prophecy is never in opposition to the teachings of the Bible). A third test is the inner witness to the truth, for genuine prophecy will meet with agreement in the spirits of those who test and judge it. Prophecy today may take many forms: reading or sharing a portion of Scripture with another, preparing and delivering a sermon or teaching a lesson, giving a word of loving encouragement to another - all these may be considered aspects of prophecy. Other divinely inspired or prophetic messages may be brought forth during a counseling session, during a time of praise and worship such as in a prayer group, or during a gathering of the body of Christ whenever it is appropriate for the gifts of the Spirit to be in operation. Lay readers, teachers, writers (prophecy may be in written as well as in spoken form), and all those who lead groups should desire the gift of prophecy in order to bring God's messages of truth to others. Always suspect, however, are prophecies that seem harsh or unloving or those that "tell others what to do." Ever a gentleman, the Holy Spirit will always be loving, gentle, and never in violation of a person's free will. True prophets behave in this same manner.

The Gift of Tongues: Jesus said of those who believe that they "shall speak with new tongues" (Mark 16:17). Perhaps the most controversial and least understood of all spiritual gifts, speaking or praying in tongues is the utterance of a language (a prayer language) spoken without having to learn or understand it. The Spirit "gives the utterance." Although the believer is in control of its use (he or she may stop and start at will), the words are from the Holy Spirit. Although the emotions may be stirred and the spirits lifted, as in all times and forms of prayer, praying in tongues is not a frenzied or undignified phenomenon. It is merely a prayer language that bypasses the intellect. Although all other gifts are for the benefit of others, the gift of tongues is personal, a prayer aid for the believer. First, it is a language of praise, assisting Christians in higher, worthier praises than they are capable of offering with their limited vocabulary and human intellect. Second, it is an aid in intercession when one does not know how to pray or when specific needs of a situation are not fully known. Third, the gift of tongues "edifies the believer" (I Cor. 14:4) or "builds up" spiritually those who allow the Spirit to pray through them. Fourth, it allows a believer to yield one of the most unruly members of the body to the Lord. The tongue is an instrument of rebellion many times, but in times of praying in the spirit, there is perfect unity with the Holy Spirit and no human will or selfishness in operation. There is at such times an inherent yielding or "letting go" of control to allow the Holy Spirit to take over. Fifth, praying in tongues allows the Holy Spirit to pray through the believers about things deep in their subconscious, things about which they may be completely unaware. It allows the Holy Spirit to purify and cleanse the hidden or unknown areas of the being. Tongues are a love gift from God to assist a Christian's inadequacies in times of prayer and praise. Those involved in ministries of intercessory prayer may find the added dimension of praying in tongues beneficial. Although generally not used in corporate worship because it would be confusing to visitors and not edifying to those not in acceptance of this practice (see I Cor. 14), praying in tongues is sometimes a part of body ministry in prayer groups or small gatherings of believers who are in agreement and open to this manifestation of the Spirit.

<u>The Gift of Interpretation of Tongues</u>:  While private devotional prayers in tongues may or may not have an accompanying interpretation, when this gift is manifested in a body of Christ (someone praying aloud or giving a message in tongues at a group gathering), it should be followed by an accompanying interpretation "that the church may receive edifying."  Paul warns about the confusion that will exist in a group if no one understands what is going on (I Cor. 14:23).  On the day of Pentecost, when believers first began to manifest the gift of tongues, or praying in other languages under the anointing of the Holy Spirit, there followed a message which all could understand (Peter's sermon in Acts 2).  Tongues plus interpretation equals prophecy, or a message from God.  Anyone who prays in the Spirit at group gatherings is encouraged by Scripture to pray for an interpretation or else to pray quietly within oneself and to God.  At times, a prayer in tongues by one person becomes the key which opens the heart of another to speak forth a word of prophecy or to give a message from the Scriptures, or to give a testimony, or to bring forth some other form of revelation of God's truth.  Because the Lord desires to communicate with his people and uses many different methods of doing so, an interpretation of a message in tongues can become an aid to this end, both to individuals and to groups.  Like all other forms of prophecy and revelation, any interpretation should be judged or "tested" in order to confirm that the message is from the Lord and not the flesh.  Submitting such supernatural revelations to the clergy or to approved spiritual directors is a necessary safeguard to prevent human error and Satan's counterfeits from stumbling believers.  Zeal must always be balanced with wisdom.

<u>From Gift to Ministry</u>:  No gift of the Holy Spirit is some kind of merit badge or indication of special spirituality.  The Lord does not give gifts to people who do not want or cannot use them.  Gifts differ "according to the grace given" (cf. Rom. 12:6-8).  The Holy Spirit will always give the <u>necessary</u> gifts to those whom he has appointed to a particular task.  Just as people who have no carpentry work to do have no need of hammers and saws, so people who have callings not requiring the use of the "tools" or gifts of the Spirit may not manifest such gifts.  Not everyone has the same gifts; not everyone has all gifts:  "But all these [gifts] work by the selfsame Spirit, dividing to every man severally as he will"(I Cor. 12:11).  It must be remembered that all spiritual gifts are to be used in love.  The entire thirteenth chapter of I Corinthians is devoted to teaching that "though we speak with tongues of angels, have the gift of prophecy, understand all knowledge, and have enough faith to remove mountains, if we have not LOVE, we are nothing."  Spiritual gifts are love gifts from the Father to his needy children manifested through one to another.  Attention should never be placed upon the gifts, but upon the Giver of the gifts.  No human being "possesses" a gift anyway.  Only the Lord can bestow gifts, but how marvelous that he allows open, willing Christians to be the "delivery boys" to bring his supernatural gifts to one another!

Although all Christians may manifest one or more of these spiritual gifts from time to time, those persons who devote themselves continually to be used in practicing that gift on a frequent, recurring basis are said to have a "ministry." For instance, all loving parents become involved in teaching and counseling their children and most Christians pray for the sick, but only those who have a definite calling to do so become Bible teachers, prayer therapists, or healers as a regular ministry. Whereas I Corinthians 12 describes the spiritual gifts available for ministry, Romans 12 and Ephesians 4 give descriptions of the functions or offices in the church for specific, delegated responsibilities. The following is an attempt to define and explain these designated ministries in practical ways.

Service Ministries: Every aspect of Christian ministry can be included under the broad category of service. Service is helping others or devoting oneself to godly and worthwhile practices in the furtherance of God's Kingdom. More specifically, it is attending to any of the church functions for which laypersons assume accountability - such responsibilities as ushering, committee work, caring for the church building, lay reading, etc. All members of a church should be attuned to hear the Lord's call to their particular place of service, ready to volunteer for that place of service, and then dedicated to perform the assigned tasks faithfully and diligently. Finding a place of service is not an optional aspect of Christianity, but rather, the expected response to the admonition of Galatians 5:13: "By love, serve one another."

Teaching Ministries: Teaching is imparting information or proclaiming precepts of truth vocally, visually, or by example. Bible study leaders, Sunday school teachers, youth workers, and group leaders of all kinds become involved in various aspects of a teaching ministry. The Holy Spirit can inspire and "teach through" those who allow him to do so; therefore, professional training (while helpful) is not a prerequisite to being called to a teaching ministry. What is required is an openness to the leading of the Spirit and a willingness to give the necessary time to prayer, study, and advance preparation. Even those who assume teaching responsibilities in a limited way - parents, counselors, etc. - should join those in full-blown teaching ministries in following the example of the Master Teacher, Jesus Christ, for the teaching pattern that brings the best results: first, teaching by example (Jesus never asked others to do anything he would not do); second, teaching in terms that hearers understand, with illustrations, stories, and examples that clarify lessons; and third, teaching with applications relevant and practical in daily life ("Go thou, and do likewise").

Exhortation Ministries: Exhortation is calling forth the best from others: encouraging, admonishing, advising, or inciting to proper action. It is helping others to be more dedicated to Christ. A lay reader who proclaims the message of Scripture; those who teach, preach, counsel, witness, or lead; those who write letters to shut-ins or speak words of encouragement to the sorrowing or sinful; and those who compliment clergy or laity for jobs well done are all involved in the ministry of exhortation, a ministry to which many more Christians should become dedicated.

Giving Ministries: Giving is sharing what one is or has with others. Generosity is a sign of Christian dedication and maturity, an indication that the believer is becoming like God, who is always generously giving and blessing. Those who give offerings and tithes to the church or who support other charities for the building up of God's Kingdom (missionary offerings, contributions to spiritual projects, support of the needy, etc.) are giving their earthly treasure to heavenly purposes. Those who give of their talents (choir members, musicians, artists, decorators, gardeners, writers, etc.) to assist the church or community are investing their natural and cultivated abilities in God's service. And those who give their time (for worship, ministry, prayer, outreach, fellowship, or volunteer work) are being good stewards of the precious gift of time (for which they are accountable to the Giver of all gifts).

Leadership Ministries: What Romans 12:8 in some translations calls "ruling" may be better interpreted "leading." Leadership is setting the pattern for others to follow - by direction, instruction, guidance, encouragement, or example. Every church group, guild, committee, and programmed activity needs leadership, whether it be a recreational leader directing games, a social leader planning fellowship activities, a spiritual leader conducting a group worship service, a prayer group leader coordinating a prayer ministry, a training leader conducting a workshop or a task leader directing a work session. Those who have natural or cultivated leadership abilities (or, even without them, find themselves thrust in a place of leadership) should remember that those in authority must be under authority. Every leader should submit both to the leading and direction of the Holy Spirit and to an earthly authority who will confirm and correct the conduct of the leadership activities and approaches.

Ministries of Mercy: Mercy is kindness and compassion, especially that demonstrated to those who seem least deserving of it. Bearing one another's burdens may include forgiving those who have erred, comforting the bereaved, helping those who face a crisis, ministering to the sick, becoming a peacemaker, or offering assistance to those in need. Many various ministries of outreach encompass the showing of mercy - hospital calling, counseling, visiting, making things or giving things to the poor, befriending the lonely, greeting visitors or newcomers, and countless volunteer efforts that are outward evidences of the inner grace of mercy. All forms of ministry should be predicated on the assumption that because God is merciful, we ought to be also.

11

Ministries of Helps:  To help is to give assistance or relief from distress where it is needed.  There are more opportunities for giving to the ministry of helps than perhaps any other aspect of Christian service.  There are untold jobs, functions, and needs in a parish that await the willing volunteer to give a helping hand:  church office workers, child care or nursery attendants, kitchen workers, fund raisers, repair and maintenance workers, committee members - in fact, almost any professional or avocational ability can find an outlet for service somewhere in parish life as a ministry to the church or community.  The ministry of helps may also include those who give prayer support or who offer support services:  taking burdens from those who are called to minister in a more direct way (such as praying for those involved in evangelism or babysitting for a Bible study leader or running errands for someone who needs the time for hospital calling, etc.).

Administration Ministries:  Administration is to assume oversight for business or for the proper execution of an organization or program (being in charge of people or things).  Those with administrative abilities are needed to serve with the governing body of the church in order to assure the smooth operation of temporal functions of the church.  Administrators are also needed to oversee the church office, to conduct stewardship campaigns, and to organize people for various church functions, projects, or programs.  Financing, planning, organizing, delegating responsibilities, and problem-solving are all administrative functions.

Apostleship Ministries:  An apostle is one "called out and sent forth."  Anyone who goes about spreading the gospel by word or deed or who ministers the love of Christ to others could be called an apostle.  In the truest sense of the word, however, apostles are those who receive a definite commission from the church authorities (or from the Lord) to work in a particular area of outreach beyond their usual sphere of influence.  Such a commission might include helping to begin a new church or mission elsewhere, conducting a ministry for the poor or unchurched in the community, or becoming involved in missionary or evangelistic activities beyond the church boundaries.  Other examples might be starting a home for unwed mothers, working with widows or orphans, or providing ministry to inmates in a prison or to shut-ins.  St. Paul, the apostle, devoted his life to missionary work - spreading the gospel and establishing and nurturing churches for new converts.  Any such form of missionary outreach would be considered an apostolic ministry.

Evangelistic Ministries:  An evangelist is one who spreads the "good news" about Jesus Christ.  Evangelistic ministries include such things as witnessing, giving testimonies, visiting the unchurched or unsaved, giving offerings to assist in evangelistic work, sharing Bibles or books with an evangelistic emphasis, assisting with surveys or backing up witnessing efforts in a support capacity, taking evangelistic programs to prisons or other institutions, aligning oneself with evangelistic efforts through committees or organizations, and living a life that bears witness to the reality of Jesus Christ in the world. Every Christian is called to be a witness for Christ, and, therefore, should be involved in evangelism to a greater or lesser degree.

Pastoral Ministries: Pastoral care is the responsibility for the spiritual well-being of the body of Christ. Although this ministry is most usually a function of the clergy, the laity can assist with the oversight and care for the flock of Jesus Christ in supportive ways. One way is praying for and ministering to the clergy and being willing to assume duties they may delegate. Some churches have programs with appointed laypersons who assist in meeting the spiritual (and sometimes temporal) needs of the parish, some have deacons who fill this need, others have committees or individuals who work with the clergy in performing assigned tasks. Pastoral care, including parish calling, counseling, visitation, crisis assistance, and spiritual direction, could well become less burdensome for the clergy if there were effective lay ministries in operation - the entire congregation assuming responsibility for one another, being sensitive to the needs of one another, and becoming willing to meet the needs of one another.

## Self-Analysis of Gifts and Ministries

Once there is a general understanding of the scriptural definitions of gifts and ministries, the next step in finding one's place in lay ministry is self-evaluation and personal analysis. Examine the chart that follows. In each column, prayerfully consider the items listed which are applicable to you. For instance, determine which spiritual gifts have been manifested in your own life with recurring power and with such regularity as to lead you to believe they may be your spiritual gifts to be used in the lay ministry to which you have either already been called or in which you would like to become involved. Then, consider the natural talents and aptitudes you possess. Finally, determine the ministries you are interested in or would like to be trained to perform. For each item checked in the three columns, go back and rate the selections in order of your preferences. By comparing your first choices in each column, and then your next choices, and so on down through the lists, a preference and aptitude pattern for ministry should begin to emerge.

The survey sheet should then be discussed with someone from the clergy or other approved spiritual adviser, prayed about together, and used as a guide in finding the lay ministry for which you are best qualified.

| SPIRITUAL GIFTS and MINISTRIES I BELIEVE I HAVE MANIFESTED | NATURAL TALENTS and ABILITIES the LORD HAS GIVEN ME | MINISTRIES I AM IN-TERESTED in or WOULD LIKE to be TRAINED FOR |
|---|---|---|
| ✓ Wisdom | ✓ Teaching | Evangelistic Visitation |
| ✓ Knowledge | ✓ Leading Groups | Calling on Newcomers |
| ✓ Faith | ✓ Visiting People | Calling on Lapsed Members |
| Healing | ✓ Counseling | ✓ Calling on Elderly |
| Miracles | Singing | ✓ Visiting Sick/Shut-ins |
| ✓ Discernment | Playing Musical | Teaching the Bible |
| ✓ Tongues | Instruments | ✓ Teaching Adult Christians |
| Interpretation | Entertaining People | Teaching Sunday School |
| of Tongues | ✓ Organizing Things | Working with Youth |
| ✓ Prophecy | ✓ Managing People | Pastoral Counseling |
|  | Managing Events | Prayer Counseling (Inner |
|  | Communications | Healing) |
| ✓ Service | ✓ Hospitality/Greeting | Intercessory Prayer |
| ✓ Teaching | Financial Management | Leading Groups: |
| ✓ Exhortation | Fund Raising | Prayer Group _____ |
| ✓ Giving | ✓ Working with Children | Bible Study _____ |
| ✓ Leading | Working with Teenagers | Others: _____ |
| ✓ Mercy | ✓ Working with Adults | ✓ Social Ministries |
| ✓ Helps | ✓ Working with the Elderly | Spiritual Direction |
| Administration | Design and Layout | ✓ Outreach Ministries |
| ✓ Apostle | Drawing/Arts and Crafts | Campus Ministries |
| Evangelist | ✓ Training People to _____ | Prison Ministries |
| Pastoral Ministries | Advising People to _____ | ✓ Organizing _____ |
|  | Sports/Recreation _____ | ✓ Teaching _____ |
| Others: _____ | Acting/Drama Production | ✓ Training _____ |
| _____ | Taking Care of _____ | ✓ Serving _____ |
|  | Public Speaking | ✓ Advising _____ |
|  | Cooking/Kitchen Work | ✓ Leading _____ |
|  | Repairing _____ | ✓ Preparing _____ |
|  | Reading | Vestry |
|  | Writing | ✓ Altar Guild |
|  | Dancing | Acolyte |
|  | Gardening | Lay Reader |
|  | Letter Writing | Choir |
|  | Library Work | Musical Group |
|  | Typing/Office Work | Usher |
|  | Sewing/Needlecrafts | Committee Member: _____ |
|  | Mechanics | ✓ Diocesan Work: _____ |
|  | Audio-Visual Work _____ | Consultant Work: _____ |
|  | Researching | Worship Leader |
|  | ✓ Sharing/Witnessing | Family Counselor |
|  | ✓ Comforting and Helping | ✓ Alcohol/Drug Rehabilitation |
|  | Others | Book or Tape Library Work |
|  | Others: _____ | Fund Raising/Stewardship |
|  | _____ | Recreation/Fellowship |
|  | My Work or Profession: ___ | ✓ Church Orientation |
|  | _____ | ✓ Crisis Aid and Comfort |
|  | My Education/Training: ___ | Telephone Calling |
|  | _____ | Deliverance (Exorcism) |
|  | My Hobbies/Interests: ___ | Landscape/Beautification |
|  | _____ | ✓ Missionary Work |
|  |  | ✓ Community Outreach |
|  |  | Others: _____ |
|  |  | _____ |

The following suggestions may help you in finding your calling to lay ministry:

1. Act on Romans 12:1. Surrender. Do not put limitations or reservations around your availability for service. Remember that God's strength is made perfect in weakness, and therefore your usefulness does not depend upon your own adequacy, but God's. For those who still feel that they are too unworthy, unlearned, or unchangeable to be used of God, it might be well to remember that the Lord once spoke through a jackass (Numbers 22:28). He is not limited by human limitations, only by your unwillingness to allow the Lord to be in control.

2. Begin with the proper attitude, seeing each life situation as an opportunity for ministry. You may have received your calling already. God often will not move you to greater things until you have been proven faithful to "bloom where you are planted."

3. Wait on the Lord. God's timetable and yours are not the same. You must not run ahead or lag behind God's leading. The Lord will open the door of service in his perfect time. Moses had to tend his father-in-law's sheep for forty years before God finally moved him into the service to which he was called.

4. Worship. Not just Sunday-in-the-pew or corporate worship, but in small groups, with a prayer partner, and especially alone. Nothing better prepares an individual for service than an attitude of praise and adoration. Sometimes specific outreach ministries emerge as an outgrowth of individuals or small groups meeting on a regular basis to seek the Lord.

5. Pray. Make this a daily and constant habit of life. Pray the prayer of Jesus: "Not my will, but thine be done."

6. Listen. God speaks in different ways. Expect to hear him through sermons, through the reading of Scriptures, through the godly counsel of others, and that still, small voice inside yourself. You may be aided in your meditation by fasting or other spiritual disciplines until you "hear" clearly and completely. Write down what you are receiving as guidance each day, and then reflect over these collected revelations.

7. Avail yourself of opportunities for training and preparation. After you have listed your natural talents and spiritual gifts (see the Lay Ministry Analysis

Sheet), make note of ministries you have performed in the past and any in which you are interested for future ministry. Then determine if such ministries require special education or training; if so, ascertain how and where you can best receive such training.

8. Examine your motives. List reasons why you feel drawn to a particular type of ministry. If you want to be involved in something because of its prestige, your desire to escape a more difficult or demanding role, or for any other reason than because you feel led of the Lord to involve yourself in the ministry he has chosen for you, you must stop and pray for better motives. The real motive for any type of service is love - love for God and others.

9. Submit your ministry (or inclination toward a ministry) to be judged. Before beginning a new work, go to your pastor and discuss what you have concluded from following steps 1 through 8 above. No ministry should ever be performed without the approval and oversight of your spiritual head. The Bible warns that we are to be in submission to spiritual authorities. It is also risky to minister alone, especially if you are a novice. Jesus sent out his followers two by two. After the clergy's approval for a ministry, it is still good practice to minister with a partner if at all possible. This not only provides double the prayer power, but also is an effective check against falling into error. Even when you are sure in your own heart that you are moving as God is leading, it is important to receive confirmation and a commission from the church, the clergy, and others whose spiritual counsel the Lord will provide in order to give you the assurance that you are in the will of the Lord.

10. Act in faith. Once you have your calling correctly determined, confirmed, and approved, begin to follow the Spirit's promptings without delay. Expect God to redeem your mistakes as a leap of faith takes you beyond where you are to where you may never have been before. Do not become overly concerned with results. Although good fruits or positive results of a ministry are often good indicators that God is at work, you may not see the fruits of your labor or they may be delayed in coming. Attention should be focused upon Jesus. Give the problems and the outcomes to him, for he is the one responsible for them. Your responsibility is to be faithful and obedient.

## Summary

To summarize, we have seen that the "What?" is lay ministry - the reasonable service of _all_ Christians. The "Why?" is a response to the command to act out our love for Christ and his body, the church, through obedience and unselfish giving of time, talents, money, and energies for the ongoing of the Kingdom, recognizing that when one does not do one's part, an added burden is placed upon someone else. The "Who?" is everyone, including _you_. The "Where?" is not only at church, but whever a Christian is. And the "How?" is up to the individual (you) and God as together you set out in faith, exploring his highest will for your life.

> Not that we are sufficient of ourselves to think
> anything as of ourselves; but our sufficiency is
> of God; who also has made us able ministers . . .
> (II Cor. 3:5-6).

# 2 · Traditional Ministries of the Church

Often in an attempt to maintain that one does not get to heaven by merit of good works, the importance of such good works is underplayed. Although salvation is through faith alone, and certainly not through anything one can do apart from God's grace, people nevertheless are called to do good works as an evidence of that faith and as a response to that grace. St. James implies that good works are an evidence of a living, vibrant faith when he says, "Faith without works is dead." The church provides many opportunities for good works to be performed through numerous opportunities for service.

Many times, traditional ministries approved by the church as functions of the laity are thought of a "chores" or "duties" or even "burdens." Often the reason is that the persons performing the functions may be unsuited to the tasks, they may have received little or no proper instruction in the performance of their duties, or they may be performing from improper motives. The problem may be complicated further by giving church workers responsibilities without also instructing them as to the spiritual significance of the task. At other times, the frequency with which a task is performed may breed such familiarity as to detract from the purpose and meaning behind the sacred function. For these and any number of other reasons, church responsibilities for ministry are often misunderstood and mistakenly performed.

A great help in overcoming the problems inherent in performing church-related ministry is education. Some basic assumptions about church ministries, assumptions that should be universally taught, understood, and practiced, are as follows:

1.  Participants should see their tasks as gifted ministries, not as merely duties or chores.

2.  Participants should have a "calling" to the particular ministry they are to perform.

3.  Participants should receive adequate instruction, not only in the performance of the tasks, but also in the spiritual significance involved in any services they are requested to render.

4.  Participants should approach the ministry with the proper attitude and motivation - a sincere desire to show love, to be obedient, and to be of service, not from any self-seeking motivations.

5.  Participants should be instructed to pray before, during, and after the performance of the ministry, asking the Lord to do through them the tasks they are performing.

In order to see these general principles in a more specific light, let us examine several traditional church roles, looking at them both as perfunctory chores and as gifted ministries. Such a contrast should immediately demonstrate the preference of the latter over the former.

NOTE TO CLERGY: The following sections of this manual may be removed and duplicated in order to give them to the appropriate people in your parish - ushers, lay readers, Sunday school teachers, etc. The information and suggestions given should be helpful to those already involved in the various ministries described and to those considering involvement in such ministries.

## The Church Usher

> I had rather be a doorkeeper in the house of my God
> than to dwell in the tents of wickedness (Ps. 84:10).

Church ushers lacking in the proper insights and motivations might see their role as merely that of a distributor of church bulletins, an adjuster of thermostats, a collector of offerings, and a traffic director to monitor bottlenecks at the Communion rail. Those who see ushering as a ministry, however, find much more.

Ministering ushers would first examine their motives for ushering. They might ask themselves, "Am I doing this willingly and gladly as a service to my Lord and my church, or grudgingly because I can't get out of it without appearing in a bad light?" They might run a checklist to determine if they are ushering out of habit, duty, or coercion. The proper starting point for useful service is a proper attitude toward that service.

Once these ushers have determined that they have, indeed, found their proper calling, they might run a further checklist to ascertain how prepared and qualified they are for this ministry. They would want to find out all they could about ushering in general and specified methods of operation for their clergy and church in particular. They would want not only to receive the prescribed training offered beginning ushers, but also to continue to observe those more experienced and to learn and improve from week to week.

Realizing that the first face most worshipers see on Sunday morning is that of the usher at the front door, the person involved in this ministry will want to appear cheerful, warm, and loving, so as to set the tone for the worship experience right from the beginning. That may require getting to bed early on Saturday night so as not to be tired or grouchy the next morning. The usher will want to be in the appointed place early in order to allow enough time to become prepared physically, mentally, and spiritually. Naturally, the most important part of advance preparation will be a time for prayer and quiet meditation. What the usher prays about specifically will be an individual matter, but a general prayer outline might include an offering of oneself to the Lord for service, thanksgiving for the opportunity to minister, and petitions and intercessions for the church service, including specific prayers for the clergy and congregation.

Upon arriving, the considerate usher would check the temperature and lighting facilities, not as a matter of routine but as a matter of ministering comfort to those who come to worhsip. He or she would view the task of distributing bulletins as a way of aiding worshipers in following the service. The function of escorting people into pews where space is available would be seen as a courtesy aid to the congregation's ability to see and hear from the best available vantage point.

The ministering usher would be sensitive to observe closely those entering for the service, watching for new faces, troubled faces, lonely faces. The usher's own smile and friendly greeting may make the difference - a ray of sunshine breaking into someone's dark world - so the usher will be sincerely glad to see each passerby.

As a service to newcomers, the usher will want to make a special effort to be friendly, perhaps offering to show them around the church, help them find a Sunday school class, escort them to the coffee hour assembly, or introduce them around the congregation. For those who appear troubled, the usher may offer a word of comfort, pray silently, or mention the matter to the clergy after the service.

Taking up the offering will be more than just passing the collection plate; it will be an offering of the love gifts of the congregation before the altar of the Lord.

Escorting communicants row by row to the altar rail, in churches where this is done, will be viewed as a sacred task, performed with dignity in keeping with the holiness of the Communion service. It will be heeding the scriptural admonition to do all things in God's house "decently and in order."

At the conclusion of the service, ministering ushers will not get away too fast, but will bless those who are departing with a loving farewell. A touch, a handshake, a smile, a greeting, a friendly word will all be gifts of themselves to others, but offered as unto the Lord.

Even the final acts of picking up the used bulletins and straightening the hymnbooks in the pews will not be viewed as custodial tasks, but as loving ways of keeping God's house uncluttered and adequately prepared for those who come to worship next.

Ushers who would thus view their role as a part of the total worship experience on Sunday morning and who would give themselves to each task as to a holy calling to ministry would not only enrich the Sunday morning blessing for those entering and leaving the church, but also enrich their own lives as well.

## The Lay Reader

Blessed is he that reads, and they that hear . . .
(Rev. 1:3).

In most sacramental churches, the reading of selected Scriptures during the worship service is the responsibility of approved laypersons, and in churches of all denominations, laypersons often are called upon to read aloud from the Bible to the congregation. The following suggestions are applicable whether such Scripture reading is an official or an unofficial function.

Jesus himself filled the office of lay reader. It was his custom both to attend the synagogue services and to participate actively as a layman. The most familiar case in point is when he read aloud from the prophecy of Isaiah to the synagogue congregation in Nazareth, declaring that "This day is the Scripture fulfilled in your ears." This act alone should underscore the significance and seriousness of the lay reader's ministry.

What picture comes to mind when visualizing Jesus as a lay reader? One cannot imagine him rushing late into the synagogue after preparatory prayers, grabbing the nearest scroll, and with obvious lack of advance preparation, stumbling and halting over unfamiliar words of the text in a self-conscious monotone devoid of inflection and conviction. The biblical accounts of those who heard Jesus read and speak always declared it was "with all authority." It is an established fact that Jesus loved the Scriptures. This was evidenced many ways and many times, the very first of which was the time when, at the tender age of twelve, he spent three whole days studying with the doctors of the law. When tempted, Jesus' reply to Satan was, "It is written . . . ." When asked difficult questions by his accusers, Jesus often referred the inquirer to the Scriptures, saying, "How readest thou?" This same reverence for, knowledge of, and belief in the Holy Word of God provides the cornerstone for building an effective lay-reading ministry.

Even before the New Testament Christian church called upon the laity to assist with public worship, Old Testament worshipers were trained in reading and singing portions of the services. In Colonial times in America, when available pastors were scarce, the laity filled in as the leaders of worship. The inclusion of the laity in public worship was then, as now, the worthy symbol of the active participation of those other than clergy in the worship experience. While the clergy is the symbol of Jesus Christ, the High Priest and Intercessor, the lay reader is the symbol of the congregation, the body of Christ as joint heirs and co-workers with the Lord in his Kingdom on earth.

While specific duties of lay readers may vary from church to church, the most frequent functions include the ministry of the Word (reading the assigned Scripture lessons for the day) and leading the congregation in the prayers and responses appropriate to the litany or the service. In some cases, it becomes necessary for a lay reader to substitute for the clergy in conducting the service (except for the celebrating of Communion, pronouncing absolution, or giving the priestly benediction). Some churches give lay readers a function in administering the chalice during the Communion service. However limited or broad the lay reader's responsibilities, there are some necessary qualifications and preparations which should be precedent to this ministry.

Although there may be exceptions, most lay readers in sacramental churches are licensed by their bishop prior to performing the office of lay reader. As far as spiritual qualifications are concerned, lay readers should, by life and example, be worthy symbols of the godly laity they personify and represent. They would want to take advantage of any training courses offered to aid them in gaining a helpful background in the Holy Scriptures, prayer books, hymnals, church history, church doctrines and creeds, conduct of public worship, appropriate canons of church law, and any other instruction that would aid in understanding and performing their ministry. Such persons would take seriously the biblical admonition to "Study to show thyself approved unto God, a workman that needeth not to be ashamed, rightly dividing the Word of Truth." Certainly, one's knowledge of the Scriptures and, hence, one's ability to impart them meaningfully and rightly can be enhanced in no better way than by daily Bible study and meditation upon Bible truths. It is reasonable to assume that those who would lead the congregation in a proper understanding of Scriptures must themselves first seek to understand them.

In addition to the spiritual preparations for this ministry, there are some academic and practical measures to be considered as well. Of all the methods of delivery in oral communication, the least effective is "reading" to an audience. It is not a natural form of communication; eye contact is limited; and most people have not mastered the techniques of reading effectively enough to project sincerity, emotion, inflection, clarity, and nuances of meanings. If at all possible, a lay reader should receive some public speaking training. Short of that, a critique of the speaking voice should be given, either in "try-out" sessions or by tape recording the lessons to be read for self-evaluation by the lay reader.

The best speakers do not strive to be dramatic or oratorical. Artificiality detracts from what is being read and places attention upon the reader. Scripture reading and prayers should be offered naturally (although with enough volume so as to be heard), as in speaking to a friend - which, of course is the case. Care should be given to proper pronunciation (saying words correctly) and enunciation (saying words clearly). Appropriate pauses should be observed, both at the beginning of the reading (so as to give the congregation time to find the place) and at the end, which should conclude with a note of finality. All the verbal and nonverbal cues (gestures, body movements, postures for worship, etc.) should provide the proper leadership for the congregation to follow easily. Movements in the chancel or at the altar should always be dignified, deliberate, and in keeping with the prescribed customs of the service so as not to detract in any way. Although random movement should be avoided as distracting, appropriate movement at the altar area may need to be slightly exaggerated in order to be seen from the back of the church.

There is a distinct difference between lay readers who see their responsibility as that of merely reading a few passages of solemn words at the appropriate times because it's "expected" and because "somebody has to do it" and lay readers who approach the task as a sacred call- ing to minister God's Word in the congregation of the Lord's people. A typical Sunday morning for a ministering lay reader might go some- thing like this:

After reviewing and meditating upon the assigned Scriptures throughout the week and looking up the pronunciations of uncertain words or unclear passages, there is a last minute review of the day's readings before leaving for the church. There is also a prayer of dedication, a calling upon God to anoint the reading of the sacred words that the reader is privileged to proclaim. With notes and checklist of special orders or procedures for the day in hand, the lay reader arrives in plenty of time to robe unhurriedly so as to be in the proper place for the preparatory prayers. The reader prepares himself in three ways: first, physical preparation, including atten- tion to grooming and to the cleanliness, neatness, and fit of the vestments in order to present a worthy picture to the congregation he or she represents; second, attention to one's emotional state, by re- moving from the mind any problems, distractions, or unrelated thoughts that might detract from full concentration upon the worship service; third, spiritual preparation by entering wholeheartedly and reverently into the confessions and preparatory prayers, adding to those one's own petitions and intercessions for the clergy, congregation, choir, and service in general.

When the service begins, the lay reader processes or enters the chancel with reverent dignity, sings the hymns with volume and con- viction, and participates fully in all aspects of worship (not just when it is his or her time to lead the service). The lay reader's role is seen as an integral part of the corporate worship of clergy and laity, a cooperative venture in faith, with neither "starring roles" nor "walk-on parts." The entire service becomes a holy sym- phony, the blending of many parts into a meaningful whole.

At the appointed time, the lay reader stands to read, striving to impart more than verbalized words from a printed page, endeavoring to impart understanding and meaning into every passage. Reading with a steady, even pace, punctuated with pauses, conversational rhythm, and emphasis upon words or phrases which need to be stressed, the lay reader projects the voice so it can be heard throughout the congrega- tion without bellowing. The reader remembers to pause before and after the readings and at points of emphasis throughout the passages. Each motion bespeaks dignity and an awesome reverence for the place, the task, and the Lord in whose name all is being done.

When the service concludes, the lay reader maintains the same decorum while carefully putting away the vestments worn, and remaining accessible to the clergy and others for any further assistance it may be possible to offer. In emergencies, the lay reader is available to fill in for an absentee or to read for more than one service, or to do any of the many unexpected but necessary functions that arise from time to time.

Like Aaron and Hur, who assisted and supported the weary Moses, lay readers may not be in the thick of the battle, but they perform a ministry of indescribable significance as they "hold up the hands" of their clergy at the sidelines.


## The Acolyte

Serve the Lord with gladness . . . (Ps. 100:2).

Acolyte (from the Greek, meaning an attendant or one who assists) is an office found in sacramental churches and is usually filled by young people, while adults fulfill the office of lay reader. This, however, is not always the case. In some instances, especially if the parish is small and the available lay assistants few, the functions may be combined. For that reason, the preceding section (The Lay Reader) should be read in conjunction with this section on the acolyte, as many of the same principles apply to both positions.

An acolyte's main purpose in ministry is to assist the clergy and people with preparations for worship and the receiving of Communion. There are many desirable qualities to be sought in qualifying one to perform the office of acolyte, but two prerequisites head the list. First, acolytes should desire the responsibility and see the position as an honored service they will delight to perform; and second, acolytes should be dependable, willing to forgo Sunday beach trips and other recreational activities rather than leave their position at the altar vacant on Sunday morning. Too often youngsters are coerced by well-meaning parents into becoming acolytes, or they reluctantly accept the position out of an improper motivation. They perform because the pastor expects it or because their friends are acolytes or because they want to "show off" in front of the congregation to gain attention. Candidates for acolyte should be screened and should have their motives explored to assure that they understand the significance of the role they are to play in the worship service. They should be encouraged to accept that role for the right reasons.

Although the desire to serve and dependability may head the list of acolyte requirements, there are other considerations which should be noted also. Just as those who take holy orders are expected to live exemplary lives, it is expected that acolytes who minister before the holy altar will be Christians whose lives will not bring a reproach upon the service they perform. A seriousness of purpose about and a reverence for the things of God should dominate the attitudes of those who assume this ministry. Serving at the altar is not to be taken lightly or to be approached irreverently. Willingness to assume additional associated responsibilities is, likewise, inherent in holding such a position; this would include a willingness to attend all training sessions (regularly scheduled and specially called practices for additional services or programs), promptness, proper care of the vestments, neatness in grooming, and making arrangements for a substitute when unable to perform.

Perhaps part of the reason for a lack of enthusiasm on the part of some youth when it comes to becoming acolytes is a lack of understanding. Too often, training sessions stress the "what" and "how" but forget to include the "why." In order for acolytes to approach their Sunday morning altar duty from the proper perspective, they must see the purpose behind the functions. The following brief description of acolyte duties and their spiritual significance may be of help.

1. Genuflecting and bowing: In order to reverence the holy presence of the consecrated elements, the cross, and the holy altar, which is representative of Christ's table at the Last Supper, obeisance is shown upon arriving, upon leaving, and whenever passing by. It would be most impolite to pass in front of someone without acknowledging tht person's presence, and certainly one wishes to be courteous to our Lord and those emblems which remind us of him. We worship, not just with our lips, but with the whole body as we kneel, genuflect, bow, and stand at appropriate times. An acolyte who assumes these postures reverently and deliberately aids the congregation in assuming proper attitudes of reverence. By example and leadership, the acolyte helps to set the pattern for meaningful worship.

2. Lighting the candles: Jesus, the light of the world, is symbolized by the lighted candle. The acolyte who thinks of Jesus as he or she lights the altar candles in preparation for worship calls the attention of the congregation to the One in whose name they are gathered for praise, prayer, instruction, and Communion.

3. Preparation: One does not rush unbidden into a neighbor's house, partake of food and hospitality, and then depart with no words of greeting, thanks, or farewell. In the same way, when we come to the house of the Lord, we must remember to express courtesy, especially words of appreciation for the privileges and blessings awaiting us at the Lord's table. The preparations for worship and ministry at the altar include confession and adoration. We would not want to pour clear, refreshing water into a dirty cup. The Lord, likewise, desires a clean vessel into which to pour his Spirit. A part of preparation for service is, therefore, the "emptying" process, the cleansing and opening of the heart to be as usable as one can possibly be. Psalm 43, part of which often is read in the time of preparation, begins, "Judge me . . . ." When the Lord judges us, he makes us aware of unconfessed sin. At that point we must judge ourselves. We must confess and repent of sins, not ignore them or try to cover them up. When the psalm says, "I will go to the altar of God, unto God my exceeding joy . . ." there is an indication that those who serve at the altar should do so joyfully.

The receiving of forgiveness of sins during the preparation time is certainly something which should gladden hearts and cause God's servants to rejoice. A sour look or an attitude of unconcern will assist no one in worship, while the acolyte who approaches this ministry with a joyful countenance and a heart of praise will help others to adopt those same attitudes. Each person who is to serve should have a private moment of preparation, asking God to cleanse and sanctify (make holy) the vessel of self for worthy service before going forth in an attitude of reverent joy and praise to the assigned ministry that day.

4. Procession: The processional march at the singing of the opening hymn is more than just a convenient way of getting all to their appointed places. Everyone in the procession follows behind the Crucifer, the bearer of the cross. This is symbolic of the Christian's duty to take up one's own cross to follow Jesus. If there is a banner in the procession, this reminds everyone not only of the solemn beauty of the Christian walk and the assurance that "His banner over us is love," but also of the fact that Christian soldiers follow the standard of the King, our Lord and Saviour, in the march of victory against all foes. The designs upon the priestly robes, the cross, the symbols on the banners, and other trappings are more than decorations. They are to call attention to something sacred, to turn eyes away from earthly things toward heavenly things. The mind should not be allowed to wander at this time, but should be focused upon the heavenly counterpart to all the earthly symbols in the procession.

5. Torchbearers: Although historically the torchbearers performed a very practical function, that of lighting the way for processions at night, the significance of this ministry is more than just adherence to tradition. The Scriptures tell us, "Ye are the light of the world" and that we should "let our lights so shine that others may see our good works and glorify our Father in Heaven." Jesus warned against "hiding one's light under a bushel," which meant being a secret follower rather than openly witnessing for the Lord. The torchbearers should remind us all of the responsibility of being a faithful follower and active witness as we seek to "walk in the light" we are given.

6. Servers: Jesus took upon himself the role of a servant to wash the disciples' feet, saying, "He who would be greatest among you, let him be servant of all." There is no higher calling than to be a lowly servant for the Lord by following his own example to us. Although the servers' functions do have a practical side (someone must bring things to the clergy, ring bells, receive the offerings, etc.), ministering acolytes will see their responsibilities from the spiritual side as well. They will see their assisting at the altar as a holy calling and a sacred task as well as an honored privilege. When they carry the alms basin or the sacramental elements, they will be aware that they are holding holy things. At the ceremonial washing, they will be reminded of the inner cleansing received through the washing away of sin, the cleansing qualities of Christ's blood, or per-

haps the regeneration evidenced by the waters of baptism. At the ringing of the sanctus bell, they will remember that all the hosts of heaven are joining in the singing of "Holy, Holy, Holy" unto the Lord. In Old Testament days, the ringing of bells signified the entering of the priest into the holy place. Today the bells indicate the ability of all Christ's followers - laity as well as clergy - to draw near and to come into the holy presence of God. The ringer of the bell is, in actuality, summoning God's people into the presence of the Creator. Thinking about these things and other symbolic or spiritual counterparts to the things involved in a server's duties will keep the mind from wandering and will help to focus on the real reason for being involved in these sacred tasks in a holy place.

7. <u>Thurifers:</u> If incense is used in worship, there should be an understanding of its use. From earliest days, worship and offerings to God were accompanied by the burning of incense, perfumed gums and spices that emitted a fragrant smoke. The rising of the smoke toward heaven was an outward and visible symbol of the grace of God in receiving the prayers and offerings of the worshipers, whose petitions rose toward God. Because all the senses should be involved in worship, the smelling of the fragrant incense is an appropriate accompaniment to the seeing, hearing, speaking, singing, and touching of worship. The ones who carry the thurible of incense would do well to recall that frankincense and myrrh were among the very first offerings made to the Lord Jesus, and that their incensing of the church and people also can be such an offering.

Whatever the acolyte's functions, whether or not they include one or more of the responsibilities described above, it is certainly a good thing to begin serving the Lord at a young age, while the mind is quick and pliable and while there is time for further growth. The foundation established in childhood is the base upon which to build throughout years of further service. Too often we put all responsibilities for leadership in the church into the hands of adults, forgetting that children and youth are the church too. What better way to assure the health and stability of the church of the future than by involving the young in service and leadership roles? Serving as an acolyte is one such way of underscoring the importance of present and potential church involvement.

Perhaps the best advice to give an acolyte or any young person serving in the church is that given young Timothy by St. Paul at the beginning of a fruitful ministry begun at a tender age: "Let no man despise thy youth, but be thou an example of the believers, in word, in conversation, in charity, in spirit, in faith, in purity . . . . Neglect not the gift that is in thee" (I Tim. 4:12, 14).

## The Teacher

The servant of the Lord must be apt to teach
(II Tim. 2:24).

Jesus, the greatest teacher who ever taught, left his followers the Great Commission, to "go and teach." Although not everyone may have a Sunday school class or lead a Bible study group, everyone is, to a greater or lesser degree, a teacher. We all teach others more by our example than by precept; we all influence one another when we give a word of advice, take a stand for our convictions, or verbalize our beliefs. Parents teach their children, employers teach their workers, and friends inspire those who look to them as examples.

Beyond this general teaching ministry to which everyone is called, however, there is the gift of teaching mentioned in Ephesians 4 (along with other gifted ministries such as apostleship, prophecy, evangelism and pastoring), which is the teaching ministry of the church set apart "for the perfecting of the saints, for the work of the ministry, for the edifying of the body of Christ." Those involved in this ministry have both a fulfilling and rewarding work and a grave and demanding responsibility.

Most churches have difficulty in finding dedicated teachers. The excuses for not teaching include "I'm not trained as a teacher". . . "I've never done it before". . . "I don't know enough myself to teach others". . . "I've already served my time and I deserve a rest". . . "I don't relate well to children (or teenagers or whomever they are asked to teach)". . . and a host of other logical-sounding reasons for avoidance of teaching. Because the demands upon this ministry include a great deal of time and energy, busy people are reluctant to make a commitment to it and those who have been involved (and are personally aware of the responsibilities) often try to sidestep such involvement again. Such attitudes put the Christian education program of many churches into desperate straits. Another reason for ineffective teaching ministries in churches is the lack of proper instruction and preparation of the teachers. People often are button-holed by a desperate pastor or Sunday school superintendent who is frantically trying to fill a teaching position, given a curriculum guide, and then thrust into a class about which they know little or nothing. This is unfair both to the teacher and to the students.

In order for a church to have an effective teaching ministry, it must be patterned after the ministry of Jesus. He did not send his disciples out until after he had properly instructed them, worked with them, and checked on their progress, giving both encouragement and correction where needed. The Christian education program of a church should be a top-priority investment in terms of time, resources, money, and talent.

Another often neglected aspect of the church educational program is overall planning. There are some basic questions that should be answered by those in charge of the teaching-learning ministries of the parish.

1. Where have we been in Christain education? This question should include an evaluation of curricula used in the past, the quality of teaching, the meeting of goals and expectations in past efforts, a determination of strengths and weaknesses, and a plan for implementing any changes necessary.

2. Where are we now in Christian education? There should be an evaluation of the present curriculum, the teaching methods to be used, and the goals expected to be achieved in the present program. Often a curriculum is selected casually, without consideration of the students' needs. Those responsible for teaching programs need to ask, "Where are our students spiritually and educationally, and where should they go from here?" Planning for an effective program should include a determination of the parish philosophy of education (where emphasis should be, approaches to take, etc.); class sizes and structures (self-contained classes, combined age groups, team teaching, or other special details peculiar to the particular program); leadership and resources available (who will be in charge and where teachers can go for further help); training to be provided (weekly or monthly teachers' meetings, workshops, conferences, etc.); and methods of evaluation (clergy interviews with teachers, observation of teachers, surveys for parental responses, regular methods of feedback and reporting of problems, etc.).

3. Where are we going in Christian education? Ineffective programs are the result of ineffective planning for future growth, spiritual development, upgrading of teaching methods and programs, and expansion of horizons. There can be no apathy or resting on laurels, but there must be continual efforts to realize dreams of bigger and better things in education. Some considerations for achieving future goals include (a) clergy support (the sheep follow the shepherd); (b) commitment and dedication at all levels including financial backing and teacher support and appreciation; (c) prayer support and emphasis parishwide of the importance and priority of Christian education; (d) opportunities for teacher training, effective leadership and assistance for teachers, and resources and teaching aids readily available; (e) definite evaluative methods for continual upgrading; and (f) open, creative atmospheres wherein teachers are free to try new ideas, tap creative resources, and grow.

Once the church has established such goals and determined a workable program in Christian education, the job of recruitment of teachers begins. Too often those responsible for recruitment forget that the Lord wants the right teacher in the right classroom even more than they do. Rather than trying to fill vacant classes with just anyone who can be persuaded to take the responsibility, recruiters should pray and claim by faith that the Holy Spirit will call forth those he has chosen for a teaching position. A notice in the church bulletin calling the entire parish to pray for the instructional program and challenging each member of the parish to seek the Lord's guidance as to whether or not he or she is being called to teach or assist in some way is preferable to other methods, which often result in the wrong person in the wrong classroom.

Next comes the question "Who should be a teacher?" Those who have received the calling. The problem is that many never "hear" their call. Sometimes the calling is ignored because people fear even the term teacher. It sounds too professional or academic for one who has never had training in education. There must be an understanding of the need for a balance between the error of feeling that only specially educated and academically qualified people can teach and the opposite and equally erroneous notion that no preparation or advance screening is necessary before placing someone in a classroom. It has already been noted that much prayer and advance preparation should precede the assignment of teachers. Although a teacher should be as capable, experienced, qualified, and dedicated as possible before teaching (as before assuming any ministry, for that matter), there must be a starting place for everyone, and a lack of past experience should not deter one from beginning a teaching ministry. In the book of Exodus, there is an account of Bezaleel, the craftsman, whom God "put in his heart that he should teach." This indicates that it is the Spirit of the Lord which will put the desire in one's heart as well as the information which must be taught and the ability to teach it. It should be a great comfort to those who want to teach but who have never done so that "the Holy Ghost shall teach you in the same hour what ye ought to say" (Luke 12:12). The Holy Spirit is referred to throughout the New Testament as teacher, guide, helper, and advocate, One who will anoint the ministers and bring forth the truth through those who yield to his control.

There are some additional misconceptions which need to be cleared up, erroneous ideas about what a teacher is and does. First of all, a teacher is not a babysitter who merely keeps children out of parents' hair until the worship service or coffee hour is over. Furthermore, a teacher is not a dictator, show-off, "Good Time Charlie," or infallible fountain of all wisdom. A teacher is someone whom God has called to share his love and impart his Word in an atmosphere of reverence, discipline, mutual acceptance, and respect. A teacher is someone whose own desire to study and learn enhances the desire to share with others, one who is committed to the Lord and the ministry of teaching to the extent of giving the needed time for the preparation and personal involvement with students. A teacher loves students and knows that what is said may not be remembered, but a loving teacher will leave a lasting imprint upon the minds and lives of the students, the imprint of God's love. A teacher lives a life that strives to practice what is taught, realizing that those who teach are held accountable to live up to their teachings. A teacher realizes that it is necessary to rely upon the Lord for new ideas, ways of coping with difficult students, and unexpected situations. It is especially important to rely upon the Lord for patience, especially the kind needed at the end of the teaching year when such patience is in short supply. A teacher is someone who learns that good teaching involves talking little and finding better ways of presenting lessons such as visualizing, demonstrating, dramatizing, using creative aids, and involving the pupils in participation activities. A teacher is someone who is sensitive to a pupil with a problem, who takes extra time with one who needs it, and who makes personal calls and visits to pupils (not just absentees) outside regularly scheduled class time.  A teacher is one who is loving enough not to allow pupils to be disruptive or disinterested in class, but who teaches that being a disciple means being disciplined.

However, a teacher does not usually walk into a classroom the first time with all these notions and abilities down pat!  Becoming an effective teacher is a process, much like Christian life itself, which is a continual learning and growing experience.  The first step is attitudinal.  The proper attitude for a beginning teacher is an attitude of love - a genuine concern for the church education program in general and the specific class or group in particular.  It also involves a love for the Bible as God's Word, the teachings and doctrines of church tradition, and the students as unique individuals with special gifts and value  as human beings.  There should also be a love of learning and sharing with others.  A teacher's commitment goes beyond the dedication to be in a particular place each week to teach; it must be a commitment of time to the necessary out-of-class activities, which are equally important - prayer, study, planning, teachers' meetings, finding and preparing resource materials, con-tacting absentees, etc.

In order to have a learning situation, three ingredients are necessary: someone to give the lesson (the teacher), someone to receive the lesson (the students), and something to be learned (the curriculum or lesson materials).  Of the three, the teacher is the key ingredient.  Although the curriculum should certainly be chosen carefully and prayerfully in order to meet pupils' needs at their level of growth and understanding, an effective teacher will not be limited by an ineffective curriculum or even a nonexistent one.  A teacher in tune with the promptings of the Holy Spirit and the real needs of the pupils can improvise, add to, adapt, and create curricu-lum.  Such a teacher will realize that the emphasis is to be on teaching students, not on teaching subject matter.  Such a teacher will realize also that the students themselves should become an active part of the curriculum, bringing with them something to be shared and learned from one another.  The best learning is self-learning, so the teacher's role becomes that of a creator of an atmosphere of learning, exploring, sharing, and growing together.

Every teacher will have an individual philosophy of education (ideas about what is needful and important in order for learning to take place).  Five assumptions that would be appropriate in such a philosophy are the following:

1. Learning should be enjoyable.  Church should be
   thought of as a happy place where pleasurable
   experiences can occur.  There is nothing that
   says education must be painful!

2. <u>Learning should be relevant</u>. What is taught, whether it is a Bible story or something else, should be related to some practical application in daily living, something to be practiced, not just learned.

3. <u>Learning should be varied</u>. Noting creates boredom more quickly than doing the same thing the same way with no outlet for creativity, experimentation, or novelty. A variety of methods and materials will keep pupils alert and expectant for "what's coming next."

4. <u>Learning should involve as many senses as possible</u>. Pupils should not only hear a lesson, but also sing about it, draw pictures of it, dramatize it, write about it, discuss it, research it, see it visualized, and even play games with it. In lecture, only about 10 percent will be retained, but in activities involving pupil participation using sensory appeals, 90 percent retention is possible. A lesson should be restated and reinforced in many ways using as many different senses as can be worked into the lesson activities.

5. <u>Learning should have a message easily understood</u>. Teachers should avoid trying to crowd too many concepts into one lesson. Focus upon one or two main ideas or objectives and clearly state these to pupils rather than assuming they will get the point of the lesson indirectly. Memorizing a key verse that explains the Bible message in a nutshell, reciting aloud the key ideas of the lesson, or getting pupils to put the object of the lesson into their own words may be helpful ways of ensuring that the lesson "got across." (A helpful method of lesson reinforcement is remembering the acrostic, R-A-M: <u>r</u>eview the lesson, <u>a</u>pply the lesson to a life situation, and <u>m</u>emorize the key idea or concept the lesson teaches.)

A typical Sunday morning for a dedicated teacher would be the result of a week of preparation, not only prayerfully studying the lesson materials and planning the class activities, but also praying for each pupil by name. The teacher would arrive early to get the classroom in readiness, making the room attractive and inviting, perhaps with pictures appropriate to the lesson or with an interest center to focus on the day's theme. A checklist of necessary materials, audio-visuals, and resource supplies would ensure no last-minute slip-ups such as missing teaching aids or something forgotten at home. Each pupil would be greeted by name and made to feel accepted and appreciated. A relaxed and pleasant atmosphere would be balanced with the reverent seriousness which should bespeak the importance of attention to the lesson. The lesson would not be all "talk" but would be given in a visual or dramatic way. There would be follow-up to the lesson involving pupil activities to reinforce the "message" and to serve as an outlet for pupil creativity. The lesson would be summarized into one or two brief statements (the learning goal for the day) and each pupil would be able, at the end of the class, to tell "what the lesson was about." There would be a challenge to apply the lesson concepts at home during the week or some practical suggestion given for putting the lesson into practice. Pupils would be given responsibility for helping to clean up and care for the appearance of the room before leaving. The teacher would be relaxed and unhurried at the end of class, remaining to visit with a lingering pupil or to give special attention to one who needs it.

Unless teaching adults, teachers would want to get to know pupils' parents in order to keep communication lines open and to understand the home situations of pupils. This is often helpful in giving insights into individuals with problems, those who need extra love and attention, or those needing help with overcoming some difficulty. The final act of the day for a teacher would be an evaluation of the class and the effectiveness of the learning that occurred. Notations would be made as to pupil reactions and other data such as better ways, different ways, or never-to-be-repeated ways of doing things.

Just as the pastor is the shepherd of the congregation, the teacher should become the spiritual shepherd of the little flock that meets regularly. It is, therefore, a part of the teaching responsibility to evangelize as well as instruct. The teacher will want to introduce Jesus to each pupil in such a personal and intimate way that they will become comfortable talking about him and to him.

None of this is an easy task. Nor can these things be accomplished quickly or without making mistakes. The teacher is not responsible for 100 percent effectivness or for perfect results every time. It is, however, good to have some ideals, some goals to work toward as a guide along the way.

The main responsibility for teaching is for a teacher to be faithful and dedicated to do the best possible in what is often a demanding and thankless ministry. The fruits of the teacher's labor may never be fully known in this life, but the Lord of the Harvest is certain to reward those who have scattered the precious seeds of truth and prayed the psalmist's prayer:

> My tongue shall speak of thy Word, for all thy
> commandments are righteousness. Let thine hand
> help me, for I have chosen thy precepts. Make
> me to understand the way of thy precepts; so shall
> I talk of thy wondrous works.

33

# The Church Governing Board

> Brethren, look ye out among you men of
> honest report, full of the Holy Ghost
> and wisdom, whom we may appoint over
> this business (Acts 6:3).

Probably because of the arbitrary separation of things ecclesiastical from things temporal, a person serving on a church governing board is seldom thought of as having a spiritual ministry. Such a one usually is pictured as someone who is "all business" - one who leaves the spiritual aspects of church leadership to the clergy. While it is true that the responsibilities of these leaders are restricted to administrative functions, these very functions should be approached with the same reverence as that with which the pastor approaches the altar or pulpit. If it is God's business, it is sacred business.

The title of the governing board varies from church to church: Official Board, Parish Council, Session, Vestry, etc. Whatever the designation, the stereotype of the person serving on the governing board remains: a person who is willing to endure occasional committee meetings in order to make rubber-stamp decisions about preplanned clergy programs; one who sits, listens, nods approval, drinks coffee, doodles on the agenda sheet to stay awake, and goes home, thankful that the job is over until the next called meeting. This is certainly not the picture of board members who see their duties as a call to ministry.

Even though serving on a board usually is an elected office and carries with it a position of honor and earned respect, it should not be thought of as a political "plum" or popularity prize. Neither should it be considered a position of demagogue, figurehead, or dictator. Board members should see their roles as those of servants, representing the congregation in the oversight of civil responsibilities. The governing body serves as a board of directors of the church, taking charge of the administration of the buildings, grounds, budget, policies, and decisions concerning the welfare and smooth operation of nonecclesiastical matters.

Requirements for membership on a governing body vary from church to church (as specified in the canons or laws of the specific church, which should be consulted), but all indicate the need for leaders who are regular in attendance and faithful in contributing to the church both financially and in other supportive ways. Beyond the call to a commitment of time, the board member is also called to a commitment of personality. The qualifications for a worthy representative should include the following:

1. <u>A person of maturity and good judgment</u>. The
   board is a decision-making body and demands the
   steadiest of hands at the helm.

2. A good listener. The board operates as a team and calls for those who can hear all sides of a question with an open mind in an atmosphere of give-and-take.

3. A flexible person with a cooperative spirit. Stubborn, domineering, or belligerent people have no place on the board.

4. A person of prayer and spiritual insights. Decisions need to be prayed about and considered from the viewpoint of "What would the Lord have us to do in this situation?"

5. A person of dependability. Those who serve on the board are often called upon to go the second mile in serving on committees, spending extra time investigating or reporting on various aspects of church business, and taking on additional responsibilities. When such an extra assignment is given, a member must carry his or her share of the burden and not let the others down.

6. A person motivated to serve from a loving heart. There should be a devotion to the church and a sincere desire to see that all aspects of church business are done decently and in order.

7. A person of commitment. Board members must be dedicated to serving the Lord and the church, not easily discouraged, not prone to give up when things get difficult.

8. An accessible person. As a representative of the congregation, a board member must be in touch with the feelings and recommendations of fellow church members, willing to communicate, and acting as liaison for input to and from the board and other lay people. The board member must be available for specially called meetings in addition to regular business sessions.

9. A person whose personal life is a worthy example. The reading of the third chapter of I Timothy would make an appropriate guideline for selecting one to serve on the board. Here the probing question is asked, "If a man know not how to rule his own house, how shall he take care of the church of God?"

10. A person with the calling to and gift for administration. The board member should not only have an aptitude for business matters, but also have a sincere desire and willingness to serve the Lord in the ministry appointed.

Duties of board members necessitate some practical suggestions for those who view their functions as ministries unto the Lord. Such suggestions might include things like planning time wisely: clearing calendars well in advance for regular meetings, board retreats, and other related functions. Preparation time is more than setting aside a night for regular meetings. It may include a time of meditation and prayer, thoughtful reflecting upon issues of business to come before the meeting, and a continual offering of oneself for useful service. It also includes praying for fellow members, especially those with whom there may be disagreement.

In some parishes, the spouses of board members meet for prayer as the board is in session, asking God's guidance upon all that takes place. Whether or not there is a formal meeting for such prayers, the family of the board member should be committed to and supportive of that person's ministry. If there is a retreat or orientation program prior to a new term of office, inclusion of the family often underscores the importance of this supportive role. A word of caution, however, is called for when it comes to board matters of discretion. There must not be loose talk about church business, and any privileged information of board meetings must be considered the same sacred trust as that of a priest in a confessional.

A conscientious board member will want to be as informed and efficient in the performance of duties as possible. Since this may require extra time and effort, both the board member and the family must be willing to make sacrifices when necessary. Priorities must be established, and often social engagements or family commitments must take a back seat when the Lord's business has to be performed.

Because a pastor cannot possibly do all the administrative functions of the parish, and because the governing body's role includes assuming burdens of overwork and details that will free the pastor for spiritual ministries, the board becomes the strong, supportive arm of the clergy. Board members should not wait to be requested or instructed to act, but should be alert for signs of fatigue or overwork and take the initiative when the pastor needs a helping hand. A considerate board member will volunteer rather than waiting to be asked when a job needs to be done. A pastor is always befriending and ministering to others, constantly giving of self. And so the pastor needs times of refreshment, times to take in as well as give out. A church governing body will want to be available to minister to the pastor, offering friendship, encouragement, prayer, and support whenever and wherever possible. This includes more than providing for the pastor's financial welfare; it includes a ministry to spiritual and emotional welfare as well. Exactly how this may be accomplished will depend upon the pastor, the situation, and propriety, but ministering board members will be sensitive and alert to act when prompted by the Holy Spirit.

Whether a board member is attending meetings, prayerfully considering weighty matters of church business, investigating and solving problems, recommending budget expenditures, or ministering to the needs of the parish or clergy, there must be the attitude of Colossians 3:17: "Whatsoever ye do in word or deed, do all in the name of the Lord Jesus . . . ."

The Bible does not differentiate between the spiritual and the secular as people often do, but rather, indicates that all aspects of life should be done in reverence as unto the Lord. Those who minister as board members should keep this foremost in mind in the performance of their duties.

Perhaps the key verse for all vestries should be the following reminder:

> Be not slothful in business; be fervent in spirit, serving the Lord (Rom. 12:11).

## Housekeeping in the House of the Lord

> Every one whom His Spirit made willing, they brought the Lord's offering to the work of the tabernacle of the congregation, and for all His service, and for the holy garments (Ex. 35:21).

There is nothing inherently fascinating about washing, ironing, scrubbing, cleaning, waxing, polishing, and dusting. There should be, however, a holy fascination for things sacred such as ministering at the altar of the Lord, preparing the elements for Communion, creating an environment for worship through decorating and beautifying the sanctuary, preparing clean and attractive robes or vestments for use in services, shining brass and silver so that only untarnished vessels are used in setting the Lord's table.

Most churches have committees or special groups whose designated task is to perform such housekeeping duties. It may be a volunteer committee, a committee appointed by the pastor, a church service or social club that has accepted the responsibility, or (as in the case of a sacramental church like the Episcopal Church) a committee established by canon law and known as the Altar Guild. People who feel called to this ministry may submit their names for consideration, even in churches where it is normal for the clergy to select individuals as pastoral assistants.

Since the attitude of such persons is the determiner of whether these activities are seen as wearisome chores or joyous services, ministering in the proper frame of mind is of primary importance. The Altar Guild prayer of the Episcopal Church, which might be an appropriate meditation before beginning any regular or special duty, embodies the essence of the proper attitude:

> Almighty God, grant that I may handle holy things with reverence, and perform my duties with such faithfulness and devotion, that they may rise before Thee with acceptance and obtain thy blessing. In Jesus name, Amen.

In addition to the proper attitude for this ministry, other qualifications include the following:

1. <u>Dedication of time</u>. It must become a family ministry, for often special services, weddings, or funerals will necessitate that a parent not be in the home as often as the children would like, or that a spouse not be available on a special holiday because the church commitment takes priority.

2. <u>Willingness to sacrifice</u>. Personal interests and appointments must often be set aside when one is scheduled for church-care duty.

3. <u>Aptness to learn</u>. A sincere desire to be trained for particular duties is necessary for adequate preparedness. Because each church may do things differently, a member must be willing to adapt to a particular pastor's preferences and to become familiar with specific do's and don'ts.

4. <u>Attention to detail</u>. This is especially important in sacramental churches where workers must be acquainted with the proper colors, symbols, liturgies, and operating methods in order to assure a coordinated and appropriate service in keeping with the church season and order of service. Even the smallest duties must be approached with thoroughness and care.

5. <u>Cooperation with others</u>. This service to the church is essentially group ministry, involving working with others, submission to authority, and consideration for those who follow up and build upon the services performed. The next person who will be serving deserves to find things in order.

6. <u>Willingness to work without complaining</u>. An uncomplaining attitude is a practical necessity in any atmosphere where accidents can happen, hard work must often be repeated, and few are available to give recognition or applause to a "behind-the-scenes" effort.

7. <u>Spiritual disciplines</u>. Working behind the scenes, often with little recognition, and assisting those involved in sacramental rites such as weddings and funerals, church-care workers need discipline, decorum and humility. There is a passage of Scripture that serves as a reminder of the holy calling and attitude with which this ministry is to be performed. It embodies the focus with which all ministry should be performed.

> Walk worthy of the vocation wherewith ye are
> called. With all lowliness and meekness, with
> longsuffering, forebearing one another in love;
> endeavoring to keep the unity of the Spirit in
> the bond of peace (Eph. 4:1-2).

## The Choir

> They ministered before the dwelling place of
> the tabernacle of the congregation with sing-
> ing (I Chron. 6:32).

Because singing is enjoyable and an aspect of church worship in which everyone can participate, the ministry of the choir is often overlooked and underappreciated. The ease with which the choir seems to perform misleads many people into believing that being a church musician is a casual or effortless avocation. What may not be realized is that the seemingly effortless delivery of the music is the result of much hard work, dedication, and sacrifice.

The choir members should not be considered "entertainers" for the congregation, nor people who fill time while the offering is collected. The real purpose of the church choir is to lead the congregation in worship and praise and to complement and supplement the rest of the service with an inspirational message set to music. Whether the choir is singing an anthem or leading the congregational singing, the emphasis should be upon the meaning of the words and the focusing of attention upon Him to whom the words are sung.

Singing has a long history in corporate worship. Moses and his sister Miriam were acting as the first choir directors as they led their people in songs of praise, rejoicing over the defeat of their Egyptian enemies. At the Jerusalem temple, singers were appointed to minister before the Lord. Nehemiah 11:22 describes how the Levites and singers aided in worship, saying, "the singers were over the business of the house of God." There was even a time when an important battle was won, not because of the military know-how of the soldiers, but because of the faithfulness of King Jehoshaphat's choir, who "went out before the army" singing praises. David and the other psalmists are also reminders of the significant part music plays in the expressions of praise, thanksgiving, and petitions to the Lord during worship.

Many feel that unless they can read music or are specially trained musically that they cannot participate in the choir. Nothing could be further from truth. While it is true that an ability to read music and a good singing voice are definite assets to the choir, most choir directors would rather have dedicated hearts and willing (albeit un-trained) voices than professional soloists. Since it is a group ministry, the weaker voices are complemented by the strong. Those who cannot read music can learn from listening and imitation. The emphasis is always on "making a joyful noise unto the Lord" rather than on showmanship.

What, then, are the qualifications for a choir member? Most directors agree that at the top of the list should be "faithfulness." A person who is late or irregular in attendance at rehearsals cannot execute the music as it should be performed. The beauty, continuity, and worship, which are the end products, come only after the mechanical and technical details are mastered. A halfhearted musician creates problems for the entire choir.

Another requisite is the wise planning of time. The choir members must not only set aside time for rehearsals, Sunday services, and special holy day programs, but also plan their days so that heavy schedules are delayed until after rehearsals or at times other than when a music ministry is to be performed. One who comes to the choir exhausted has nothing to give to the music, which always demands an enthusiasm, a heart-felt energy, and the giving of one's best efforts.

It goes without saying that one's dedication of talent (or one's dedication of self in spite of a lack of talent) should precede the joining of the choir. There can be no "prima donnas" in the Lord's music ministry. It is a body ministry, a group which must work as a unit in a spirit of cooperation and love. There must be, therefore, an attitude of humility and a willingness to be disciplined, to take direction, and to become only one small part of a more meaningul "whole."

Preparation for the Sunday morning worship service should begin long before the choir members arrive at church. The rehearsal of the music should be accompanied with a readiness of mind, a preparedness to worship and a desire to minister. The "Chorister's Prayer," often used among Episcopalians to aid the choir in achieving the proper mindset before singing, suggests a type of meditation appropriate for many church choirs:

> Bless, O Lord, thy servants who minister in
> Thy Temple. Grant that what we sing with our
> lips we may believe in our hearts, and what
> we believe in our hearts we may show forth in
> our lives. Through Jesus Christ, Our Lord. Amen.

Choir members should always be aware that their function goes beyond processing in and out or singing an anthem at the appropriate time. As leaders of the congregation, they should actively participate and concentrate upon every aspect of worship, whether or not it is accompanied by music. The singing of the special music should not be thought of as a "performance" but, rather, as an offering to God and an aid to the congregation's centering in on things spiritual.

Usually the director will select music appropriate to the day (perhaps after consultation with the pastor) in order to reemphasize the theme of the Bible lessons or sermon topic. In such instances, the choir has a part in the teaching ministry as the music says, in a different way, that which has been read or spoken. But even when the music is different from Scripture or sermon, the purpose is the same: to open the ears and hearts of the congregation, to inspire, to instruct, or to aid in worshipful praise and adoration.

Often the choir will do more than just sing together. Some choirs have formed themselves into a prayer group in order to share mutual concerns and intercessions. Even if no such formal group is formed, choir members should be in prayer - not just prior to and during services, but throughout the week. Such a praying, caring body will make new choir members feel comfortable and accepted and will add a spiritual dimension that will both enhance the music and enrich the lives of the musicians.

Some choirs have a retreat or workshop as a new church year begins. This allows the choir members to hear other musicians or receive inspiration from a retreat or workshop leader. It also serves as a type of "pep rally" to get the music program off on the right foot - enthusiastic, expectant, and ready to go. Furthermore, it gives an opportunity to see the music ministry long-range, and it affords a chance to rehearse for a longer time than is possible in the brief, weekly sessions. Such advance preparation and planning gives the choir a sense of the entire, coordinated music program for the coming seasons.

A word should also be given to the importance of the ministries of junior and youth choirs. Nothing is more important to a youngster's development in appreciation for worship than choir training. Participants acquire the disciplines of music and become better worshipers as they learn to follow the order of service through their active participation and leadership in the services. Parents must sometimes make sacrifices to provide transportation or rearrange schedules to get youngsters to rehearsals and services, but it is time well spent in terms of training and supporting the spiritual development available through music. In this sense, it becomes a family ministry.

There is no more joyous service to perform than that of singing to the glory of God and leading in the church music ministry. Those who "come before his presence with singing" find that they not only bless those who hear them, but also that abundant blessings are in store for themselves as well.

# 3 · Ministries of Helps

## Beyond the Traditional Ministries

There are any number of services that lay people can perform in addition to the "traditional" ministries mentioned in chapter 2. These additional services often are overlooked or left undone because no one took the initiative to get them done or because the demon of complacency whispered in people's ears, "Don't get involved." Many times professionals are hired to do work that easily could be done by volunteers - either individuals or committees. Volunteer efforts would not only save the church money, but also give the lay workers an opportunity to expand their stewardship by dedicating talents to the service of the Lord. There is virtually no vocation, hobby, aptitude, or interest that cannot be utilized in some aspect of church life.

Usually the problem is "getting started." Churches, like people, fall into comfortable routines of "the way it's always been done." Some functions, which have outlived their usefulness, continue because no one thought to terminate them; others, which may be desperately needed ministries, are unfulfilled because no one assumed responsibility for them.

A church that found a workable solution to this problem initiated a "Talent Pool" instead of holding an "Every Member Canvass" at stewardship time, the regular time for subscribing the church budget and making pledges. Rather than requesting members to pledge money to meet the church's needs, the focus was on human involvement and the giving of time and talents. There was a survey taken to determine which part of the parish life and outreach each individual would become personally responsible for. On "Accountability Sunday" the pastor and the governing board vocally reaffirmed their commitments to areas of ministry, and the congregation submitted pledge cards (for services they would perform) during a special part of the worship service, followed by Communion. In this way, the church needs, which had been previously publicized, were matched up with volunteers who had particular interests in meeting those needs. The result was personal and specific ministry.

At another small church, the annual meeting was utilized as a time for listening for and answering "calls." After a time of fasting, prayer, and seeking the Lord's guidance for parish direction, people who felt inclined to involve themselves in particular aspects of ministry would rise and say, "I feel a call to---." Those who shared the same concerns would then meet as a group to organize and determine areas of responsibility in answering the call to that particular ministry.

Although these suggestions may not be applicable in every parish, the principles underlying them are. It is not difficult to survey the membership to determine resources and then match these abilities to church needs. (The Lay Ministry Analysis Sheet on page 14 may be a useful tool in such a survey.) Church growth is often in proportion to involvement. Even though the initial push to get people started often takes some doing, once people become actively involved and see the results of their efforts, there is an inherent concern, an attitude of caring, a feeling of belonging, and a personalization that begins to replace feelings of detachment and restraint.  People no longer feel they are on the outside looking in but, rather, that they are at the center arena where they can be part of making good things happen.

Once a church determines that more lay involvement is needed, what then? There are some additional questions that must be answered before arbitrarily matching up a church need with a willing volunteer. What if the volunteer is unsuited to the task and only _thinks_ he or she can perform adequately?  Who will be responsible for screening and checking on the work of volunteers? What safeguards can be built into the program to assure that volunteers do not overstep their approved responsibilities or fail to do them? Obviously, some organization, planning, and establishing of boundaries must precede the implementation of a full-blown lay ministry program of helps. The survey guide on the following page may be helpful in the preplanning stage.

## Helping Ministries

What Romans 12:7 calls "ministering" and I Corinthians 12:28 calls "helps" may be terms too general for any clear idea of specific implementation. When lay people are told they should be "ministering" they often wonder, "Ministering what? Ministering how?" If asked to evidence the gifts of "helps" they may ask, "Helps to whom?" Even though each church's needs and resources are uniquely different, perhaps the following list of helping ministries categorized and supplemented with suggested methods of effecting them may be beneficial:

### Personality Helps

Human beings are not only endowed by their Creator with certain inalienable rights, but also endowed with certain characteristics of personality. We say that a person is outgoing, efficient, friendly, understanding, neat, generous, or any number of other descriptive adjectives which set him apart from others. In determining suitability for particular ministries, it would be well to do an inventory of characteristics (a personality profile) in advance. There are various ways this can be done, including professional tests which may be secured and taken by prospective helpers. The simplest way, however, is to have an individual make a list of adjectives (describing both positive and negative characteristics) about herself or himself and then have several people who know the person well prepare a similar list for comparison. If time permits, the clergy or a qualified counselor may go over the lists with the person to help define the most outstanding personality assets suggested. Obviously, a shy, retiring person by nature should not be given the same responsibilities as those better suited to an extrovert's personality, nor would it be advisable to appoint a sloppy person to a job requiring orderliness. Once the human elements of ministry are understood, they may be more wisely invested in tasks suited to personality aptitudes and preferences. If the entire parish (or a group within the parish) gets involved in such a survey, a record file of "People Suitable for---" can be determined and be readily at hand

## Survey of Lay Ministries for --- Church

1. What is our church's definition of lay ministry?

2. What lay ministries are available in this church at the present time?

3. What are the strengths and weaknesses in present ministries?

4. What are the priorities for ministry (what is needed, listed in rank order)?

5. What ministries need a "funeral" (have outlived their usefulness)?

6. What makes ministry "happen" (prerequisites for effective ministry)?


## Tests for Starting a New Ministry

1. Do we have the resources (money, people, materials, etc.)?

2. Is there really a need for this ministry?  How do we know this?

3. Is the clergy in support of this ministry?  Is it scripturally sound?

4. How much time and effort will be required?  Will the results make this investment of time and energy worthwhile?

5. Have prayer and careful planning preceded implementation of this ministry?

6. What, if any, are the blocks (problems expected) which may occur? How will these problems be dealt with and by whom?

7. What are the purposes and expected results of this ministry?

8. Have both long-range and short-range goals been determined?  Whay are they?  Has everyone involved been made aware of these goals?

9. Who will be in charge and provide leadership?  What qualifications do the leaders possess?

10. Have responsibilities for sharing in this ministry been fairly apportioned?  Are those assigned particular responsibilities committed to the support and success of this ministry?

11. What criteria will be used in selecting and evaluating volunteers? (Qualifications, aptitudes, time required, etc.)

12. Has this ministry been "tested" on a small scale first?

13. What boundaries and safeguards have been established?

14. How will this ministry be followed up, evaluated, and perhaps modified in time?

15. How will Jesus Christ be glorified in and through the efforts of this ministry?

when needs arise.  Here are some personality characteristics corresponding to particular ministries to serve as examples of personality helps:

1. Edification:  To edify is to build up or strengthen another.  A vocal, outgoing individual could perform this ministry by giving compliments, offering words of encouragement, or counseling.  A shy, reticent person could write a note of encouragement or appreciation, give a gift, or just be available for listening. Clergy and leaders, who usually receive more criticism than approval, are especially in need of edification.

2. Comfort:  When sickness, death, or tragedy strikes, there are any number of ways of offering comfort. Those with personality characteristics and the training to do so can share Scriptures, prayers, or words of consolation, while others may send sympathy cards, gifts, or flowers. Bringing food or offering to do chores or run errands can also be a source of ministering comfort at difficult times.  Warm, generous, and sympathetic personalities will always find a place of service at such times.

3. Outreach:  This ministry may mean anything from evangelism and missionary efforts to interchurch or community services to funding relief and welfare programs - anything that extends the love of God beyond established boundaries.  Implementation may take the form of sophisticated organizational programs such as stocking a food pantry or clothes closet for the needy or conducting a survey of welfare needs of the community.  An organized person with leadership qualities would most likely design such programs, while those with personalities appropriate to detail work and assisting in a follower's role would provide the leg work and support efforts.  The same would hold true for other organized outreach activities such as taking witnessing teams into prisons or institutions, visiting the unchurched of the community, or participating in various types of missionary activities.  On the other hand, outreach may take the form of nonorganized activities such as friendly individuals bringing neighbors with them to church services or altruistic individuals donating money or service hours to charities of their choice.  It could include as simple a thing as providing transportation to a senior citizen or as complex a program as serving daily meals to the hungry. The kind of outreach involvement, naturally, will depend upon needs, interests, and available resources in individual parishes. Where there are interested people with the ability to promote and maintain complex programs of outreach, there will be requirements like money, personnel, and maintenance.  Where these resources are lacking, it can take the form of a small number of people conscientiously concerned for meeting the needs of others just by showing their love, sharing their talents, or giving their time.  Although outreach ministries frequently spotlight the "doers" and the "take charge" people, there is also the need for the quiet followers who support these efforts with their money, prayers, or behind-the-scenes endeavors.

4. Pastoral Care:  Just as a flock of sheep needs the shepherd's care and guidance, congregational flocks need shepherding also.

The pastor is the over-shepherd, but often one person cannot even know about, much less minister to, all the needs and concerns of the church. In some parishes, the membership is divided into geographic locations with an "under-shepherd" given specific parish families for which to be responsible. These helpers visit and check on the welfare of the portion of the congregation in their designated area, inform the clergy of needs or problems, and act as a liaison between the home and the church. Such pastoral responsibilities may include involving children from broken homes, the divorced, or the widowed in the helper's own family outings or providing counseling services such as to single families or teenagers in need of guidance. Even when such a program is not maintained on an organized basis, and even when such a pastoral helper may lack the leadership qualities of the clergy or trained counselors, the people of any parish can be trained to assume responsibility for one another in informal ways. Families may be matched up to pray for each other regularly. Mothers in a specific area can meet to share concerns and insights about maintaining a Christian home. Businessmen can support each other in efforts to witness for Jesus in a materialistic society. One woman in a medium-sized parish who took pastoral responsibilities to heart assumed the duty of writing letters every week to different people in the parish. Sometimes it was a word of cheer and encouragement or a compliment for a job well done at some church function. Other times it would be sharing a passage of Scripture or a teaching she had heard. On rare occasions it would be a gentle but firm rebuke given in love when a sheep seemed to be straying from the fold. This woman knew that all sheep go astray when they are untended, and she neither ignored the situation when it occurred in the parish nor expected the clergy to assume all responsibility for meeting of parish needs. Care must naturally be exercised here, for there is a fine line between being controlling, nosy, or critical and the Christian responsibility to support, encourage, and respond to needs. It goes without saying that invading the realm of the clergy's pastoral responsibilities should be done only with the approval and support of such clergy. Most clergy are delighted to have the assistance of submitted and dedicated lay people who are willing to become responsible for one another - either by overt roles of leadership or by quiet displays of loving concern, but such ministry must be guided, judged, and approved. People of differing personality types can and should become involved in following St. Paul's admonition, which is the essence of pastoral care: "When others are troubled, needing our sympathy and encouragement, we can pass on to them this same help and comfort God has given us" (II Cor. 1:4, Living Bible).

Vocational Helps

In much the same way that personality profiles provide a useful tool in matching up people with needed ministries to which they are suited, a survey of occupations in the church can provide for additional needs. For instance, single women are often taken advantage of in the business world, especially if they are not familiar with the service, product, or methods involved. A list of Christian businesses and merchants would be of invaluable help for such a woman alone who may need to purchase a new car, have repair work done, or plan for financial investments. In times of economic problems, a "job corps" ministry could be started from such a list. Those out of work could be matched up with Christians who need dependable employees. Such a survey also would assist the church when vocational services might be needed on the church property. Rather than hiring work done, the church could call upon members to volunteer services as a part of their stewardship pledge. Almost any vocational know-how can be put to use in some aspect of church life, but the following categories should be a starting point for organizing the parish into vocational resource areas:

1. Church Business Operations: The clergy, the church governing board, and the church office staff (for churches large enough to require such a staff) can utilize the talents of many different occupations such as bookkeepers, administrators, stenographers, financial planners, personnel managers, and office assistants. Retired people or housewives can volunteer time on a regular basis to work in the church office. If necessary, babysitters can volunteer to take care of children while mothers address envelopes, type and mail out church bulletins, or do the numerous clerical tasks that are required to keep the church running smoothly. Tax experts, accountants, insurance workers, real estate brokers, lawyers, business machine operators and clerk-typists can be organized on a rotating basis for weekly service, or they may be "on call" to come in and give assistance as needed. Even young people (teenagers after school or college students on vacation) can get into the act putting materials together, running errands, signing out library books or tapes, and answering the telephone. Usually people are willing to offer a few hours of service time utilizing the skills and talents they possess to help out at church. They just have to be asked. Someone has to survey the talents and professional services available in the parish and then organize the volunteer efforts.

2. Purchasing Needs: Churches buy a lot of products and supplies. Often, these needs could be met by people willing to make donations or to give items to the church at a discounted price. A survey of the merchants and dealers in and around the parish (including nonmembers who may be approachable) can provide the church with a list of purchasing sources. Whether the need is for groceries, paper goods, office supplies, machinery, or furnishings, there is usually someone willing to make a donation either as a tax deduction or as a part of their stewardship pledge. More money could be given to missions and outreach programs if less could be spent upon internal operations, so wise purchasing becomes a stewardship opportunity not only for the individuals who make donations but also for the church.

3. Maintenance and Repairs: When things around the church break down, whether it is the minister's car or the air conditioning

system, there is frequently a member of the church who is trained to fix them. Or members have relatives or friends who are willing to lend a helping hand. Here again, the key is knowing who does what. Having a list of skilled carpenters, plumbers, painters, landscapers, interior decorators, mechanics, and other maintenance-repair people will be invaluable when breakdowns occur or fix-up time comes around. Naturally, people must work for a living and are sometimes unavailable when needs arise, but this problem can be circumvented by having "work days" at the church on weekends or by utilizing retired people. Work-day projects can be a great deal of fun if they are combined with things which appeal to the workers - food, entertainment, contests, fund-raisers, prizes, or awards.

4. Services: When the church is in need of special services, it is advantageous to know the right person to call. Advertising and publicity people, florists, educators, recreation leaders, printers, janitors, librarians, social workers, counselors, funeral directors, photographers, musicians, and a host of other occupational services can be made available both to the church and to individual members of the parish. Most Christians would rather deal with and give business to other Christians if given the choice, so a list of occupational services can find many needful and varied uses.

## Avocational Helps

Hobbies and extracurricular interests of adults and youth should also be considered as outlets for ministry. An artistic person can paint a mural on the nursery or Sunday school class wall; skilled needle workers can create banners or wall hangings to decorate the church; seamstresses can make robes or vestments; gardeners can make flower arrangements for the altar and floral centerpieces for banquets; sports-minded individuals can organize church teams, coach, or provide recreational programs for youth; actors and musicians can put on special programs for holy-day services or entertainment; cooks and bakers can plan church suppers; woodworkers can make toys for Sunday school preschoolers; fishermen and hunters can provide the main course for a church cookout - and on and on. Summer vacation Bible school programs or special Lenten weeks of study are good times to teach skills and make useful things for the church. Christmas, Easter, and other holy days are also good target dates for making things or getting involved in creative projects as special "offerings" unto the Lord. Instruction classes or special-interest groups can be formed at the church in order to encourage the dedication of creative talents to a useful purpose.

## Committee Helps

It has been said, "A camel is a horse designed by a committee." The inference is that the more people involved in a project, the "lumpier" the result. Committees are supposed to provide an efficient way of doing business, but often the differences in personalities, methods, and ideas for procedures result in more friction than facilitation. The added dimension and "plus" for the church committee, however, is that Christ can dissolve differences to bring people into unity Christians who work together and prayerfully consider alternatives find that the Christlike qualities of sharing, submission, cooperation, and mutual respect will result in outcomes committees are designed to effect.

The need for a particular committee arises and dissolves depending on existing situations. Churches, like clubs and most other organizations, have two kinds of committees: standing committees (those of long duration, which continually exist for ongoing programs) and temporary or special committees (short-range groups, which meet only until the need for them ceases to exist).

Usually, the standing committees are subgroups associated with church organizations such as the governing board or service organizations - committees such as membership, finance, outreach, and Christian education. Temporary committees are usually social, investigative, or fund-raising. Examples would be a group to plan a Christmas social or program, a committee to do a feasibility study, or a fund-raising group to put on a rummage sale or pancake supper.

People who serve on any kind of church committee should see their function as a ministry, entering into the work with the same spirituality and decorum sitting on that committee as sitting in the pew. The reason this is not always the case is twofold. First, committee work is often focused on functional aspects of problem-solving rather than on spiritual principles. Second, clergy or committee heads often do not take time to educate the workers to approach their tasks as lay ministries. There must be a balance of the spiritual and the temporal. Obviously, a committee that spends all its time praying and exploring the spiritual aspects of the function but never gets to work on the practical operation to be performed has gone too far in the other direction. Good committees require people with their heads in the clouds but their feet on the ground.

Time and effort should be given to surveying the need for church committees and for evaluating the efficiency of committee operations within the church. Such committees may be either the personification of the biblical gift of helps or a complete waste of time.

Time and effort should also be given to educating those called to serve on various committees before they are thrust into an activity for which they are ill-prepared and unsuited. Committee members deserve to know (1) what the purpose and goals of the committee are; (2) how and why they were selected to serve on the committee; (3) how much time and effort will be required to complete the task at hand; (4) what preparation and training, if any, will be needed for the task; and (5) what is expected of the individual as a member of the committee.

# Survey To Determine Committee Efficiency

I. Type of Committee:

1. What standing committees exist in our church and for what purpose?

2. What temporary committees have existed and for what purposes?

3. What committees beyond the local church level (e.g., district, diocesan, provincial, conference) does our church participate in?

4. What community or interchurch committees does our church take part in?

5. Evaluate the effectiveness of these committees in terms of benefits to our church and the spreading of the Kingdom's work.

II. Membership of Committee:

1. How are members chosen (appointed, elected, volunteer, other)?

2. How is leadership for committees determined?

3. What determines the compatibility and suitability of the membership?

4. Evaluate the effectiveness of methods of selecting leaders and committee members. What better methods of selection might be tried?

III. Size of Committee:

1. Who or what determines the size of a particular committee (tradition, canon law, bylaws, personal preferences, other)?

2. Is the size appropriate to the committee's function (too few, too many, appropriate)? Give reasons to justify reply.

3. How are committee members removed or replaced? How is the size of the committee enlarged when necessary? Are these methods workable? What "safeguards" for avoidance of hurt feelings, if any, have been built in to avoid exclusiveness and at the same time ensure proper utilization of those best qualified?

IV. Spiritual Considerations:

1. Does the committee open and close with prayer?

2. Does the committee have a Christ-centered purpose? What is it? How is this purpose implemented through committee functions?

3. Does this committee have the full approval of the church, clergy, and/or governing board?

V. Efficiency of Meetings:

1. Are committee meetings regularly attended by all members?

2. Are meetings conducted punctually (open and close on time)?

3. Do meetings run smoothly and in a businesslike fashion (use of parliamentary procedure or other orderly process to ensure disposal of business without getting sidetracked or bogged down)?

4. Is there an agenda published in advance? Is there a planned program?

5. Are members kept informed (published minutes or other methods of communcation before, during, and after meetings)?

6. Does the meeting proceed with orderliness, openness, and positiveness? (Are attitudes expressed those of cooperation and mutual respect? If not, why not?)

7. Evaluate the effectiveness of -- committee head

-- committee members

-- committee functioning (overall)

NOTE: Each church or committee may have its own criteria for evaluation, but a few guidelines might be as follows:

Chairperson - leadership qualities, fairness, organization, ability to work within allotted time frame, able to stay on target, etc.

Committee members - cooperation, dedication, freedom from personality quirks (not a "yes person" or "do nothing" or troublemaker, etc.)

Productivity - accomplishments, efficient use
of time and resources.

VI. Problems of Committee:

1.  What problems are inherent in the group?  Are they func-
    tional or personality conflicts?

2.  What are the contributing causes to these problems?

3.  What suggestions for solving the problems have been
    offered?  Have they been "tested"?  If so, with what
    results?

4.  Have members met together to pray about the difficulties?

5.  When the solution to a problem is determined, do all members
    cooperate to effect a solution?

VII. Improvements:

1.  How long has it been since the committee was changed, up-
    dated, revamped?

2.  Does the committee have a suggestion box or other method of
    getting feedback?  Are outside suggestions for improvement
    considered?

3.  Evaluate the committee in terms of overall proficiency:

                    -- efficiency

                    -- productivity

                    -- spirituality

The survey chart above may offer some helpful guidelines in
evaluating church committees and setting goals for productive committee workers.  Every committee head should answer these or similar
questions prior to beginning any committee function in the church.

## Conclusion

Whether one is giving of personality, vocational talents, or
avocational interests, the ministry of helps offers far-reaching
and many-faceted opportunities for a layperson to become involved in
a personal way in the service to Lord and church.  It was said of
Jesus, "He went about doing good."  Jesus calls his followers into
this same kind of life, saying, "Whosoever will be great among you,

let him be your minister, and whosoever will be chief among you, let him be your servant" (Matt. 20:26-27).

For a true-life experience of how the ministry of helps changed one church's outlook on volunteer efforts, take the case of the church hostess who got tired of calling the same people on the phone all the time for donations of refreshments for the kitchen. This particular church was famous for hosting numerous receptions, parties, and social events at which refreshments were served. People began to be irritated at so many requests for baked goods, so the hostess said one day, "Okay, Lord. If you want refreshments served at this church, you'll have to get the people to bring them in." With that, she put a notice in the church bulletin saying that she would make no more appeals for refreshments, but that the Holy Spirit could remind the women of the kitchen's needs instead. She went on to suggest that the congregation set aside an extra portion of baked goods whenever they were doing their regular family cooking - an extra dozen cookies, half a cake, an extra batch of hors d'oeuvres, etc. The little extra would be designated as an "offering for Jesus" and brought to the church freezer at everyone's convenience. Such a system was not only a convenience that allowed people to help at times when they were already involved in cooking anyway, but also an opportunity to serve the church and see the kitchen at home as a place of ministry. After a year's time, the hostess reported, "The Holy Spirit did a much better job at reminding people about providing for our needs than I could have done on the telephone. We never lacked for refreshments at a single function, and no one was burdened about helping because it was done voluntarily and lovingly."

When word of the success of this method got around the church, other committee heads and church leaders began to follow suit. The Christian Education director, for instance, put a similar notice in the church bulletin when it was time to recruit Sunday school teachers for the coming year. No telephone calls, no arm-twisting, no pleas for support were issued, just a simple request to pray and ask the Lord to nudge the people he had chosen for a teaching ministry that year. The church began to see that the Lord was interested in every church project and function and that he wanted to provide for every need of every organization. If he could provide baked goods for the church freezer, he could also provide volunteers and workers to carry out every ministry of the entire church. The steps were few and simple: (1) make the need known; (2) pray about the need; (3) trust the Lord to provide the necessary solution (volunteer) to meet the need.

There are abundant resources and talents in each and every church congregation. But regardless of the many or limited talents one may possess, and even if a person is actively involved in other traditional or special ministries, one can always become involved in the ministry of helps. Like the dutiful Scout who finds a good deed to do daily, the church volunteer who will diligently seek the Lord's will in finding a particular area of service can find needs to be met at church. Activities in the home, at the job, from leisure time or from committee work can all merge into fulfilling ministries whenever God's people will take the time to plan for and implement these gifts of helps.

# 4 · Ministries of Prayer

If Jesus, the perfect Son of God, found it necessary to get away in quiet to commune with God, even to the extent that he "continued all night in prayer" (Luke 6:12) - and if the miracle-working saints of the early church gave themselves "continually to prayer" (cf. Acts 6:4, 1:14) - should not all of God's people, who fall far short of their spirituality, seek to follow and even exceed their examples? The people whom God uses to accomplish his purposes on earth are people of prayer.  The biblical examples and personal testimonies of those so used by God attest to the fact that when people pray, the hand of God moves.  II Chronicles 7:14 is only one of many promises in God's Word proclaiming God's readiness to hear and answer prayer: "If my people who are called by my name will humble themselves and pray, and seek my face, and turn from their wicked ways; then will I hear from heaven, and will forgive their sin, and will heal their land."

Prayer is such an integrated part of church worship and such a common practice that oftentimes its significance and power are over-looked.  Prayer is much more than a shopping list of personal wants to present to God.  It is more than reading of specified passages in a Prayer Book at appropriate times.  It is more than a religious ritual or spiritual "duty." Prayer is communing with God.  Such communication is a two-way street: speaking and the courteous response of listening. One would think it quite rude if someone called upon the telephone and never let the other party do any of the talking.  Yet Christians often do this to God when they monopolize the conversation in prayer, never listening or expecting to hear God's response.

Although there can be no set patterns or hard-and-fast rules governing all methods of prayer, there are some guidelines to be con-sidered by which to measure one's personal prayer life.  For instance, an acceptable pattern for prayer, if it is to be balanced rather than narrow or exclusive in scope, would include the following: meditation, silence, listening, praise, adoration, thanksgiving, confession of sin, intercession for others, and finally, petition - one's own personal needs.  By placing the personal requests at the end of the list, there is not only balance in the prayer (attention to God and others as well as to self) but also an attitude of worship and humility that comes from centering the thoughts away from self, lest selfishness dominate the sacredness of prayer.  I Timothy 2:1 speaks about this important balance in the prayer life: "that, . . . supplications, prayers, inter-cessions, and giving of thanks be made for all men."

In addition to balance, there should also be variety in the form of one's prayers.  To recite well-known, established prayers may be very beneficial at times, but one also needs to learn to be conversa-tional with God.  People were created that they might have fellowship, an intimate friendship, with their Creator. God does not care about flowery language or specific forms of prayer; a sincere, heartfelt simplicity is preferred to fancy, Pharisaic phrases. An intimate friendship can hardly be established when there is no frequent communication. Therefore, various modes of prayer can enrich and expand the intimacy of communing with the Lord. Prayers may be offered with others or alone, aloud or silently, in quiet humility upon the knees or in the midst of the busiest activities, in the Spirit and with the understanding, at the church altar or at the family dining table. Will not the Father, whose love of variety is evidenced in the fingerprints of creation, delight in the creativity of his children's prayers? To heed the scriptural admonition to "pray without ceasing" is to be constantly in an _attitude_ of prayer, a keeping of the heart attuned to God, whether washing dishes, mowing the lawn, driving down the street, or kneeling in church. Prayers may be read, recited, written, paraphrased, whispered, thought, spoken, sung, or even whistled, but as I Timothy 2:8 says, "Men [should] pray _everywhere_."

To the guidelines of praying with spiritual ears open to listen, with balance, and with variety in prayer, consistency should be added. There should be a definite time set aside for prayer each day. That is not to say prayers should not be offered spontaneously as needs and desires arise at a time other than the regular prayer hour. It is to say that there is something special about having a quiet time daily, an appointed time for being alone with God. It does not matter whether the time is early in the morning, to start seeking God's direction for a new day; the last thing at night before retiring, to offer the day to the Lord as a final offering; or at some time between, such as the lunch hour or a coffee break. The important thing is having an uninterrupted block of time in a quiet place where one may consistently keep a divine appointment with the Almighty.

## Getting Started

For beginners, prayer is often awkward. Like any new venture, it takes time and practice before it becomes an easy, relaxed, and natural function. Sometimes it seems to beginners in prayer that their prayers are a waste of time. They may not feel different or see any astounding results of their prayers. It may seem that God either did not hear their prayers or that God does not really care about people's needs. Such beginners need instruction and help in understanding what prayer is all about and how they fit into the purpose of prayer. Prayer is not for the purpose of calling down God, like some kind of divine Butler, to meet one's every request. Prayer is better thought of the other way around: it is getting in touch with God to determine how we fit into God's plans and purposes. Jesus set the proper tone for prayer when he prayed, "Not my will, but Thine be done."

A novice must also be made aware of the fact that God's hearing a prayer request and responding to a prayer request are not one and the same. God always hears a prayer, but he may not always respond in an expected way. Just as parents always hear their children's petitions to them but do not give the children each and every thing asked for, so God, as a loving Father, often withholds that which would not be best for his children. God always answers prayers, but his answers may be (a) yes; (b) no; (c) wait, for now is not the proper time; or (d) I've got something better in store for you.

If God's purposes and his will must be foremost, rather than humanity's needs and desires, why bother to pray anyway? Because people need to pray, because prayer is edifying to people, and because people are commanded to do so. Just as loving parents would never turn away a child, saying, "Don't bother me until you have a really important thing to say," so God is interested in the smallest concerns of his children. He wants people to come to him with their feelings, problems, joys, and sorrows - not so that people can tell God something he does not already know, but because a loving Father wants to share all of these things with his children. Prayer changes people's thoughts, attitudes, and actions because communication with the Almighty has a transforming effect. Prayer becomes a release, a method of unburdening and receiving reviving refreshment and cleansing. All this is going on whether or not one realizes it.

But what can be said to the person who wants to pray and tries to pray, but who feels unfulfilled or unsuccessful at each attempt? The answer is, "Keep praying." One should not trust one's feelings in such matters. The assurance of God's ear being open to a person's prayers rests not upon one's emotional reactions (changeable and unreliable at best), but upon faith that what God's Word says is true: ". . . before they call, I will answer; and while they are yet speaking I will hear" (Isa. 65:24). One should continue to pray, even when answers seem to be delayed or when God seems far away. Praying out of love and obedience, rather than from the motivation of receiving immediate rewards and uplifting feelings, will, in the long run, make one a stronger, more spiritually stable individual.

## Patterns for Beginners

When the disciples said to Jesus, "Teach us to pray," the pattern for prayer offered them was the Lord's Prayer, sometimes called the "model prayer." For those who have difficulty in feeling comfortable with extemporaneous (spontaneous) praying or for those who have had little experience with conversational prayer, praying aloud before other people, or even speaking intimately in private with the Almighty, the Lord's Prayer can be a great source of help and instruction. Praying this prayer or other memorized prayers is perfectly acceptable as a starting place for learning to pray.

Reading and meditating upon prayers in devotional classics such as the Book of Common Prayer can also be a good place to begin. The Lord does not care whose words are spoken as long as the intents of the heart are pure and the petitions are sincere. There is nothing wrong with offering up the prayers created by others as long as the words are personalized.

Reading psalms from the Bible will also be helpful, for many of these are prayers. Read a passage aloud, reflect upon it, then read it aloud again, making it a sincere message to the Almighty from a heart of love.

There will undoubtedly come a time, however, when one will want to move beyond the reading or reciting of preconceived prayers. How does one learn to speak to God as easily as one speaks to others? By practice! A relationship, whether it be with the Lord or with a new acquaintance, takes time to grow close and intimate. One must give time, faithfully and regularly every day, to the cultivation of a prayer life. One way to begin is by paraphrasing other prayers. The Lord's Prayer, for instance, contains several different types of prayers. Following is a sample of a paraphrased version of these various aspects of prayer. After reflecting upon these, a beginner can compose his or her own version of the Lord's Prayer or any other prayer.

| Prayer Object | Lord's Prayer | Paraphrased Version |
|---|---|---|
| Worship, Recognition of God's Lordship | Our father, who art in heaven . . . | Dear Lord in heaven, thank you that you are my Father and I am your beloved child . . . |
| Adoration | Hallowed be thy name . . . | I give you praise and honor and glory. I magnify your holy name! |
| Submission | Thy kingdom come; thy will be done in earth as it is in heaven. | I acknowledge you as my Lord and King. I want to be in your perfect will this day. |
| Recognition of Blessings | Give us this day, our daily bread . . . | Thank you for this day and for supplying all my needs. |
| Confession | And forgive us our trespasses . . . | I am truly sorry for my sins. Please forgive me for ---. |
| Intercession | As we forgive those who trespass against us. | Help me to love and forgive those who have hurt or abused me, especially ---. |
| Petition | And lead us not into temptation, but deliver us from evil . . . | Thank you for loving me just as I am and for wanting to help me improve. Please help me overcome the temptation to ---. |
| Praise and Exultation | For thine is the kingdom, and the power and the glory forever. Amen. | I love you, Lord. Thank you for being my Friend. Thank you for the evidences of your power at work in my life. May I help to bring your Kingdom to earth this day. Amen. |

In addition to paraphrased prayers, reciting memorized prayers, and reading of the prayers of others, another method for beginning a prayer life is by writing out one's thoughts, feelings, hopes, fears, needs, etc. It is sometimes easier to write out one's thoughts than to speak them. Such a written prayer may be in the form of a daily spiritual diary, a journal, or a letter to God. All that is required is a quiet place where one can share oneself with God by writing down those things which are on one's mind and heart. The following outline sample may be an idea-starter for composing written prayers:

Dear God,

　　　Today I am planning to ---. What do you think of this? If you have another plan for me today, then please put me where you want me and bring the people into my life today I need to meet. I am really happy and excited about ---. Thank you for letting me experience such joy. Lord, I don't understand why --- has happened. I'm confused and unhappy about it, but please help me to trust you to work out everything in this situation. I love you, God.

　　　　　　　　　　　　　　　　　　Your child,
　　　　　　　　　　　　　　　　　　---

Here is another version of the written prayer:

I give you this day and ask you to lead me as I ---.

I worship and praise you today because ---.

I am especially thankful for ---.

I feel guilty about --- and I ask your forgiveness for ---.

Please bless (protect, heal, help) ---.

My greatest needs right now are ---.

I need your guidance and direction for ---.

I'm having trouble loving (forgiving, understanding) ---.

I'm overly concerned about ---. I know that worry is a sin, so please take this burden and give me your peace.

I am weak spiritually in faith (temperance, patience, unselfishness, etc.).

My greatest desire (goal, ambition, dream) is ---.

Show me your will concerning ---.

Teach me how to pray (understand the Bible, overcome temptation, etc.).

Speak to my heart now as I meditate in silence and let me hear clearly what you want to say to me today: _____

(Write impressions or revelations you receive here.)

# Intercessions

As well as being a regular and important priority in one's personal daily life, prayer also can become a ministry to others. One form of prayer ministry is intercession. To intercede - to pray on behalf of others - is a priestly ministry. The priesthood of the Old Testament was established for this purpose to entreat the Lord's favor for others, to lift up the needs of the sinful, and to make oneself available for offerings and sacrifices on behalf of God's people. There is no higher calling than to be an intercessor standing in the gap between God and those in need of his help, guidance, comfort, or forgiveness. Many accounts in Scripture reveal how an intercessor "turned the tide" for others. Moses interceded many times for the rebellious Hebrews; Esther's maidens fasted and prayed for her mission to save the entire Jewish community; Nehemiah and many of the other prophets wept before the Lord for the whole nation. To further emphasize the importance of this holy calling, we are taught that even Jesus and the Holy Spirit are given the ministry of intercession to assist humankind in all aspects of life.

Many churches provide for intercessory prayer during worship services. Some practical approaches to additional ministries of intercession are suggested below:

1. Church Prayer Lists: Most parishes have a weekly or daily prayer list available to parishioners for calling in names of those in need of prayer. In small churches, the list may be read during regular services or published in the church bulletin as a reminder for individual intercessions. Where such a list is lengthy, it may be placed on a bulletin board or made available at special prayer services. Such a list becomes a useful tool for calling the intercessors together in unity and for bringing the intercessors' attention to the needs and requests of others. Furthermore, a prayer list provides those needing prayers a convenient way of making the need known.

2. Church Prayer Services: The ministry of Sunday worship may be extended into weekday or evening services that emphasize intercessory prayer. If there are clergy available to conduct such services, those in need of prayer can come to the altar for the laying on of hands, or for holy unction if the need is for healing. In some churches, the climax to the litany or order of service is to break up into small groups for prayer ministries one to another. Separate areas may be designated for those in need of healing, those praying for guidance, those burdened for others in difficulty, etc. Sometimes these services are called healing services, prayer and praise services, or intercessory prayer vigils. By whatever name, they extend and personalize the prayer ministry of the church beyond the more formal services of Sunday mornings.

3. Altar Ministry: Following the Sunday morning worship service or at appointed times approved by the clergy, people are invited to come for prayers at the altar. If qualified and trained lay people are available, the clergy may be assisted by them in praying for those who come forward for prayers.

4. Prayer Request Boxes:  Some churches have receptacles in convenient places for the purpose of dropping in prayer requests. These
written requests are then available for clergy and/or lay people to
pray over, either individually or collectively.  In other churches,
prayer requests are placed in the alms plate.

5. Intercessors' Meetings:  Laypeople who feel called to such a ministry may meet with others who share this call on a regular basis
for the purpose of intercession.  There are several ways to approach such a ministry. There may be a sign-up sheet for individuals wanting to volunteer for a prayer vigil, a setting apart of
time for being at the church to take a turn interceding each week,
or formal groups may meet regularly to pray for the needs of the
parish. Sometimes there is a group appointed as prayer support for
particular leaders or activities of the church, such as those who
pray regularly for the clergy, specific organizations, leaders,
committees, and specified programs or activities. It is preferable
to pray specifically instead of generally. For instance, it would
be better to pray for "The Reverend Dr. Brown" than for "our pastor" or to pray for Sunday school teachers by name and class rather than
saying, "God bless our Christian education program." Sometimes these
groups are informal, with no specified leadership - just concerned individuals who come together to petition the Lord about mutual concerns.  The
form of intercession at such meetings also is varied. There may be a
printed litany to be read, the meetings may be conducted in silence (unspoken prayers by individuals), conversational prayers may be offered
one by one, or a leader may pray aloud while others pray in silence. The
exact format should be left to the discretion of the individuals involved.
There must be one common consideration for all of these intercessory
groups: a definite way of communicating prayer requests to the intercessors. The church prayer list or entries in a prayer request box may
be made available to such groups, or a leader may become responsible for
receiving any calls for prayer from those who are unable to meet but
who want the group's intercessions.

6. Prayer Partners:  Many individuals have found value in having a
prayer partner, a designated person upon whom to call in time of
need and with whom to "swap" prayer requests. A church organization may pair up individuals for this purpose or it may be an
individual matter of choice. If the pair meets face to face for
prayers, it is best to let the selection of partners be by choice
in order to eliminate any difficulties in relating to someone
with whom one would not be comfortable. Busy people who cannot
meet regularly with a prayer partner can still become involved
by promising to pray daily for a partner, who, in turn, will do
the same. Telephone calls to alert a prayer partner of special
requests can replace meetings. This ministry can be expanded to
include "family partners." One family in the parish can "adopt"
another family for which to pray on a regular basis.

7. "Hot Lines":  For emergencies, crisis comfort, and even less
pressing needs, a church or home telephone ministry can be established.  Often pastors  will have an answering service to
whom calls are referred if they are unavailable.  But where
such a service is not established or where the needs are many,

then trained volunteers can be assigned regular duty manning a "hot line" telephone. Often a prayer spoken over the phone or a word of comfort is adequate until professional help or spiritual guidance can be obtained from more qualified people. Lonely people may need to hear a friendly voice, depressed people may need to talk to someone who will express genuine concern, and people with problems may just need to unburden themselves to someone who has faced a similar difficulty. Such a "Dial a Prayer" or "Dial a Friend" service can give homebound people a ministry if, on a rotating basis, their phone number is included for particular hours of a day.

8. Individual Intercessors: For those who do not want to belong to an organized group or for whom regular meetings are a problem, the ministry of being an individual "prayer warrior" is always available and needed. This may be as simple a thing as having a list of prayer requests posted on the kitchen refrigerator as a reminder to pray for individuals with needs. The church is always in need of people who will make a commitment of time each day to set aside to remember the church, the clergy, and specified requests. Those who are the more vocal and active participants in ministries that are in the limelight always need the prayer support of the unseen ministers who, in the secrecy of their prayer closets, lift them up in prayer. To such intercessors goes the promise of Christ: "Thy Father which sees in secret shall reward you openly" (Matt. 6:6).

9. Adoption Intercessors: Similar to adopting a prayer partner or family for which to pray, this ministry involves members of church organizations or individual volunteers who are assigned specific aspects of church life and/or particular church leaders, which they "adopt" as their special prayer intentions for a specified time. For instance, one individual will be assigned a daily prayer commitment to the clergy, another will take the church secretary, someone else will take a board member, another a Sunday school teacher, etc. Others may be assigned a particular church ministry such as praying for the choir, outreach programs, youth organizations, or church finances. Intercessors may keep their prayer responsibilities permanently, or there may be a rotation program whereby, weekly or monthly, a new prayer assignment is given. Such a prayer ministry assures that the entire church and all its programs and leadership people are being undergirded by prayer.

10. Family Intercessors: Sometimes church leaders get so busy with the Lord's business, ministering to those who come to the church with needs, that they forget the responsibility to minister in their own homes. Children are in the home many more hours than at church; therefore, they must see and practice the principles they are taught at church for those principles to become real and effectual in their lives. One of the most important ministries a parent can perform is involving the family in home worship, including teaching the children to pray. Prayers at mealtime and bedtime are the most widely accepted practices of family devotion, but these should be supplemented with a regular time for family worship which may include singing, reading of the Scriptures or a Bibly story book, sharing of experiences and spiritual insights,

and - most importantly - allowing everyone, from the youngest to the oldest, to lead in prayer. Intercession for one another can be expanded to include prayers for those outside the family unit - relatives, friends, and church members. Children learn by imitation, so it is important for mothers and fathers to become the kinds of intercessors who will set an example for the children to follow. Strong churches are made up of strong families. Families receive their strength from making Christ the center of the home, not just relating to Christ as someone they hear about for an hour on Sunday, but a personal friend with whom they talk each day. In an era when divorce and broken homes are so prevalent, it is especially important to remember the old saying, "Families that pray together stay together." The ministry of intercession, like charity, begins at home!

## Prayer Chains

Prayer chains provide an efficient and prompt way of involving a number of people in the ministry of intercession for a specific need. Usually a published list of intercessors is made available to those who will become part of the chain. The intercessors' names and phone numbers appear on the list along with instructions such as the following:

> Anyone can start the prayer chain. When you have a prayer need or know of someone who needs prayers, simply call the number of the person whose name appears after yours on the list. If that person is not at home, call any name on the list. When you finally reach someone, state the request, giving only brief and necessary details. That person will then call the next person on the list, and so on. Each person on the chain should actually contact another intercessor, not giving up, putting off the call, or leaving a message. The circle is complete when the original caller is called back with the request.

Sometimes it is better to have several prayer chains of a few people than one long list that takes a great deal of time to complete. There may be interconnecting chains, with the phone number of a chairperson from one group appearing on the list of other groups. Such a system allows for several prayer chains to be operating simultaneously.

Obviously, there must be a person or committee who will assume responsibility for typing up the lists, making telephone number changes, adding or deleting names as it becomes necessary, distributing the lists, and handling any problems that arise.

A less sophisticated way of conducting a prayer chain ministry is simply to have an understanding among several friends who can call each other for prayers and ask that the request be "passed on." Prayers may be said over the phone if both parties agree, or the ministry may merely become that of reporting the requests.

Whether the chain is formally organized or informally conducted, this kind of ministry can serve both the purpose of intercession and the purpose of getting people involved in an important lay ministry who might otherwise feel they had no talent or contribution to make toward the work of God's Kingdom.

In addition to parish prayer chains, there are interchurch and communitywide groups, which expand this ministry geographically. In such cases, the name of the person in charge of another church chain would appear on the local list. There are even more expanded programs in existence, whereby connections to prayer chains all over the United States provide a network of intercessory prayer that can be placed in operation by one telephone call.

The prayer chain ministry is sometimes facilitated by the publication of a booklet listing names, addresses, and phone numbers of individuals or prayer groups that will accept requests. Such a booklet is often useful when one is traveling to another state and in need of information, assistance, or prayers.

## Prayer Calendars

Prayer reminders in the form of weekly, monthly, or yearly calendars have proven useful in churches and parish organizations. Much like the "adoption" intercessions described earlier, but much wider in scope, such a calendar allows numbers of people to be in prayer unity concerning particular people or ministries even though separated geographically. A weekly prayer calendar can be published in the church bulletin, while the more comprehensive ones will require special efforts for composition, printing, and distribution.

Church prayer calendars may be duplicated and picked up regularly at the church or mailed out to subscribers. A decorative annual calendar, which may include Scriptures, art work, recipes, inspirational messages, or other items of interest, could become the sponsorship project of a church group in order to raise money for a worthy charity.

For small groups, birthdays and anniversaries may be included on the calendars as reminders to remember those celebrating special occasions. For the larger groups, the items listed will need limiting because of space. As each church organization plans its individual calendar of events for the coming year, a composite of all such events may be itemized on a master calendar. If individual copies are not duplicated, a large single version may be posted on a church bulletin board or displayed in another strategic place as prayer reminders for passersby. Such a prayer calendar will keep important dates and specific events included in the intercessory prayers of the parish.

The exact format and makeup of a prayer calendar may vary from church to church. There is no required size, shape, or composition. The end result may be simply a typewritten list of services, those hospitalized, shut-ins, special coming events, birthdays, and families

Sample Prayer Calendar

Pray for the People and Organizations Listed for Each Day This Month:

Pray for Parish Families: (J - P)

The Month of April

Special Intentions for April: Lenten Disciplines and Programs, Men's Retreat, Prison Ministry, GOOD FRIDAY and EASTER SERVICES

| SUNDAY | MONDAY | TUESDAY | WEDNESDAY | THURSDAY | FRIDAY | SATURDAY |
|---|---|---|---|---|---|---|
| | | | | 1<br>James Family<br>ECW Program | 2<br>Jinx Family<br>Pastor's Birthday | 3<br>Jones Family<br>Lenten Supper and Study Program |
| 4<br>Kapp Family<br>Shut-ins | 5<br>Karns Family<br>Healing Service | 6<br>Kawalski Family<br>Hospitalized and Ill | 7<br>Landry Family<br>Prayer/Share Groups Meet | 8<br>Lovelace Family<br>Senior Citizens | 9<br>Lucas Family<br>Quiet Day Ushers | 10<br>Luna Family<br>Youth Programs |
| 11<br>Mabb Family<br>PALM SUNDAY | 12<br>Martin Family<br>Healing Service | 13<br>Mitchel Family<br>Church-care Workers | 14<br>Mullen Family<br>Prison Ministry Penance Service | 15<br>Napier Family<br>Missionaries Prayer Vigil | 16<br>Nelms Family<br>...MEN'S RETREAT... Good Friday | 17<br>Nixon Family<br>...MEN'S RETREAT... National Church Leaders |
| 18<br>Nobb Family<br>EASTER SUNDAY | 19<br>Nye Family<br>Healing Service | 20<br>O'Day Family<br>Church Staff and Volunteers | 21<br>Oldham Family<br>Prayer/Share Groups Meet | 22<br>Oliver Family<br>Board Members Budget Committee | 23<br>Owens Family<br>Lay Readers | 24<br>Oxford Family<br>Sunday School Teachers |
| 25<br>Papp Family<br>Clergy | 26<br>Patton Family<br>Healing Service | 27<br>Pepper Family<br>The Choir | 28<br>Peterson Family<br>Library and Tape Ministries | 29<br>Pevey Family<br>Young People Serving the Church | 30<br>Pulver Family<br>Leadership Training Course | NOTES<br>Additional Prayer Requests: |

Names of Hospitalized: _____  Newly Baptized or Confirmed: _____  New Church Members: _____

or individuals with particular needs. A weekly calendar can include special prayer requests of a more specific and short-range nature, while monthly or yearly calendars must be more general. Calendars may be published as part of a church directory, with pictures of members of the parish family and specified times for praying for each one.

The sample prayer calendar on the preceding page should suggest one method of developing such a tool for intercession.

## Prayer Groups

An increasingly popular method of group ministry is the prayer group. There is a broad differentiation of makeup and format from group to group. Some groups meet at the church, others in homes or another designated place. Some groups have a structured program, while others are "open" meetings with a changeable and free-flowing format.

The prayer group idea is certainly not new. The book of Acts describes how the early Christians went from house to house for teaching, fellowship, and prayer. Such meetings should never be considered replacements for corporate worship in the church but, rather, supplemental meetings on a more intimate level. To receive all that is available from worship and prayer, one needs to become involved in three ways: first, the coming together of the body of Christ at Church; second, smaller parts of that body coming together for more personal involvement and interrelated ministry; and third, private worship, whereby a person relates personally and intimately on a one-to-One basis with the Lord. Such a balance will assure that people do not function at one level only, but that they relate to the Lord and others in ever widening spheres to give and receive the utmost in their spiritual lives.

The following ideas and guidelines are just that: suggestions for those who may be thinking of starting a group but who need some basics to "get going", or helps for existing prayer groups for comparing, evaluating, and obtaining fresh or different ideas.

## Purpose

There are two questions that should be asked before starting a prayer group or participating in one. The questions should be asked individually by each member of the group and collectively by the unit that must function as a body: (a) What is needed? and (b) What does God want to do in this group?

Because people are at different stages of spiritual growth and because differences in personality and experience make one type of prayer group more appealing than another to certain individuals, it is important to choose the right body to which to commit oneself.

Usually people are drawn together because of some common bond or interest. But even in the most compatible group, there will be individual differences and interpersonal relationships which may present problems. It is important to start from the premise that <u>our group will have unity of the Spirit even when there is disunity of opinions</u>. Ephesians 4 should be the theme chapter for every prayer group because it is a call to unity, forebearance, love, and longsuffering among the body. The following verses in particular should give direction and purpose to a group:

> Walk worthy of the vocation wherewith ye are
> called, . . . endeavoring to keep the unity of
> the Spirit in the bond of peace. . . . for the
> perfecting of the saints, for the work of the mini-
> stry, for the edifying of the body of Christ: Till
> we all come in the unity of faith, and of the knowl-
> edge of the Son of God, unto a perfect, unto the
> measure of the stature of the fullness of Christ
> (Eph. 4:3, 12-13).

Since no one has arrived at that place of perfection yet, there must be a forgiving spirit and a tolerance for others rather than criticism for the mistakes of those in the group. Nothing will doom a prayer group to failure more quickly than rigid, unrelenting people who must see things done "this way." To summarize, the basic answer to the question, "What is needed?" is "A group of people who will be loving and committed enough to each other to be patient with each other's mistakes along the road to spiritual maturity."

The answer to the second question, "What does God want to do in this group?" will differ according to the purpose of the group and the needs of the moment. Once the need for unity is seen as the general, or universal, purpose for the group, members must go about the business of finding out the more specific purposes for any prayer group gathering. Most likely, any group will include one or more of the following:

1.  <u>Worship and Praise</u>: Where the emphasis is upon worship,
    the prayer group becomes a small replica of the church
    - people who sing or speak praises to God to honor him
    and to bear witness to his importance in their lives.
    It may be an ordered service or an informal gathering
    (e.g., people on the floor with guitars and song sheets)
    "making a joyful noise unto the Lord."

2.  <u>Prayer</u>: Whatever else is included, prayer is a pre-
    dominant element in any group. The method of praying
    may vary from group to group, but every gathering
    should begin and end with prayer and offer opportu-
    nities for remembering special needs and intentions
    at some time during the meeting.

3. Fellowship and Sharing: It is important, especially for new Christians, to have the friendship and support of others who understand the trials as well as the triumphs of the Christian life. In such a group, members find a refuge from the world where people often "don't speak their language" or have the same interests. The fellowship includes more than just enjoying each other's company; it provides members with an opportunity to share experiences of a newly found or more deeply awakened faith, to give and hear testimonies of what the Lord has been doing in individual lives, and to find and give acceptance to others "where they are" spiritually. Fellowship time at prayer groups may or may not include the serving of refreshments, but there is always an atmosphere of loving acceptance and warm congeniality.

4. Instruction: No matter who you are or how long you've walked with the Lord, there's always further to go. Because no one ever reaches a point in earthly life where he or she has "arrived" and needs no further guidance, training, or correction, many prayer groups give time to providing for this need. It may include a training program, Bible study, guest speakers, or listening to instructional tapes. Whether the group has a regular leader for this purpose or it is an informal learning experience, a time of instruction will be a valuable supplement to the regular program of Christian education of the church. Most clergy are anxious for the spiritual growth of church members to take place, be it at the church or elsewhere, but any speaker or teaching should have the approval of the clergy as a safeguard against error being taught.

5. Ministry: The most mature aspect of group activity is that of body ministry - praying for, counseling with, and helping fellow Christians and others who may be brought into the group with specific needs to be met. The type of ministry may be evangelistic (introducing people to Jesus), intercessory (praying for individuals or expressed needs), or consoling (giving comfort and support). The prayer group should be a kind of spiritual "hospital" where the troubled in body, mind, or spirit can find spiritual "doctors" who can ease pains and aid the casualties in the battlefield of life.

Once the format of the prayer group is determined, there still needs to be a refining of the specific purposes and intents of the individual meetings. The first question to be answered is, "Why are we here?" Unless people know what they are expected to give and/or receive from the group, the group will not function effectively. Although the structure of the group may change with time, there should

67

be some underlying goals.  One way to open up the possibilities is by asking each individual to respond to these questions:

> Why am I here?  What do I expect to happen from prayer group participation?
>
> For what purpose do I believe the Lord has drawn us together?
>
> What do I think the Lord is trying to say to this group?
>
> What, in particular, does the Lord want to happen at this meeting?
>
> What can I expect from the others in the group?
>
> What can the others expect from me?
>
> Where am I spiritually?  Where do I want to go from here?

## Leadership

There is no such thing as a totally "Holy Spirit led" group.  Although there is freedom in the Spirit and times when leadership may move from one to another, people who come to a meeting with no one in a place of authority may be in for some unfortunate surprises.  Certainly the Holy Spirit wants to guide a meeting, but the Spirit must work through people.  The Bible often speaks of the importance of being "under authority."  That does not mean bondage or totalitarian rule.  It does, however, denote the need for the group to have one or more people responsible for the oversight and direction of the group.  Just as the church has divisions of responsibility under the headship of the clergy, and just as heaven itself is divinely ordered with submission to the Kingship of the Father, so any group needs a recognized leader.  The Lord will lay it upon the hearts of the individuals who are called to such leadership, and, if it is prayerfully and carefully considered, the group will confirm the one so called by an inner witness within their own spirits.  In addition to the mutual agreement of all concerned and the inner witness as to the call of God upon the leadership, what other qualities should a prayer group leader possess?  Here are some suggestions:

1.  A Maturity in the Spirit:  How can people expect to lead others where they have not walked?  This does not mean that leaders must have all knowledge or know all answers or have had all collective spiritual experience.  Who does?  The maturity of leadership expected is to be found in someone who has been a Christian long enough to have acquired some understanding of many of the problems and at least some

of the workable solutions to them. This maturity comes from a deep commitment to Jesus Christ and to serving him fully and earnestly.

2. An Exemplary Life: Those who would lead must set the example. The biblical criteria for leadership is someone "of honest report, full of the Holy Ghost and wisdom." St. James reminds us of the difference between earthly and heavenly wisdom: "The wisdom that is from above is pure, peaceable, gentle, easy to be entreated, full of mercy and good fruits, without partiality, and without hypocrisy." A leader who seeks to be this kind of person will not only be wise, but also a worthy example to inspire confidence from those he or she leads.

3. A Humble Spirit: The person in authority must be under authority. Jesus never pushed his weight around or tried forcibly to control anyone. A leader should always consider the role as that of a servant, remembering Jesus' words, "The greatest of you must be servant of all."

4. A Listener: A good leader listens both to the Lord for direction and to those he or she leads for what the Lord may be saying through them.

5. A Warm, Accepting Attitude: A love for the Lord and a love for people (regardless of their personalities or inadequacies) is fundamental. No person in leadership should misuse the power of authority to achieve personal gain or to hurt another. The proper motivation for assuming a leadership role is that of obedience to the Lord and the sincere desire to pass on God's love and truth to others.

6. An Openness Toward Others: A leader should always be open and approachable, someone a person with a problem would go to without reservation, confident that there would be understanding and trust personified in the leader.

7. A Stable, yet Flexible, Character: The stability that comes from being centered in the Lord will bring forth the flexibility that can adjust to difficulties and meet problems without falling apart. A leader needs emotional maturity and the ability to cope with problem people and unexpected situations.

8. A Sense of Responsibility: A leader already has built-in responsibilities to the Lord (to be obedient, to follow the direction of the Spirit, etc.) and to the group (being there when needed, fulfilling the jobs

assigned as competently and faithfully as possible, etc.), but even beyond these, a leader must be responsible to self. There must be a basic honesty, with no game-playing or mask-wearing. Assuming a role of leadership does not make one a saint or privileged person; it carries with it a grave accountability to be oneself, but the best self one can be. In order to be a stepping stone rather than a stumbling block, leaders must always remember, "Unto whom much is given, much shall be required."

9. **An Ability to Communicate:** Leaders must be able to articulate a message, an idea, or a direction to the group in understandable terms. Although leaders need not be polished public speakers, they should be able to speak to a group with the kind of authority and self-confidence in their voice that commands respect and acceptance from the group.

10. **An Aptitude for Management:** Quite simply, a leader must be able to lead. Leaders find themselves thrust in positions where they must guide and direct people, organize, and make things happen. Such a responsibility requires that the leader be able to inspire action or acceptance from the group and also be able to initiate and administrate whatever is supposed to happen.

11. **An Enthusiasm for the Work:** No one gets excited about following someone who does not appear interested in what is going on. A good leader will approach the tasks with conviction and enthusiasm.


## Procedures

The exact procedure to be followed in conducting a prayer group will vary, depending upon the purpose and changing situations that may occur. For instance, in a group where the emphasis is upon worship, a great deal of time will be spent in praising or singing; in groups stressing fellowship, the emphasis will be upon sharing love and exchanging witnesses or personal experiences; in instructional groups, the emphasis will be upon receiving edification; and in ministry-centered groups, the emphasis will be upon praying for and ministering to the needs of those with problems or prayer requests. Some groups may involve themselves with all of these activities in a regularly followed, structured pattern, such as opening with praise and worship, having a brief teaching or Scripture devotion, gathering for intercessory prayer, and ending with a fellowship hour that may include refreshments. But in the event there is a special need for deeper study, a call from the Lord to more concentrated worship, a person with a very pressing need that requires time and attentive ministry from the group, or a real need to share mutual concerns or express more love through fellowship, one activity may take the whole session one time, while another may be dominant at another meeting. The best way to determine the direction for a particular meeting is to begin with a period of silence, a waiting before the Lord to discover what _his_ purpose will be. As everyone prays and seeks the Lord's guidance, he will reveal the procedure to be followed. The Lord is, after all, more anxious to have his people in his will than they are to know what it is!

Often there will be a theme or dominant thread that will weave its way through a particular gathering. If everyone is centered-in on picking up that direction, there can begin a flowing with the Spirit that far surpasses any human-ordered business. There must be a delicate balance between having such a rigid and predetermined program that the Spirit is quenched from any promptings to the contrary, and such a hang-loose, nondirected gathering that the meeting ends in futility or confusion. The Lord gives his people minds and expects them to be used, but he also expects that those minds be placed under the order and control of the Holy Spirit for direction.

Two basic procedures may be followed for the gathering. Sometimes these two procedures will reverse or intertwine. It is impossible to give specifics or absolutes because the Holy Spirit is free to rearrange, undo, correct, or modify any existing plan. We can never know him completely because he is infinite and we are finite. That is what gives the Christian life so much pleasure and excitement; it is also what keeps Christians on their toes and dependent on heavenly guidance. With all that in mind, here are the two procedures:

1. The Directed Meeting: Here the responsibility for the progress of the gathering is in the hands of the leadership. Members of the group take their cues from the leader, in much the same way the church congregation follows the direction of the clergy during formal worship. Even in such a directed meeting, however, there should be an atmosphere of give-and-take. A good leader is sensitive to those she or he is leading, and often takes cues from the suggestions or corrections of the group.

2. The Open Meeting: Here the progress of the meeting is in the hands of the body - different individuals making contributions under the leadership of the Holy Spirit and the watchful eye of the prayer group leaders(s). Since everything that comes from the lips and hearts of even the sincerest Christians may not be free from error, it is scriptural to "judge" what comes forth. These kinds of meetings are sometimes called "Hatha" meetings because they reflect the procedure outlined in I Corinthians 14:26. "When you come together, every one of you hath a psalm, hath a doctrine, hath a tongue, hath a revelation, hath an interpretation. Let all things be done unto edifying." Often the Lord will prepare several offerings for one meeting: someone may have a Scripture to share, another a song, another a

testimony, and so on. Obviously, such a meeting requires maturity and a sensitivity to the Spirit's movement among those who come prepared to share.

## Guidelines for Prayer Groups

Following are some suggestions that may be useful for prayer groups, regardless of the type of meeting or the various procedures used:

1. After the purpose of the meeting is determined, seek to flow in the prescribed purpose in unity with the brethren.

2. Authority for leadership should be placed in responsible people who will act, challenge, and correct in love whenever necessary.

3. Each meeting of the group should be considered a new and unique experience. Do not try to repeat past experiences in order to work up past blessings or results. Let the Lord be in the driver's seat!

4. Although the edifying of the brethren will be an important aspect of the group activities, people should not come always expecting to receive, but to give. (Maturity in Christ means producing more than you consume.)

5. Meetings should be considered more Jesus-oriented than need-oriented.

6. There should be a basic commitment from all concerned to become responsible for one another's welfare and edification. A "family" atmosphere is the goal toward which all members should work.

7. Prayer is the basic element in prayer groups. Emphasis should be placed upon prayer, not only at the meetings, but before and after them - prayers of preparation before going, prayers for the leadership and purpose of the meeting, prayers daily for the people and their revealed needs, prayers of follow-up and thanksgiving after people have received ministry or answers to prayers, and prayers for anything relevant to the group or individuals in it.

8. Care should be given to the size of the prayer group. Everyone who comes should be welcomed and made to feel a part (no exclusiveness or cliques), but when the group gets so large that individuals are "lost in the crowd," consideration should be given to splitting to form two groups.

9. Prayer groups should have a definite beginning and ending time. It is possible that people needing special ministry or those desiring to linger for additional fellowship will want to stay beyond the closing hour, but courtesy to those who must leave should include an appropriate time for them to depart without causing an interruption.

10. Consideration should always be extended to newcomers or visitors who may not understand what is going on. The Holy Spirit would never lead a group to do anything to embarrass, confuse, or hurt another.

11. Even though there will be designated leaders for the group, each person should be considered an equally important part of the gathering and should have the freedom to express, in love, his or her views. No one should ever feel excluded or diminished because of expressing ideas that are "different." Love must be the focal point around which all prayer group activity revolves.

## Patterns of Prayer for Prayer Groups

There are many different modes of prayer that may be adapted for a group gathering. It is not necessary to follow the same pattern week after week. Some groups follow the prayer forms in one of the several denominational prayer books available or they use a printed litany, with blanks to be filled in for appropriate responses from individuals or for special prayer requests. Prayers may be offered in silence or by a prayer leader. But the goal toward which all groups want to strive is to become conversational in prayer and to have as many voluntary participants as possible. People get more from that in which they become personally involved than from those things in which they are merely spectators. The following patterns are suggested as an aid in developing such a spontaneous, conversational approach to prayers.

1. Sentence Prayers: Going around the prayer circle one at a time, each person offers a brief sentence reflecting his or her prayer need or thanksgiving. "Amen" may be said first by the petitioner and then repeated by the group in unison as a sign that the group is unified in agreement with the prayer. If there should be someone too shy to pray aloud or someone with an unspoken request, that person may pray in silence and then say "Amen" to indicate that the prayer burden has been released to the Lord.

2. Silent Intercessions: Holding hands in a circle, the group ministers to one another first by praying in silence for the person standing on the right, and then by praying silently for the person on the left. Silent intercessions may also be offered as a leader reads a general prayer for a particular category (for the sick, for spiritual awakening, for comfort, for assistance with a problem, etc.) and then allows a period of silence for participants to remember by name those in each category.

3. Patterned Prayers: Following the pattern for balance in the prayer life (adoration, thanksgiving, confession, intercession, petition, and meditation), members of the prayer group take turns offering up prayers that fit these categories. Although the following example may be expanded and modified as members become more comfortable with conversational prayer, this is a good way to start off a beginning prayer group.

Adoration – Each person, in turn, offers a phrase of adoration, such as "Praise God," "Bless the Lord," "Hallelujah," "Glory to God," "Hosanna in the Highest," etc. (If it is a very new group, the praise words may be assigned in advance so each one will know what to say.)

Thanksgiving – Each one expresses thanks for a blessing in turn, such as "Thank you, Lord, for ---."

Confession – Each takes a turn asking forgiveness for sin. It is not necessary to be specific. A person may merely say, "Forgive me, Lord, for all my sins" or "I'm sorry for what I did today."

Intercession – Needs of those present or absent are offered up one at a time. This may be as simple as saying, "God bless ---" or "Lord, help ---." Or, at the indication of a leader, names may be spoken aloud with no further explanation.

Petition – One's own needs and requests are spoken. For those who have no special intention, they may repeat a predetermined phrase, such as "Lord, be merciful unto me," or "Help me, Lord, to grow in grace."

Meditation – The listening portion of the prayer circle may be observed merely by keeping a period of silence in which each person centers thoughts upon Jesus, reflects upon the goodness of God, or tries to "hear" what the Spirit is saying to that one individually.

4. Written Requests: The group is given paper and pencils to write out petitions and intercessions. These may be gathered together in a container, all may lay hands upon them, and one or more people may pray aloud a general prayer for all requests.

5. Group Liturgy: Following a printed liturgy or prayer service, the group may read it together and, at appropriate times, mention thanksgivings, confessions, or petitions. The leader may read portions and the group respond with an appropriate predetermined phrase. For instance:

| Thanksgivings | Individual: | "For ---" |
|---|---|---|
| | Group: | "Father in Heaven, we thank thee." |
| Confessions | Individual: | "For the sin of ---" |
| | Group: | "We pray thee, Lord, forgive." |
| Petitions | Individual: | "I beseech your mercy for ---." |
| | Group: | "Peace be unto you." |

6. Group Meditations: A leader reads aloud a passage of Scripture or other inspirational devotional thought. After a specified time of silence in which the group reflects upon what the passage means and how it may be speaking to an individual or the group, these thoughts are shared aloud. If preferred, the meditations may be written down and thought about without vocalizing them. Another form of group meditation is to give everyone paper and pencils and to keep a period of silence in which participants are encouraged to write down the thoughts, impressions, or revelations from the Lord they receive during the silence. Sometimes these meditations are written in first person as a personal message from the Spirit to the individual doing the writing. (Caution: This in no way should be considered something akin to automatic writing or some sort of occult divination. Some of the messages may be the person's own thoughts and some may be divinely inspired, but all meditations should be tested by prayer and accepted doctrines of the church and scriptural teachings.)

7. Two-by-Two Ministry: Draw names for prayer partners for the evening, after first praying for the Lord to "match up" those who should share together. Let the partners go off, two by two, to separate areas to share insights, discuss needs, pray for one another, or otherwise minister to each other as they may feel led.

8. Group Confessions: As a leader mentions a general sinful area (such as pride, greed, intemperance, lust, jealousy, worry, resentment, unforgiveness, etc.), the group writes down the specific confessions that may be appropriate. At the conclusion of these private confessions, all the written lists are gathered into a container (which is flame-proof) and the papers are lighted with a match.

A prayer of thanksgiving for forgiveness is then of-
ferred as the smoke goes heavenward, a symbol of
forgiveness and God's mercy to receive the prayers
of the penitent. (The burning of the written confessions often must be done outdoors.)

9. "Hot-Seat" Prayers: A member of the group with a prayer
   need sits in a chair (the "hot seat") in the middle of
   the room as the group gathers around to lay on hands and
   pray (silently or audibly) as each may be led to do for
   each expressed prayer request. Touching the person in
   need of ministry is an effective and scriptural way (cf.
   James 5:14-16; II Tim. 1:6) of making a point of contact
   and expressing love.

10. Conversational Prayers: When the group is ready to move
    in this direction, someone may be appointed to open, and
    another to close, the prayer time. Others will either
    take turns in order as they are seated to pray, or prayers
    may be said spontaneously as people feel moved to pray.
    Those who wish to pray aloud do so while the others pray
    silently. No pattern is followed but, rather, the parti-
    cipants talk to the Lord about whatever is on their hearts.
    Some prayer groups appreciate having a second person pray
    about the same request before a new petition is made
    known; in this way, the "two-in-agreement" promise of
    the Bible is made manifest (cf. Matt. 18:19).

There are, doubtless, other ways to pray as a group and as individuals within the group. Whatever is most comfortable and appropriate
should be the criterion, for there is no "right" or "wrong" way to pray.
A sensitivity to the feelings and desires of the people in the group
as well as a submissiveness to the promptings of the Holy Spirit will
provide all the groundwork necessary for a fulfilling prayer group
ministry.

### Prayer Groups for Children and Young People

A familiar proverb says, "Train up a child in the way he should go
and when he is old, he will not depart from it." The younger the age
at which people learn to pray aloud, the less inhibited and embarrassed
they will be about doing it in later life. Many churches have begun
weekly prayer groups for younger people or have devoted a part of the
regular Christian education program to the expressed purpose of developing habits of prayer for youth. Youngsters should learn to pray, both
as a private and individual discipline and as a group activity. Confirmation classes and youth choirs are likewise setting aside a time
for young people to pray for one another and for special intentions.
Whether in Sunday school, other church activity, or home, children and
teenagers should be taught to pray.

The only real requirement for starting a children's or teens' prayer group is a qualified leader. Because young people are naturally uninhibited and trusting, and because they are usually more easily led than adults, prayer groups for children are often more spontaneous and effective than those of their more inhibited counterparts, the adults.

Any suggestions on preceding pages may be adapted to a youngster's level. Singing is a good way to bring the group into unity and will give an outlet for expressions of praise and worship. Some songs even give the added dimension of teaching. The currently popular singing of Scriptures is especially effective, both as a unifying procedure and as a teaching device (learning the Word of God in an easy and enjoyable manner). There are a number of cassette tapes designed for children; they provide both teaching and music, which may be included in the prayer group program. A word of caution here, however. The younger the child, the less lecturing and inactivity he can tolerate. It is best to keep listening (either to tapes or to the leader/teacher) to a minimum and opt for participation activities - singing, clapping, sharing, discussing, doing. Even the youngest children can catch on to the patterned prayer techniques described earlier, and soon they will be involved in conversational and spontaneous prayers. A shy child should never be put on the spot or forced to participate in anything until ready. Usually, seeing and hearing others as they participate will be all that is necessary to get even the most reticent child going.

The language used in prayer is secondary to the intents of the young hearts. Youngsters should be encouraged to talk to God in their own vocabulary and at their own level of understanding rather than to adopt flowery prayer phrases with a ring of artificiality. Just as parents are interested in their children, regardless of how big or small the child's need, so their Heavenly Father is interested in each youngster's concerns. Young people can pray about their friends, their pets, their school activities, or any other aspect of their lives. It is important to stress this point, especially to teenagers who should be encouraged to pray about their dates, social lives, career choices, and changing feelings of adolescence.

To illustrate the point that the intentions of the heart are vastly more important than the choice of words or topics of prayer, consider the true story of a young teenage girl who had to be in a program at church. She was suffering from a case of stage fright and had prayed for "perfect calamity." She thought the word calamity was a form of the word calm. Her testimony to the prayer group afterwards was that God had heard and answered her prayer for calamity at the performance. It was evident to everyone that God had fulfilled the request of her heart and not that of her lips.

## Conclusion

Although this treatment of the various aspects and methods of prayer for individuals and groups is by no means exhaustive, there should be enough food for thought to stimulate interest in the opportunities available for the different prayer ministries. Whether one finds oneself praying alone in the privacy of the home, together with a prayer partner, with loved ones around a family altar, or with a larger group, each individual should see prayer as not only a central part of the Christian life, but also an occasion to serve one another and the Lord in a ministry of love. Everyone can and should be involved in some aspect of the ministry of prayer.

# 5 · Ministries of Social Outreach

People are by nature gregarious. They want to communicate with, touch, react to, and get involved with other people. During war, those who wish to break down the resistance of a prisoner know that the worst form of punishment and the best way to get an enemy to talk is by ostracism. It has been said that the only thing harder than living with people is living without them. Because of this basic need to interact with others, Christians have a responsibility to develop skills of communication and interpersonal relationships in ministries of social outreach. The shyest of individuals can be a part of such a ministry. Even though it be on a very small scale (within a limited group or one to one), everyone gets into the act of building and maintaining relationships.

Sales people know there is nothing more successful for business than person-to-person contact. Christians are in the business of "selling" Jesus to the world; therefore, they need to know how to approach one another in the best possible ways. Just as sales personnel represent and speak for a company or product, so Christians represent the church and Jesus Christ. The favorable or unfavorable impression upon others has far-reaching implications.

## Greeting Strangers

Almost every church has some method of welcoming visitors and newcomers. Sometimes the ushers are assigned the duty of spotting and greeting nonmembers as well as the regular congregation. In some churches there are official greeters who assist the clergy either as a regular assignment or on a rotating basis. There are two basic approaches:

1. Structured Methods: Official greeters are stationed at strategic places (front door, welcoming table, coffee hour assembly) for the purpose of meeting and assisting visitors. The advantage of this method is its efficiency and the assurance that the job will be done. The disadvantage is that it may sometimes become more perfunctory than sincere.

2. Unstructured Methods: Everyone in the congregation is alert to observe, identify, and assist newcomers. In very small churches where a new face is easily recognizable, this works better than in larger congregations. The disadvantage of this method is that there is no guarantee that people will voluntarily respond to the need to greet visitors. Those who do extend a hand of friendship voluntarily, however, usually make a better impression than someone easily identifiable as an official host or hostess whose "job" it is to serve as a

greeter. The key is for both the official and unofficial greeters to be motivated by love and a genuine
desire to be courteous and helpful to strangers.

Because the first impression a visitor gets on a visit to a new
church is usually a lasting one, it is vitally important that the greeting ministry be carefully planned for and integrated into the total
church program.

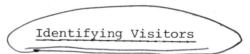

## Identifying Visitors

Except perhaps in very small congregations, there needs to be some
tangible method for identifying nonmembers. Suggested identification
methods are as follows:

1. Guest Book: Visitors are asked to sign a registry as
   they enter. The ushers or greeters are assigned the
   responsibility of checking the guest book and transferring data about guests to the church office.

2. Visitor Card: Cards to be filled out by visitors are
   placed in the pews and attention is drawn to them from
   the pulpit. Cards may be placed in the offertory or
   collection plate when it is passed or collected by
   ushers.

3. Identification Badges: A ribbon, a small cross, or
   other object for identification purposes is attached
   to the visitor card or handed out by the greeters.
   Visitors wear these to alert members to extend a
   welcome.

4. Name Tag: Where the size of the congregation permits,
   name tags may be used, with one color for regular parishioners and another color for visitors. This is most
   helpful in allowing people to address each other by
   name.

5. Welcoming Table: Greeters are stationed at a designated
   place where the visitors are requested to go to receive
   a welcome and necessary information in exchange for filling out a visitor card. Such a welcoming station may
   provide refreshments, information sheets about the church
   and its activities, or small remembrances for the visitors.

6. Recognition: At an appropriate time during the worship
   service, the visitors are greeted from the pulpit. Depending on the preferences of the church and clergy,
   visitors may be asked to stand, raise hands, or otherwise identify themselves. They may introduce themselves
   or they may be introduced by a member of the congregation.
   One church, in particular, rather than requesting visitors to

stand (some people don't enjoy being singled out in that way during a service), asks them to remain seated as "honored guests" during the singing of a specific hymn. The standing members take note of those who remain seated and greet them after the service.

7. Receiving Line: Greeters stand at the front door with ushers to welcome those entering and to identify visitors, or they stand with the clergy at the door to meet visitors as they leave.

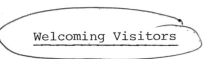

Welcoming Visitors

There are many different ways to make a visitor feel welcome - anything from a simple handshake and a friendly word to one of the following:

1. Bulletin Announcements: A special written message to greet visitors appears in the order-of-service bulletin. Names of prior week's visitors may be included also. This may be a regular feature of the church newsletter, a copy of which may be sent to visitors along with an expression of appreciation for their presence at the service and an invitation to return.

2. Escort Service: Ushers or greeters offer to escort visitors to Sunday school classes, to the coffee hour assembly, or to other areas of interest. This may include a tour of the church grounds and explanation about the history of the church and present programs and activities.

3. Special Introductions: Before or after the service, visitors are introduced to other parishioners. The greeters should find out something about the visitor (occupation, home area, interests, etc.) to mention so that those who are introduced have a starting place from which to begin a conversation. Alert greeters will seek out members with something in common with the visitors so that there will be a common ground upon which to build.

4. Receptions: A visitors or new members coffee hour (or other social event) may be planned in order to honor newcomers. Sometimes it is good for greeters to make arrangements for the nonmember to be transported to and from such an event so the new person does not come alone or feel strange in the new group.

5. Personal Letters: In large congregations a form letter is automatically sent out to each person who has filled out a visitor card, signed the guest book, or otherwise

been identified as a visitor. In smaller churches, a personal message can be sent. Letters generally express pleasure in having the person attend and the hope that the visit will be repeated.

6. Sending Greeting Packets: In addition to the church bulletin, a packet especially designed for visitors may be sent out. Such a packet may include a brochure about the church, a list of the services and activities with times and dates of meetings, and the name and phone number of a contact person who is assigned to assist newcomers. Such a greeting packet may be sent along with the follow-up letter after someone has visited the church, sent separately as an additional method of follow-up, or delivered by hand on a personal visit.

7. Telephone Contact: A telephone call inviting the visitor to another service or to extend a further welcome will personalize and supplement mail-outs.

8. Personal Visits: By far the most effective method of making visitors feel welcome is a personal visit to their home (assuming they live in the area). Clergy, a visitation committee, church greeters, church leaders, or any individual who takes note of visitors may assume responsibility for this ministry. Those who call upon visitors should be prepared to answer questions and to extend the follow-up to include additional contact with the persons - planning to sit together in church on a particular Sunday, seeing each other socially, attending midweek church activity in which the visitor may have an interest, etc.

## The Visitation Ministry

It is commonly reported that some denominations lose one out of every two people gained. The loss is due, primarily, to indifference and a lack of follow-up from clergy and parishioners where newcomers are concerned. Most people cannot get excited about attending a church where they are ignored. The visitation ministry, therefore, is one of the most fundamental and needful ministries in the church.

1. Visiting Newcomers: Perhaps the easiest to call upon, newcomers have "opened the door" by expressing interest through their first visit to the church. Generally, newcomers fall into one of these categories: people who have moved to town and who wish to transfer their church membership; people who have a personal or spiritual need and who are looking to the church to help; people who are "shopping around" for a church where they can feel comfortable and accepted; those who have been brought to the service by a friend or relative; and the curious, those who have heard about the church and/or pastor and who wish to check out the chruch for themselves. For those whose ministry it is to call upon newcomers, it is best

to ascertain into which category the people to be visited fall. Here are some suggestions to consider before visiting a newcomer:

Pray for guidance and direction before attempting to visit.

Find out as much information as possible about the person in advance of the visit (check the visitor card, ask the clergy or others who may know something about "where the newcomer is").

Try to determine what the newcomer's basic need is; then determine how the church can best help meet that need.

Know as much as possible about the church, its programs, and its various age-group activities in order to provide information to all members of the family to be visited.

Take along a church bulletin or schedule of services to leave for the newcomer's later reference.

Leave follow-up information. A visitor from the church should write his or her name and telephone number on a church bulletin or on a piece of paper for the newcomer's future reference (or leave a calling card).

Know about the community in which the newcomer lives. Be ready to offer assistance such as locating shopping centers or schools if the family is new in town. A map and list of community services will be most helpful.

Be prepared to listen to the newcomer, answer questions, and, if the person is receptive to the idea, to pray together. Take cues from the newcomer and proceed carefully, going only as far as the person seems comfortable in going. Don't do all the talking. Take notes (preferably mental) about the newcomer's background to pass on to the church office or to those making later visits.

Be sincerely happy to visit and let it show. A visitor from the church should not appear to be going about this churchly duty with a "canned" speech to give, but as one who is sincere and has a genuine interest in the newcomer. Make every effort to help the newcomer feel accepted and welcome in the fellowship.

Be prepared to do additional follow-up. Don't visit once and then ignore the newcomers. Offer to sit together at church, introduce them around, invite them to a social affair, or in some manner continue the friendship that begins with the house call.

2. <u>Visiting Lapsed Members</u>: A lapsed member is someone who used to attend church but does no more. In most cases, an incident precipitated the dropping out, or the refusal to attend church was a silent cry for help of some kind. Usually, lapsed members feel let down if no one takes notice that they have stopped attending services, and the sooner a visit is given, the better the chance of recovering the member. Reasons for dropping out may include any one of these:

Conflict: A personality conflict occurred between the member and the clergy or the parishioners. A misunderstanding and hurt feelings are often involved in this type.

Trauma or tragedy: A spiritual set-back due to a death, tragedy, moral problem, or other incident that is non-church-related.

Expectations not met: Some members feel the church does not meet their spiritual expectations or needs. Some may want more Bible study, shorter sermons, more or less evangelism, different prayer book services, higher or lower churchmanship, more or less involvement in renewal movements, or other procedures more to their liking.

Interest in another church: Either for convenience or for conviction, another church offers greater appeal.

Overwork: Member backed off from too much responsibility.

Underwork: Member was never asked to become involved and so felt left out.

Apathy: Once the habit of skipping church took hold, it became ingrained and the member lost interest.

Lack of commitment: A nominal Christian with little depth of faith often sees little value in church attendance.

Because of the inherent problems in visiting lapsed members, those who assume this ministry may require more preparation and training than those who visit newcomers. Some suggestions for visiting lapsed members follow:

Pray for guidance and proceed cautiously.

Determine whose responsibility the visiting of the lapsed member should be. In some cases the clergy can handle the problem best; in others, a layperson is more readily received.

Research the background of the lapsed member. Determine where the person was before leaving the church, but look for vital information only. Don't be nosy!

Don't take sides if there was a conflict that caused the member to give up church. While remaining neutral, be a sympathetic and understanding listener if the former member wishes to discuss any problems connected with church.

Let the lapsed member know how much he or she has been missed.

Push for a reconciliation (if a conflict was the reason for dropping out of church) and for forgiveness (if someone mistreated the lapsed member). Explain that the church is nothing more than a hospital for sinners, and that while human beings may let one down, Jesus never will.

If apathy or lack of personal commitment to Jesus are the reasons, seek to lead the lapsed member to such a commitment.

Be a friend, not just a church visitor. Get involved with the person socially and personally. Never give a speech that is obviously preplanned, artificial, or insincere.

Encourage others in the parish to call or visit. (Be sure the additional attention does not come off as a "set up" but, rather, as a real concern and interest on their parts.)

If the lapsed member is receptive, pray together about the person's reasons for leaving the church, asking the Lord to heal any wounds.

Do not condemn or be judgmental in any way. The member should not be made to feel "naughty" for being absent from church. The person likely already has enough problems without having more guilt added to the list.

Center the conversation on Jesus, not on the personalities or irregularities of the church. Churches and people are imperfect, but Jesus will have appeal no matter what the circumstances.

Encourage the person to give the church one more chance. Emphasize the positive results and blessings of restored membership. Stress the importance of regular worship, Christian fellowship, and receiving of Communion.

Follow up the visit with additional attention, gestures of love, and a Christlike attitude. The church representative who visits may be the only part of the church that brightens an otherwise dismal outlook for the lapsed member. Do not become overbearing or pushy, but by the same token, do not give up, regardless of the response. When all else fails, just keep praying!

3. <u>Visiting Prospective Members and the Unchurched</u>: Those who have never been involved in a church fellowship usually will not understand its importance or relevance to their lives. Those who have no personal relationship with Jesus Christ will see little reason for going to church at all. Although methods of witnessing and more specific evangelistic ministries will be considered more fully in chapter 6, a few guidelines may be mentioned here:

> Pray for the Lord to prepare the heart of the individual to receive ministry before approaching him or her. Pray to speak only the words the Lord will give.

> Wait on the Lord for the proper time to approach the person. Do not "come on strong" or become "pushy."

> Be a friend, allowing the love of Jesus to pour out to the individual. Even before speaking of spiritual things, the person should have seen something different or special in the visitor's life.

> Think about the people whose lives were influential on you (e.g., those who were instrumental in your conversion experience). What made their approach acceptable? Make a mental list of a visitor's "do's and don'ts." Avoid tactics that turn people off.

> Give your personal testimony - what Jesus has done in your life. This should come across naturally, not like a sermon or prepared speech.

> If the prospect is open to it, bring books, instructional tapes, or tracts that may aid spiritual development.

> Introduce the prospect to other Christians. Invite the prospect to a church social or other event where he or she can see that church people are enjoyable company and "okay" people, not fanatics or abnormal types.

> Invite the prospect to accompany you to church as you would invite him or her to any other place. Be certain to tell the prospect something about the church in advance - the method of worship, what is customarily done, and any special do's and don'ts.

> Seek to lead the person to make a commitment to Jesus. Church attendance, stewardship, good works, and all other Christian activities are outgrowths of a personal relationship to the Saviour, never ends in themselves. Knowing Jesus is "step 1"; going to church is "step 2." But since the church may become the means by which one comes to know Jesus, it is a good and conducive atmosphere into which to bring a prospective Christian.

Make a personal commitment to pray for the prospect daily. Often when no visible signs of change are evident, the Holy Spirit is at work in mysterious ways. The prayers of the faithful assist in that work.

## Training Programs for Outreach

Some churches have a regular and formally structured visitation program, while others take a very informal approach to visiting, people paying calls only when requested to do so by the clergy or when individually inspired to do it. An outline for a formalized training program might go something like this:

### Visitation Training Outline

1. Instruction: The visitation committee or those who feel called to such a ministry of outreach agree to meet together for a time of instruction prior to going out into homes to visit. The length of time for the instructional program will be determined by the amount of knowledge and past experience of the trainees and the judgment of the clergy or training program leader. Instruction should include techniques of effective visiting and personal experiences and/or insights from those who have been involved in the ministry previously.

2. Role Play: It is most helpful to have a "dry run" before going out visiting for the first time. Situations comparable to real life can be acted out in role play, discussed and evaluated by the group, and brought to logical conclusions for determining general guidelines. Determining proper responses to difficult people or situations before actually being confronted by them in real life will give more confidence to the visitors and greater freedom from mistakes. For instance, what should be a church caller's response in the following cases?

    a. A lapsed member who can't stand the new pastor?

    b. A newcomer whose feelings were hurt by a thoughtless member of the congregation?

    c. An unchurched individual who is sour on life and who blames God for a tragedy or unhappy situation?

    d. Someone who won't come to church because of the changes in liturgies and forms of worship? (The old ways are best.)

    e. An apathetic member who sleeps in every Sunday morning or has a golf game scheduled at the hour of morning worship?

  *f.* Someone who is sincerely looking for a deeper
   spiritual experience, but who feels too guilty
   for past sins to approach God?

  *g.* Someone who feels ignored and unappreciated at
   church?

  *h.* Someone who wants to be a Christian but does not
   know how.

  In addition to acting out scenes between a church
caller and people such as those named above, members of
the training group can recall actual true-life experiences they have met for role play and discussion.

3.  <u>Making Assignments</u>: Information cards with the names,
 addresses, and pertinent data on those to be visited
 are distributed to the church callers. Any questions
 as to background and/or approaches to use should be
 directed to the leader. Information cards are made up
 from information on visitor cards or from referral information. "Difficult" cases should be reserved for
 the clergy or those most experienced in visitation
 techniques.

4.  <u>Making the Visits</u>: Going out to make the calls two by
 two is both a scriptural method of ministry and a built-
 in safeguard. It is good to match up a novice with
 one more experienced if possible.

5.  <u>Recording Data</u>: Some method of recording the visit and
 its results should be instituted. This may take the
 form of recording data on the bottom of the information
 card after the visit or providing callers with special
 printed forms for this purpose. An alternate idea is
 to request that all callers keep a notebook in which to
 record a log of visits and the outcomes. Reasons for
 successful or unsuccessful visits should be noted.

6.  <u>Reporting Back</u>: A time limit for visiting should be
 set, and at a predetermined hour, all the callers
 from the church should return for follow-up and evaluation. By discussing the visits, further insights and
 learning will take place.

7.  <u>Prayer Involvement</u>: It goes without saying that the
 entire visitation ministry should be constantly undergirded by prayer. A pastoral blessing or an invoca-
 tion should be given before the callers depart; callers
 should be praying as they go, either individually and
 silently or aloud with the other caller going along;
 and prayers for those called upon should be offered
 when everyone returns to report. Names of those visited

may be added to the church prayer list and included in other intercessions throughout the week.

8. Support Services: For members of the congregation who do not feel called to visit, there are many support services which they can perform. A group may remain at the church to pray as the callers go out; kitchen workers can prepare refreshments for the callers upon their return; others may conduct surveys or pass on names of prospects or members who have missed several services; still others may type up the information cards, mail out literature to prospects, or do record-keeping.

## Helpful Hints for Visiting Laypersons

The following suggestions apply to any visitation situation:

1. Depend on the Lord, not on human ability or "methods," for effective ministry.

2. Don't be overly concerned about results. Successes and failures cannot be determined by human standards. As long as a caller is faithful to plant the seeds of love, the Lord will take care of the "harvest."

3. Make Jesus and the church attractive to others through your own enthusiasm and spirituality. Actions speak louder than words.

4. If possible, telephone before visiting to determine the best time to come. Try to avoid dinner hour and other inconvenient times.

5. Time the visit carefully. Don't breeze in and out without taking adequate time to communicate. Neither is it advisable to make a lengthy visit, overstaying the welcome.

6. Remember that people are at different stages of spiritual development and will require different approaches. Predetermine the person's need and then tailor the approach to meet it.

7. The larger the parish, the more organized the visitation program must be. Care must be taken that no one is overlooked or made to feel unimportant in a large congregation.

8. Communication is a vital element. Visitors must communicate not only with those they are calling upon but also with the clergy and leaders to whom information should be passed on for follow-up, assistance, and suggestions.

9.  Strive to get the person "involved." A person who is actively serving has less time for nursing old wounds or criticizing the church. Basic needs of people include the need for acceptance, adventure, and accomplishment. The church provides outlets for all three if one will only take the time to find one's "niche."

10. Be sincere. People can spot a phony, so don't try to fake anything.

11. Assure the person that she or he is "wanted" and "needed." No one else can fill that person's particular place in the body of Christ, and the person needs to know it.

12. Write things down. Don't trust your memory. Keep accurate records of visits and results for future ministry. If no one is at home when you visit, leave a note. In fact, two notes are in order: one for the prospect and one to yourself as a reminder to call again.

13. Follow-up is necessary. Keep supporting the person with prayers, additional visits, and "helps" for spiritual welfare.

14. Although training is desirable, the real requisite for being an effective church visitor is a heart of love.

15. Don't become discouraged or worried about bad experiences. The Lord can redeem mistakes. He prefers a sincere effort that may backfire every now and then to halfhearted efforts for fear of making a mistake.

16. Be alert for visitation prospects - new people in the community, unfamiliar faces at Sunday worship services, referrals from the clergy. Don't wait to be asked to extend a welcome or friendliness to someone, even if that person has not been assigned to you for a visit.

17. Don't lose sight of the fact that this is a ministry unto the Lord as well as to others. Jesus says, "In as much as ye have done it to the least of these, ye have done it unto me."

## Fellowshiping

Christians often speak of "fellowship." Sometimes they mean a party or social event. Sometimes they mean one accord or a unity of spirit among the brethren. Other times they are speaking of the whole church as a "fellowship of believers." It may even denote a friendliness of personality, as one who likes to interact with others in comradeship - an attitude of fellowship.

While all of these are aspects of the broad scope of fellowship, when the Scriptures speak of fellowship it is with a much more profound meaning and a deeper spiritual significance. Bible references indicate that true fellowship involves a separation from sin and a blending of the personality into that of Jesus Christ in such a way as to zero in on a new plane of existence. Some Christians try to tip their hats to the Lord while continuing to walk in ways contrary to his teachings, fully expecting that what they do during times other than Sunday morning worship time in no way relates to a broken fellowship, an unenriched fellowship, or a nonproductive fellowship.

Consider these Scriptures: "Ye were called unto fellowship of his Son Jesus Christ our Lord" (I Cor. 1:9); "Be not unequally yoked with unbelievers, for what fellowship has righteousness with unrighteousness? And what communion has light with darkness?" (II Cor. 6:14); "Ye may have fellowship with us, and truly our fellowship is with the Father and with his Son Jesus Christ" (I John 1:3). The thread that runs through all of these verses seems to be, "One cannot have true fellowship of any sort apart from fellowship with Jesus, and such a fellowship demands a changed and separated lifestyle." In the description of the activities of first-century Christians, fellowship is given equal importance along with "doctrine, breaking of bread, prayer, and miracles" (Acts 2:42-43). It is not described here as a sideline or a less spiritual aspect of Christianity.

Once an understanding of the spiritual implications of fellowship is achieved, the next step is determining how fellowship can be implemented as a lay ministry. Some people have a natural talent or "gift" for planning social events and extending hospitality. These people should see such abilities as stewardship opportunities for Christian service. Those to whom the responsibility falls for planning socials, get-togethers, and recreation programs should do so from a Christ-centered viewpoint. Jesus wants to be Lord of all areas of a Christian's life, including the social life. Such a spiritual approach will not, as some believe, make the event dull, "churchy," or less inviting. To the contrary, Jesus is the best party-planner one could consult. He was often the honor guest at dinner parties and social functions of his day. And, after all, it was he who did not wish the host at the wedding party at Cana to be embarrassed because of a slip-up in planning the refreshments. In fact, a prayerful and Spirit-directed planning of social and recreational programs will enrich them and give an added dimension no such secular program could ever produce.

Of the four main functions of the church (worship, instruction, service or outreach, and fellowship), the two that usually receive most attention are worship and fellowship. The beauty and reverence of most worship services need no further comment; understandably, the highest-attendance function is the Sunday morning service. Also well attended are events such as church suppers and social events. The same cannot be said, however, for Bible study, teacher-training session, missionary project, or work day. Perhaps the key is to combine some of the most appealing aspects of church life (worship and fellowship) with those less popular (instruction and outreach). Although space will not permit a comprehensive and detailed rundown of all possible kinds of spiritually uplifting and instructional fellowship activities, the following samples should present the basic pattern for approaching fellowship as an opportunity for ministry.

No host or hostess would invite dinner guests without deciding on the menu to be served. Neither should the spiritual "food" to be offered at a fellowship time be overlooked. Questions to be considered are the following:

1.  Who will be coming? (The whole parish, a particular age group?)

2.  What are the needs of those coming? (Interests, spiritual maturity, likes and dislikes, etc.)

3.  What theme (spiritual "message") should be dominant?

4.  How can Jesus Christ best be honored at this function?

### Church Fellowships

Church fellowship activities generally fall into one of three categories: church suppers, recreation programs, money raisers.

1. Suppers: The ubiquitous covered-dish supper seems to be the most popular of all social events at church. Whether on a regular basis or at special occasions, this is a convenient and inexpensive way of gathering the church family together for a meal and friendly, relaxed conversation. The instructional aspect of ministry can be added to such a supper program in one of several ways - by providing a devotional, teaching, or audio-visual program following the meal; by dividing the tables into discussion groups to consider solutions to problems of Christian living or other topics of interest; by the inclusion of spiritual music (either group singing or special music provided by guest singers or instrumentalists); or by providing a group project or activity before or after supper (such as banner-making, collages, posters, puzzles, quizzes, etc.) which carry out the theme or instruccional purpose of the event. An outreach emphasis can also be added to the program by collecting money, food, clothing, or other items for the needy as a part of the "admission price" to the supper or by inviting the elderly, needy, or orphans from local institutions to be guests at such events. The covered-dish-supper participants may also elect to make something or work on a project for a deserving charity, to write cards or letters to shut-ins or hospitalized members, or to hold a work session at the church following supper for any repair or maintenance work that needs doing. As an example of combining fellowship with outreach, one church decided to bring money instead of a covered dish to a church supper (the amount of money that would have been spent if a dish of food

had been prepared). The money was donated to a fund for relief of the hungry. Participants that night ate a meager supper of bread and soup, which was provided by church kitchen volunteers, to remind themselves of God's blessings and to practice the discipline of self-denial while at the same time remembering those less fortunate. Such a program provided a good object lesson for children and adults alike.

2. Recreational Programs: Church recreational programs may range from team sports and outside activities to inside functions such as game nights, family night gatherings, and coffeehouse meetings for youth and young adults. It goes without saying that church teams which compete against other churches in the area have a built-in instructional program emphasizing good sportsmanship, team work, and principles of Christian interaction, even with rivals. Pep talks from coaches and empirical learning from experiences on the softball field or basketball court are excellent training grounds for practical Christian living. Leaders who coach or support such teams should never overlook the opportunity for ministry before, during, and after a game. Instruction can likewise be "slipped in" and integrated into inside programs in palatable and natural ways. The idea is not to be preachy or heavy-handed in an instructional-program approach but, rather, to make the fun activities even more meaningful because they spring from a spiritual and moral foundation. Rap sessions are natural functions at social gatherings. Why not structure the regular conversation a bit by providing topics, questions, or study guides relevant to problems the group is facing in daily life or problems of society that can be approached from a biblical standpoint? Music, films, Bible scavenger hunts or games, discussion drama (role playing of problem situations followed by evaluation and discussion by the entire group), and the sharing of testimonies can all be incorporated into a recreational program. The production of a play or a musical production (with a "message") can also be a source of excellent learning experiences as well as recreational therapy. The Youth Club program, which many churches use totally or in part, is an example of this idea of integrating a corporate meal with worship, instruction, music, and fellowship. In such a program, adults and youth get to know each other and relate to each other in harmonious ways. The church cannot compete with the secular world when it comes to offering entertainment. Instead, the church must offer something the world cannot offer - that which is spiritually uplifting and personally rewarding. That, after all, is what most people are hungering for.

And what of outreach ministries? Can they also be incorporated into a recreational program? Yes. Whether a church has a structured recreational program provided on a regular basis or has recreational activities as an integral part of other organizations (Sunday school, youth programs, guilds, Men's Club, etc.), there are innumerable opportunities for lay ministry. Retreats, lock-ins (overnight sessions at the church), special emphasis programs, and other such events can emphasize evangelism, missionary projects, assistance to the needy, or stewardship of time, tithes, or talents. Games, which are an inherent part of recreation, involve competition. It is easy to sponsor tournaments for games (table tennis, checkers, cards, shuffleboard, Scrabble, or whatever) and make the entrance fee the donation of money or some usable item for a worthwhile charity or sponsorship. Since everyone is not necessarily game-oriented, contests can be held for art work, essays, or speeches - any area of interest to the particular recreational group. The theme for such entries might be something like "What My Faith Means to Me" or "How Jesus Would Solve the Problem of --- ." There is also the opportunity for outreach by the taking of programs or gifts to a retirement center, jail, orphanage, or detention home for delinquent youth. Such a program might include music, testimonies, drama, refreshments, and the giving of hand-made gifts or cards. Any group that meets on a regular basis (for even a brief period) can involve itself in a service project. This is transforming Christianity into a workable and practical function rather than viewing it as merely a theological ideal or theory. Programs may involve all sorts of things - improving the self-concept, building loving relationships with others, participating in work projects at church or in the community, collecting for the needy, witnessing, sharing with others, developing leadership qualities, learning about churchmanship, or anything else that is needful. Whatever the theme, the Dewey educational philosophy of "learning by doing" is certainly applicable to recreational programs among Christians. Nothing is as much fun or as rewarding as involving oneself in a worthwhile cause. Church recreation not only gives a desirable alternative from the world's ideas of diversion, but also encourages God's people to become involved in giving out rather than always taking in.

3. <u>Fund Raisers</u>: Money-raising functions at churches take all forms - bake sales, spaghetti dinners, rummage sales, pancake suppers, bazaars, talent shows, carnivals, dinner-dances, card parties, bingo games, fashion shows, auctions, and an unending list of other offerings designed to satisfy some basic human need for fun, food, entertainment, pleasure, or material gain. The basic need for spiritual nurture need not be overlooked in the planning of such functions.

To incorporate instructional aspects into a money-raising project will not be difficult, provided those in charge remember what motivates people to support a project with their presence or their pocketbooks. People like to be inspired as well as entertained. There are many Christian films, music groups, and speakers that people will pay to see and hear. Such offerings can be included in the price of a supper, bazaar, carnival, or whatever else is going on. Talent shows, likewise, can feature Christian music, monologues, dance, choral speech presentations, or skits. Often humor in the form of satire is a painless way of pointing out human foibles and will sometimes work when a lecture or sermon on the subject would not.

Outreach is built into any money-raising project, provided it is for some worthy cause or charity. Whoever plans, sets up, cleans up, or sells tickets is involved in service, but often participants are so taken up with the mechanics of a project that they forget to stress the reason behind all the activity. Think of the possibilities: someone's artwork or handcrafts are sold at a church auction; someone's needle-work is purchased at a bazaar; someone else's home-made baked goods are sold at the morning coffee hour; another's talents are involved in an evening's entertainment; someone's book-keeping abilities are utilized in planning the budget for a fund raiser; someone's salesmanship ability is put to good use selling tickets; and another's public relations talent is put to work in publicizing the event. In the midst of the flurry of activity surrounding any such pro-ject, someone needs to call the participants' attention to the way in which they give of themselves, that it be done as an offering unto the Lord. Prayer should precede all other preparations. The guidance of the Lord should be sought in each aspect of the project.

Perhaps the most successful type of fund raiser to em-phasize outreach is the kind that utilizes the skills or ta-lents of the individuals involved. An auction can include services (such as an evening of babysitting or a day of yard-work); groups can put on car washes, dinners, or paint-up/fix-up campaigns; or organizations can sponsor "Rent a Helper" programs in which volunteer services can be purchased.

Another way in which to stress outreach is through publicity about the fund raiser. Posters, bulletin announce-ments, and publicity in the media can stress the sponsorship project (the way the money will be spent) so that even those who buy tickets will feel a part of helping the outreach ministry.

Home and Community Fellowships

The same spiritual principles also apply to social events held out-side the church. Many people belong to business organizations, clubs, and neighborhood civic groups and become involved in all kinds of ser-vice projects, yet never see their activities as opportunities for ministries of outreach. Often the unchurched and uncommitted get their first glimpse of Christianity in the lives of those with whom they meet and work together in committees or community activities. God's people should see these involvements as opportunities to extend the outreach of the church and to sow seeds of love. In addition to community in-volvement, there are also opportunities for social outreach when inter-church functions, interdenominational fellowships, or special programs take place.  Serving on committees or working with those of different faiths or fellowships strengthens the body of Christ and gives opportunities for exchanging ideas, broadening horizons, and sharing ministries.  The church needs to stress these ideas and provide instruction in methods of outreach, indirect evangelism, and day-to-day witnessing techniques that can be incorporated in business, community, and social relationships.

Even something as commonplace as home entertaining can be viewed as an outreach ministry.  The Bible says that a servant of Christ should be "given to hospitality."  Visitors who come to a Christian home should be able to sense the presence of the Lord, not just from tangible clues such as Christian symbols on door-knockers, religious pictures on the walls, or bumper stickers on the cars in the garage.  It is even more than saying grace before meals or getting involved in conversations about the church or one's faith.  There should be a peace, an atmosphere of love and acceptance that permeates the household and manifests itself in the warm and smiling faces of the family.  It should be obvious to all that Jesus is the unseen honor guest at every family get-together, dinner party, or social function.  Since Jesus wants to be Lord of all aspects of one's life, it makes sense to pray about the parties one plans and the invitation list and what to serve and any problem involved in the many facets of entertaining.  The Living Bible interpretation of I Peter 4:9 says, "Cheerfully share your home with those who need a meal or a place to stay the night."  Some Christians have taken the verse to heart and established an "Elisha room" in their homes.  Just as the widow of the Old Testament kept a room ready and waiting for the prophet Elisha whenever he passed by and needed lodging, so they keep a guest room available for anyone the Lord may send to them for lodging.  Other Christians have opened their homes to take in the needy or have become foster parents to homeless or troubled youth.  Still others heed the biblical admonition to "go into the highways and hedges" when they give a party by entertaining the lonely or poor - people from institutions or those who cannot repay the invitation.  Sometimes several families or individuals from the church will band together to support such outreach ministries of hospitality and love.

A true-life example of the benefits of letting Jesus plan a social event can be found in the case of a Christian couple who, although they lived on a modest income, felt led of the Lord to provide a buffet dinner for friends, neighbors, and casual acquaintances to whom they were witnessing.  The guest list totaled over a hundred, which presented not only problems of where the money would come from to feed so many, but also problems of space.  Their small home would hardly accommodate one hundred dinner guests!  Still, they felt the Lord was leading them to offer this gesture of love and friendship to each one on the list.  After praying for guidance, they were led to invite the guests to come between the hours of 5:30 P.M. and 8:30 P.M., open-house fashion.  With a budget of barely $50, they were able to feed the hundred people who came a beautiful buffet of ham, turkey, salads, hot dishes, rolls, desserts, punch, and coffee.  Exactly one-third of the guests came in three shifts during the evening, timed perfectly to be accommodated by the thirty-three seating spaces they managed to arrange throughout the house. The Lord even gave the hostess a different and creative idea for an attractive centerpiece for the serving table. The centerpiece, which featured the theme of love and friendship in the form of Christian symbols, flowers, and the theme, "God loves you and so do we!" let each person who came know of the purpose behind the invitation. At the end of the evening, the couple said, "We'll never plan a party without the Lord's help again. He does miracles!"

## Hospital Calling

In some churches all visits to hospitals are made by the clergy. More and more, however, as the clergy are overworked and as lay ministry efforts increase, lay people are being trained to assist in this important form of outreach. Everyone who has ever been hospitalized knows that there are times when a visitor is most welcome, and other times when conversation is the last thing needed. For that reason, it is most important that hospital callers be discerning individuals who will be sensitive to the apparent needs of those to be visited. As was suggested for those who will visit newcomers or lapsed members, a training program (or at least a long talk with one's pastor) is suggested prior to launching out on a hospital calling ministry for the first time.

The role-play technique is very effective in such a training program. By allowing prospective callers a "dry run" in practice sessions, the various kinds of situations to be encountered may be dealt with in a safe and supportive atmosphere before the real thing occurs. If only one or two individuals in a parish are approved for hospital calling, they may receive direct training from their clergyman - either in private discussions or through "on the job training" obtained by accompanying him to hospitals to observe first-hand the approved techniques and procedures. If, on the other hand, there are members of a hospital calling committee or a large group of individuals from one or more churches in the area to be trained, a formalized training program should be instituted. Although there are basic principles which can be pointed out, there can be no hard and fast rules. Each hospital caller will develop his own style and will perform the ministry in the manner in which he is most comfortable and in the way he feels led of the Lord to perform it. There occasionally will be exceptions to all the rules or methods one learns. With all that in mind, the following suggestions are offered:

Suggestions for Hospital Callers

### Advance Preparation:

Clergy approval and advance training should precede this ministry. The training may take the form of discussions with the clergy, reading of books or tracts on the subject, taking workshop courses, and/or serving as an apprentice, accompanying a seasoned caller.

Personal aptitudes should include sociability - a genuine liking for people; cheerfulness - a pleasant and winsome personality; faith - not only a personal commitment to Jesus Christ, but also a firm belief in his power to heal those sick in mind, body, or spirit; wisdom - a discerning spirit that will be sensitive to the needs of others with an inner witness of when to speak, when to pray, when to counsel, when to remain silent, when to leave, etc. Also needed is physical and emotional strength and stamina. Not everyone has the stomach for a sick room; not everyone can observe suffering without becoming ill.

A calling to this ministry should be felt by the hospital caller and confirmed by others. If prayer and a time of waiting upon the Lord has preceded the involvement in hospital calling, the Lord will open the door and prepare his servant properly.

A general knowledge of Scriptures and prayers for healing will be most beneficial.

A personal philosophy about sickness, wholeness, the place of faith in the recuperation process, and feelings that are associated with illness should be determined in advance and then checked out by the clergy. Writing down this philosophy will help to clarify thoughts and make it easier when you are called upon to "give an answer for the hope that is within you." It will also give the clergy an opportunity to clarify or correct before an error is perpetuated.

Predetermine and check out various approaches that might be called for in different situations. For instance, what would be the proper approach to take with one only slightly ill? Someone recuperating from a major operation? Someone following childbirth? Someone with a lingering and debilitating illness? Someone with a terminal illness? Someone at the point of death? Unless these and other similar questions are faced and answered ahead of time, the hospital caller can be caught off-guard.

Before the Visit:

Find out as much as possible about those to be visited ahead of time. Check with the church office, the hospital, the family, and others before going in "cold."

Pray. Give time for personal meditation and prayer to prepare yourself; pray for those to be visited; pray for guidance to be able to minister God's love in the way the Spirit directs; pray for the family of the sick person and those who minister healing gifts to the person.

Check out the hospital rules ahead of time and be certain to observe them. Many hospitals limit the number of visitors allowed, have definite visiting hours, etc. It is also good to check on special instructions about the patient. For instance, a special diet would restrict the bringing of food-stuffs, or a NO VISITORS sign on the door may or may not include authorized callers from the church. Patients may ask the caller for forbidden items (cigarettes, sweets, etc.), so the caller should know what is and is not acceptable ahead of time.

## The Visit

Be sure to knock or announce yourself before entering in order to avoid finding the patient in an embarrassing situation.

Be observant. Try to identify the patient's greatest needs, whether they are physical, emotional, or spiritual - or all three. Take note of the patient's response to your coming. Is he or she glad to see you and anxious to visit? Is the patient in pain? Sleepy? Depressed? Would it be better if you came back at another time? Adjust the visit to the needs of the patient.

Determine the dominant purpose for your visit. Are you there primarily to socialize, to offer comfort, to pray, or to minister in some other way? Know what needs doing before attempting to do it.

Time the visits carefully. Conversation can be very tiring to someone who is ill. Do not overstay. Do not force the patient to talk if it is obviously an effort for the person to do so. On the other hand, if the patient is lonely and desirous of your company, do not brush him or her off with a hasty retreat. Take your cues from the patient's condition and attitude and the obvious circumstances. Use common sense and good judgment.

Focus conversation in the direction of the patient's needs and interests. Bring some news about the church, friends, and things to which the patient can relate. Do not bore with in-formation about which the patient knows or cares little. Don't spend all the time talking about yourself. It would be better to focus attention upon Jesus, his power to heal and comfort, and his ability to meet and overcome all difficulties in life. DO NOT DISCUSS PROBLEMS OR DEPRESSING TOPICS!

Don't pump the patient for information about his or her condi-tion. Unless the patient volunteers to discuss such physical problems with you, don't dwell upon the illness at all.

Keep three things out of a sick room:  fear, worry, and doubt.
Let your attitude be one of confidence and assurance.  Do not,
however, be insincere. Do not, for instance, tell a patient,
"You look wonderful," when in fact, just the opposite is true.
Although humor is often a good device for releasing tension,
use good judgment here.   Some situations are definitely not
a laughing matter.

Ask the patient's permission to pray together.  Usually, the
response will be affirmative, but never violate a person's
wishes. If an offer to pray is refused, you may say that you'll pray
silently or that you'll keep the person in your private prayers
each day, or you'll put him or her on the prayer list at church,
or some similar response.

Carry a calling card to leave with the patient who is asleep
or out of the room when you call.  If these have a printed
prayer, Scripture verses or inspirational message, it will be
another form of ministry, especially in situations described
just above.

Offer to be of service.  Leave your phone number on the card;
offer to visit again, run an errand, or minister in any other
way indicated as needful.  The patient may want you to read a
portion of Scripture or a selection from an inspirational book.
Have such things at hand for such situations.

Don't ignore the person in the next bed.  If a patient shares
a room with others, extend your ministry (as it is accepted)
to all who need it.

Don't forget the power of touch.  Unless the patient's condition prohibits it or unless the patient reacts negatively to
your touch, hold the patient's hand during prayer, shake hands
upon entering and leaving, embrace, and express your love
through the point of contact you make through appropriate gestures - a gentle pat, a kiss, or a touch.  Naturally, how well
the caller knows the patient, the sex of the person, and propriety must be considered when determining appropriate gestures
of Christian love.


## After the Visit

Continue to pray for those visited.  Keep a notebook or file
of those called upon with pertinent information as to their
condition, attitude, needs, etc.  Indicate answers to prayers
when the patient regains health, and be certain to offer prayers
of thanksgiving at such times.

Keep lines of communication open.  Keep in touch with the patient,
and pass along information about the person's condition to
the church and clergy.

Follow-up may include additional visits, referral for a visit or further ministry by others. For instance, the patient from a sacramental church may want to make a confession or to receive Communion. Be certain to get this type of request to the pastor immediately. Even after he or she is healed, the patient should feel your love and concern; not just at the time you are functioning in your "churchly duty" of hospital calling, but at all times.

Helpful Prayers and Scriptures Related to Healing: Members of churches that have printed liturgies and prayer books will find therein model prayers of thanksgiving, recovery, and of healing, as well as prayers for the despondent and dying.

A sample prayer for the sick follows, and after it are printed some appropriate Scripture passages.

> Dear Lord Jesus, you are the Great Physician, the Source of all life and health. We look to you for strength, comfort, mercy, and wholeness, asking that you abundantly pour out your healing love upon ---. We give you thanks and praise for hearing this prayer of faith, which we pray in the name of our Lord and Saviour, Jesus Christ. Amen.

The prayer of faith shall save the sick (James 5:15).

I wish above all things that thou mayest prosper and be in health (III John 2).

Jesus bore our sins in his own body on the tree, that we, being dead to sins, should live unto righteousness; by whose stripes ye were healed (I Pet. 2:24).

Jesus himself took our infirmities and bore our sicknesses (Matt. 8:17).

I am the Lord that healeth thee (Ex. 15:26).

Unto you that fear my name shall the Sun of Righteousness arise with healing in his wings (Mal. 4:2).

In the fear of the Lord is strong confidence; and his children shall have a place of refuge. The fear of the Lord is a fountain of life, to depart from the snares of death (Prov. 14:26-27).

God is our refuge and strength, a very present help in trouble. Therefore, will not we fear (Ps. 46:1-2).

He said unto me, "My grace is sufficient for thee; for my strength is made perfect in weakness." Most gladly, therefore, will I rather glory in my infirmities, that the power of Christ may rest upon me (II Cor. 12:9).

If thou canst believe, all things are possible to him that believeth (Mark 9:23).

# Crisis Comfort

James 1:27 describes true, undefiled religion before God the Father as "visiting the fatherless and widows in their affliction." Perhaps the most difficult and, at the same time, the most rewarding function of social outreach is ministering to someone at a time of crisis. Although a pastor is usually the first person called at a time of difficulty or sorrow, there is much that a layperson can and should do.

The word <u>crisis</u> means not only a crucial time, but also a turning point. It is important for those in this ministry to remember that problems are a common meeting ground for all Christians, but that there is victory on the other side. Jesus said it this way: "In the world you shall have tribulation, but be of good cheer; I have overcome the world" (John 16:33).

Each person may react a little differently to tragedy. For some, it becomes a life-shattering experience; for others, it becomes a life-changing experience. For some, wounds heal quickly; for others, the healing process is painfully slow. In some cases, people turn away from God or blame him for their misfortunes; in other instances, people become stronger in a faith that is tested and found to be all-sufficient. Because each situation will be different and those involved will react in unique and individualistic ways, there can be no magic formula to plug into a crisis situation to make the hurt go away. God deals with his children as individuals, and we, likewise, must do so with each other. There are, however, some generalizations which can be made. What can a Christian layperson do to help a suffering fellow human facing the slings and arrows of life?

1. <u>Give empathy, not sympathy</u>. To empathize with someone is to "feel with" the person — to experience what that person has experienced, to put oneself into the other's shoes. People do not want pity, but it helps to know someone can share the hurts, or, as it says in Romans 12:15-16: "to rejoice with them that do rejoice, and weep with them that weep, being of the same mind one toward another."

2. <u>Pray</u>. Nothing is as sustaining in a crisis as prayer. Whether the prayers are offered in or out of the person's hearing, the effects of intercessory prayer will be felt and appreciated. "The effectual fervent prayer of a righteous man avails much" (James 5:15).

3. <u>Be there</u>. Although there are times when a sorrowing person must be alone with grief, a person usually needs someone to walk through the "valley of the shadow" with her or him. Often just the presence of a caring, loving individual will ease the pain. "Stand fast in one spirit" (Phil. 1:27).

4. <u>Listen</u>. Psychiatrists and psychologists attest to the healing therapy of "talking out" one's problems. It is not good to

suppress or bury hurts. Often the best ministry one can offer is just listening. "The hearing ear, and the seeing eye, the Lord has made even both of them" (Prov. 20:12).

5. Comfort. Uttering words of comfort and consolation may take many different forms. The Scriptures are full of words of promise and strength and should be a ready source of help at such times. A good example is Psalm 46, which begins, "God is our refuge and strength, a very present help in trouble." A testimony from one who has endured a similar experience and come out on the other side is likewise helpful. Words of godly counsel, when given under the anointing of the Holy Spirit, can also be comforting. When offering such counsel, however, the counselor must be careful and prayerful to say only the words the Lord wants to speak through him or her. In such instances, the Spirit will also prepare the heart of the sorrowing one to receive the words. Sometimes a written message is better than a spoken one, in that the words may be chosen carefully, prayed over, and corrected before they are given to the one to be comforted. The one ministering should be very sensitive to the promptings of the Spirit and the obvious needs in each circumstance in order to fulfill the admonition of I Thessalonians 4:18: "Comfort one another."

6. Share the burden. Depending upon the type of crisis it is, there are various opportunities for giving a helping hand to lighten the burden of the individual or family involved. There may be a need for taking care of children, preparing meals, making arrangements, answering the telephone, receiving visitors, answering questions, or any number of other duties, the doing of which will free the minds and hands of those who are troubled. Committees or individuals in crisis ministries should be alert to perceive such needs and quick to respond to them. "Bear ye one another's burdens" (Gal. 6:2).

Beyond these general principles, there are some specific preparations which those involved in crisis comfort can employ prior to making themselves available for ministry. First might be remembering crises in their own lives in order to develop a clearly defined philosophy about various problems and how they can be faced triumphantly. Questions to be considered are these:

What emotional feelings were evidenced during the crisis?

What outlets for these emotions were needed?

What helped most at the time of crisis?

What hindrances got in the way and how could such hindrances be avoided or overcome?

Second, one's own personal feelings about grief, tragedies, testings, and death need to be faced and defined. After writing out such a philosophy, it would be well to go over it with a pastor or spiritual adviser competent in the field of crisis aid. Some questions to consider in this area are these:

Who or what is the cause of tragedy and problems to be faced in life?

What part, if any, do Satan and sin play in life's problems?

What is the Christian view of tragedy?

What is the Christian view of death?

What aids are available through the church and other sources for dealing with life's problems?

How can one resolve the conflict between evil circumstances and the belief in a loving, omnipotent God?

Where does "God's will" fit into tragic circumstances?

What does the Bible teach as the Christian's acceptable response in times of crisis?

What should a Christian do when he or she cannot understand conflicting circumstances?

These, of course, are heavy questions with no easy, ready-made answers. Crisis ministers would do well to resolve their own ambivalent feelings about such questions before attempting to offer aid to others who must grapple with the same questions. The suggestion to conduct training sessions involving role play (which was made for church visitors) could be extended to include a time to deal with these soul-searching questions. Whether in role play, discussion, or private interview with a counselor, these questions should be dealt with as a preparation for ministry.


Ministry Areas In Crisis Comfort

Because there are so many different kinds of crises, and because each circumstance may require a different approach, it might be advisable to have those involved in crisis aid become "specialists" in one area of ministry. This would be particularly appropriate in large congregations. Just as a doctor specializes in one aspect of medicine, lay people may find that one is best suited to one type of crisis situation and another to a different type. Or they may begin at one level and slowly branch out to include other areas of ministry as they gain experience and competence. The following categories are offered as a means of determining such ministry areas:

1. Relationship Problems: alienation, separation, divorce, family quarrels, violence, rebellious children, runaway children, battered or neglected children, and other forms of conflict in interpersonal relationships.

2. Emotional Problems: depression, hysterical behavior, mental illness, drug or alcohol abuse, suicide, unhealed memories of the past.

3. Physical and Circumstantial Problems: accidents, emergencies, tragedies. (NOTE: Tragedies cover a wide range; what may be a tragedy to one may not be to another. For instance, one person may see a birth defect or mental retardation or physical ailment as a tragedy, while another may view it as an opportunity to grow and develop in other ways, as a learning experience in life, or as a challenge to greater spirituality. One type of person may see a home destroyed by fire or the loss of a job as a tragedy, while another may take such events in stride, thinking of them as part of life. The problem itself is not the issue so much as the victim's response to it.)

4. Spiritual Problems: loss of faith, backsliding, alienation from God because of sin or guilt, involvement in false religions or cults.

5. Death, Separation, and Dying: terminal or lingering illnesses, loss of a loved one by death or institutionalization, adjustment to grief and loneliness.

Obviously, dealing with some of these problems will require training as a counselor and spiritual adviser. Unless one has the necessary educational and theological background to handle complex problems, it might be best to limit crisis assistance to one of the following ministries which, while requiring less training and skill, are nonetheless equally important in crisis ministry:

1. Phone Calls: A brief expression of concern is preferable to a lengthy conversation. (Don't pry or demand details unless the sorrowing one volunteers such information.)

2. Cards or Letters: A personal message may be added to a card purchased in a store. Heartfelt expressions of love are more appreciated than "store-bought" messages, but they do not have to be elaborate or lengthy. A simple, "Our thoughts and prayers are with you" or "Please know how much I share in your grief" will suffice. Sometimes churches and individuals keep a supply of personalized messages of sympathy on hand for unexpected situations that arise.

3. Flowers: Unless requested not to do so, the sending of flowers is a tangible and thoughtful way of expressing loving concern or sympathy.

4. <u>Donations or Gifts</u>:  Instead of flowers, a donation may be made either to the sorrowing or in their name to their favorite charity.  The wishes of the individual and the family should be the determining factor here.  A memorial or honorarium to the church, an inspirational wall plaque, or another appropriate gift may be the means of saying, "I'm thinking of you."

5. <u>Food</u>:  At times of death, illness or sorrow, it is always appropriate to bring in prepared food.  This is not only a gesture of love, but also a way of freeing the bereaved or troubled from meal planning.  Often a committee will take turns bringing a complete meal or will volunteer to donate separate items of foodstuffs over a period of time.  The church may have an organized way of providing such a service, or individuals may do so voluntarily.  It is an extra consideration to bring food in disposable containers or, at least, to mark the containers with the donor's name, to eliminate confusion when it is time to return the dishes.


Crisis Comfort Scriptures and Prayer

Although far from an exhaustive list, the Scriptures cited below may be a source of help and comfort in meeting particular crisis needs. Following the Scripture suggestions is a sample prayer of comfort.

1. <u>Relationship Problems</u>:

     In times of persecution - Psalm 118:6-8
     Patience in family trials - Psalm 27:10-14
     In times of rebellion - I Peter 5:5
     Where there is unforgiveness - Colossians 3:12-15

2. <u>Emotional Problems</u>:

     For worry, depression, or fear - II Timothy 1:7; Psalm 138:7;
     Psalm 23
     Power over mental problems - Colossians 1:21; Philippians 4:7
     Overcoming addictions and bondages - Philippians 4:13;
     Galatians 5:1
     Assurance that prayers are heard - John 5:13
     In times of indecision - Proverbs 3:5-6
     Freedom from past hurts - Luke 4:18-21

3. <u>Circumstantial Problems</u>:

     Unemployment or financial problems - Matthew 6:25-34
     In times of sickness or tragedy - Romans 8:28, 38-39
     The purposes of suffering - I Peter 5:10
     In emergencies and turmoils - Psalm 46:1-5

4. Spiritual Problems:

When one has backslidden - Jeremiah 3:22; Isaiah 55:7
When one has been involved in false religions, cults or the practices of the occult - I Timothy 4:1; Leviticus 19:31; Isaiah 47:13-14; Micah 5:12; Jeremiah 27:9-10
When problems are the result of sin - Hebrews 12:5-11
If one cannot pray - Romans 8:26
When faith is lost - Hebrews 11:6; Hebrews 3:12-14
When one feels separated because of guilt - Romans 8:1

5. Death and Dying:

Comfort at the time of death - Isaiah 25:8; I Corinthians 15:54-57
Overcoming the fear of death - Psalm 23:4; Psalm 116:15
Promise of life after death - Romans 8:11
Rewards after death - I Peter 1:3-4; Revelation 21:4-5
For loneliness at the death of a loved one - Hebrews 13:5; Psalm 34:18-19

6. Comfort in Any Crisis:

The Lord's ability to comfort and heal - Psalm 147:3-5
Power through Jesus to overcome any problem - II Corinthians 4:8-10
Strength in a time of trouble - Psalm 37:39-40

Any of these Scriptures can be written down or printed on cards to send to one who is grieving or troubled. This is often a more lasting and ongoing source of comfort than merely quoting the verse or reading it.

Prayer: Dear Lord, when with our finite minds we cannot understand, we simply trust in your abundant mercy and infinite wisdom. We ask that your comfort, strength, mercy, and love surround ---, and that you be (his/her) refuge and very present help in trouble. We thank you that you never allow us to face more than you will give us the grace to endure. We place all circumstances and ourselves in your loving hands, confident that underneath are the everlasting arms of our Lord Jesus Christ. Amen.

## Conclusion

It is a far distance from the ministry of greeting and visiting newcomers at church, to the ministry of planning Christian fellowship programs, to the ministry of comforting the sick and grieving. What do all of these have in common?  One important thing:  they are all a part of social outreach, the building of a bridge of love into the life of another soul.

No matter what other gifts, talents, or ministries people may dedicate to the Lord, they will doubtless find themselves called upon to become involved in one or more of these social functions or outreach ministries.  It behooves every Christian layperson to be prepared for the time when he or she will be called upon to greet, visit, fellowship with, minister healing to, or comfort another in the name of Jesus Christ.

# 6 · Ministries of Evangelism

II Timothy 4:5 says, "Do the work of an evangelist." Exactly what kind of work is that? Some people's idea of evangelism is negative; they imagine street-corner zealots passing out tracts or grabbing passersby to ask, "Brother, are you saved?" Or they imagine a tent meeting and emotional responses to a fiery preacher's warnings of hellfire and damnation. Although such approaches may play a small part in the broad scope of evangelistic methods and techniques, they are only that - a small part. There are infinitely more and different approaches to evangelism to be explored.

The first question is, "What is an evangelist?" The answer: "Anyone who shares the good news about Jesus with another." The method of sharing may be open and direct, or covert and indirect. The person doing the sharing may be an outgoing extrovert or a quiet, gentle soul. There are many kinds of evangelism and many evangelistic approaches. Essentially, all Christians are evangelists in that they bear the name "Christian" and, by so doing, each is proclaiming to be a "little Christ."

Every Christian is also a witness. A witness is someone who tells the truth about what he or she has experienced or believes to be the truth. Witnessing is not an optional part of Christianity. Jesus said, "Ye shall be witnesses unto me" (Acts 1:8). He did not say, "You ought to be" or "you might be" a witness. There is no choice given in the matter. Every Christian is a witenss - whether a good one or a bad one. It, therefore, becomes a Christian's primary concern to be the best kind of witness possible, since one's very life and actions are gospels constantly being read by others.

## Forms of Evangelism

Evangelists come in all shapes and sizes. Perhaps the best way to describe the various kinds is with an analogy. In the sport of golf, for instance, there are many different kinds of golfers. There is the celebrity golfer, such as Arnold Palmer, who not only spends a great deal of time at the game, but also makes headlines doing it. Then there is another kind of professional golfer, who may not be so well known as the celebrities, but who nevertheless makes a living from golfing. Next, there is the avid golfer, who does not devote full time to the game, but to whom golfing is an important sideline. Lastly, there is the "sometime" golfer, who plays only now and then. All of these types may play the game well, but not all of them devote the same amount of time to the sport. In the same way, there is the "Billy Graham" type of evangelist who is well known and involved in proclaiming the gospel full-time throughout the world. There is also the professional evangelist who, although not as widely known and publicized, is nevertheless involved in the evangelism ministry as a full-time vocation - someone who travels about the country holding evangelistic crusades or conducting evangelism courses in churches. Next, there is the enthusiastic evangelist, who is not involved in this ministry full-time, but to whom it is an important avocation. Such persons may use either direct or indirect approaches in sharing Jesus with friends and neighbors. They do not miss an opportunity to turn a conversation toward matters of the gospel, and even their secular lives are a testimony to their active faith. Whether they are teaching Sunday school, working with business associates, or exchanging greetings with the checkout clerk at the supermarket, avid evangelists make every life situation an opportunity to let the light of Jesus shine through them. Last of all, there are the "sometime" evangelists. Although they do not actively seek an evangelistic ministry, they do proclaim the gospel by their actions - church attendance, integrity in work, setting an example for family and friends, perhaps even giving regularly to support evangelistic programs. Such people occasionally may even speak up to say a word about their beliefs, but usually, they defer to others more vocal, preferring to give silent testimony to their faith.

## Gift vs. Ministry

The "gift" of evangelism differs from the "ministry" of evangelism. It is the work of the Holy Spirit to draw people to Jesus, and Christians who have the Spirit working in their lives and hearts, under the Spirit's anointing, will be able to speak a word, answer a question, or meet a need that will plant a seed of love for God's harvest of souls. That is the gift which the Lord bestows upon all his children - the spiritual reproductive ability that draws others toward the light of Truth. Not everyone, however, has a ministry of evangelism, which is as a full-time vocation. Consider another analogy: A carpenter uses tools every day in his work. Other men, who are not full-time carpenters, have some of the same tools and use them from time to time. Often those who are not carpenters use the tools just as effectively and make things which are just as lovely and important, but using tools is not their main focus in life. Thus it is in evangelism. All Christians should learn to handle the tools of an evangelist, whether they are called to use them full-time or part-time.

## Tools of Evangelism

The tools of evangelism are first, a willing and obedient heart, and second, a working knowledge of the basic steps in becoming a Christian. Anyone who stops to consider how he or she came to know Jesus will probably associate the situation with another human being. Perhaps in early childhood, a Sunday school teacher, a Scout leader, or a family member personified Jesus' love. Perhaps a friend, minister, or spiritual counselor so reflected Christian joy and serenity that Jesus became very appealing. The point is, almost everyone comes to Jesus through the efforts or examples of other persons. God, the

Creator, instills within people this creative process that perpetuates itself and brings forth new life, not just in the physical realm, but in the spiritual realm as well. If, then, the ministry of evangelism is a natural and necessary part of the ongoing of Christ's Kingdom, and if every Christian is expected to participate in it to a greater or lesser degree, how can this work best be accomplished? By keeping it simple. Becoming a Christian is not a difficult process, and neither should talking about it to others be difficult. Jesus said it was accomplished by becoming like a little child. A child is simple, uninhibited, teachable, dependent. Even a child can understand the simplicity of the gospel. It is as simple, in fact, as A-B-C: acknowledge, believe, and confess.

Acknowledge: The first step in becoming a Christian is acknowledgment of who God is and who people are. God is perfect; people are imperfect. God has all that it takes to make human beings whole, complete, fulfilled, and at peace. Humans, without God, are lost, incomplete, unfulfilled, and insecure. People cannot save themselves, make themselves good, nor find their way alone. People have a need. That need is for God. Nothing but God can fill that need. Some try to fill the void with pleasure, success, money, or other people. But it is like trying to put a round peg in a square hole. Nothing fits, because there is no substitute for the only thing that will make people whole, the Lord himself. People cannot earn their salvation or work their way to heaven. The very best a person could do would never be good enough for the standard of perfection God demands. That is why people need Jesus. Jesus is God Incarnate, the Perfection lacking in a human being's life. People receive that spiritual and supernatural perfection in receiving Jesus. It is undeserved. It is freely given and accepted, not earned. "For by grace [the undeserved favor of God] are ye saved through faith, and that not of yourself; it is the gift of God: Not of works, lest any man should boast" (Eph. 2:8-9).

The acknowledgment of who God is and who people are includes the acknowledgment of the fact that people are sinners. "There is none righteous, no not one" (Rom. 3:10). Isaiah tells us that all our righteousness is as filthy rags in God's sight (Isa. 64:6). Romans 3:23 says it this way: "All have sinned and come short of the glory of God." But rather than being a hopeless situation, the very sinfulness of people becomes the basis for hope. Jesus paid the price for sin upon the cross. The Bible clearly says, "Without the shedding of blood, there is no remission of sin." In Old Testament times, the shedding of blood of sacrificial animals atoned for human sin. But the atonement of Jesus on the cross was a once-and-forever sacrifice that paid the full penalty for all human sins - past, present, and future. I John 1:7 says, "The blood of Jesus Christ cleanses us from all sin." In acknowledging Jesus as one's Saviour from sin, a person receives forgiveness and acceptability before God. God looks at sinful people and sees only sinless Christ. The penalty was paid in full at Calvary. God, in his mercy, gives human beings quite a deal: people give God a sinful life and a black (albeit receptive) heart, and in exchange, receive a new life, a cleansed heart. It is what Jesus described to Nicodemus as being "born again." Through an acknowledgment of Jesus Christ, people die to their old, fleshly life and are born of the Spirit into newness of spiritual life.

Believe: Jesus said, "I am the Way. No man comes unto the Father but by me" (John 14:6). Jesus did not say he was "one of the ways" or a "part of the way." Being sincere, going to church, trying to live a good life, or just any religion (whether or not it recognizes Jesus as the Son of God) will not provide the way to God. People come to God only through Jesus, for "neither is there salvation in any other" (Acts 4:12). The whole basis upon which salvation rests is belief in Jesus: "Believe on the Lord Jesus Christ and you shall be saved" (Acts 16:31). The gospel (good news) can be summed up in the most popular verse of St. John's writings, John 3:16, which says, in part, "whosoever believes on him should not perish but have everlasting life." Dissecting this verse and examining each part will give one the explanation for the wide acceptance of this one verse as the entire gospel in a nutshell:

| | |
|---|---|
| For God | The greatest deity |
| So loved | The greatest gift |
| The world | The greatest company |
| That he gave | The greatest act |
| His only begotten Son | The greatest perfection |
| That whosoever | The greatest invitation |
| Believes | The greatest simplicity |
| In him | The greatest attraction |
| Should not perish | The greatest promise |
| But | The greatest difference |
| Have | The greatest certainty |
| Everlasting life. | The greatest possession |

Belief is not just a head knowledge of who Jesus was - belief in him as a historic figure. The Bible says even the devils believe in Jesus (know who he is) "and tremble." The kind of belief necessary is an individual acceptance of Jesus into one's heart - believing that Jesus' death on the cross was a personal thing. Out of such a personalized, accepting belief will come the foundation for an intimate relationship with Jesus. People get out of the "driver's seat" and give Jesus control of their lives. This kind of belief presupposes that, upon people's acknowledgment of their sin and their need, Jesus will forgive the sin and fill the need. The beginning of this new, personal relationship starts with a simple act of faith, accepting Jesus as one's Saviour from sin, believing that old things will pass away and all things will, eventually, become new: "For you are dead, and your life is hid with Christ in God" (Col. 3:3).

112

<u>Confess</u>:  Romans 10:9-10 says, "Confess with your mouth the Lord Jesus Christ and believe in your heart that God raised him from the dead . . . for with the heart man believes and with the mouth confession is made."  After the head acknowledgment of one's needy condition and the heart response to a belief in Jesus to remedy the condition, the mouth must proclaim the truth.  God does not want a silent partner. Jesus promises, in Matthew 10:32, "Whosoever therefore shall confess me before men, him will I confess before my Father which is in heaven. But whosoever shall deny me before men, him will I also deny before my Father which is in heaven."  Christians should not be ashamed of their Lord or their faith.  Rather than hiding their newfound light under a bushel, persons who belong to Jesus should let the light shine for others to see.  It is through the confession of who Jesus is and what he means in a person's life that others are attracted to Jesus, and the work of the Kingdom continues.  The Bible says that all the angels of heaven rejoice whenever one sinner comes in repentence to Jesus.  There should, likewise, be rejoicing on earth.  Such rejoicing cannot take place unless the new Christian is willing to let others know about this faith.  Furthermore, there is something significant about voicing one's beliefs.  Words are power.  God created the world by "speaking" it into existence.  When he said, "Let there be light," there was light.  In much the same way, when a person utters a truth, it becomes real.  Saying it makes it so.  Whether a confession of one's faith is done publicly, at confirmation at church, or privately, to one's family or friends, or even individually to God as one professes acceptance of Jesus as a personal Saviour, it is important that a Christain learn early to speak forth that which he or she believes to be true.

To review, there are three steps to God, the Father, through Jesus Christ, his Son:

> <u>A</u>cknowledging one's need to be saved and one's own inadequacy and inability to save oneself.

> <u>B</u>elieving in Jesus Christ as the remedy for that inadequacy, sin, or need for love and wholeness.

> <u>C</u>onfessing Jesus Christ as Saviour and Lord, giving oneself to him as fully and completely as possible, and saying so.


This process of the second birth (or being "born again" into God's family) is very similar to birth and life in the physical world.  Giving birth to a new baby is only step one.  There is much care and much growth necessary before the newborn baby reaches maturity.  Giving one's life to Jesus, being baptized or confirmed, and being filled with God's Holy Spirit are all departure points, not points of arrival.  Then, as in the natural life, begins the maturing process.  A baby learns to walk only after many stumbling steps, much time and effort, many falls, and consecutive tries.  Baby Christians, also, grow a little at a time - sometimes stumbling, learning from mistakes, and trying again.  It must not be expected that, because one has become a Christian,

one will never sin again.  The triumph comes in knowing that there is
a Power within that is greater than that which draws one toward sin.
One becomes an overcomer by "coming over" some things.  Jesus will
provide the strength and help needed to keep growing, as Jesus did
himself, "in wisdom and in stature, and in favor with God and man."

Knowing these A-B-Cs of salvation is by no means the only tool
for the work of an evangelist.  Additional methods of explaining the
gospel are available through books, tracts, and other means, and they
may be more appropriate for a given situation.  There is no one way
to lead another to Jesus.  Each situation will be different because
each person is different.  The Lord has promised that the Holy Spirit
will give the appropriate words:  "Settle it therefore in your hearts,
not to meditate before what you shall answer, for I will give you a
mouth and wisdom" (Luke 21:14-15).  It is, after all, the Spirit's
responsibility to (1) prepare the heart of the person who needs Jesus;
(2) give the witness the right words to speak; (3) cause the words to
take root in the needy one's heart; and (4) draw that person to Jesus.
It should be a source of relief to a beginning witness to know that
she or he bears only a small part of the responsibility and that the
Holy Spirit will carry the greatest part of the load.  The results are
not the responsibility of the witness either.  The main duty  of the
witness before God is to be available to witness and to be responsive
to the promptings of the Holy Spirit to proclaim the truth in love.

Additional "tools" that a Christian may need from time to time
will always be provided.  If one truly wishes to be used in the ministry of evangelism, the Lord will be faithful to give such a one the
instruction, guidance, and equipment needed.  It all begins with prayer,
the kind that Isaiah prayed:  "Here am I.  Send me."  Whenever one begins to breathe such a prayer, the Spirit moves into action to assist
in every way.  The doors of opportunity will open, for the Lord is
anxiously waiting to send laborers into the fields that are already
white unto harvest.

### An Evangelist's Checklist

The following are some suggested prerequisites for an effective
evangelistic ministry:

1. Live a life that is a positive testimony.  Nothing can be worse
   than witnesses who do not practice what they preach.  The old
   saying "What you are speaks so loudly that I can't hear what
   you say" holds true for those who become involved in evangelism.  Certainly, one doesn't wait for perfection before offering the self to be used; if perfection were the criteria, all
   ministry would cease.  But, on the other hand, it is important that the Christian's life be as consistent as possible
   with the gospel proclaimed.

2. Love must be the motivation for everything.  One does not drag
   or force others into the Kingdom of God; they are loved in.

It is the love of Jesus that others will see in the witness that will spark the responsive chord in their own lives. Jesus' love is unconditional; it is not withdrawn when a sinner rejects it. In the same manner, the evangelist must accept the person as is without criticism or condemnation. Patience and longsuffering must often accompany love that will, eventually, overcome all barriers.

3. Begin at the person's point of need. If the person is full of guilt, begin with presenting Jesus as a forgiving Saviour; if the person is in difficulty, present Jesus as the Mighty Counselor who is the Source of all wisdom and guidance; if the person is lonely, present Jesus as the Friend who sticks closer than a brother; if depression is the problem, show Jesus as the Source of hope and comfort, etc. Whatever the need, Jesus is the answer, but the answer must fit the person's particular problem.

4. Use a method acceptable to the person in need. Some people can respond very quickly to a direct evangelistic message; others are turned off by this approach. Pray for guidance and be observant. Do some homework to discover important information about the prospect - where the person is spiritually; the person's responses to past approaches; the values, form of worship, religion of the prospect, etc. If all this is not known ahead of time, some general conversation and subtle questioning may be necessary before "plunging in." Go only as fast and as far as the person is willing and able to go.

5. Know how to present the steps to Christ clearly and simply. Because there is no set pattern or specific method of evangelism that fits every situation, it is better to have general knowledge and access to additional resources than some predetermined formula to "fit" all occasions. Whether one uses the A-B-C approach described earlier or another one, the witness needs to have a background of the following: (i) appropriate Scriptures relative to humanity's lost condition without Jesus and God's remedy through the atonement of his Son; (ii) general knowledge of one or more ways to explain the way to become a Christian; (iii) a personal testimony of what Jesus has meant in the witness's life; (iv) access to additional books, tracts, or cassette tapes which may be needed in some cases; and (v) a pattern of prayer to pray with someone wishing to accept Christ as Saviour. (None of these requirements need be involved or difficult; anyone can develop the skills of presenting each of them. Samples of all of them appear elsewhere in this manual. See, for instance, the final pages of this chapter.)

6. Envelop all aspects of this ministry in prayer. Prayer is the hub around which all aspects of evangelism revolve. Witnesses must pray for themselves before attempting to take on this ministry, praying to be used in the way the Lord, not they, would ordain. Witnesses must pray for the person in

need, requesting that the heart be open and prepared to receive the truth. They must also pray for guidance to know the right approach, the proper timing, the real needs of the person they are ministering to, and the way in which the Lord wants to meet those needs. Lastly, witnesses must be able to pray with the person who is to receive Christ, leading that person to make a profession of personal faith and to ask Jesus into his or her life. (It is best to let the new convert pray, but because there is often reluctance to do so, witnesses may need to lead in an appropriate prayer and have the convert repeat after them.)

7. Know the difference between a testimony and a witness and how to present each. In Sharing God's Love, a very helpful book on evangelistic opportunities and how to meet them naturally, the authors Rinker and Griffith differentiate between the two in this way: (a) a testimony is one's personal encounter with Jesus, how he came into one's life and changed it for the better; and (b) a witness is telling another about Jesus, who he is, why he came to earth and died, and why everyone needs a personal relationship with him. A beginning evangelistic ministry should start with the evangelist preparing, preferably in written form, a personal testimony (or at least an outline of the important events in his or her spiritual autobiography) and a few "practice sessions" giving the testimony aloud to others. It may be given to family members or friends or recorded on tape and played back for evaluation. It should sound conversational and should use natural, unsophisticated language. It should not come across as sermonizing, self-righteous bragging, or condemning of others. It should be straightforward, sincere, and glorifying to the Lord (not to the person talking). In learning to talk easily and naturally about Jesus and developing an outline for a witness to his saving grace, it may be well for one to write out one's beliefs about humanity and God, sin and punishment, repentance and forgiveness, heaven and hell. This statement of faith should be checked with one's clergy and verified for consistency with articles of faith and doctrine. Important terms that should be defined and understood include grace, belief, faith, salvation, redemption, atonement, Christian, and everlasting life. Many times these terms are used without a full understanding of what they mean either scripturally or personally in the life of a Christian.

8. Be available for and prepared to answer questions. A new convert will often have many questions about a newly found faith. Do not worry about having all the answers (no one does have them!). There are two things to do when you are asked about something of which you are unsure: (a) pray for the Lord's wisdom, for often the Lord will reveal a word of knowledge or discernment that will minister to the need at hand; (b) frankly admit that you do not know, but that you will find the answer if possible. Be readily in touch with clergy, spiritual coun-

selors, or resources (reference books, Bible dictionaries, etc.) to consult at such times.

9. <u>Be willing to follow-up</u>.  Just as a new baby needs care and attention, a baby Christian needs nurturing too.  Check on the new convert's spiritual progress from time to time; be observant for signs of a setback or problem. Keep a prayerful and watchful interest.

10. <u>Offer "after-care" suggestions</u>.  A new Christian needs a spiritual environment in which to grow.  This may include joining a prayer group or Bible study program, having a prayer partner to call in times of need, receiving counseling for unresolved conflicts, and taking on regular disciplines of prayer and study (Scriptures, inspirational books, etc.).  It goes without saying that the after-care should include regular church attendance, Christian fellowship, confession and Communion (all the regular ministries and disciplines of the church).

## When Doors Are Most Open

There are certain times when a person is more open than other times to receive the good news about Jesus.  The best time, of course, is in childhood, when the mind is teachable and not yet hardened by intellectual arguments and worldly cares and pursuits.  Because this is true, every effort should be made to introduce children to Jesus as a Friend.  A lifelong relationship can be established very early in life.  A little child, without understanding complicated terms or theological precepts, can understand God's love and Jesus' desire to live in his or her heart.  The Sunday school program of the church should devote a great deal of time and effort to evangelizing the youth.  Special instruction for doing so should be given all youth workers and teachers in the church Christian education program.

The home is another place where Jesus can be introduced and worshiped.  The church should instruct parents in how to teach their children about Jesus.  Children are in the home many more hours than at church; therefore, the concepts taught at church should be reinforced and put into practice in the "laboratory" of the home.  Confirmation classes (in churches that have them) and special family workshops should provide parents with the information and assistance needed to ensure that children are not just ushered into church membership or to the Communion rail without an understanding of the significance of these events.  Sometimes parents (or even Sunday school teachers and youth leaders) become embarrassed when expected to talk about Jesus on a "personal" level.  This embarrassment can be overcome in only one way:  by practicing talking about Jesus on a personal level.  In order to keep the church going and growing, evangelism should have a high priority on the church's list of ministries.  Training for and involvement in evangelism should be built into the total church program in order to assist the church and the home in doing the jobs they are commissioned by the Lord to do.

117

There are, in addition to childhood, other times when people will respond readily to the message of the gospel or to a testimony from a witnessing Christian. Those involved in evangelism should be alert to these opportunities:

1. <u>At a time of crisis</u>. This is what is known as "need-oriented" opportunity. People give their attention to the Lord when they are in trouble or when all other avenues of help seem closed. Often the very first experience with the Lord on a personal level comes when he ministers to some need - at a time of sickness, death, tragedy, or difficulty. When people come to the end of themselves and turn to the Lord to handle for them what they cannot handle themselves, there is an open door through which the loving, caring Saviour may enter.

2. <u>At the hearing of the gospel</u>. The Bible says, "Faith comes by hearing and hearing by the Word of God." The Scriptures are the inspired revelations of God which are sharper than a two-edged sword to cut through human barriers and arguments. God has promised that his Word will not return to him void, but that it will accomplish the purposes he sends it forth to do. That is why it is so important to know the Scriptures and to be able to handle the "Sword" correctly. Care must be given here, however. No one wants to be hit over the head with a string of Scripture verses by a Bible-thumping fanatic. The witness must prayerfully seek the guidance of the Holy Spirit to know (a) when to use Scriptures and (b) which Scriptures to use. Often suggesting that a person read the Gospels (especially the Gospel of John) will open that person's heart to a receptiveness to the Jesus met from reading these pages.

3. <u>At an emotionally stirring experience</u>. Sometimes people respond to the Lord when they observe him moving in miraculous or supernatural ways. The Bible teaches that miracles are a sign to the unbeliever. At a healing, vision, or other revelation of God's power at work, a person will be awed into an awareness of who God is. The danger here is that eyes will be on the miracles rather than on the Miracle Worker. Emotional highs are not as solid a basis for building a relationship with the Lord as is simple faith. After the "mountain-top experience" there must be a coming down to earth. Emotions can change, but the Truth of God does not; therefore, one whose attention is drawn to the Lord through emotionally stirring experiences must be instructed in a sound doctrine of faith. Otherwise, the person may always be looking for spectacular feelings or supernatural experiences rather than for Jesus.

4. <u>At the observance of Jesus in others</u>. This is the most frequent way, and possibly the most effective way, of showing Jesus to others. When Christians are truly the "salt of the earth," they make others thirsty for Jesus. Others will want what they have. Christians should be very careful to conduct themselves in such a way as to draw others to Jesus by their

demonstrations of love, concern, cheerfulness, helpfulness, and spirituality. A living faith that manifests itself in daily situations will attract others the way pieces of metal are attracted to a magnet. (It wouldn't hurt, from time to time, for Christians to check out their lives to determine how their spiritual "magnetism" is working.)

5. <u>At an answer to prayer</u>. Even people to whom prayer is an unfamiliar experience often turn to the Lord in this way if all other means to solve a problem seem hopeless. People also turn to the Lord because of the faithfulness of intercessors who, on their behalf, have prayed for their salvation. Prayers of all kinds - either those of the prospective Christian or those of others who love and care about him or her - can become the door-openers to Jesus. Prayer is often the initiator of circumstances that bring lost sheep into the fold, and should therefore be the focal point of evangelism.

## An Example of an Effective Evangelist

For anyone wishing instruction in evangelistic techniques, the example in Acts 8:26-40 provides some effective guidelines. Philip was one of the seven deacons chosen by the first-century church, so we know that he was a man of "honest report, full of the Holy Ghost and wisdom." That is a good starting place for any ministry. Since a person's lifestyle will be either a help or a hindrance to one's ministry, Philip did well to live the kind of upright and godly life that would be an asset to his calling to be an evangelist. A dependence upon the Spirit is fundamental, for, after all, it is the work of the Holy Spirit that draws people to Jesus. The other characteristics of Philip's ministry are as follows:

1. Philip went where he was sent, not reluctantly but enthusiastically. We read that "he ran" to his place of ministry after receiving the command to go. Philip did not choose when and where he would minister, but was obedient to the promptings of the Spirit in a submissive and cooperative attitude.

2. Philip permitted no differences or prejudices to interfere with his ministry. The person to whom he was to minister was of a different race, a different social class, and a different backgound. The fact that the eunuch was black, well educated, and wealthy (and Philip was none of these things) did not pose a barrier to God's love being extended.

3. Philip began by involving himself with the eunuch "where he was." Philip inquired about what the eunuch was doing at the moment reading. Philip expressed a genuine interest and a concern for the eunuch before approaching the subject of Jesus or salvation.

4. Philip asked probing questions. He wanted the eunuch to realize his own need. When Philip asked, "Do you understand what you are

reading?" the eunuch's reply was, "How can I understand except some man should guide me?" That was the opening for Philip to begin at the point of the man's need - a need for understanding. The questioning not only provided an opening for ministry and got the eunuch vocally to express his need, but also helped Philip to determine where the eunuch was spiritually. Philip began at that point and moved forward. It is most important to determine a person's readiness before a confrontation. Beginning too soon, before the heart has been prepared and made receptive by the Holy Spirit, will not effect a fruitful ministry.

5. Philip followed the lead of the eunuch. Philip did not run ahead of or lag behind his convert; he moved at the pace which the eunuch could go comfortably. A good evangelist does not attempt to give meat when the prospective Christian can take only milk. It was the eunuch himself who requested instruction and baptism. Philip might have suggested these things if the eunuch had not, but how much better for the initiation to be from the promptings of the Spirit within the one being drawn to Jesus! Too often the evangelist takes the ball away from the convert and forgets that patience (and even sometimes silence) can allow the Spirit to move the person in the direction best to go.

6. Philip taught the eunuch from the Bible. He did not use his own words or arguments; he simply "began at the Scripture and preached unto him Jesus." Notice that the Scripture they were reading was from the Old Testament (Isaiah). The entire Bible, not just the New Testament, is about Jesus. Prophecies about and preparations for the Messiah can be an effective way of showing the unity of Old and New Testaments, and any part of God's Word is an effective beginning place for soul-winning.

7. Philip led the eunuch to make a profession of his faith in Jesus. Philip did not tell the eunuch to live a good life, to keep the law, to be a moral person, or even to keep studying the Bible to be saved. Philip asked if the eunuch "believed with all his heart." It was after the eunuch said, "I believe that Jesus Christ is the Son of God" that Philip went on to the next step - baptism. A profession of faith in Jesus must be primary; other acts of piety and spiritual disciplines should be outgrowths of that faith.

8. Philip did not rest on his laurels. As soon as the eunuch was baptized and sent on his way rejoicing, Philip was off to his next place of ministy: "Passing through, he preached in all the cities. . . ." A good evangelist does not stop with one convert, but moves on to wherever the Spirit next directs.

### Sowing the Seeds

The importance of a prepared heart to receive the gospel message has already been emphasized. Becuase evangelism is a shared ministry, combining the work of one or more evangelists and/or witnesses with the work of the Holy Spirit, it is often difficult to know where in the conversion process one's efforts are being manifested. St. Paul described this sharing process when he said, in effect, "One may plant a seed, another may water it, another may nurture it along, but it is God that gives the increase [harvest]." That is the reason persons in this ministry should never be discouraged if they do not see immediate or positive results from their evangelistic efforts. Their job may be merely to prepare the soil or to plant the seeds, which someone else will cultivate later. It may take the vocal and silent testimonies of many witnesses and the prayers of many intercessors over a long period of time before a person takes the step of giving his or her life to Jesus Christ. For another person, the conversion may be accomplished very quickly and easily, perhaps because the person was instinctively open and receptive to the gospel, or because many other people already had prepared the person's heart to receive Jesus through numerous testimonies, deeds of love, and unceasing prayers.

Whether one's part in another's conversion is large or small, seen or unseen, everyone who participates in sharing the love of Jesus with another is demonstrating wisdom: "He that wins souls is wise" (Prov. 11:30). How great will be that person's joy when, in heaven, he meets someone who says, "I am here because of what you said or did to help me come to Jesus." As St. James puts it, "He that converts a sinner from the error of his way shall save a soul from death and shall cover a multitude of sins" (James 5:20).

Not every evangelistic effort will be the same. Sometimes evangelists meet resistance and problems along the way. The joy comes to evangelists, however, even in the midst of such problems or defeats because they know that they have been faithful and obedient to the Lord in sharing the gospel message. In the parable of the Sower, Jesus described the various kinds of people one may encounter in an evangelistic ministry. When the Spirit scatters the seeds of Truth abroad, the message sometimes falls upon deaf ears, or what Jesus described as the "wayside" hearers. They lack the understanding of spiritual things to make contact. They have no desire or motivation to hear. Perhaps their past experience has turned them away from religion or they have never been exposed to real Christianity before and it all seems strange to them. The parable teaches that the message of the gospel very frequently is lost to such casual listeners because Satan is waiting to snatch away the seeds as soon as they are planted. Because such a person is the most difficult type to witness to, a great deal of "soil preparation" must go into this kind of evangelism. A "wayside" hearer must be cultivated with love and attention and must have a great deal of involvement with Christians on other levels to build up an attitude of trust and respect.

The next kind of person one may encounter is the "stony-ground" hearer. This person, on the surface, seems open and eager to become a Christian, or at least expresses interest. The person springs up quickly and looks to be a promising follower of Jesus, only to die away quickly because there is no depth to the expressed commitment, no relationship beyond an emotional one. Just as the sun scorches tender plants with no strong roots, the tribulations, persecutions, and problems to be faced as a Christian will scorch and wither the shallow Christian. Such people often want the blessings of Jesus without the responsibilities that go with them. They want what Jesus can do for them, not Jesus for himself. Such people need to become grounded in the Scriptures, which tell how to cope with the troubles as well as the triumphs of Christianity. It is a disservice to new Christians to speak only of the blessings and joys of following Jesus. They must also be prepared for the cross that Jesus has said they will be asked to bear. After the emotional "high" of falling in love comes the day-to-day growth in commitment, establishing of a unified relationship, resolving of conflicts, and enduring of testing periods. This is true in marriage, and equally true when one becomes the "bride" of Christ.

A third person one may meet in evangelistic work is the "thorny" hearer, one who looks, talks, and acts like a Christian. Some people call this person a "nominal Christian," but such a one does not have much time for Jesus, the church, or spiritual pursuits - not because of being a "bad" person, but because of being too busy doing other things. The "thorns" of worry, money, business, social interest, or personal matters grow up to choke out fruitfulness as a Christian. Instead of taking Jesus into his or her secular life, the "thorny" hearer shuts Jesus off from everyday activities. Because of confusion in priorities, this type of person never seems to have time for a deeper commitment to Jesus Christ. Such people need to be helped to "weed out" the thorny pursuits choking their Christian witness, stealing their time, and sapping their strength. Making Jesus Saviour is only step one; next comes step two - making Jesus Lord. When Jesus rules the secular life, priorities fall in line, time is correctly spent, worries are released, and Jesus (not money, success, or pleasure) will be enthroned in first place in the heart. It is the church's responsibility and the responsibility of individual Christians who are mature in their faith to instruct the "thorny" Christians and to correct (in love) those who have only a halfhearted devotion to Christ. The Bible speaks harshly to lukewarm believers, and the church should, therefore, never become casual about a convert's lifestyle when it hinders spiritual growth. Jesus says, "I wish you were cold or hot. So then because you are lukewarm and neither cold nor hot, I will spue you out of my mouth" (Rev. 3:15-16). Planting seeds of love for this type person may also involve some necessary "weeding." Here the evangelist is not asking someone to embrace a newfound faith, but encouraging the person to deepen commitment and to put first things first. That, too, is being a good witness.

The last type Jesus described in his parable is the "good-ground" hearer, the one who, at the hearing of the gospel, responds readily, understands, makes a commitment, and begins to bear good fruit (works or righteousness). The reason such people are able to do so, according to the parable, is because the soil of their heart is rich and fertile, receptive to the seed, and prepared to nourish and protect it. Such open responsiveness in a person makes witnessing easy and the encounter a joy. Such a one was the eunuch to whom Philip proclaimed the message of Jesus: eager, inquisitive, decisive, and enthusiastic. Evangelists do not find this type of hearer frequently. Usually, the work of the Kingdom, much like the farmer's work of tilling the soil, is not a spontaneous crop which springs up uncultivated and unattended. It usually requires careful planting and prayerful attention before fruit is brought forth.

Because there are so many different kinds of people and so many different approaches one may take, a witness must prayerfully consider when to speak, when to listen, when to share a Scripture, when just to be a friend, and when to remain silent and pray. Whatever the condition of the "soil" of a person's heart, the Holy Spirit knows just the remedy to enrich and prepare it. If the witness will spend the necessary time in prayer for guidance, the promise of the Scriptures is a bountiful harvest that will ultimately bring forth fruit - "thirty, sixty, and a hundredfold."

## Roadblocks

Here are some of the roadblocks that get in the way of "wayside," "stony," or "thorny" hearers and cause them to reject or ignore the gospel:

### "Wayside" Roadblocks

<u>Lack of understanding.</u> People have never heard or read the gospel, and, therefore, do not understand their lost condition apart from God.

<u>Feelings of not being "good enough."</u> Guilt feelings prevent some people from coming to Jesus. They think they have to give up habits or become drastically different from what they are before being acceptable to the Lord.

<u>Blocked by error.</u> Sometimes people are involved in false teachings, occult practices, or religious cults whose activities are contrary to the Scriptures, and such involvement keeps the truth from their ears.

<u>Fear of "losing control."</u> Many feel that they do not need God, the church, or what they consider to be religious crutches for the weak. They want to stay in the driver's seat and make Self the god of their lives.

### "Stony" Roadblocks

<u>Turned away by circumstances.</u> When tragedy or problems occur, God is blamed and rejected. Perhaps a prayer wasn't answered to one's liking.

Let down by others. When an insincere or hypocritical Christian does not measure up to certain standards, faith is rejected or felt to be meaningless.

Fear of persecutions. The price of Christianity is considered too high if it means being laughed at, set apart as "different," or rejected by others.


## "Thorny" Roadblocks

Other gods come first. Money-making, business matters, social pleasures, family involvements, personal goals, prideful ambitions, or other secular pursuits are more important. Some people feel they will have to "give up" things they value and they do not wish to do so.

Intellectualism. A skeptical or atheistic attitude is often the result of an education which is not oriented from a Christian viewpoint. Some feel they are too "smart" to believe the Bible or Jesus' miracles or other things which must be accepted by faith rather than proven scientifically.

Looking at things, rather than Jesus. At times a church's ritual or worship practices turn people off. Their faith is choked by religious trappings, which they incorrectly assume are the be-all and end-all of Christianity.


## Witnessing in Roadblock Situations

Although there are no easy answers or formulas to meet every situation, the following suggestions are offered for witnessing to people with problems described above as "roadblocks."

Obviously, for the person who has no understanding of the gospel or the plan of salvation for mankind, the solution is instruction. It is most important that this person be dealt with gently and slowly. Someone in the dark can be blinded by too much light until he or she has, by degrees, adjusted to it. The witness should never expect to see all the "bread of life" swallowed in one bite. Give a little instruction and large doses of love and understanding.

For those who feel guilty because they are aware of their sinful condition, this is a very healthy sign. The good news is that they do not have to wait until they have cleaned up their lives or taken on different habits before they will be acceptable to Jesus, who said, "I came not to call the righteous but sinners to repentance." Salvation is by grace, the free and undeserved gift of God, so no one need ever fear they will be turned away because they are not "good enough." No one is, but God's mercy is far greater than anyone's sin. The changes that are needed in lives are to come as the natural result of the new birth after, not before, conversion.

Those who have a mental block because of false teachings, errone- ous religious beliefs or practices, or involvement in occult arts must renounce such things. Naturally, people are reluctant to discard what they believe to be true, even after hearing convincing arguments to the contrary. If, after giving appropriate Scripture references revealing the error of such things, such a person seems unconvinced, the best approach is to say something like this: "None of us, includ- ing myself, wants to believe or teach a lie. Will you pray and ask God to show you the full truth about this matter? If your belief in --- is wrong, the Lord can bring circumstances that will prove it to you if you are open and teachable. Do not rely upon my words, but test what I have shared with you through your own prayers and study." The witness might also suggest making an appointment with a pastor or spiritual adviser in whom the person has confidence or the reading of approved books on the subject being debated. These approaches will leave the initiative of "proof" up to the individual, so that person does not have to become defensive or protective of the beliefs under attack. No one has to be right or wrong if both the person and the witness promise to pray and to be open to further truth from the Lord on the subject. God is always faithful to honor a sincere request for knowledge of his will, and any small opening will be flooded by his light as soon as the matter is turned over to him. It is not unreason- able for anyone to be asked to pray for greater wisdom or enlightenment, and often this small step will be the beginning of a turn-around for the seeker of truth.

The people who want to stay in control and who fear turning them- selves over to Jesus might be asked, "How well is it going with you in control? Are you happy? Fulfilled? Do you have peace of mind?" etc. If the answer is no, then the door is open to further ministry. The person who appears to be satisfied with life without Jesus may be prompted to "try it the other way" for a period of time for comparison, just to see if there is more to life than the person imagines or has previously experienced. Sometimes a trial-period proposal becomes the crack in the door at which Jesus is knocking. If the person will not try Jesus even on a trial basis, then it may be best to back off, to keep praying for God to engineer circumstances which will draw the person out, and to continue to be a loving and attentive friend. A witness must always accept the prospective convert, no matter how con- trary the prospect may be, and must never assume that a rejection of Jesus is a personal rejection. Furthermore, it is good to explain to such controlling kinds of people that putting Jesus in control does not make one a mindless puppet. On the contrary, Jesus knows far better what makes one happy and fulfilled than the person concerned knows. Because Jesus loves people so, he never violates their free will but, rather, wants only the best for them. Jesus can direct a human being's life in new, exciting, and rewarding dimensions, but the person must first give Jesus permission to do so.

For a person rebelling against God for some tragedy in life, an explanation of the origin of evil may be helpful. There are problems and tragedies in the world for the same reason there is sickness and death - because of the fall of humanity through sin. Thorns began to grow among the flowers in Eden and the problems came into the perfection of God's creation because of Satan's influence and humanity's rebellion. God is Love. He is not responsible for evil. On the contrary, he can transform the difficulty into a victory, if only one will let him. It sometimes helps to describe how Jesus or the disciples dealt with tribulations, or it may be appropriate to share a similar situation faced by the witness or another to emphasize how God can bring good from that which a human being considers evil. If none of these approaches work, it might be well to point out the end result of staying angry with God. To continue in rebellion is to separate oneself from God, the only source of comfort and help at this difficult time. The underlying question, of course, once it has been pointed out that the end result is separation from God, is "Is that what you really want?" The spirit of God in every individual craves companionship with the Father, and the honest person will admit to not really wanting estrangement. If all else fails, give it some time. Once the agony of the initial hurt subsides, and the atmosphere is less emotional, try again.

For those who are critical of insincere or hypocritical Christians, explain that the church is not composed of flawless saints, but only of sinners saved by grace. Satan is always at work, trying to cause a Christian to make a misstep in order to stumble another who may be watching. A judgmental attitude and unforgiveness are just as sinful in God's eyes as whatever the Christian has done wrong. Try to turn the person's attention away from being let down by people and toward being lifted up by Jesus, who never fails. People make mistakes; Jesus does not. Ask, "Is your unforgiving attitude (hurt, resentment, or whatever is being felt) worth the price of separation? . . . Are you happy feeling as you do? . . . Wouldn't you like to unburden yourself of these bad feelings you have against ---?" etc. The Lord alone can judge another, and we must leave that job to him. Seek to turn attention away from other people and their sins to the individual's attitudes that may need healing, and seek further to bring that person into a closer relationship with Jesus, who loves and accepts everyone (even the hypocrites) "as they are."

If persecution, rejection, or ridicule are prices too high to pay for being a follower of Jesus, some instruction about the claims of Christ upon a person's life needs to be given. Jesus never promised in the Bible, "Follow me and I'll give you a rose-strewn pathway with everyone loving and accepting you for the great person you are." No, instead he promised a Christian the same treatment he himself received - "for the servant is no greater than his Master." Jesus commanded, "Deny yourself, take up the cross, and follow me." (Many Christians try to do step three without first doing steps one and two.) Jesus was not accepted in his hometown or among the religious leaders of his day. Even his closest friends deserted him when he needed them most. One who truly wants to be like Jesus not only will want to feed the hungry, teach the gospel of love, and help the needy, as Jesus did, but also will be ready to suffer for the sake of righteousness the way Jesus did. Many blessings and heavenly rewards are promised those who endure hardness as soldiers of Christ and who are persecuted for their beliefs. But there has to be the cross before the crown.

No one can outgive God, and no one ever gives up something for the Lord without receiving something much better in return. Many people, however, are afraid Jesus will interfere with their lifestyle or their values in life. Those who do not have time for Jesus or those who make no place for him in the midst of devoting energies to making money or attaining personal goals are missing out on laying up real treasure - the treasures of heaven. All that they do in life will pass away and have no lasting meaning unless it has been Christ-directed activity. There is a little poem that says it well: "Only one life/'Twill soon be past/Only what's done for Christ will last." For the too-busy person, some teaching on stewardship may be in order. The Lord requires not only the tithe of one's material wealth, but also a tithe of one's talents, energies, time, and devotion. It is idolatry and certainly a breaking of the first commandment to put anything in first place ahead of the Lord. Sometimes in an effort to be loving, witnesses hesitate to speak out a word of warning to someone who needs correction. It is not loving to allow others to proceed in error upon the wrong path. Although words of rebuke should never be given judgmentally, it is certainly one's Christian responsibility to speak the truth in love. Even if people react in anger or disapproval, the words of warning may slip into their subconscious mind and be used of the Holy Spirit at a later time to bring about conviction and amendment.

When witnessing to an intellectual or scientifically oriented skeptic, or to an atheist, don't argue. One cannot "prove" God to anyone. These kinds of people usually try to find contradictions in the Bible, find fault with church doctrines (such as the virgin birth or the Trinity), or prove the fallibility of faith. If such people cannot take a leap of faith in order to "test" the substantialness of belief in Jesus Christ as the Son of God, try a thought-provoking approach, perhaps like this: "Let's say, for the sake of discussion, that you are right and I am wrong. Let's say the Bible is just a human-written collection of fables and that Jesus was a mere man and not the incarnate Son of God. Then we both die. If what you say is true, I really haven't lost anything, because the Christian life has been for me a happy one, and if all I will get are these earthly rewards, it has been more than enough. But if my belief is right and yours is wrong, and we both die, then what? If the Bible promises are true, I go on to be with the Lord and live in bliss everlasting, and what becomes of you?" Unless the person specifically asks what the Bible teaches about those who die outside of Christ, it is best not to paint a dark picture of eternal punishment. Often the question "What happens to you if you die and Jesus turns out to be who he said he was?" is enough to get the person thinking in the right direction. Usually the more educated and thoughtful the witness, the more open to acceptance the person will be. Really intelligent people listen to other intelligent people with respect and even give each other the right to be wrong. Under no circumstances allow tempers to become inflamed. Love is the only force strong enough to overcome the barriers a person can place between self and the Lord. If the witness is calm, accepting, unruffled by attacks, and fully persuaded of his or her convictions, it cannot help but make an impression.

For people who cannot accept a particular church's form of worship or religious practices, the answer is simple. Find another church, prayer group, or place of worship. Even as each personality is unique, so churches, which are made up of people, are unique. People need to feel "at home" in the form of their approach to God. Those who are emotional and vocal in their worship have difficulty in a quiet, contemplative congregation. The opposite is true of those who prefer a reverent form of worship. Put them among the handclappers and "Hallelujah" types, and they are most uncomfortable. Even within the same denomination there are various preferences - high church people, low church people, traditionalists, evangelistic advocates, liberals, conservatives, charismatics, and those who have no real personal preferences. People do not have to accept others' preferences, but they do have to accept others and give them the freedom to follow their own beliefs. God is not as interested in the outward form of worship as in the intents of the hearts of his people. Emphasis needs to be placed upon Jesus and the common beliefs to which all Christians subscribe in unity, not upon rituals, forms of worship, or religious trappings. If people cannot be led to ignore the outward forms and concentrate on a personal relationship with Jesus in the congregation where they are, then prayerful consideration should be given to making a move. It is important to note, however, that no church is perfect and a certain amount of acceptance of differences must be given wherever one may be worshiping.

### Practical Helps in Witnessing

#### Some Important Don'ts

1. Don't forget to listen and find out "where the person is" before witnessing; start there.

2. Don't push, argue, or manipulate. Often enthusiasm leads to errors in good judgment.

3. Don't answer questions that have not been asked. Give only as much information as the person can assimilate at one time.

4. Don't try to take people further than they are prepared to go. Keep the witnessing need-oriented.

5. Don't forget to pray before, during, and after the witnessing session.

5. Don't become overly concerned about failures, spectacular results, looking foolish, or anything else. Keep attention upon being a faithful and obedient witness who follows the leading of the Holy Spirit.

7. Don't stop loving, accepting, and forgiving the person, even when that person may send forth rejection.

8. Don't give up on anyone, no matter how long the conversion takes. After all, God does not give up on anyone, so why should the witness?

9. Don't hide your light under a bushel. Let what you wear, say, do, and think always glorify Jesus. Even one's attitude is a witness.

10. Don't forget that object lessons are often useful if used in good taste and with sincerity, not for showing off. A Bible, bumper stickers, a cross on a neck chain, or other Christian symbol or device may be a conversation starter that leads someone to ask about Jesus.

11. Don't forget to be a loving friend as well as a witness. Always avoid any form of condemnation or judgment of a prospect's beliefs or actions. People can be sensitive to even hidden attitudes of criticism.

12. Don't feel you have to defend God, the church, or your personal beliefs. Refuse to become upset when these are attacked.

13. Don't think you have all the answers. All you really have is the Answer, Jesus Christ. Witnessing results are his responsibility, not yours.

14. Don't forget to be "real." Be sincere and straightforward without self-righteousness or spiritual pride poking out. A witness who seems so spiritual as to be completely removed from down-to-earth, everyday living may have problems relating to ordinary people in acceptable ways.

15. Don't get sidetracked. Emphasis should always be on a personal relationship with Jesus Christ - not on the gifts of the Spirit, the church, good works, doctrines, other people, or any other substitute for the "Way."

16. Don't forget to sow seeds anywhere and everywhere. A word, a smile, a kind or unselfish deed, a Christian response to another's unkindness, a cheerful attitude in the midst of difficulty - all these will bear witness to a real and workable faith.

17. Don't forget to practice what you preach. A testimony should be consistent with the lifestyle of the witness.

18. Don't forget to follow up. See that those who are witnessed to receive needed training, prayer support, fellowship, and ministry to their needs.

19. Don't forget that the words of the Bible have greater authority and impact than any words from the human intellect or feelings. Use the Scriptures whenever appropriate to do so, but use them prayerfully and carefully.

20. Don't think you have a choice about whether or not to be a witness. You already are a witness - either a good one or a poor one. Pray for the Holy Spirit to direct your actions to be the best witness possible and to open up opportunities for your witness to be given in the right times and places.

## Scriptures Useful in Witnessing

The gospel in a nutshell:  John 3:16

Man's condition apart from God:  Isaiah 53:6; Romans 3:23

God's judgment of sin:  Revelation 20:12-15

God's justice and mercy:  Exodus 34:67; John 3:1

God's grace:  Ephesians 2:7-8; Romans 3:24

God's willingness to hear our prayers:  I John 5:14-15

How man comes to God:  John 14:6; Romans 5:1-2

The only way to salvation:  Acts 16:31; Acts 4:21

The need for a blood atonement:  Hebrews 9:22; Hebrews 9:14

The need for confession of sin:  I John 1:7-9; Acts 3:19

The need for a new (spiritual) birth:  John 3:3

The need for obedience:  Hebrews 5:9

Everyone accepted by God (no exceptions):  Joel 2:32; II Peter 3:9; John 6:37

Why Jesus came to earth:  Luke 19:10

How a person must initiate a response to Jesus:  Revelation 3:20

Avoiding delay in accepting Jesus:  II Corinthians 6:2; Matthew 24:44

Punishments and accountability:  Galatians 6:7-8; Romans 14:12

Promise of new life:  II Corinthians 5:17; Ephesians 4:22-24

Promise of forgiveness and freedom from condemnation:  Romans 8:1-2; I John 1:9

Promise of rewards:  John 14:2-3; Hebrews 11:6; II Timothy 4:8

What to say to receive Jesus:  Acts 8:37; Mark 9:24

What to do after becoming a Christian:  Matthew 28:19-20; Acts 1:8

## Sample Witnessing Approaches

Each person will relate the gospel in his or her own words, but the basic content of any witness should include these concepts:

Who Jesus is: John 1:1-4. Jesus is the Son of God made incarnate in flesh.

What Jesus did: Philippians 2:6-11. Jesus left the glory of heaven to become human.

Why Jesus did it: Hebrews 9:12. Jesus became human to redeem us from sin.

What Jesus' action means: Hebrews 4:15 and II Timothy 2:5. Jesus is able to understand us and identify with our needs, and He can mediate for us before God.

How Jesus' life affects us personally: Romans 5:8-9. We can be saved and justified by Jesus' blood sacrifice for our sins.

What our appropriate response is: Acts 16:30-31 and Romans 12:1. We should believe and give our lives to the Lord.

## Sample Witnessing Patterns

A witness to an adult might go something like this:

"Because we are all the children of Adam, we are born with the stain of original sin upon us. This sin separates us from God. But God loves us so very much that he takes the initiative to provide a way out of our separated condition. The way is through his Son, Jesus Christ. Jesus paid the full penalty for the sins of the whole world when he died for us upon the cross. This means that Jesus was our substitute, the "Lamb of God that takes away the sin of the world." Even before the foundation of the world, Jesus was willing to lay down the glory of heaven, to take on the form of human flesh, and to give himself as a sacrificial offering for the sins of those apart from God. Jesus stands at every heart's door knocking, waiting to be invited in to bring human beings back to God, the Father. We can accept or reject the salvation offered to us by Jesus Christ. The doorknob is on the inside. Jesus will never force himself upon anyone; he waits patiently for an invitation to come in. What he did on the cross was not just for the world in general, but for you in particular. He wants to be your personal Saviour. Won't you ask him into your life right now?"

A witness to a child might go something like this:

"Here is a picture of three colored hearts. When you were first born, your heart was black, like the first one, because of the wrong things that everyone says and does. Jesus died on the cross to take away the blackness. His red blood on the cross will wash away all the black dirt of sin. Then your heart looks like the red heart here. When Jesus' blood washes a heart clean, it becomes snowy white like the third heart. Jesus wants to come and live in your heart and be with you always. That is because he loves you so very much. There is a verse that tells how much you are loved and how much Jesus wants to be your best Friend. Let's read it together and put your name in the verse: 'For God so loved (name), that he gave his only begotten Son, that if (name) believes on him, (name) will not perish, but have ever-lasting life.' That means that if you ask Jesus to live in your heart, he will be with you always - to love you and watch over you, and help you forever and ever. Would you like to ask him to do that now?"

Another way of presenting a witness is through the "grabber" - a question designed to turn minds toward spiritual things in an indirect way as a natural part of a conversation. Some grabbers are:

What do you think happens to you after you die?

What is the most important thing to you in life?

What would it take in life to make you truly happy and fulfilled?

What is your greatest goal or ambition in life?

What is your greatest fear (need)?

What was the most difficult problem you ever faced in life? How did you cope with it?

If you were to die today, where would you be tomorrow?

Any of these can be a lead-in to discussing things of the Lord. Depending upon the openness of the individual, the conversation can turn sharply or casually in a spiritual direction. Finding out what someone believes about life-after-death leads very naturally into dis-cussions of heaven, hell, belief, and unbelief. A more direct question ("Where would you be tomorrow if you died today?") must be handled with great wisdom. People should never feel that they are being put on the spot or that their views are being attacked. It is better for the witness simply to state what he or she believes without any sug-gestion of attack upon the other person's beliefs, regardless of how erroneous or unscriptural they may be. Go no further unless asked to explain why you believe as you do.

When inquiring about a person's values, goals, or secret desires in life, it is quite natural for the witness to speak of his or her own, describing how the Lord has changed or directed these things. Jesus, of course, is the only source of genuine and lasting happiness and satisfaction, but if people do not know that, the witness must say

so in a nonthreatening way.  One of the following approaches might
be in order:  "When I came to know the Lord, (a) my values changed;
(b) life took on a new dimension; (c) I discovered new meaning in ---;
or (d) I realized my dreams for --- ."

When the conversation moves toward coping with fears and problems,
the witness has a perfect opening for describing how he or she overcame a fear or a problem through the help of the Lord, through prayer,
or through another spiritual aid.

## Sample Testimonies

Each person's private encounter with the Lord is different.  Some
people have dramatic and exciting conversion experiences, while others,
whose relationship with the Lord is just as valid, may have very ordinary stories to relate.  It is not necessary to embroider the account.
When giving you testimony, just state briefly the following: (a) what
life was like before encountering Jesus personally (optional); (b) how
you came to know Jesus; (c) what differences he has made; (d) why you
feel that a personal relationship with Jesus is vital.

It is not necessary to dwell on how sinful or indifferent you
were in the past; the emphasis should be upon your relationship to
Jesus Christ here and now, what you have learned that has made life
richer and more fulfilling, and the help it has been to have someone
to lean upon during the growth processes of life.

Four sample testimonies follow:

"I was only six years old when a Bible teacher asked for those who
wanted Jesus in their hearts to raise their hands.  I raised mine.  I
did not understand the scope of that simple action, but I did know
that riding home on the bus that day, I felt elated, joyful, clean,
and safe.  I was not baptized until about six years later, but I always knew from that moment I raised my hand that Jesus was with me.
From that day to this, I have had the assurance that I was in the
Lord's hands.  There have been times when I have turned my back on
him, but he has never turned away from me.  I could never have survived
the cruelties of a rejected childhood, the rejection of a husband who
left me, and many other painful rejections throughout my life if I had
not had the sustaining love of Jesus that was so real and powerful that
I knew he would never reject, leave or forsake me.  After the pain
of divorce and the despair of being alone with two small children to
raise, I cried out to the Lord, saying, 'I've made a mess of things
and my life is in pieces, but if there's anything left of me you want
to use, I'm yours.'  The Lord answered that plea.  He put the pieces
together, brought to me a Christian husband who adopted the children,
and gave us a life of unity and security - the things for which I'd
sought all my life long.  Today I no longer hurt because of rejection.
I am happy and at peace.  As soon as I turned over the reins of my
life to the Lord, he redeemed all the mistakes, set my feet upon a
sure path, and healed all the hurts and wounds of my past.  He has made

the difference between brokenness and wholeness, despair and peace of mind. I have learned that for whatever the problem in life, Jesus is the Answer!"

"I cannot tell you the date and time of my conversion. I was not a hopeless, godless person one day and a convert to Christianity the next. It seems that I have always had a relationship with the Lord, even though I can't pinpoint the exact start of it. There were certainly people along the way who helped my awareness of the Lord to grow. A Boy Scout troop which met at an Episcopal church brought me into the church and introduced me to the reverence of the liturgical form of worship, which, for me, was very appealing. As a youth, I was impressed with the priest and the words he spoke from the pulpit, and I desired to be confirmed in a faith, which by this time was taking deep and lasting roots. Gradually, sometimes by leaps and other times by tiny steps, the faith began to grow. I guess the high point in my spiritual autobiography came when, at age twenty-nine, I prayed for a wife. All of my buddies were married by that age, and I felt very empty and alone. The Lord heard and answered that prayer almost immediately. I learned from that experience that God wants to give us the desires of our hearts and to fill our lives with good things, but we have to ask him for his help. He doesn't force himself upon us. Since that first experience of a definite answer to a specific prayer, I've asked his help in my home life (being the head of a family isn't easy, and I need all the wisdom of the Lord I can get), in my business life, and in my social life. As I continue to grow, Jesus just keeps getting better and better to me, and I keep finding more and more meaning to life. The Lord has begun to use me to witness to other businessmen and to counsel and pray with people having problems. I don't have any answers for these people, but the wisdom of the Lord is always available to me when I ask for it. The more I learn through Bible study and prayer, the more open doors of service I find waiting. Somewhere back there - and I don't remember where or when - a tiny seed of faith was planted in my heart, and it just continues to grow and grow!"

"I was one of those people who thought I could work my way into Heaven. I was at church every time the doors were open and sometimes when they were not. I served on every church committee and was well known for being the typical "good Christian." And then one day I realized that I was not doing all my good works for the Lord. I was doing them for myself. I liked the praise and recognition that came to me. My life was being filled with busy things to do simply because my life was empty, and I wanted to fill it with something worthwhile. One day at a Faith Alive Weekend Conference at our church I heard a witnessing layman say that these things could be substitutes for the only really fulfilling Thing in life, Jesus Christ. He stressed the importance of a 'personal' relationship with Jesus, and I realized that I didn't have that at all. Oh, I knew who Jesus was, but I didn't know him in any personal way. I felt like the people in the Bible who said, 'Lord, Lord! Haven't we done all these good things in your name?' and to whom he replied, 'I never knew you.' Suddenly, I wanted more than anything else to know Jesus. I decided to stop being so busy doing things for him and to take time to find out who he was. I asked him to forgive me for my spiritual pride, and I gave him my life to do with as he saw fit. What a change! Instead of feeling pressured to be busy all the time or guilty if I weren't doing something every minute, I learned to be at peace with myself - to sit quietly in his presence and to meditate upon his Word, something I'd never had time to do before. I have learned that there is no substitute for Jesus. Even good things can keep us from the best. Now that I have the Best, I can speak from experience when I tell you to 'accept no substitutes!'"

"My wife was a Christian and I wasn't. It really bugged me. I guess I secretly was jealous of her relationship with Jesus. I felt shut out. I thought when she became a Christian she'd be running off to prayer groups and church services all the time, leaving me behind. But instead, she just got more and more loving and attentive to me every day. She didn't try to convert me or leave tracts in the bathroom the way a friend of mine said his wife had done. Slowly, I began to see that Jesus hadn't taken her away from me. He had just made her more lovable. It was that love that finally broke down all my resistance. I didn't know what she had, but it sure was nice! I started to go to church with her (she didn't pressure me to do it; I just wanted to). I met other Christians who were regular guys. I learned that to be a Christian didn't have to make somebody weird or fanatical. It wasn't long before I wanted Jesus too. Now my wife and I are even closer than ever. If you want to make a good marriage even better, just let Jesus be in on the partnership."

Sample Prayer Patterns

Just as each witness and testimony is different, so the methods of prayer used in evangelism vary. Simple words are preferred to formal prayers. Following are some suggestions:

Prayer for Someone to Come to Jesus: "Dear Lord, thank you that (*name*) is your child and that you love (him/her) so very much. Help (him/her) to respond to that love. Draw (him/her) to yourself and open (his/her) heart to a saving knowledge of Jesus Christ. Thank you, Lord. Amen."

Prayer at the Time of Acceptance of Jesus: "Dear Lord, thank you that (*name*) comes to you right now in simple faith, asking that you come into (his/her) life and make (him/her) a new creature in Christ. Thank you that old things will pass away, and that you will give (him/her) abundant new life. As (he/she) accepts, by faith, the atoning sacrifice of the cross, I pray that (he/she) may be a worthy follower of (his/her) Saviour, our Lord Jesus. Amen." (Note: The prayer may be prayed by the new convert, substituting the pronouns "I" and "my" for "he/she" and "his/hers.")

Prayer of Repentance: "Dear Jesus, I confess that I am a sinner. I know that I cannot save myself. I need you. Please take away my sinful past and receive me as I offer myself to you. Thank you, Lord. Amen."

<u>Prayer for More Faith</u>:  "Lord, I'm not sure if you're real or not. If you are, I want to know you better and feel your presence.  Please reveal yourself to me.  I give you as much of myself as I can. Amen."

## Five Frequently Asked Questions on Evangelistic Outreach

1.  What ways are available for indirect witnessing and evangelism (as opposed to direct-confrontation witnessing)?

Praying for those who need Jesus and praying for evangelists; giving out Bibles, tracts, or Christian literature; sharing tapes; inviting people to church or to evangelistic meetings; introducing people to those with an evangelistic ministry or those who evidence the gift of witnessing; living a life that will bear a silent testimony to the saving power and love of Jesus Christ; and supporting evangelistic work financially.

2.  What is the best way to receive training in evangelism?

In addition to reading on the subject, one may take advantage of workshops and courses offered from time to time.  Observing others who are involved in this ministry will also be helpful, perhaps accompanying someone of experience and serving as a back-up prayer partner in evangelistic ventures.  The best way to learn, however, is through the instruction program the Holy Spirit will give those who offer themselves for service.  Praying for guidance and then relying on the Spirit's direction will be the most effective way of learning.  One may read books on swimming and watch others swim, but one has to get in the water sometime to function as a real swimmer.  The same is true of evangelism. You learn it by doing it!

3.  Evangelistic efforts are frowned on in my church.  What can I do?

Sometimes the terminology is at fault.  If you say you are going to involve yourself in "sharing God's love with others," probably no one would object, but if you say "evangelism," you often find negative connotations involved.  All ministry at a parish should be approved and judged by the clergy.  Proceed slowly and prayerfully, waiting for open doors before doing things that inflame other brothers and sisters in Christ.  There are many indirect methods of witnessing, which may be employed before a full-blown evangelistic program is instituted. Just keep praying and waiting upon the Lord to open doors.

4.  How can a church expand its evangelistic outreach?

If the pastor approves, a group of interested people may band together to study, pray, and "practice" evangelistic techniques.  The role-play method is good for trying out various approaches and finding answers to problems.  Consider also inviting in a team of people involved in successful evangelism to conduct training programs.  Prayer groups may expand their ministry from praying for the lost to bringing them in to the meetings for ministry or sending out approved visitors to talk to others about Jesus. Programs of outreach may also be given in jails, detention homes, and other institutions. Often a program of special music and refreshments can also include testimonies from several people who want to share Jesus with others.

5.  What terms should a person know in order to speak the language of evangelism?

Grace - the undeserved favor of God; a free gift. God's free gift of salvation is ours by his grace: God's Riches At Christ's Expense.

Belief - conviction based upon **knowledge** or personal experience; a heart-knowledge rather than a head-knowledge where Christ is concerned.

Saviour - one who saves. Someone who jumped in to save a drowning child would be the child's "saviour," or rescuer. Jesus saves God's children from sin and death. Therefore, he is a Saviour.

Redemption - to "buy back." After enough green stamps are collected, one takes the books of stamps to the "redemption" store to get back a prize. We cash in our sinful lives at Christ's cross and get back the prize of eternal life. Jesus buys us with the price of his blood.

Atonement - to make amends for an offense. Jesus makes up for our sins with his atoning sacrifice of himself. This makes us one with God. It is "At-One-Ment."

Repentance - a change of mind with regard to the past. One who "repents" turns away from sin and back toward God.

Justification - made just or acceptable before God. Jesus' death on the cross "justifies" us before God (*JUST AS IF I'D* never sinned).

Salvation - the saving of humanity from the consequences of sin; deliverance from eternal damnation.

## Conclusion

Evangelism has been discussed from many aspects and viewpoints. But one could master all the methodology, have an evangelistic routine down pat, know all the definitions, forms, tools, guidelines, Scriptures, and answers, and still miss the boat when it comes to evangelism. If all that were done without love, it would be as sounding brass. Basically, evangelism boils down to letting people know that God loves them. It's letting them know that the evangelist loves them too. God is love. Because God loved, he gave. This, too, is the reason for all evangelistic efforts - to spread abroad and perpetuate the unfathomable love of God evidenced in Jesus Christ through the lives of those who have experienced something special from touching the hem of his garment. Because we love, we give. Whether it is the giving of a testimony, a witness to the saving power of Jesus Christ, a direct confrontation, or an indirect method, everyone should be about the business of sharing the gospel. Jesus commands it. He says to us what he said to the man delivered from the legion of demons: "Go home to thy friends, and tell them how great things the Lord hath done for thee. . ." (Mark 5:19).

# 7 · Ministries of Counseling

Counseling is an important aspect of Christian ministry for two very good reasons:  first, because everyone has problems and will need some form of counseling during life, and  second, because counseling is such a broad and many-faceted ministry that it touches and overlaps all other forms of ministry.  It would be well to examine the broad scope of counseling by categories in order to see the structural parts of the whole:

## Forms of Counseling

1. <u>Simple listening</u> - acting as a sounding board for one who is troubled.

2. <u>Informal counseling</u> - giving opinions or casual advice when asked to do so by a friend or relative.

3. <u>Formal counseling</u> - professional assistance by trained doctors, psychiatrists, psychologists, or counselors.

4. <u>Spiritual (pastoral) counseling</u> - a type of formal counseling which combines some methods of professionalism with the added "plus" of Bible instruction, spiritual and moral guidance, and prayer.

Obviously, the more involved in counseling one becomes, the more training that is necessary.  Everyone gives informal advice from time to time, whether it be a parent counseling children, an employer counseling an employee, a teacher counseling a student, or a friend counseling a friend.  Even in the simplest forms of counseling, however, one needs to rely upon the guidance of the Holy Spirit rather than humanistic methods or predetermined pat answers.  The book of Job teaches the folly of offering preconceived notions as advice.  Job's three friends were learned men who gave a lot of seemingly sound advice based upon their past experience and humanistic thinking.  Unfortunately, it was not God's message they proclaimed to Job, but their own ideas.  Not until the younger man, Elihu, spoke to Job were the words of the Spirit heard.

Even the most informal counseling over a cup of coffee in the kitchen  should be preceded by prayer and should be guided by the Spirit of God.  This is because real counseling is nothing more than getting "hooked up" to the Mighty Counselor, the Source of all Wisdom and Knowledge.  The book of Isaiah describes Jesus as that "Wonderful Counselor" to whom was imparted the spirit of "counsel and might, wisdom and understanding, knowledge and fear of the Lord" (Isa. 11:2).  Our finite minds cannot begin to grasp all the ramifications of a problem; we see in part, but we cannot know all truth.  That is why the best counselors are those who get in touch with the Infinite and let his wisdom be brought to bear upon the problem at hand.

## Comparison of Counseling Methods

There are two equally erroneous conceptions about professional counseling that need to be avoided:  first, the belief that psychiatrists are the only people who should be sought out for answers to mental or emotional problems and that they have all the answers to life's difficulties; and second, that professionals have none of the answers and need to be avoided in times of difficulty.  All good things come from God, including good professional help.  The danger that lies in exclusive reliance upon psychological or psychiatric care (apart from any spiritual guidance) is twofold:  first, many professionals do not take into account that a human being is also a spiritual being and may have a spiritual problem at the root of her or his problems; and second, there is an inherent disagreement between the basic assumptions of strictly humanistic methods and spiritual methods, which the following formulation pinpoints:

Basic Assumption in Humanistic Counseling:  People are basically good, and have, within themselves, resources for overcoming problems and finding fulfillment.  Guilt is destructive and must be seen as an inhibitor of personal growth.  People must be in control of their own destiny ("do your own thing").

Basic Assumption in Biblical Counseling:  People are basically sinful and, apart from Jesus Christ, can find no lasting peace or fulfillment.  Guilt is God's "early warning system" to alert people to their sinful ways.  The Lord must be put in control of a person's destiny ("do God's thing").

The discerning counselor will be able to receive those things that are helpful and productive in psychiatry and psychology and discard those that are in opposition to biblical teachings.  The following chart may be of help:

### Counseling Comparisons

| Counseling Method: | Psychoanalytic Psychology (Freud) | Nondirective Counseling (Rogers) | Transactional Analysis (Harris | Reality Therapy (Glasser) | Biblical Counseling (Adams) |
|---|---|---|---|---|---|
| Man's Basic Problem: | Repression of Desires, Sexual and Social Maladjustment | Lack of Self-Understanding | Noncommunication; Reacting from Past "Script" | Blame-Shifting; Escapism | Sin |
| Treatment: | Psychoanalysis (Socialization) | Autonomy (Insight and Self-Awareness) | Adult Reasoning; Change in Life Script | Accepting Responsibility | Deny Self; Obey God |

The foregoing is by no means a comprehensive overview of all counseling assumptions and treatments, but it does give a capsulized view of several well-known schools of thought as to people's problems in life and how to solve them. Any counselor must understand where he or she is in terms of a philosophy about humanity's basic problem and how it can be cured. The Christian counselor naturally begins with the biblical approach and uses all other methodology supplementally as needed and only wherever applicable.

While strictly humanistic methods are often helpful in finding causes for a particular problem, they are not always successful in providing the necessary answers or the healing that may be needed. Nor can they provide a remedy for the guilt that is attached to sins of the past. Scriptural counseling is the only method that gives a person real hope. If the problem is social maladjustment, lack of self-understanding, inability to communicate, or blame-shifting, a solution may or may not be found. But if the problem is sin (a failure to adjust one's life to the commandments of the Almighty as presented in the Scriptures), there is great hope. Jesus took care of sin upon the cross. He has promised to continue to forgive sin and to heal hurts and to set people free (even from the sins of others that may be inflicted upon the innocent).

"Sin" is not a popular word today. It is easier to place the blame for people's problems upon society, unrealized goals, or suppressed psychological urges.

The advantage of biblical counseling is that the counselor does not rely upon textbook methods or case histories for a guide, but upon the Holy Spirit, who can not only reveal the real source of one's fears, grief, bad habit, guilt, anger, or other symptom, but also provide the means for healing all of those things. The power of God's love is the best possible medicine for a troubled soul because it ministers to the whole person - not just the will or the emotions or the intellect, but to the spirit as well. Rather than just treating symptoms, the Holy Spirit ministers to the root-cause of humanity's ills.

This brings up another aspect of comparison between humanistic and spiritual counseling methods. Almost all forms of counseling see a person as a trinity or three-part being. But there is a decided difference of opinion as to which part of the person to put in the dominant position of control over life choices. The diagram on the next page may make this difference clearer.

At a glance, one can see that only the biblical view recognizes the spiritual part of a person's nature and makes accommodations for it. The danger of putting one's mind or reasoning powers in the driver's seat is that a human being's judgment is often wrong. Proverbs 14:12 says, "There is a way which seems right unto a man, but the end thereof are the ways of death." A person receives guidance from three sources: God, Satan, and one's own conscious and subconscious thought processes. It is most certainly advantageous to have the Spirit in control of one's mind and body. When the fleshly desires of the body,

the emotional responses, intellectual processes, and decisions of the
will are controlled by the Spirit of God, this brings a person into
harmony with self, God, and fellow human beings. It is, of course, the dis-
harmony that comes from being out of the will of God that brings on
emotional, mental, physical, and spiritual problems in the first place.

The Trinity of Person

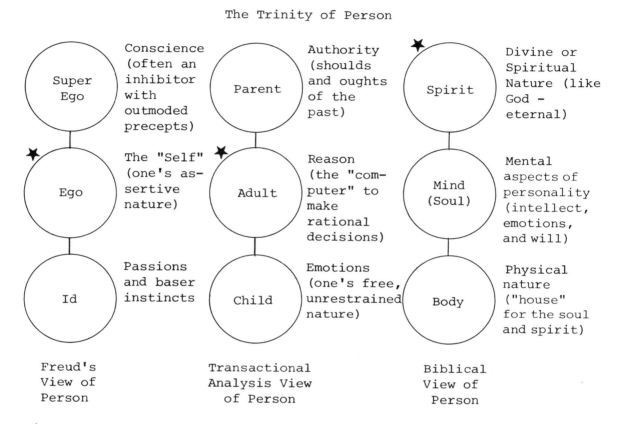

Freud's              Transactional         Biblical
View of              Analysis View         View of
Person               of Person             Person

★ = What to put in "control" of a person's attitudes, actions, etc.

## Mental and Emotional Disorders in Human Beings

It has been said that a person cannot break God's laws; they break
the person in the nonobservance of them. If, for instance, a man over-
works or neglects his health or overindulges in improper food or drink,
his body will break down. If a woman harbors resentment, jealousy,
anger, or other negative emotions, her mind will break down. If one
neglects worship, prayer, confession, and moral obligations, one's
spiritual health will break down. Each of these various aspects of
human nature can and will affect the other. The physical body may
reveal the results of a disease of the mind; both mind and body may
be affected by a spiritual problem. Because each part of human nature
will affect and interact with other parts, a counselor must be aware
of this and suggest the proper treatment that will get to the actual
cause of a problem, not just mask symptoms. There are four basic
causes for a person's "dis-ease," which may be described as follows:

141

1. <u>Physical Cause</u>: This may involve heredity, brain damage, glandular disturbances, harming the body or mind (through drugs, disease, injury, fatigue, etc.).

2. <u>Emotional Cause</u>: This may be the result of physical disorders affecting the emotions - psychosomatic problems or the mental strain of physical sickness. Also, any number of stresses of daily living such as depression, a poor self-image, grief, unhealed memories of the past, etc., may be involved.

3. <u>Spiritual Cause</u>: This purely and simply is sin, that is, breaking God's laws, rebellion, moral problems, unforgiveness, etc.

4. <u>Demonic Cause</u>: Demon oppression or possession of the soul or body of a person. A problem of demonic origin usually starts in the flesh from "dabbling" in sin. If unchecked and unconfessed, the person may be anointed by an "unholy spirit," at which point the demon powers take over. For instance, a person may start out having anger, but if allowed to go uncorrected, a spirit of anger eventually may have the person. There is also the oppressive activity of demons brought about from a curse upon a family or individual. (This subject will be discussed more fully in the chapter on healing, which includes the problems of occult involvement, the need for inner healing for traumatic experiences, the breaking of bondages, and related subjects.)

Since a person's problems may stem from any one of these four causes - physical, emotional, spiritual, or demonic - it is essential that the counselor have the guidance of the Holy Spirit to determine both the cause and the necessary remedy. Humanistic methods of treatment cannot provide remedies if the problem is spiritual or demonic; only the church can. The chart on the following page may picture this more clearly.

Thus, it may be noted that the ministry of the church through spiritual counseling methods has the remedy when humanistic methods may have none. This is not to say that the work of doctors and psychologists is not important in the ministrations of mental health; it is to say that these healing arts should be supplemented by spiritual means when this is what is needed.

### Remedies Available for Man's Dis-Ease*

| "DIS-EASE" | CAUSE | REMEDY | CHURCH AID | HUMAN AID |
|---|---|---|---|---|
| Spiritual Ills: | Sin | Confession; Repentance | Penance; Communion | None |
| Emotional Ills: | Original sin; Sins of others; Stress; Past pain or guilt | Inner healing; Change in life-patterns; Renewed mind and emotions | Prayer and Counseling | Psychiatrists; Psychology |
| Bodily Ills: | Disease; Psychosomatic disorders; Injuries | Prayers of faith for physical healing | Laying on of hands; Holy unction (anointing with oil) | Doctors; Medicine; Therapy |
| Possession or Oppression: | Demonic influences | Deliverance | Exorcism | None |

Counselors should be aware that most mental problems are progressive. What may start out as a character deficiency (sin) can progress to some type of psychological or psychosomatic disorder (a breakdown in mind or body), and then go on to create a neurosis (abnormal behavior patterns). The earlier a problem is detected and treated, the better the opportunity for a rapid and complete recovery.

The progressiveness of mental disorders may be observed in many schizophrenics. James 1:8 refers to a "double minded" person as "unstable in all his ways." This is the classic behavior pattern of someone suffering from schizophrenia (or split personality). Schizophrenia may begin as a disturbance in the personality, and then go on to a cause distortion of the personality, and finally, a complete disintegration of the personality. Usually it begins with rejection in some form. Perhaps parents did not want a child or showed no love for the youngster. This blocks the person's ability to give and receive love. Then the counterfeit balance of rebellion is set in motion to compensate for the feelings of rejection and inferiority. If the condition continues, it may develop into paranoia, a completely deluded personality out of touch with reality.

*This is an adaptation of a similar chart in Father Francis MacNutt, Healing (Ave Maria Press, 1974), p. 167.

Eve might be called the first schizophrenic. In II Corinthians 11:3, her condition is described as the result of having been "beguiled through the subtilty of Satan and corrupted from the simplicity that is in Christ." Satan is very interested in controlling the minds of God's people. He wants to turn people away from the ways of God, which is the beginning of subsequent problems and "hang-ups" resulting from separation from the Creator. Eve's double-mindedness came when she was tempted to break God's law for personal gain. She wanted super-natural knowledge; she wanted to be as a god. All humankind since then has suffered from the same dilemma - whether to obey God single-mindedly and keep peace of mind, or whether to disobey and suffer the consequences of double-mindedness and mental breakdowns. Not all mental problems and psychological disorders are the result of sin, but very many are.

A survey taken several years ago revealed that Catholics had the lowest percentage of mental problems and emotional illnesses. The reason given was the frequency of confession among people of the Catholic faith. Rather than allowing the sin to build up and progress to deeper levels with accompanying complications, Catholics are en-couraged to rid themselves of potential mental problems at the con-fessional booth regularly. One of the greatest preventive measures against mental problems is repentance. In fact, the Greek words for mental illness and repentance are related:

paranoia - "beside the mind" (a condition when one
        is out of his mind)

metanoia - "change of mind" (repentance, or turning
        away from wrong-doing or wrong thinking)

Is it not reasonable, then to conclude that a failure to repent could cause one to be "out of his mind"? Every counselor should keep this fact in mind while counseling. Many patients who spend years on a psychiatrist's couch could speed up the time of recovery with a time on their knees for a "house-cleaning" of buried sin and guilt. This is yet another reason to advocate spiritual counsel-ing. Many professional counseling methods call for the negation of guilt rather than the corrective action of repentance. When a homo-sexual or a spouse-swapper is told to "accept the lifestyle if the relationship is meaningful" or is admonished not to feel guilty "because you must accept yourself as you" are or is told that "every-one is doing such things today because moral values have changed," the problem goes unsolved. God has placed within every human being a conscience (the Spirit of God, or whatever other name one wishes to call it). When a person sins, this inner alarm clock goes off and makes the person uneasy inside. Although one can ultimately silence the alarm clock after repeated times of sinning, the guilt only goes under-ground and sets up another problem. The guilt may be transferred to ulcers, a heart condition, nervous disorders, emotional distress, or depression - but it doesn't go away until it is confessed and forgiven.

## Building Blocks to Emotional Health*

As people progress in their spiritual walk with the Lord, the battle for the mind increases. Satan wants to trip up the heels of God's people at every point along the road. That is why it is important for Christians to receive training in countering these attacks. A pictorial view of the Christian life might look something like this:

| (A) BIRTH | (B) SIN | (C) ENCOUNTER WITH JESUS | (D) DAILY WALK . . . . | (Z) HEAVEN |
|---|---|---|---|---|
| natural birth | original sin | supernatural birth - being born again, receiving water and Holy Spirit baptism | growth in grace and in power as one matures spiritually | perfection |

It is important to distinguish between (C) and (D) above. The encounter with Jesus is the work of the cross done for a person by Jesus Christ. The daily walk or growth process is the way of the cross done by Jesus in a person. It is a process, and not an event. Some new Christians mistakenly believe that once they accept Jesus, there is smooth gliding all the way to heaven. The fact is that the blessings are in proportion to the victories - and there can be no victories without some battles. Some Christians put all the emphasis on getting to point (C), and then stay there. More and more churches need to be assisting Christians in getting from (D) to (Z), or working toward reaching the perfection for which all are striving. Some scriptural guideposts along the road from (D) and (Z) are:

Build upon the proper foundation - I Corinthians 3:11 (building life on Jesus)

Use a proper guide for living - Psalm 119:11, 105 (following the commandments of the Lord as outlined in Scripture)

Purify the soul and renew the mind - I Peter 1:22-23; Romans 12:2 (following the Spirit's leading away from fleshly pursuits toward spiritual insights and godly purposes)

Discern the difference between truth and error - John 16:13 (allowing the Spirit to direct choices toward right attitudes and actions)

---

*This section is an adaptation of a teaching by Bob Mumford, Christian Growth Ministries, Ft. Lauderdale, Florida.

## Building the Foundation

Jesus Christ is the only sure foundation upon which to build a life. Those who try to build upon their own selfish desires or upon sinful practices will find everything collapsing like the house built upon the sand. Unless Jesus is the center of a like, a life is "off center."

## Using the Proper Guide

The word of God, the Holy Scriptures, must be the guide for life if one expects stability. Listening to the teachings of the world - no matter how educated or right-sounding they may be - will not bring peace of mind but only confusion. Often trends such as the New Morality or modern interpretations of traditional beliefs confuse people as to what is right and what is wrong. The Bible's teachings do not change with modern technology and updated fads. The Lord has promised that "heaven and earth shall pass away but my words shall not pass away" (Matt. 24:35). If the Scriptures forbid it, it should not be done - no matter who says it is an acceptable practice in today's modern-thinking world.

## Purifying the Soul and Renewing the Mind

The soul becomes purified by obedience and the mind becomes re-newed by discipline - putting off old fleshly habits and taking on the godly habits of the new life in Christ. Every aspect of the sin-ful past may not go at once. Some things take time, effort, prayer, and continued watchfulness. There will be tests and problems. But Jesus supplies the power for one to be an overcomer. A lazy Christian who is satisfied with half-measures and halfhearted devotion to Christ will find life lacking in real peace and stability. Such a person can-not be "together" with one foot in the Kingdom and one foot in the world, but will be the double-minded person St. James speaks of as "wavering like a wave of the sea driven with the wind and tossed."

## Discerning between Truth and Error

The Bible teaches that spiritual things are spiritually discerned. Someone who is not a Christian has great difficulty in understanding the things of the Lord. To a non-Christian they may seem foolish. It is most important that a Christian rely upon the Holy Spirit for leadership into truth and away from error. Satan's error is often dressed up in religious robes or acceptable trappings (truth mixed with error). Even in Jesus' day this was true. Jesus' friends thought he was "be-side himself" and the scribes thought he was "possessed of a devil" (Mark 3:21-22). The prophets were thought to be "fools and the spiri-tual man is mad," according to Hosea 9:7. Satan wants things upside-down. He likes people to thing bad is good and right is wrong. To be emotionally on target, a Christian must be able to discern the truth,

even when it is clouded and disguised or even when everyone else thinks
he or she is wrong.  The Christian must have the courage to choose the
truth as God seems to be revealing it, even when everyone calls the
person a fool for doing so.

## The Church's Responsibility

Part of the problem of emotional instability results from the
fact that churches have not done enough to prepare Christians for the
warfare they must face in their spiritual pilgrimage.  Many denominations
spend all their time evangelizing, as though getting people into the
Kingdom of God is the only necessary thing, the end result.  That is
just giving birth to the baby.  Many, many years of growth, maturing,
and struggle follow the conversion experience.  There are problems
and setbacks along the way.  The church needs to provide instruction
and assistance in dealing with these problems and needs to give aid to
the Christian soldiers who fall on the battlefield of life.  Obviously,
the clergy cannot counsel everyone on a one-to-one basis.  There is
not time enough.  In some instances, people who do not really need a
pastor's attention take his or her time and energy so that those who
really need counseling go unattended.  What is the answer?  There are
several.  First, group counseling and instructional sessions can be
instituted.  Training seminars can be started, not only to provide
individuals with training in solving their own problems, but also to
give approved candidates training in counseling methods in order to
help others.  Each church should have a cadre of counselors to minister
to people with emotional and spiritual problems.

Naturally there are problems that need to be worked through in
establishing such a spiritual counseling center at the church (or in
the community, if several churches are involved).  The first problem
is the barrier of prejudice.  Many people feel that, when they are in
trouble, only a pastor can help them.  There is a lack of confidence
in lay counselors, even those who have been professionally trained
and whose ministry has been proven.  Only time and education will overcome this problem.  A second barrier is often found among the clergy
themselves.  There is a reluctance to turn over the members of the congregation to lay people; this is a natural outgrowth of the clergy's
feelings of responsibility for the flock.  Clergy may well question,
"What if the counselor does more harm than good?"  This problem can
be solved only by having the lay counselors approved by the clergy
and working closely with them until such time as there is mutual
agreement that counselors are ready to minister outside of the pastor's
watchful eye.  Even then, lay counselors should check in with the
clergy and keep the lines of communication open.  Every ministry
should have the approval and direction of the church and clergy, but
in none is it more necessary than in the ministry of counseling.

## Who Can Be a Counselor?

Any committed Christian may, under the guidance of the Holy Spirit, speak a word of wisdom or offer advice, but deep counseling should be approached cautiously and only after adequate preparation. There is a danger in either extreme of attitude - that of saying, "Only completely stable, well-trained and qualified counselors should ever minister to others" and the opposite extreme of saying, "One needs no preparation, only simple trust in the Holy Spirit's guidance." No one is really ever worthy, completely and fully qualified, or adequately trained (in human strength) to face all the problems thrust upon humanity or to offer flawless advice every time; but it must be remembered that the Spirit flows best through a life that has been cleansed and prepared for service. No one would want to go for treatment to a doctor who had not first been schooled, tested, and approved during internship. Likewise, no one wants a counselor who has not been trained and approved for ministry. There is a delicate balance between trusting in training and trusting in the supernatural guidance of the Holy Spirit. Both are necessary. One should be as qualified and trained as possible, but at the same time, one should not let a lack of professional training or past experience ever prohibit the moving of the Spirit through one's life if one is being called to counsel. Of the two extremes - never leaping out in faith for fear of making a mistake, and going off ill-prepared to serve the Lord in areas beyond one's ability - it would seem that the Lord would be more pleased with ventures of faith, however feeble, than with fears of failure that would bid one to bury talents like the unfaithful servant. The Lord can redeem mistakes and even use them further to instruct his servants. The best course of action is to avoid either extreme: to be both trained and yielded to the Lord's guidance, which may often lead one into areas beyond textbook or classroom instruction.

## Characteristics of a Good Counselor

1. Openness: Although there are various counseling methods, one requirement of all counselors is an open and honest approach to this ministry. There must be openness between the counselor and the one seeking counsel. If there is hesitation or if confidence is lacking in the counselor, the Holy Spirit will be hindered from getting down to the root of the problem. The counselor must be open, both to accept the counselee and to the leading of the Spirit. The counselor must inspire confidence from others as one who is capable and as one who is relying upon a higher power than self for an effective ministry.

2. Love: A counselor must be free from even secret or hidden condemnation, from even the slightest judgmental attitude. Such an attitude can be picked up by any counselee who is the least bit sensitive. The Lord accepts and loves us, no matter how wrong our choices may be. As his representative, the counselor must evidence this same loving attitude.

A love for the Lord and a love for others must be the motivation for entering the counseling ministry.

3. <u>Noncontrolling Attitude</u>: Counseling is never a license for controlling others or telling them what to do. The Holy Spirit guides and gives gentle reproof, but he does not force or coerce. Counselors must give people freedom – even the freedom to be wrong. If God Almighty does not hinder a person's free will, neither should a counselor. It is certainly right to point out error when it is found, but the counselee must not be rejected if the error is not corrected.

4. <u>Trustworthiness</u>: A counselor must be trusted never to betray a confidence or to repeat what goes on during a counseling session. Nothing will destroy a counselee's confidence quicker than a talkative counselor who shares what has gone on without permission. A counselor must also be trusted to keep his or her word. A promise for continued help or a pledge of any sort must be relied upon.

5. <u>Listening Ability</u>: Listening is of the utmost importance during counseling. Most counselors talk too much and listen too little. The best kind of listening has three aspects: listening to the actual words spoken by the counselee; listening for hidden meanings and unspoken words not verbalized but which are indicated by facial expressions, inflections, body language, or emotional overtones; and listening to the Lord for guidance. Some counselors make the mistake of not only doing almost all the talking but also finishing sentences for the counselee when there is so much as a moment's hesitation. This often leads to offering advice about things other than the counselee's real needs. A counselor should not try to "second guess" a counselee, nor should the counselor come to a counseling appointment with any preconceived notions about the person or the person's problems. Two people with similar problems may require entirely different corrective action. The Lord is not bound to operate today as he did at the last counseling session, so each appointment must be approached as a fresh, new experience. Since a counselee's deepest hurts and needs are often glossed over or hidden completely (often below the awareness level of the counselee) it is necessary for the counselor to be in constant prayer, offering up everything being said and done to the Lord. Rather than fearing silence, a counselor should use quiet periods from time to time throughout the counseling session to listen to the Lord for further direction. The only effective counseling comes through Jesus, the Mighty Counselor, so a lay counselor must rely totally upon him at all times, waiting for his guidance and correction, and never relying upon human reason for the answers.

6. Patience: A counselor should not attempt to "hurry" or "help" the Holy Spirit do his work. Counselors who run ahead of the Lord or their counselees will find themselves alone with the problem. The counselor should move only as fast as the person is able and willing to go, and go only as far as the Lord directs - no matter how much more the counselor thinks he or she knows about the situation or how to remedy it. There should also be patience with the counselee, a longsuffering attitude toward mistakes and any lapses. A counselor must be prepared to give the needed time for the counselee (several sessions may be necessary) and the needed time for the Holy Spirit to complete his work.

7. Questioning Ability: A good counselor knows how to ask the right questions at the right time. If the Holy Spirit reveals a word of knowledge about the person's problem, the counselor should know how to probe gently and carefully, never forcefully, lest the counselee feel threatened. The counselor should not hesitate to mention anything that comes into his or her awareness; it may be the Spirit bringing up from the subconscious the key that will unlock the mystery of the person's unhappiness. If the counselee has difficulty communicating or cannot seem to get started, the counselor should have some questions ready to ask - questions such as these: "When did you start feeling unhappy?" . . . "What is it you would like to change?" . . . "What is your earliest recollection of this problem?" . . . "What feelings or reactions come to mind when I mention the word --- [Whatever the Spirit has revealed]?" Even a simple, "What can you tell me about yourself?" can get the conversation started and help the counselee to open up.

8. Ability to Affirm: The counselee needs constant reassurance and affirmation from the counselor. Many people feel that their sins, their lives, or their problems are worse than anyone else's. It is good to assure a counselee that others have walked the same road or have had the same (natural) reactions, or that there are no new sins. A counselor may feel led to share a similar experience he or she has had, but it should be remembered that emphasis ought to be placed upon the counselee's needs and upon Jesus' ability to meet them, not upon the counselor's life story or someone else's problem. Sometimes just a simple "I can understand your feeling that way" is an affirmation that says the counselor accepts and appreciates the counselee as a human being.

9. Prayer-centered Attitude: If a Christian counselor has been sought out for assistance, there is an unspoken assumption that there will be reliance upon a Power outside the counselor. Prayer should be a dominant part of all Christian counseling - at the beginning of the session to offer up the time together to the Lord and to invoke his guidance and blessing, and at the conclusion to release all that has been said and done into the Lord's capable hands, and at any time throughout

the session as the Lord leads. The counselor should also
be praying silently throughout the session, for prayer
is the power-source for effective counsel. If the counselee
should not be open to prayers offered aloud, the counselor
can still pray silently. But whenever possible, it is
good to have the counselee pray aloud. Even if this is a
new experience and even if the counselee must repeat words
suggested by the counselor, this will lay the groundwork for
building a relationship of intimacy and communication with
the Lord in the future.

10. <u>Awareness of Limitations</u>: Counselors must be humbly aware
of their weaknesses as well as their strengths. They should
not attempt to counsel "over their heads," nor should they
allow a counselee to become overdependent upon them. They
should know when to refer the counselee to another and when
to ask the clergy or another spiritual counselor for assistance. Counselors should never make the mistake of
trying to carry the burdens of those they counsel. This
is the Lord's responsibility alone. Every person and
situation should be completely released to the Lord at the
end of the session. That does not mean that counselors
will not continue to pray for the counselee, be available
for futher help, or be interested in the counselee's
welfare; it does mean that they will not become excessively
burdened with another person's problems, and that they will
not try to be the total source of another's guidance or
welfare. Counselors must also know the limitations of their
own strength and schedule. Each counseling appointment
should be checked out with the Lord in advance, and there
should be no guilt attached to saying No if a person's
request for counsel is not confirmed by the Holy Spirit.
Counselors cannot be all things to all people; they must
be able to determine which counselees are their responsibilities and which ones belong to other counselors. They
must also know when the Lord is saying that their bodies
need rest so that they do not overextend themselves -
always giving out and never taking in. Listening to the
Lord and not the demands of other people (or even their
own sympathetic nature that may suffer from guilty feelings
if requests for counseling are denied) must be kept upper-
most in mind at all times.

11. <u>Scripturally Oriented</u>: Although a counselor certainly does
not have to be able to quote the Bible from cover to cover,
it is advantageous to know what the Scriptures say about
typical problems in life and how they should be confronted.
The Holy Spirit will never lead anyone to an action forbidden
in the Bible. (The Holy Spirit, after all, is the one who
inspired the Holy Scriptures, and he would not go against
his own words.) The counselor who knows biblical answers
has the added assurance that his or her counsel is author-
itative and according to the will of God, not the ideas of

people. Jay Adams's book <u>The Use of the Scriptures in Counseling</u> will be helpful to a counselor for this purpose. (It contains a section of alphabetically listed problems and related Scriptures for them.) There is also a similar list in the questions-and-answers section of this chapter.

12. <u>Courage</u>: A counselor is expected to speak the truth in love. Sometimes love must be tough. It is not loving to say only what the counselee wants to hear, even if it is wrong. Often a counselor must say the unpopular thing or the difficult thing. Counselors are answerable to the Lord for their faithfulness to speak his message, even when it is not what a person wants to hear and even when it makes a person uncomfortable or angry. Counselors must be prepared for rejection at times, just as Jesus had those who "walked no longer with him" when the teaching was not to their liking.

13. <u>Discernment</u>: Because a problem may have its origin in any number of causes (physical, emotional, spiritual, demonic), a counselor must have the gift of discernment in operation to determine a counselee's real needs and the necessary treatment. Often symptoms mask the real trouble, which is deeply hidden in the subconscious. A Spirit-filled counselor who is relying upon the power of the Holy Spirit to be at work in each counseling situation can cut through the smokescreen and see with spiritual eyes the real root of the problem. Like all gifts, discernment is the supernatural work of the Holy Spirit manifested through people, but its effectiveness can be increased with use and practice. The counselor may manifest several or all of the nine gifts of the Spirit during a counseling session, but the Holy Spirit is the initiator of them. The counselor responds in faith to follow the leading of the Spirit. After repeated experiences of such faith, the counselor will begin to "hear" more clearly and respond more readily, working in cooperation with the Spirit.

14. <u>Calling</u>: The most important requisite for a counselor is a call from the Lord to the counseling ministry. Counseling is not an activity for the nosy, the well-meaning "do-gooder," or those seeking a place of authority or recognition. One who feels the call of God to perform a counseling ministry should have that ministry submitted, judged, and approved by the church authorities. Otherwise, the counseling, no matter how effective, will be out of divine order. The Lord will confirm through recognized authorities those whom he has called to this work.

## Characteristics of Good Counsel

The following criteria are suggested as a means of "testing" counsel for biblical accountability:

1. <u>Is it Jesus-centered</u>? Psalm 73:24 says, "Thou shalt guide me with thy counsel." It is most important that Jesus (the "Mighty Counselor" of Isa. 9:6) be directing and guiding every counseling session.

2. Is it scriptural? The Bible teaches that all Scripture is inspired by the Holy Spirit; therefore, the Lord would never lead a counselor to advise someone in opposition to Bible teachings. Psalm 119:24 says, "Thy testimonies also are my delight and my couselors."

3. Is it spiritually inspired? The third chapter of James contrasts earthly and heavenly wisdom. The wisdom that comes from the Spirit is "pure, peaceable, gentle, easy to be intreated, full of mercy and good fruits, without partiality, and without hypocrisy" (James 3:17). Spiritual counsel does not have to come from the lips of superintellectuals or educated professionals. In II Samuel 15 and 20 there is the illustration of Ahithophel, King David's highly respected counselor, and an unnamed, obscure woman who advised Joab. The Lord overthrew the counsel of Ahithophel and blessed the counsel of the simple handmaiden. The Lord spoke through the lips of a dedicated spokeswoman, but he brought to naught the words of a man who was known as the "oracle of God" (II Sam. 16:23). When Ahithophel realized that his words were not heeded, he hanged himself in frustration. The humble, unnamed woman was proclaimed a wise counselor and the saviour of an entire city. Certainly the lesson to be learned is that the Lord uses a servant submitted to him, but he withdraws his blessing upon any words spoken from the flesh and not from the Spirit.

4. Is it discerning? Counselors must discern that which is of God and that which is not from God. Because Satan disguises himself as an "angel of light," a counselor must determine the truth by testing all guidance, lest there be deception by counterfeits of God's wisdom. "The Lord will bring to light the hidden things and make manifest the counsels of the heart (I Cor. 4:5). The Lord will give each of his counselors a special way (an "inner knowing" or sign) to indicate proper choices in questionable situations.

5. Is it judged for accuracy? Proverbs 11:14 says, "In the multitude of counsellors there is safety." Every ministry should be judged, corrected, and supplemented by others in the body of Christ. It is especially important for a beginning counselor to have his ministry judged. There should be no "stars" or "lone rangers" in the counseling ministry. Just as the prophets are subject to the prophets, so counselors should be subject to other counselors. Counselors also need to go for counseling themselves from time to time, to keep their own channels open and unclogged.

6. Is it mature? At the death of King Solomon, his son, Rehoboam, took the throne. Rehoboam did not follow the advice of the elder counselors but, rather, "chose to consult the young men he had grown up with." The result was rebellion and disunity. A good counselor will seek out the wisdom of those of

experience and learn from them. The advice of immature counselors is often impetuous and needs the complement of seasoned advisers against which to test it.

7. _Is it unblocked?_ In I Samuel 14:37 King Saul asked counsel of God and did not receive it because there was unconfessed sin in the life of Saul's son. The implication is that counselors must not only keep their own lives in tune with the will of God, but also see that their families are, likewise, in divine order before the Almighty. Those who advise others in the name of the church must be certain they have their own houses in order. There are, of course, some situations beyond a parent's control, but wherever possible, the home should be a carbon copy of the church in holiness, respect, obedience, and submission to authority. Confession, repentance, and restitution whenever necessary are prerequisites to an effective counseling ministry.

8. _Is it conviction-based?_ Wishy-washy counselors with no strong convictions will hardly inspire confidence from those they counsel. Whenever spiritual counsel is given, counselors should not back down from it or water it down to please others. "Be steadfast, unmovable, always abounding in the work of the Lord, forasmuch as you know that your labor is not in vain in the Lord" (I Cor. 15:58).

## A Self-Test for Counselors

Following are some questions that prospective counselors (and experienced counselors, too) may want to ask themselves in order to look at their ministry objectively:

1. Have I been "called" to this ministry? How do I know?

2. Have I discussed this ministry with my clergy and with others? What advice have I received concerning my counseling ministry?

3. Have I been counseled myself? Have I been prayed for by a spiritual authority?

4. Am I waiting upon the Lord to open doors for ministry, to provide the right timing, and to prepare me adequately for his service?

5. What are my real motives for wishing to perform this ministry?

6. Who will receive glory from my ministry (all or part of the recognition)?

7. What aptitudes for counseling do I have? What preparation and training?

8. What is my counseling philosophy? (What branches of psychology, accepted methods, techniques, and guidelines am I in sympathy with and how do I plan to implement them? How does this philosophy compare with scriptural teachings and church doctrine?)

9. To whom is my ministry submitted (both directly and indirectly) for judging and correction?

10. Am I more in the Spirit or in the flesh when I counsel? How did I know?

11. Have I evidenced the Holy Spirit's gifts of wisdom, discernment, knowledge, miracles, prophecy, etc.? In what ways and to what extent? What were the results?

12. What kind of spiritual example is my life? What kinds of spiritual examples are my home and family relationships?

13. What kind of fruit (results) has my counseling ministry brought forth? What kind of fruit do I expect it to produce in the future?

14. What are my greatest strengths? Weaknesses? What can I do to capitalize upon the strengths and to compensate for the weaknesses?

15. How much of my time each day is spent in prayer? How well do I "hear" what the Spirit may be saying to me? How can I learn to listen better during times of meditation?

## Directive vs. Nondirective Counseling

Because counselors use different counseling techniques, one of the first questions Christian counselors must ask themselves is, "Am I a directive or a nondirective counselor?" The Rogers school of nondirective counseling calls for the counselor to act as a sounding board, reflecting back to counselees their own thoughts. The theory is that people have within themselves the untapped resources for finding solutions to their problems. A nondirective counselor does not suggest a plan of action or give advice. The nondirective counselor's purpose is to help people get insights into themselves to find their own answers.

Directive or confrontation counseling, on the other hand, involves the counselor in giving directions for suggested changes deemed necessary in the counselee's life. Here the supposition is that personality is not changed by insight but by action. This is the kind of counseling that Jesus did. Jesus did not act as a sounding board for the scribes and Pharisees, hoping that they would discover the source of their needs through insight. Jesus confronted them directly about their sinful ways and suggested amendment, warning them that they should give an account of themselves in the day of judgment for their idle words (cf. Matt. 12:36). When the rich ruler came to Jesus for advice, Jesus did not tell the ruler to launch a self-discovery program to find out what was lacking in his life. Jesus spoke directly: "You lack one thing. Sell what you have and give to the poor" (Luke 18:22). Even when Jesus taught by parables, he gave the explanations or "lessons" which his followers were expected to receive and put into practice in their lives. This is directive counseling.

The Bible itself is a directive counseling book. The entire book Proverbs gives directions, warning, and suggestions for living. The commandments given to Moses were directive (do's and don'ts for daily living). The description of Scripture given in II Timothy 3:16 declares that these writings were "given by inspiration of God and profitable for doctrine, reproof, correction, instruction in righteousness." Reproof, correction, and instruction are directive terms.

An important aspect of any counselor's philosophy is his or her approach - whether it will be directive or nondirective. Naturally, there may be times when a particular situation will call for a different approach, but a counselor should have made some basic assumptions about general procedures. It is also important to determine whether a counselor will follow a prescribed counseling method or combine various methods or develop one of his or her own. It is wise to know both the strengths and the weaknesses of various counseling systems. Most humanistic and unscriptural counseling processes underestimate people's problems in life and the necessary solutions. Freudians, who say a counselee is the victim of poor socialization, believe that an analyst can undo a human being's problem because it was brought on by a human being. The Rogerians (nondirective counselors) believe they can draw out of a counselee the answers for problems because people are basically good and have a far greater potential than they realize. Behaviorists, who say problems stem from poor learning and faulty conditioning, state that the solution is in education and reconditioning. Transactional Analysis (TA) says crossed transactions in human relationships are at the root of human problems. TA advocates learning to make adult communication transactions and accepting oneself and others ("I'm OK - You're OK"). Reality therapy asks people to assume responsibility for their own actions without blaming others, to become masters of their own fate rather than victims of the actions of others. Although there is a thread of truth running through all these philosophies, the one thing missing is the biblical view of a person as a sinner. It may be easier to believe we are all "OK" than to see ourselves as sinners, but if the problem is sin, one is certainly working from a faulty premise. There are really only two ways of going about solving problems - God's way and all other ways. Either a Christian believes that God has laid out all the necessary answers to life's problems in his Word, or the Christian must see the Bible as incomplete, a half-measure which must be supplemented with other methods and beliefs.

## Biblical Counseling

Biblical counseling presupposes a need for a change in the counselee. Starting from the premise that humanity's basic problem is sin this method advocates adjusting one's life to the teachings of Scripture. Sometimes a counselee is the victim of another's sins. In such a case, the counselee may have to change an attitude rather than an action. If a counselee was mistreated, hurt, abused, or misjudged by others, the counselee's unforgiving attitude, resentment, or revengeful thoughts may have to be dealt with. The teachings of Jesus to "turn the other cheek, go the extra mile, forgive seven times seventy times, overcome evil with good, and pray for them that despitefully use you" become more than just good sermon topics. They become practical (albeit difficult) ways of dealing with real problems.

Jay Adams, professor of practical theology at Westminister Theological Seminary in Pennsylvania, has written several books expounding what he calls "nouthetic counseling." The term comes from the Greek word for mind, or reason (nous). Nouthetic counseling is biblical counseling in that it approaches problem solving from the standpoint of warning, teaching, confronting, admonishing, and disciplining counselees. This does not mean becoming dictatorial or controlling of a counselee. It merely means pointing out the biblical view of the problem and admonishing the counselee to adjust to it. According to Adams, the use of Scriptures in counseling involves five essential factors:

1. A Biblical understanding of the counselee's problem

2. A clear understanding of the Holy Spirit's telos (purpose) in Scriptural passages appropriate to both the problem and the solution

3. A meeting of man's problem and God's full solution in counseling

4. The formulation of a Biblical plan of action

5. Commitment to Scriptural action by the counselee[*]

The following Problem-Solving Guide, created by Dr. Adams, is a useful tool in counseling according to this method.

## Problem-Solving Guide

| What Happened (The Problem) | My Response (Describe) | What I Should Have Done (Bible Reference) | What I Must Do Now (Bible Reference) |
|---|---|---|---|
|  |  |  |  |

---

[*]Jay Adams, The Use of Scriptures in Counseling (Baker Book House, 1977), p. 17.

Let us say, for example, that the counselee is a rebellious teen-age boy who is unhappy at home because of the restrictions placed upon his independence by his parents. He may want to tell the counselor how unreasonable his parents are and how justified his feelings of resentment are. In biblical counseling, the counselor starts from the premise that the only sins that can be confessed are the counselee's. If the parents are guilty of wrongdoing, they may need counseling also, but the matter at hand is the teenager and how he will deal with the problem from his standpoint.

The Bible has some very clear teaching on the subject of child-parent relationships, rebellion, and resentment. A biblical counselor might begin the biblical understanding of the problem with a similar situation described in I Samuel, chapters 1 and 2. Eli, the priest, has two sons who rebelled against their father and the teachings of God. The Lord not only held the sons accountable for their actions, but also held father Eli accountable. When Eli did not take the proper steps to correct the actions of his sons, the Lord said, "I will judge Eli's house forever for the iniquity which he knows because his sons made themselves vile and he restrained them not" (I Sam. 3:13). One of the first principles to be understood here is that parents are accountable before God for the actions of their children.

The teenage counselee may protest that he has done nothing wrong, as Eli's sons did. Although this is doubtful, let us assume, for the sake of argument, that it is the case. Even so, the Bible speaks quite clearly about a child's attitude toward parents. Whether or not the parents are doing their job correctly, God still holds children accountable to observe the commandments to (1) "Obey your parents in all things [not some things or the things you agree with] for this is well pleasing unto the Lord" (Col. 3:20); and (2) "Honor your father and mother, which is the first commandment with promise: that it may be well with you and you may live long on the earth" (Eph. 6:2-3). The counselor may ask the teenager if his rebellious attitude honors his parents - if his way of speaking to them and about them and his way of responding to their demands is honorable before the Lord. As long as children live under the roof of their parents, they are expected to submit to parental authority. That is not a popular belief, in this day of "do your own thing," but nevertheless, God's Word says it: "Be subject unto the higher powers. For there is no power but of God; the powers that be are ordained of God" (Rom. 13:1). Every authority on earth (whether it be one's parents, one's employer, or one's pastor is given for people's good. To rebel against authority is to rebel against God, for all authority is ordained of God. Although the Roman government was not God-fearing or even benevolent to the Jews, Jesus said, "Render unto Caesar the things that are Caesar's." Jesus knew the destructiveness of rebellion against the authorities God has given humanity for its own protection and well-being.

So then, the real problem with which the teenager must come to grips is his rebellion. No matter how justified he may think his feelings are, the Bible speaks plainly on the subject of rebellion and calls it sin: "Rebellion is as the sin of witchcraft, and stubbornness is as iniquity and idolatry" (I Sam. 15:23). The counselee must realize that his sin of rebellion is just as wrong before God as any sin of which he may think his parents guilty. Once these things have been made clear, the next step is formulating a biblical plan of corrective action. There are any number of appropriate actions that may be deemed necessary, depending upon the particular circumstances, but some general principles that apply here are the following:

1. The sin of rebellion needs to be confessed and repented.

2. The son needs to ask forgiveness, not only of God, but also of his parents.

3. There needs to be a changed attitude toward parental authority.

4. Positive steps need to be taken toward building up, rather than tearing down, a relationship between parents and child (discussing problems openly and lovingly, praying together, forgiving each other, working together in love to find workable solutions, etc.).

If the teenager were filling out the "Problem-Solving Guide" it might look something like this:

1. <u>What Happened</u>: "I did not get my way about --- ."

2. <u>My Response</u>: "I rebelled (became angry, left home, yelled at parents, etc.)."

3. <u>What I should Have Done</u>: "Obeyed my parents in <u>all</u> things " (Col. 3:20).

4. <u>What I Must Do Now</u>: "Take positive steps toward reconciliation with my parents and toward changing my attitude of rebellion against authority" (Rom. 12:17-21).

Naturally, this is an oversimplification of a problem that may have far-reaching ramifications and require further steps to be taken toward finding adequate solutions. But the underlying principle of adjusting behavior to scriptural teaching will apply in any situation.

In a real-life situation, a counselee came to a pastor for advice. The counselee was a man who had been homosexual all his life and who had married a very masculine woman, not out of love but in an effort to cover up his deviate behavior. Although the wife loved the husband, he had only contempt for her and for the part of himself of which she was a constant reminder. In time, the counselee had met a more feminine woman, renounced his homosexuality, and then gone to the pastor to get the church's blessing on his decision to divorce his wife and marry his lover. The counselee had all kinds of convincing arguments as to why this was advisable - his present wife brought out his baser instincts, he did not love the wife and had married her for all the wrong reasons, his girl friend was a Christian and together they could have a promising life in accordance with God's will for husband and wife, and he was certain that God wanted him to be happy, not miserable as he was with his wife.

Had this man gone to a humanistic counselor, he might have been told to find answers within his own heart, or to make an adult or rational decision, or to refuse to feel guilty about normal feelings and sexual drives of any sort, or to do whatever he was willing to accept responsibility for doing. But because he went for Christian counseling to a pastor committed to the teachings of Scripture, he was told what the Bible had to say about adultery, homosexuality, fleshly lusts, and divorce. The counselee's argument about "being in the will of God" in his proposed solution to the problem melted away in the authority of God's Word. Since the only scriptural ground for divorce is unfaithfulness, and since the wife loved and remained faithful to the counselee in spite of all his indiscretions, the counselee's only course of action before God was to confess his sin, give up his adulterous liaison, and begin to work toward making his marriage what God wanted it to be in the first place. Both husband and wife were in need of further counseling to aid them in working through their sexual problems, their identity problems, and their spiritual understanding of godly marriage. Once they made a commitment to adjust their behavior to God's standards, they received the supernatural power to bring about the changes that eventually brought happiness. When the counselee stopped seeking to fulfill the desires of his flesh and started seeking to fulfill the commandments of God through obedience, a new and beautiful love was born in his heart for his wife. Obedience (an act of the will) came before feelings (an act of the emotions), and God honored that commitment by giving the counselee the thing he had always wanted - a warm and beautiful relationship of love.

People are never truly happy and fulfilled apart from being in God's will. Satan will try to confuse the issue and make people think they are happy in the midst of their sin, but the pseudo-happiness eventually falls away to reveal the devastating misery and pain of separation from God. The Bible says that Satan is a thief and a liar. He wants to rob people of their peace of mind, their happy family life, their relationship with the Lord. He lies and tells people that right is wrong and sin is good and obedience to God will make them unhappy or unfulfilled. It is up to Christian counselors to set the record straight!

## Principles of Biblical Counseling

1. <u>Biblical counseling gives authority to the counselor</u>: The counselor is not offering his or her own words or the words of a psychological school of thought, but the infallible word of God.

2. <u>Biblical counseling is directive</u>: Like the counseling of Jesus, this method gives specifics rather than vague or ineffective suggestions for correcting improper behavior.

3. Biblical counseling is efficient: Rather than wasting a lot of time dealing with a counselee's feelings and insecurities, this method gives a practical and workable course of action to be followed. It gets to the heart of the problem quickly and sets the counselee on a course of corrective action immediately.

4. Biblical counseling requires commitment and discipline: The words discipline and disciple come from the same root. Following the teachings of Jesus in problem solving causes people to commit themselves to patterns of disciplined living which will make of them what God (and they themselves) would like them to be. Disciplining people is a natural result of biblical counseling.

5. Biblical counseling is based upon honesty: There can be no sugar-coating of sin or any blame shifting in this method. Counselees must assume responsibility for their own actions and their reactions to others. When this is done, it is the first step toward getting the problems solved.

6. Biblical counseling is sufficient: There is no greater textbook on psychology or interpersonal relationships than the Word of God. This is not to say that biblical counseling should not be supplemented with other aids when they are called for (medical care, good nutrition and health habits, valid psychological principles, etc.), but in the mainstream of daily life, the solution for every problem may be found somewhere in the Scriptures. Learning to apply these principles of Scripture to life is basic to people's happiness and security.

7. Biblical counseling is reliable: Those who practice the teachings of the Bible are bound to get results because God had promised to bless his Word as it is applied in life. God's Word never returns to him void; it accomplishes the purpose he sends it forth to accomplish - healing, reconciliation, forgiveness, or whatever is needed in each life situation.

8. Biblical counseling is supernatural: Counselors who apply Bible principles to problem solving have all the power of heaven behind their efforts. They are not dependent on professional techniques, great thinkers, or humanistic methodology. They are dependent upon God Almighty and all his resources - not only to reveal the problems but also to straighten them out. Biblical counselors are participating in God's will of sanctification for his people (bringing about change through holiness).

9. Biblical counseling requires confrontation: People tend to deal with problems in very negative ways. Some people just ignore their problems and pretend they are not there. Others try to work around their problems, never getting them solved, but making the best of things as they are. Still others give up and say there is no possible solution, or they get a substitute problem (alcohol, drugs, physical symptoms, etc.) to

cover up the source of the trouble. Biblical counseling causes people to confront the problem head-on, to give it a name, and to apply God's prescribed solution to it. This type of counseling forces people to look at their problems realistically and to look at themselves in light of the truth.

10. <u>Biblical counseling is total counseling</u>: Other methods leave out the spiritual side of human nature and deal with only one or two aspects of a person's personality. Through biblical counseling comes wholeness in mind, body, and spirit, integrating the person into a whole and holy being.

## Health for the Self

Every counselor and counselee will need a framework for building a healthy self-concept and an emotionally healthy attitude toward life. The following guidelines are suggested as a starting place for building one's own philosophy. A counselee and a counselor together may work through a list such as this, adding to it or modifying it to meet particular life needs. The final product should be typed up and placed where one can refer to it from time to time.

### My Philosophy of Life

1. I am God's child. Although I am self-centered and subject to Satan's attacks, I can never do anything so bad as to separate myself irrevocably from my heavenly Father, who loves me and forgives me each time I ask.

2. Conflicts and problems are part of life. I am not unique in my struggle to overcome trials, tests, and temptations.

3. I must admit, not hide, my problems. I must confront honestly my problems, myself, my family, others, and God.

4. I am responsible for my choices and my responses to others. No one can hurt me unless I let it happen. I can choose to let Jesus be the buffer between me and the forces that come against me.

5. I can change for the better. No situation in my life is beyond the scope of God's healing, sustaining grace. No habit or attitude must remain as it is today; with God's help, it can be different tomorrow.

6. I can pray honestly and specifically about any problem in life. God will not be embarrassed by, or disinterested in, whatever I tell him. He already knows how I feel inside anyway, so I cannot hide anything from him. He is interested in whatever interests me and wants me to share my feelings with him.

7. I must be patient with my growth as a person. I must keep remembering that the reconstruction of my personality, the changing of old, self-centered habits, and the attaining of a renewed, spiritual nature is a process that does not happen overnight.

8. I must always forgive and release all feelings of resentment toward anyone who hurts me. Nothing will damage my spiritual life more or affect my emotional stability as adversely as harboring old hurts and grudges.

9. I can retrain my mind to think and react positively by affirmations of the truth. I must counter all negative thoughts with these positive affirmations.

10. I must avoid negative cycles of conduct that pull me downward.

11. I must avoid substitutes for Jesus. Even good things such as church work or giving to charity must not have the first place in my heart that is reserved for Jesus Christ.

12. I must keep "short accounts" with the Lord by frequent confession and spiritual disciplines. I must not allow sin to build up in my life or "go underground" by my avoidance of confessing it.

13. I must continually examine my motives. I must love God for who he is, not for what I get from him. I must want the Lord more than his blessings.

14. I must trust when I do not understand the circumstances I face. Recognizing the "turbulence" involved in my "reconstruction" process and firmly believing that "all things work together for good" will help.

15. I must not fear being "transparent." I must be real to myself and others. I must avoid all game-playing and phoniness.

16. I must submit to my authorities. Even when they are wrong, I must remember my place of submission, pray for them, and respond to them in love.

17. I must be careful about what I see, read, hear, and wear. I must be discerning in my choices and avoid even the "appearance" of evil. I must avoid allowing myself to be placed in tempting situations to which I am vulnerable.

18. I must know what my convictions are and stand up for them. I must remember that people who stand for nothing fall for anything.

19. I must find a place of usefulness. By seeking God's will in my life and fulfilling that purpose, I will find fulfillment and happiness.

20. I must read the Bible daily and have a quiet time of prayer and meditation for my spiritual nourishment. I must not just read the Scriptures, but I must seek to live by them.

21. I must constantly reflect an attitude of praise, no matter what the circumstances. God deserves my praises even when I do not feel like offering them. I can be as happy and joyful as I make up my mind to be.

22. I must avoid worry. I need to learn to unwind and relax, releasing all my problems and anxieties to God. He can do something about them, whereas all my fretting will only make matters worse.

23. I must give up all the past to the Lord. I must not let Satan "blackmail" me over my past mistakes. The Lord covers my sins in the sea of forgetfulness. So must I.

24. I must open my whole self to God - surrendering everything I hold dear, including the giving over of my reputation.

25. I must learn to stay in balance. I must avoid extremes of any kind. Even the "good" extremes can get me off-center.

26. Love must be the dominant force of my life. I must love God, myself, and others (even the unlovable!), and never let anything shake that love.


## Blocks to Communication and Wholeness

In Dr. James Mallory's book The Kink and I there are some practical and down-to-earth suggestions for getting along with others and avoiding what he calls "twisted living." Dr. Mallory is a Christian psychiatrist, one who sees people's basic problem as sin and their corrective course of action as following the teachings of Jesus Christ as outlined in the Scriptures. The following categories drawn from Dr. Mallory's book have been modified somewhat, but basically they are presented from the author's viewpoint.* These typical human reactions, which set up barriers between people, should be recognized by Christian counselors. When such a reaction occurs, the counselor should help the counselee not only to identify it as an unacceptable mode of behavior but also to correct it as quickly as possible.

1. Withdrawal: "I'm not going to listen to this." This reaction is a form of escapism. Confronting a problem must replace withdrawing from it.

---

*James D. Mallory, with Stanley C. Baldwin, The Kink and I: A Psychiatrist's Guide to Untwisted Living (Victor Books, 1973), especially pp. 223-226.

2. <u>Disallowance</u>: "You shouldn't feel that way." People often do this to others - especially parents disallowing the feelings of their children when it is evident that the feelings are unacceptable. Even if another's feelings are unjustified or exaggerated, it does not help to have one's feelings belittled. Feelings are not right or wrong; they just are. Allow others to have their feelings, but seek to help them go on from there.

3. <u>Defensiveness</u>: "I'm not like that." This usually comes when someone has been confronted about negative behavior. It also may come when one's views have been attacked and he or she takes the assault on those opinions personally. The natural reaction is to defend oneself (or beliefs) and to deny the accusations. The Bible says to "agree with your adversary early." It will take the wind out of the accuser's sails if the response is, "I'm sorry if that's the way you see me. Please pray for me to do better." Christians do not have to defend themselves anyway. The Lord has promised to do that job. If the accuser is wrong, all the counterarguments in the world will not convince the accuser of it. If the accuser is right, defensiveness will not help the situation.

4. <u>Counterattack</u>: "Well, you're worse than I am." This is another defense mechanism that often accompanies the defensive attitude. The object is to point out a worse failure in the life of the accuser. No one wins in such a situation. This reaction only leads to angry words and further breakdowns of communication. Try "overcoming evil with good" by finding something nice to say to the accuser. (This must be said sincerely or it comes across like sarcasm instead of oil on troubled waters.)

5. <u>Super-Guilt</u>: "I'm so awful . . ."or "After all I've done for you . . . ." Both of these approaches belong to the martyr category. In the "I'm so awful" approach, the object is to make the accuser feel sorry for the accusations by hearing an exaggerated replay of them and then to cause the accuser to say, "Aw, you're not so bad." In the "After all I've done for you" approach (used skillfully by possessive mothers) the object is to use guilt as a wedge to get one's own way. "After all I've done for you" is followed by "the least you should do for me is ---" (whatever the person is after). Both approaches are designed to arouse false guilt in others; they should be avoided because they are both phony and manipulative.

6. <u>Peace at Any Price</u>: "Whatever you say" . . . . "Do whatever you want" . . . or "You win. Just leave me alone." Such approaches, used when it is obvious that the person does not really agree, avoid confronting a problem for the sake of peace and quiet. Henpecked husbands often use this response with nagging wives, the kind who know if they harp long enough they can get their own way. This is another escape mechanism which does not bring real, but rather a counterfeit, peace. If neither party can agree with the other, a compromise should be sought. To give in constantly to another causes one party to become domineering (a form of idolatry) and the other to become dependent and lacking in self-respect.

7. <u>Substitutes for Jesus</u>: "I'll use 'methods' to get relief." People often turn to methods or things in an attempt to avoid dealing with a problem or person scripturally. Unacceptable habits such as drugs, alcohol, cults, humanistic self-help programs, and pleasures of the flesh are used to mask over the problems. Even "acceptable" substitutes are sometimes used: doctrines, legalism, good works, emotional highs, status, moral codes, etc. None of these substitutes will bring lasting relief or solutions. Jesus must be given first place, and his guidance must be sought for problem solving.

8. <u>Inability to Love</u>: "I want nothing more to do with you." This reaction often follows when the loved one has caused hurt, disappointment, or disapproval for failure to "measure up." There are only two kinds of relationships - a "control" relationship and a "love" relationship. In the control relationship, love is withdrawn when someone falls short of expectations; in the love relationship, love is constant and never withdrawn, regardless of the actions or reactions of others. Love, to be like God's agape, must be unconditional. Often prayers for hurts of the past must be prayed before the blockage to love will go away. This is especially true of those who have received great amounts of rejection. Some people cannot love God, themselves, or others. They must be helped to see that love is not just an emotional feeling, but an act of the will. People can make up their minds to love and do loving things, even when they do not "feel" loving. Love is unselfishness, an action verb that says, "I want to meet others' needs; I will put myself last;

I will live by the theme of Romans 12:10: 'Be kindly affectioned to one another with brotherly love; in honor prefering one another.'"

9. Negative Patterns: Often people who have been rejected set up patterns of behavior which bring on more rejection. Such people expect to be rejected, so they do negative things which cause others to reject them further. They collect bad feelings like collecting green stamps. They can then "cash in" all the collected bad feelings as a big rejection pay-off and celebrate with a pity party. It is not that the person really enjoys the results of such behavior, but it is the behavior pattern that is most comfortable (a kind of life script that is written in one's mind, something one is used to, and something one cannot break away from without help). Such negative patterns of behavior must be interrupted and supplanted by a relationship with Jesus which will then lead to an acceptance of the self and an acceptance by others. Scriptures and affirmations of a positive kind must be repeated, believed, and confirmed by others until the subconscious mind is programmed with the new life-script.

10. Negative Cycles: Very similar to the negative pattern described above, a negative cycle further intensifies a poor self-image. People with a bad self-concept often reinforce the image they have come to accept by negative behavior. This, in turn, brings negative reactions from others, which then further breaks down self-image. Once on this downward spiral, the self-concept is reduced over and over again in this vicious circle. Scriptural teachings, prayer, and Christian counseling are necessary to change the course toward an upward spiral.


## Dealing with Anger

Some schools of psychology advocate transference of aggression. If a little girl hates her mother, she is told to pretend a pillow is mommy and to take out her anger on it. She then hits and yells at the pillow rather than assaulting mommy. This is nothing more than teaching the child to commit murder in her heart. The Bible says, "As a man thinks in his heart, so is he." Jesus' Sermon on the Mount showed how persons can commit adultery in their hearts or "kill" somone in their hearts by calling that one a fool. Rather than helping the child to deal with hostile feelings, transference of aggression encourages violent reactions and aggressive behavior. Jesus' approach advocated "agreeing with an adversary, turning the other cheek, going the extra mile, loving enemies, blessing them that curse you, doing good to them that hate you, and praying for them that despitefully use you and persecute you." These, of course, are not natural reactions. They must be supernatural reactions. It is vital that Christian counselors know how to help people work through their anger and hostilities by the use of effective confrontation methods. The following guidelines, also adapted from Dr. James Mallory's The Kink and I (pp. 193-98), are suggested:

1. <u>Take your responsibility</u>: Do not say, "You made me angry." Say, "I feel angry." Do not place the blame for your reactions upon another person. Assume responsibility not only for your actions, but also for your reactions.

2. <u>State feelings honestly</u>: Say, "I feel hurt" or "I feel disappointed." Confront without condemnation. Speak the truth, but speak it in love. It is not loving to be dishonest about your feelings or to act as though everything is fine when it is not. A relationship must be built upon frankness and honesty.

3. <u>Describe the results</u>: Say, "This situation separates us" or "We are too emotionally wrought up now to communicate in love." This is not placing blame, but merely describing the situation.

4. <u>Allow reaction</u>: Say, "Express your feelings on this." There are always more ways than one to look at a situation. Try to empathize with the opposite viewpoint. Acknowledge and affirm the other person's right to feel as he or she does, even if you cannot accept that viewpoint.

5. <u>Push for reconciliation</u>: Say, "Will you forgive me?" You may not think you are wrong, but it never hurts to ask for forgiveness of even imagined wrongs. Being right is not as important as being in one accord.

6. <u>Let is rest</u>: If the other person will not forgive or work toward a solution to the problem, give it some time. Remain available and risk it again at a later time.

7. <u>Turn it over to the Holy Spirit</u>: Pray for the Spirit to work in the other person's life to bring about reconciliation. If you have done everything in your power to make things right, you must leave the final results to the Lord. Continue to "pray without ceasing" for God to bless the one you are alienated from and to show you anything further you need to confess or rectify. (Don't just pray for God to "change" your opponent; pray for God to "bless" the person too.)

As Dr. Mallory, the Christian psychiatrist, puts it, "Face anger honestly, restrain and control it; allow it to motivate you to action that resolves conflicts and brings healing."

## Counseling Surveys

Before a church or an individual can offer counseling services, some preliminary investigation needs to be done.  Such a survey would include identifying the needs of the community (church, group, etc.) and determining the services available to meet those needs.  It might also involve training for prospective counselors where needs exist and no people or resources are available.  The survey following is an example of the kind of questionnaire that might be helpful to fill out and discuss prior to beginning a counseling ministry.

### A Counseling Survey

1. What counseling services are available locally (professional services, church services, informal Christian guidance through prayer groups or spiritual leaders, etc.)?

2. Evaluate the quality of available services:

3. What changes or improvements (additions, modifications) in counseling services presently available would be desirable?

4. What needs exist that are not being met by present services available?

5. A. What training for prospective counselors is available?

   B. What training would be desirable that is not presently available?

6. Where would one go for help for the following problems?

   A. Family problems (parent-child relationships):

   B. Marital or sexual problems:

C. Depression:


D. Deeply rooted emotional disturbances:


E. Financial problems:


F. Bondage to food, drugs, alcohol, etc.:


G. Guilt feelings:


H. Uncontrollable behavior:


I. Personality conflicts:


J. Bondage to other people (dominant-dependent relationships, etc.):


K. Other problems (spiritual, emotional, physical, mental):


7. What kind of self-help or instructional programs would aid people in coping with problems before they reach gigantic proportions?


8. What can I do (individually or through my church, prayer group, family, community, etc.) to foster emotional and spiritual health?

## Questions and Answers about Counseling

1. What kind of advance preparation is suggested before one begins a counseling ministry?

A blind person cannot see to lead others. Counselors should be as emotionally "together" as possible. They should seek prayer and counseling for themselves to discover if they have any unresolved conflicts. The Lord will provide his servants with the training needed. It may take the form of reading on the subject of counseling, going to training retreats or workshops on counseling, attending academic classes on counseling, sharing and exchanging ideas with those in the counseling ministry, or obtaining professional instruction. The main requirement is waiting upon the Lord. He will open the door of service in his timing and send the people to counselors for help when the time is right.

2. What kinds of help are available to those needing counseling?

Those who cannot work through a problem without outside help may go to a pastor, a spiritual elder, a professional counselor, or a Christian friend who has passed through a similar difficulty. It depends upon the nature and severity of the problem as to which kind of counselor you choose. The first step is prayer. The Lord will bring the one in need and the one who is to minister to that need together if his will in the situation is being sought. A physical check-up also is often a desirable first step. Low blood sugar and other physical ailments often produce emotional reactions and depressions.

3. How does one know if one needs counseling help or not?

Pray about it. The Lord may choose to work through various means to bring about wholeness. He is not bound to operate according to a set plan (or even the way he operated yesterday). He may want to minister directly to the individual as that person prays through a problem. He may want to use professionally trained people or the person next door. Those in the counseling ministry should be aware of the biblical admonition to "lay hands suddenly on no man." The caution indicated is that each counseling session should be confirmed through prayer to determine which people are which counselors' responsibilities. Let the Lord open the doors. If there is a genuine need for counseling (beyond routine advice and prayer support) this will be confirmed and made clear both to the counselee and to the counselor the Lord has chosen to minister to the person.

4. What should be done if a simple-sounding problem develops into something the counselor feels inadequate to handle?

Again, the first step is to pray. If the Holy Spirit does not give an answer, ask him to reveal the name of the one he has chosen to continue the ministry to this need. Counselors should have a ready list of advisers upon whom to call in emergencies. There is an advantage to counseling at the church, in that a pastor is usually nearby for emergency situations. It is also good to counsel in pairs in order to utilize the insights of more than one counselor. It is good to consult frequently with another counselor (clergy or lay) about problems. Without revealing the identity of the person involved, guidance and prayer may be requested. Sometimes silence or delayed guidance are the signals to wait upon the Lord. He may be wanting everyone to wait for him to work in the situation or to engineer circumstances that must take place before the final answer comes. It is always better to admit not having answers than trying to "fake it" or counsel outside the guidance of the Spirit. No one person can be all things to all people, so counselors should carry their responsibility only as far as they are led.

5. What are some inherent dangers of counseling?

As the Lord blesses and a counselor sees fruitful results of ministry, there is the danger of pride getting in the way and the counselor beginning to believe that he or she somehow has a corner on the oracles of God. The glory belongs only to the Lord for any successful counseling session, and when people try to share even a little of it, they are in trouble. There is also the danger of a counselee transferring dependency to the counselor and the counselor enjoying the role of rescuer to an unhealthy degree. A man and a woman should not counsel alone together, for the obvious dangers that such a situation might create. Even happily married people have been tempted sexually in ways they never imagined possible in such situations, and should no such problem ever come up, it is still good to abstain from even the "appearance of evil." Another danger is in the possibility of allowing Satan to enter the session so that the counselor hears counterfeit discernment or gives fleshly (rather than spiritual) advice. There is also the possibility of making mistakes, but it is comforting to know that the Lord can redeem them. Having a counseling partner to back up, pray, and test guidance for confirmation is good insurance against these last two dangers. The fact that there are dangers in counseling (as there are in any ministry) should not make one fearful to follow the calling the Lord sends out. To avoid the problem of overdependence upon the counselor or transference of gratitude from the Lord to his servant, the counselor should keep pointing to Jesus and encouraging the counselee to rely upon him more and more and to thank him for every step along the path to wholeness. It is good for a counselor to stay somewhat aloof, yet loving, and to encourage fellowship with other Christians, Bible study, and other spiritual disciplines that will involve the counselee with other people and various means of spiritual maturing. It might even be well to encourage the counselee to find someone less fortunate to give help to (in ways that the counselee is capable of giving it) in order to pass on the loving concern that has been shown to him or her.

6. What preventive measures can be taken to avoid the need for professional counseling?

A basic step is a personal commitment to the Lord Jesus Christ and involvement in Christian opportunities for fellowship and instruction. Participation in prayer-and-share groups will often give one the opportunity to unburden a problem and receive ministry. It is also good to have a prayer partner or close Christian friend in whom to confide and share prayer requests. A family conference table for discussing problems and praying for one another in the home is also a wonderful dose of preventive medicine. Often just writing out one's feelings and problems (whether or not this is shared with others) is a way of getting things out in the open where they can be dealt with and examined objectively. Frequent confession is also suggested as the foremost method of "preventive medicine" in emotional and spiritual health.

7. What biblical counsel can be offered for specific problems?

Some of the most common problems are listed below, and following each one is a series of appropriate biblical citations.

Anger - Ephesians 4:26-32; James 1:19-20; Proverbs 29:8; Matthew 5:22; Proverbs 15:1.

Bondages to people or things - Exodus 20:3; I Corinthians 10:14; I John 5:21; Colossians 3:2; Matthew 10:37-28; Matthew 6:33.

Carnality - Romans 8:6-8; John 6:63; James 4:4; I Peter 2:11; Titus 1:15-16; James 4:7-8.

Depression - II Corinthians 4:8-9; Romans 8:35-39; Psalm 51: 8-12.

Divorce - Jeremiah 3:1; Matthew 5:31-32; Matthew 19:3-8; I Corinthians 7:10-16, 39-40.

Drugs, Alcohol, etc. - Ephesians 5:18; John 8:32-36; Ephesians 1:6-7; Philippians 4:13; Proverbs 23:20-21; James 1:2-5, 12-25; Colossians 1:12-14; Romans 8:2-18; James 4:7-10; Romans 8:26-27; Romans 12:1; I Corinthians 6:19-20; I Corinthians 9:27; Proverbs 20:1; I Corinthians 10:31; I Corinthians 3:16-17.

Finances - Luke 6:38; Proverbs 16:8; Malachi 3:8-12; Proverbs 11:25; Proverbs 3:5-6, 9-10; Psalm 118:8; I Timothy 6:9-10.

Fornication and Adultery - Acts 15:20; I Corinthians 5:9; I Corinthians 6:13-18; Jeremiah 3:1; Proverbs 6:26-33; Leviticus 20:10; Matthew 5:27-32; Galatians 5:19; I Corinthians 6:9; Hebrews 13:4; James 4:4.

Guilt - I John 1:9; Romans 3:23-25; I John 2:1-2; John 3:17; John 5:24; I John 5:14-15; Romans 8:1; Joel 2:13.

Immaturity - Hebrews 5:12-14; I Peter 2:2; I Peter 1:14-16; Ephesians 4:14-15.

Inability to Love - Jeremiah 31:3; John 15:9; I John 3:1; Matthew 5:44; Proverbs 25:21-22; Romans 12:9-21; John 13:34; I John 4:20-21; I John 3:14-18.

Judgmental Attitudes - Romans 2:1; Matthew 7:1-5.

Marital Problems - I Corinthians 11:3; I Timothy 3:4-5;
I Corinthians 11:8-9; I Timothy 2:12; Ephesians 5:24;
Colossians 3:18; I Corinthians 7:13-16; I Peter 3:1-2;
Genesis 2:18-24; Ephesians 5:25-33.

Parents and Children - Colossians 3:20; Ephesians 6:1-3;
I Peter 5:5; I Timothy 3:4-5; the following verses from the
book of Proverbs: 23:13-14, 19:18, 13:24, 22:15, 29:15,
17:1-2, 22:6, 29:17.

Poor Self-Concept or Rejection - Matthew 10:29-31; Matthew
25:34; Exodus 34:6; I Timothy 1:15-16; John 15:9, 16;
II Peter 3:9; Isaiah 42:5-6, 16.

Pride - Proverbs 11:2; James 4:6; Proverbs 16:8; Timothy 3:6;
I John 2:16; Matthew 20:26-27; Matthew 23:11-12; I Corinthians
10:12.

Rebellion - Isaiah 30:1; I Samuel 15:23; Psalm 68:6; Deuteronomy 21:18-21; James 4:7-10; Ephesians 5:21; I Peter 2:13-15.

Self-Pity - Jude 1:16; I Corinthians 10:10; Philippians
4:11-13; I Timothy 6:6-8; Hebrews 13:5.

Sexual Perversions - Leviticus 18:22-23; Deuteronomy 22:5;
Romans 1:24-27; I Corinthians 6:9; Leviticus 18:6; Deuteronomy 27:20-23; Leviticus 18:17-18.

Temptations - II Peter 2:9; Revelation 3:10; I Corinthians
10:13; Proverbs 3:6; James 1:14-15; Galatians 5:16-17;
I Corinthians 10:6.

Unforgiveness - Matthew 6:14-15; Matthew 18:15; Mark 11:25;
Luke 17:3-4; Ephesians 4:32; I John 1:9-10; James 5:9;
Hebrews 12:15; Luke 6:37.

Worry - Matthew 6:24-34; Philippians 4:6-7; I Peter 5:6-7;
II Timothy 1:7.

Wrong Companions - Romans 16:17-18; I Corinthians 5:9-13;
II Corinthians 6:14-18; James 4:4; Proverbs 9:6, 13:20,
14:9, 22:24-25, 23:20-21, 29:24.


## Conclusion

The whole idea of offering a guide to counseling in these few
pages is somewhat absurd. There is no way in this brief space to
cover the whole gamut of counseling methods, services, and procedures.
It has been the purpose, rather, to offer some guidelines and suggestions, some thought-provokers to lead the prospective counselor to

further study and contemplation. Because "the fear of the Lord is the beginning of wisdom," it is only through seeking the Lord's guidance that a person develops any skills as a spiritual counselor and lay minister. So whether you follow a prescribed counseling method or develop one of your own, may you be guided by the Mighty Counselor into all truth as you seek to minister in his name.

# 8 · Ministries of Healing

The Bible says that Jesus "went about healing all manner of sickness and all manner of disease among the people" (Matt. 4:23). It also says that the things Jesus did we are to do - and even greater things. One of the signs of Christ's followers is that they "shall lay hands on the sick and they shall recover" (Mark 16:18).

Although everyone does not have a ministry of healing to the extent that one devotes full time to this purpose, everyone can be a prayer channel for the sick. The Christian's attitude toward illness is knowing it is not God's highest will. Jesus already paid the price for our healing: "Himself took our infirmities and bare our sicknesses" (Matt. 8:17) and "by His stripes ye were healed" (I Peter 2:24).

The main ingredient in prayers for healing is <u>faith</u> - the belief that the power of Jesus to heal as he did long ago is still available today. Even Jesus did not do many miracles where there was unbelief. It is not the faith that does the healing, however. Only Jesus does that. It is not like a formula ("get enough faith worked up and you get a pay-off"). In fact, there is nothing a person can do - be good enough, have enough faith, say the right words, etc. The action is not the person's, but God's. He is the source of healing and wholeness. People relinquish themselves and submit themselves to a God of love who wants only the best for his children, which includes, of course, healthy minds and bodies.

Some people pray for the sick rather negatively; they give themselves a loophole by praying "if it be thy will." Jesus never prayed that way for the sick. Healing (or wholeness) is always God's will. It's just that some healings are instant and miraculous, some are gradual and progressive, and some are never completed in this life. But as in all ministering, the results are not the responsiblity of the minister. Those involved in healing ministries are but to pray positively, in faith believing, and then leave the rest in the loving hands of the Almighty.

Where should the healing ministry be practiced? Anywhere it is needed. It is time Christians became less self-conscious about the business to which they have been called and commissioned. When one reads the book of Acts, it becomes apparent that the early Christians got involved in the healing ministry wherever they were. Even though the church was considered a "hospital" of sorts, where people went to receive ministry, the main thrust of the early healing ministry was out in the world, where the needy people were. In addition to the healing of the lame man at the temple (Acts 3:2-8), there were healings in many places other than church: in the streets (Acts 5:15), in homes (Acts 9:33-34), in nearby cities (Acts 9:38-42), and in distant places (Acts 28:1-9).

This pattern of healing both in and out of the church locality should likewise be followed by modern-day believers. The church is the first and foremost place where the healing ministry should be in operation; however, God's people also should be willing to pray for others at work, in their homes, and wherever else they may be. Often through a physical or an emotional healing someone is introduced to Jesus. The Bible teaches that miracles are a sign to unbelievers, and a healing (no matter how large or small) is certainly miraculous.

How should a healing ministry be practiced? There are many formal and informal means through which the Lord may work to bring about wholeness. He is so creative that he is not bound to use one type of person or one single method. It is important that all Christians become aware of the possibilities and begin to bring their faith in line with the mighty works that the Lord wants to perform. Without faith it is impossible to please him. Many times people see no miracles of healing because they expect none.

There is no set pattern to use as a guide for beginning a healing ministry. The Scriptures describe many procedures. What follows is by no means an exhaustive treatment, but it covers several useful methods.

## Healings through the Church

Many practices of the church are, by their very design, instruments of healing. The receiving of Communion, for instance, symbolizes the receiving of the Lord Jesus, who is Perfect Wholeness. There have been many testimonies given by people who have received a healing at the Communion rail. Penance (confession) is likewise a healing process. Whenever one confesses sin, there is a cleansing of the spirit and the soul, which is preventive medicine for many physical and mental ills. (Therefore, there should be more emphasis on confession for the health of the body of Christ!) Many times in Jesus' healing ministry he said, "Thy sins are forgiven thee" at a time of physical healing, which underscores the interaction of the body with "dis-ease" of the spirit. Holy unction (anointing with oil) is a very scriptural way of administering the healing gifts of the church. In James 5:14-16, the basis for several practices of healing are set forth: (1) prayers for physical healing through intercession; (2) calling on a minister or an elder of the church when in need of healing; (3) anointing with oil; (4) confession of sin in conjunction with the prayer of faith for healing; and (5) the promise of results to be expected:

> Is there any sick among you? Let him call for the
> elders of the church; and let them pray over him, anoint-
> ing him with oil in the name of the Lord. And the prayer
> of faith shall save the sick, and the Lord shall raise
> him up; and if he have committed sins, they shall be for-
> given him. Confess your faults, one to another and pray
> one for another, that ye may be healed. The effectual
> fervent prayer of a righteous man avails much.

177

## Outer Healing

### Laying on of Hands

There are many instances in the Bible where the power of touch became the point of contact for the Lord's healing power to flow to one who was ill.  Jesus often touched those to whom he was ministering.  Peter's mother-in-law, Jairus' daughter, the leper of Matthew 8 were all healed at the touch of Jesus.  There was even an instance of a woman being healed who merely touched the hem of Jesus' garment.  The laying on of hands became a traditional way of imparting God's grace, whether it was to set apart and send forth someone for ministry (Acts 13:3), to ordain deacons (Acts 6:6), to impart the gift of the Holy Spirit (Acts 8:17-18), or to impart the gift of healing (Mark 16:18).  St. Paul and St. Peter often used the ministry of touch in their healing work (Acts 3:2-8; 28:8-9).  To touch someone is to say, in effect, "I care about you and I want to identify with your suffering as I become a channel of God's healing love to flow through me to you."

There is nothing "magical" about the laying on of hands.  When Simon the sorcerer wanted to give the apostles money in exchange for the power he saw evidenced with the laying on of hands, he was told, "Your money perish with you, because you thought that the gift of God may be purchased with money.  You have neither part nor lot in this matter, for your heart is not right in the sight of God.  Repent therefore of this wickedness" (cf. Acts 8:18-24).  This admonition implies that the one who lays hands upon another must first examine his or her motives and be certain that the heart is right before the Lord.  The laying on of hands in the ministry of healing is much like watering a plant.  The hose does nothing more than bring the water to the thirsty plant.  It is the water, not the hose, that performs the necessary function.  Those involved in healing become "hoses" to bring the Water of Life to those thirsty individuals who need the sustaining power of the Almighty to give them life and health.

### Speaking the Word of Faith

Psalm 107:20 says, "He sent His word and healed them."  In addition to intercessory prayers for the sick, there is the added function of speaking words of healing as Jesus did.  Our only pattern for anything we do is Jesus and what he did.  There are many instances recorded in Scripture where Jesus but spoke a word and there was a healing.  Matthew 8:16 tells us that Jesus "cast out the spirits with his word and healed all that were sick."  Other healing words of Jesus include these:  "As you have believed, so be it unto you" (Matt. 8:13); "Great is your faith; be it unto you as you will" (Matt. 15:28); "Your son lives" (John 4:50); "Arise, take up thy couch, and go into thine house" (Luke 5:24); "Lazarus, come forth" (John 11:44).  These and other passages emphasize the importance of word power in promoting faith for healing miracles.  A wishy-washy minister who is uncertain of God's power to heal or who lacks the confidence to believe in God's miracles can hardly inspire the sick to have an unshakable faith.  Although one does not presume upon God, order him about, or dictate to him the course of action to be followed in any given situation, it is important to stand in the authority of the believer in matters of healing. If a minister has prayed for guidance in advance and feels led to pray for someone's healing, then it should be a positive prayer accompanied by words of affirmation and confidence. Claim the Lord's wholeness wholeheartedly and allow no doubt to overshadow the act of faith being performed.

## Prayer and Fasting

When Jesus' disciples were unable to heal the child possessed of a deaf, dumb, and epileptic spirit, the reason Jesus gave was, "This kind can come forth by nothing but by prayer and fasting" (Mark 9:29). Often the means by which a healing is accomplished is the sacrifice of the intercessor who is willing to fast and pray for the one who is ill. There have been many miraculous healings as a result of indiviudals or groups who became such sacrifical intercessors for others. In one true case, there was a woman who had undergone every physical and psychological test to determine the cause for her bizarre behavior and many painful symptoms. The woman was unwilling to submit for prayers of deliverance, even though her psychiatrist felt that hers was, at bottom, a spiritual problem. The woman's daughter, who was a Christian, called upon members of her prayer group who were believers in the supernatural healing power of Jesus Christ to join her in fasting and prayer for her mother. Much to the surprise of the doctors, the woman, and her husband, the symptoms left, and the woman's mind and body began to function normally again. No medical explanation or psychiatric treatment could be credited – only the willingness on the part of the body of Christ to fast and pray in believing faith.

## Doing Something Needful

There were times in Jesus' healing ministry when he demanded something to be done before healing took place. Sometimes it was an act of faith required on the part of the sick person ("Stretch forth your hand" or "Take up your bed and walk"). At other times it was a gradual process requiring several steps to be accomplished before the healing was complete ("Go to the priest, make an offering, cleanse yourself with water"). In the case of the blind man of Bethsaida, Jesus first took the blind man out of town and anointed his eyes. When the healing at that point was only partially completed ("I see men as trees, walking"), Jesus then put his hands again upon the blind man's eyes and made him look up. At that point the blind man saw clearly. From this illustration, it would seem that every healing is not instant or complete with one prayer or one method of healing applied. People are complex beings. The cause of the physical manifestation may be deeply rooted and very involved. There may be several kinds and methods of prayer needed, several people needed to minister, and several days or years required for the process to be completed. Perhaps the person who is ill needs to perform an act of faith such as claiming healing before physical symptoms are gone. Perhaps there is sin in the person's life that needs to be repented of or a situation needing to be remedied by reconciliation or restitution. Perhaps there is a blockage to healing that must first be removed. Those involved in the healing ministry must be attuned to the Spirit to hear clearly from the Lord how he plans to bring about the necessary healing and what steps need to be followed.

### Rebuking the Devil

Satan can bind a person spiritually, emotionally, and physically. There are many examples in Jesus' ministry of healing where it was necessary for him to rebuke the devil or cast out an evil spirit before healing took place. In fact, physical healing and deliverance from demons were grouped together in descriptions of Jesus' ministry: "He healed many that were sick of divers diseases and cast out many devils" (Mark 1:34). . . . "They brought him many possessed with devils, and he cast out spirits with his word and healed all that were sick" (Matt. 8:16). . . . "Jesus rebuked the devil and he departed out of him, and the child was cured from that very hour" (Matt. 17:18). Those performing ministries of healing must be aware of the possibility that a person's illness may be demonic in nature. If such is the case, the person needs to be taken to one called to and approved for the ministry of exorcism. When Jesus sent out his disciples, he gave them some marching orders, which have not been revoked for modern-day followers: "heal the sick, cleanse the lepers, raise the dead, cast out devils; freely you have received, freely give" (Matt. 10:8). The body of Christ is often failing to use all the power and various means available to bring about healing.

### Having the Proper Emphasis

Sometimes sick people put all their attention upon their ailments and symptoms when attention needs to be placed upon Jesus. The Lord needs to be honored and worshiped whether or not he is solving the physical problems according to human desires and according to human timetables. Proclaiming Jesus Christ Lord of one's life is often the first step toward wholeness. The Lord is interested in the totality of people - their spiritual as well as physical well-being. Often getting right spiritually must come before getting right physically is possible.

### Kinds of Healing Needed

Because people are made in the image of God, they, like God, are a trinity - a body (the physical exterior), a spirit (the immortal manifestation of God within man), and a soul (the conscious and subconscious mind consisting of the will, emotions, and intellect). Sometimes the soul and the spirit are confused with one another. The soulish part of people is not the Godlike part, not unless it is submitted to the Holy Spirit's control. Satan is ever at work in the soulish areas of people's lives to take over their emotions, their will, and their intellect. Thus, many ailments of the mind are the results of Satan's work in the soulish nature. It naturally follows that people, as a trinity, are capable of three kinds of sickness. They can be physically ill, spiritually ill, or emotionally or mentally ill (a dis-ease of the soul that may exist below the awareness level). Any one of these ailments can and does affect the other areas. The following kinds of healing may be necessary:

Repentance: Confession of sin and repentance (a change of direction) are often the means by which spiritual healings come.

Prayers of Faith: Intercessory prayer for others or believing prayers for oneself are a part of the healing process for physical ailments.

Inner Healing: Prayers to offer up the past with all its hurts, guilt, and unhappy memories are needed when the soulish areas are bound by circumstances of the past. Often actions of the present are deeply rooted in experiences of early childhood or even prenatal experiences of a child in the womb.

Exorcism: Deliverance from demonic oppression is necessary when the mind, body, or spirit may be influenced by demon powers.

It may be concluded, then, that methods of praying for and ministering to the sick may take different forms. Formal methods may include any of the ministries of the church (confession, receiving Communion, anointing with oil, laying on of hands, prayer, counseling, inner healing, exorcism). Individual or "informal" methods of healing may include intercessory prayer, speaking forth words of faith for healing, fasting, binding or rebuking hindrances to healing, joining in one accord with other believers to "claim" a healing, or relinquishing the total life (not just the ailment) to the Lord in a commitment of surrender. Any one or all of these methods may be necessary to bring about wholeness. Or the Lord may choose to bring about a healing in a totally different way, one never before encountered. Although people can discover some principles about healing and the way God usually works, they can never totally understand it. If people could, they would know as much as God. A great part of the excitement of the healing ministry is seeing the Lord do the unexpected.

Who should become involved in the ministry of healing? Although there may be certain people especially anointed for a healing ministry (those who devote a great deal of time and energy to this form of outreach), it must be remembered that everyone can and should offer self as a prayer channel for the sick. Wherever the opportunity arises, Christians of all walks of life can participate in the healing ministry - whether it be a parent praying and believing for a sick child, an employee praying for a co-worker's headache, a student praying for a teacher's temper that may need healing, or an entire family or prayer group fasting and praying for someone's deliverance or wholeness.

## First and Second Aid

Because the Lord works through a variety of means to tailor-make each healing unique and suited to the individual in need, the healing gifts of doctors and other professionals must not be overlooked. The important thing is to have priorities in order. First aid is prayer; second aid is medicine or professional help. It does not show a lack of faith for a Christian to take medicine or to consult a physician--not if, after prayer, it is determined that medical treatment is called for. It is, rather, a decided lack of faith to ignore the treatments and professional assistance the Lord has provided as aids to healing. The key is balance. Any extreme is to be avoided: that of trusting only in medicine and never trusting in medicine; trusting exclusively in supernatural power for healing and disbelieving in supernatural power for healing. There must be an openness to the leading of the Holy Spirit, for the Lord will not be boxed in by a set of predetermined rules. Prayer is the only sure foundation upon which every means of healing can confidently rest.

## How and Where?

More and more, churches are including healing services in their total program. Not only are there special midweek services at which the healing ministry is regularly performed, but also many churches offer an altar call or remain open at the conclusion of Sunday worship for those who wish to receive individual prayers for healing. As lay ministers are trained and approved, they are assisting clergy in praying at the altar for those who request such prayers. Prayer groups, prayer lists for intercessions, and prayer chains are also useful tools of the church in the healing ministry. For details of various church-related programs such as these, see chapter 4, "Ministries of Prayer," and chapter 5, "Ministries of Social Outreach" (sections on Hospital Calling and Crisis Comfort) in this manual.

In addition to the church's various ministries of healing, there are also opportunities for healing powers to be evidenced in daily life. In the home, for instance, parents should be instructing their children to see Jesus not only as Saviour and Lord, but as their Source for everything - including good health. Jesus is the Great Physician, but too often children see their parents reach for a bottle of pills or call a doctor without so much as a brief prayer about their ailments. It is rather incongruous to send a child to Sunday school to hear about Jesus' miraculous healing power and then never rely upon it in real life. Children should be taught to pray for themselves when they are sick and to intercede for others who are ill. The father, as "priest" of the household, should lay hands upon his family whenever there is a need; mother can offer up prayers for healing along with the usual

functions of kissing hurts, putting on Band-aids, and applying oint-
ment to skinned knees. It also is good to instruct the family members
to seek the causes for their maladies. If the illness is the result
of poor health habits or physical reactions to sin, there needs to be
corrective action as well as prayer and medication. The corrective
action may include confession. In fact, it is never amiss to ask the
Lord to reveal any hidden sin or the reasons for suffering, as this
will be a step toward treatment of the causes and not just the symptoms.

In one family where prayers for healing were a regular part of
the household routine, a mother once overheard her young daughter
playing house with a neighbor child. Both little girls' dolls were
"suffering" from tummy aches. While the neighbor child applied a toy
hotwater bottle to her doll's stomach, the other little girl laid her
hands on her doll's midsection and closed her eyes. "Dear Jesus,"
she prayed, "please make my baby well. Thank you. Amen." The mother
was gratified that lessons of Christian living were being learned and
practiced even by her youngest child. Children become what they are
taught, and they always learn more from example than from precept.

The church and the home are not the only places where the ministry of healing should be practiced. Once a Christian gets over the
initial embarrassment of breaking the ice, he will find that people
generally accept the suggestion to be prayed for during an illness or
difficulty. Sometimes, if there is a reluctance on the part of the
person who is suffering, the prayers must be offered silently. But
most times, if the suggestion for prayer is put in the form of a
question (such as, "Would you like me to pray for you?"), there will
be a positive response. The prayer does not have to be long or formal.
The important thing is turning the attention away from the problem and
toward the One who can do something about it.

Praying for fellow workers (at luch time, coffee-break time, or
before or after work) is both a ministry to the sick (or troubled) and
a witness to the Christian faith. People, even those who may disagree
with the witness's denomination or doctrine, cannot help but be touched
by one who is unafraid to call upon God on behalf of others. Such an
act says more about loving concern for others than all the words in the
world.

It may be appropriate here to share a true-life example of how a
praying Christian shared God's healing love and her own testimony for
Jesus at work. The woman was employed at a place where prayer and
Christian witnessing were not popular - the public school system. She
was a high school teacher, known among the students as "The Queen of
the Jesus Freaks." Even though she took a great deal of ribbing, both
gentle teasing and overt criticism for her faith, she was always available to offer prayers and help to the students. Even those who felt
the most threatened by her would come to her secretly (when none of
their peers were around to ridicule) and say, "Hey, my dad is going
into the hospital for surgery. Will you pray for him?" or "My girl
friend needs your prayers." This woman met with a group of students

before school each morning for a prayer time. They prayed for the school, the faculty, the students at test time (both examinations and the tests and trials of life), and any individual's needs as they were made known. When this teacher directed a school play, each rehearsal began with prayer. To the surprised actors and crew she would quip, "We need all the help we can get!" Many miracles and healings resulted as prayer became a regular part of the production - praying for help in memorizing lines, praying for faulty sound equipment, praying for attitudes that needed healing. The most impressive and miraculous answered prayer came on opening night. The production was a musical and the pianist was too ill to perform. She was a Jewish girl who was coming down with strep throat. She was running a high fever and was ready to leave for home, which would have meant the cancellation of the show. The other students in the production, in desperation, brought the Jewish girl to the teacher for prayer just a brief time before the curtain was to rise. The teacher told them, "It's obvious we need a miracle if the Lord wants us to put on this play tonight, but I don't know how to pray except through Jesus Christ. I know the Jewish faith doesn't recognize praying to Jesus . . . I know! I'll pray in the name of your Messiah because I believe that's Jesus anyway." When, at the conclusion of the prayer, the Jewish girl looked up with tear-filled eyes, she said, "The pain in my throat and the fever are gone. I think I like your Jesus!" Many of the young people who stood around observing either became Christians or had their faith strengthened as a result of a simple prayer for healing offered in a very unlikely place by a woman who was unafraid to put her faith on the line. People everywhere need to take the healing power of Jesus with them to work, to social events, and to their neighborhoods. How many missed opportunities for Jesus to touch a life have been the result of a Christian's reluctance or lack of courage to pray?

There may be Christians who find such overt confrontations offensive or who simply are too shy to pray aloud for anyone. But they can still be used as prayer channels. They can distribute books on healing or give a prayer card (an appropriate prayer for healing printed on a small calling card). Others have found an effective ministry in sending cards with faith-building Scriptures on them to those who are suffering. By adding a simple, "I'm praying for you" to the card, there is the quiet testimony of faith brought forth. By whatever method one is led to minister, everyone in the body of Christ can have a part in sharing Jesus' healing power and love with those in need of them.


The Use of Scriptures in Healing

Faith-building Scriptures which may be effectively used in the healing ministry include the following:

"I will permit to be put upon you none of these diseases, for I am the Lord that heals you" (Ex. 15:26).

"Jesus Christ makes you whole" (Acts 9:34).

"Attend to my words, for they are life unto those that find them and health to all their flesh" (Prov. 4:20-22).

"He gave them power against unclean spirits to cast them out, and to heal all manner of sickness and all manner of disease" (Matt. 10:1).

"Heal the sick, cleanse the lepers, raise the dead, cast out devils; freely you have received, freely give" (Matt. 10:8).

"Heal the sick and say unto them, The Kingdom of God is come nigh unto you" (Luke 10:9).

"Beloved, I wish above all things that you may prosper and be in health, even as your soul prospers" (III John 1:2).

"He that believes on me [Jesus], the works that I do shall he do also; and greater works. Whatsoever you shall ask in my name, that will I do" (John 14:12-13).

"The prayer of faith shall save the sick, and the Lord shall raise him up. The effectual fervent prayer of a righteous man avails much" (James 5:15-16).

"Unto you that fear my name shall the Sun of Righteousness arise with healing in his wings" (Mal. 4:2).

"If you can believe, all things are possible to him that believes" (Mark 9:23).

"[Jesus] healed all that were sick that it might be fulfilled which was spoken by Isaiah the prophet, saying, Himself took our infirmities, and bare our sicknesses" (Matt. 8:16-17).

The Bible is an excellent source book for those involved in healing or those interested in learning more on the subject. First, the Scriptures are a source of comfort to those in misery, whether it be of body, mind (soul), or spirit. Second, the use of Bible verses such as those quoted above can build faith and turn the ailing person's thoughts toward the Great Physician. Third, the study of Scripture (especially those parts which tell us how Jesus and the early apostles ministered healing gifts) provides a guide to emulate and a reference source for those interested in healing. Fourth, the Scriptures have healing power inherently within them because they are not the words of human beings but the supernaturally inspired revelations of the Holy Spirit. The Word of God is life and health (cf. Prov. 4:22). The Scriptures give hope when all hope is gone: "Whatsoever things were written aforetime were written for our learning, that we through comfort and patience of the Scriptures might have hope" (Rom. 15:4). Last, the use of the Scriptures in the ministry of healing will act as a safeguard against error. There are many false doctrines and peculiar beliefs about healing throughout the world. The safest place to check them out for accuracy is with the Word of God. Any pattern for administering healing that is in opposition to scriptural patterns should be suspect. Those who minister healing gifts must remember to be cautious, for "You do err, not knowing the Scriptures" (Matt. 22:29).

## Hindrances to Healing

There are many reasons why some people who are sick do not get well, even after much prayer for healing. It is good to know some things which can clog up the prayer channel to hinder God's healing power from flowing freely and some reasons why every prayer may not be answered according to man's immediate desires and expectations. It should be noted that none of these hindrances are insurmountable barriers (for God's grace, after all, knows no limitation). The following areas should be examined, rather, as points of inquiry whenever healing is needed.

1. Sin: Psalm 66:18 says, "If I regard iniquity in my heart, the Lord will not hear me." Sometimes a prayer channel is clogged by unconfessed sin. At other times, the sin may have been confessed to the Lord, but there are wrongs that need to be righted. One cannot just say to God that he is sorry for stealing from his neighbor or for offending someone, and then not take the necessary steps toward restitution and reconciliation which the individual situation requires. Although any sin can be a barrier to physical, mental, and spiritual health, there are four areas that may need special attention.

   (a) Unforgiveness: Forgiving and being forgiven are keys to healthful living. Unforgiveness becomes like a cancer that eats away at its victim. Even though one may not approve of the actions of others, he can, like Jesus, say, "Father, forgive them; they know not what they do." Bitterness, anger, resentment, revenge, and many other sins often spring from the sin of unforgiveness, causing the spiritual, emotional, and even physical degeneration of the one harboring the unforgiving spirit. It is important to remember that forgiveness begins in the will and not the emotions. The moment one determines by an act of his will to forgive, the door to a healing begins to open.

   (b) Sexual sins: Problems in the area of sex are universal. Satan always wants to pervert the beauty of sex as it was intended by God for married love. One remains vulnerable to such evil influences until he becomes the sexual being God wants for him to be by surrendering the life force and passions to the control of the Holy Spirit. This includes renouncing all sexual practices contrary to Scripture: fornication, incest, concupiscence (lust), adultery, bestiality, perversion (homo-

186

sexuality, sodomy, etc.), and even lust turned inward (masturbation, illicit fantasies, etc.). Guilt feelings attached to such sexual practices can bring about ill health; moreover, good health in mind, body, or spirit may be deterred until such guilt feelings are dealt with from a Christian viewpoint.

(c) Occult involvement: Research has indicated that the two most prevalent results of occult involvement are mental disorders and suicide. Today's Health, a magazine published by the American Medical Association, gave warning of the dangers in this way: "The new occult craze - and that is just what it is - has given rise to all manner of flimflam and hocus-pocus with people's health."* Any dealings in the occult realm - divination, supernatural psychic experiences, spiritualism, witchcraft, occult games, astrology, ESP, hypnotism and the like - are not only potential health hazards but also idolatry (a breaking of the first commandment by looking to a source other than God for knowledge, aid, or guidance). The Scriptures say that such activity is "an abomination to the Lord." When one looks to mediums, horoscopes, Ouija Boards, or cults rather than to Scripture, prayer, and the church, some form of ill health may result, not to mention the separation from God that such unscriptural practices portend.

(d) Abortion: Those who have either had an abortion or given advice or aid to someone seeking an abortion often have unresolved guilt feelings, sometimes on a subconscious level, which can create a poor self-concept, strange compulsions, or other symptoms of "disease." In the author's counseling experience, it has become customary to encourage those so involved to confess abortion as "the sin of murder." Even though abortion is a controversial subject upon which even clergy do not agree, the therapeutic value of confession cannot be disputed. The taking of a life is not the unpardonable sin (Moses and David were murderers who were forgiven and used of God in mighty ways). For many people, to excuse or condone abortion is to leave the problem unresolved, to allow the emotional trauma of the experience to lie underground and to fester in the subconscious mind, only to have the guilt attached to it reappear in other symptoms or ailments. But once it is given a name, confessed, and forgiven, there is a resulting release from guilt (whether or not the guilt is consciously acknowledged).

---

*Glen F. Loyd and Theodore Irwen, "How Quackery Thrives on the Occult --Devil Doctors and the Gullible," Today's Health, November 1970, p.21.

Even though trends of modern thinking tend to put a stamp of approval upon sexual permissiveness, the occult, abortion, and the like, there is within each person a desire for moral and spiritual purity which has been nurtured by the Holy Spirit and Judaic-Christian morality and tradition. No matter how many surveys or people of authority say that such things are acceptable, if the conscience says something different, the resulting conflict will breed fertile soil for some form of degeneration - ill health, mental problem, or spiritual unrest. Confession should always accompany a prayer for healing. Jesus himself often said "Thy sins are forgiven thee" as well as "Take up thy bed and walk." Because the ills of mind, body, and spirit are so intertwined, confession of sin is often the first step toward wholeness. And because the four areas mentioned above are strongholds from which Satan can wage further warfare, special attention should be given to them. For instance, participation in the occult can lead to demonic possession, mental problems, or even suicide. Resentment and an unforgiving attitude can result in physical manifestations such as arthritis, ulcers, or high blood pressure. An abortion can lead to depression, guilt-induced anxiety, or self-hatred. Sexual impurity may lead to unnatural or violent acts, emotional breakdowns, or spiritual bankruptcy. Sin begets sin, one problem leading to another on a downward spiral. For healing to take place, the root of the problem must be discovered and dealt with before outward manifestations or related symptoms will go away.

2. Insufficient Instruction: Many people go unhealed because they are ignorant of God's will to heal them, ignorant of the teachings about healing in the Scriptures, or ignorant about the power and authority of a believer over the debilitating influences of Satan. There is sickness in the world for the same reason there is sin - because of the fall of humankind. As a liar and thief, Satan wants to tell humanity that it cannot be healed, and he wants to rob humanity of health in mind (soul), body, and spirit. The Lord is the Healer, Deliverer, Restorer, and Reconciler, but oftentimes people, in their great ignorance, look to every other source for their well-being. Such insufficient instruction is overcome by sufficient instruction. Or, as St. John puts it, "The truth shall make you free" (John 8:32).

3. Unbelief: Signs and wonders, including the wonders of healing, are promised to "them that believe" (Mark 16:17). There are all kinds of unbelief that hinder the healing ministry. Those who are not attached to a believing body suffer the consequences of "community unbelief." Even Jesus had problems in Nazareth because of the lack of faith there, and he could not do the miracles he wanted to perform. There is the problem of doubt that creeps in both before and after a healing. For that reason, those involved in healing minis-

188

tries should keep all doubters out of the sick room while they minister. (Remember how Jesus took only his closest followers with him into the room where Jairus' daughter was placed? The doubters were left on the other side of the door.) The minister must not doubt God's power to heal: "Neither be of doubtful mind" (Luke 12:29). Many people, like doubting Thomas, must "see" before they will believe. But Jesus said the blessed ones were those who believed without seeing, for Christians are expected to walk by faith, and not by sight. Often it is necessary to think and act like one who has already been healed, even before symptoms disappear. At other times, a person who is weak in faith can be aided by an intercessor who will believe for him or her. Whether one is on the giving or receiving end of healing, there must be confidence in God to perform the healing necessary: "Now the God of hope fill you with all joy and peace in believing . . ." (Rom. 15:13).

4. Erroneous Thinking: Not only have many people been deprived of the truth about healing, but also many have been filled full of false teachings. Human traditions and unscriptural philosophies have a way of sounding right when they have been perpetuated long enough. There are many people who believe that all sickness is God's will, that the age of miracles has passed, and that the healing gifts of the Holy Spirit belonged to a past dispensation, but are no longer at work today. Even churches often become tangled in erroneous doctrines. Healing practices and beliefs must check out with Scripture or they can become Satan's counterfeits designed to bring on more problems rather than to solve the ones at hand. Some erroneous methods to be avoided include healing through spiritism (mediums or psychic healers); through hypnotism or other mind-controlling methods; through witchcraft or "spells" or other occult means; through self-help or humanistic methods that advocate mind-over-matter techniques apart from the power of the Holy Spirit; and through bloodless cult practitioners.

5. Avoidance of Natural of Health Laws: Improper diet, over- or under-eating, lack of sleep or rest, lack of exercise, overindulgence in tobacco, drugs, or alcohol, and any other over- or under-indulgences that create an imbalance in God's natural order of things - any or all of these things can become barriers to healing. The body must be maintained as the Temple of the Holy Spirit; otherwise, it will break down as does any machine not cared for properly.

6. Improper Living Habits: Overwork and worry are concommitants of twentieth-century life. Everyone is in a hurry, working under pressure, and suffering from free-flowing anxiety. Doctors say that the majority of the patients they see have psychosomatic disorders (physical

ills brought on by mental or emotional strain). One of the greatest barriers to health is the failure to keep a quiet time daily, a time to let the spirit catch up with the body, which moves in perpetual motion. Isaiah 30:15 says, "In quietness and confidence shall be your strength." There are many, many Scripture verses that advocate "waiting upon the Lord." For those who are too busy to do so, the price is broken strength, broken bodies, broken health. Silence is an unexplored world to many people, a world associated with unfruitfulness and powerless inactivity. Nothing could be further from the truth. Silence will open up new vistas of understanding; it will be therapy to an overwrought mind and body; it will renew the spirit, it will draw one nearer to God; it will cause one to grow. Listening - deep, concentrated listening to the still, small voice of the Infinite - and regular times of quiet meditation are re-storers. For those whose energies are sapped and whose minds are weary and anxious, there is a place of renewal which it is risky to avoid: "They that wait upon the Lord shall <u>renew</u> their strength" (Isa. 40:31). This is not trans-cendental meditation or out-of-body experiences, which have become popular counterfeits of healthful restoration. It is a regular divine appointment of drawing apart from the frenzy of a busy schedule to get one's life regulated, one's priorities in order, and one's body and mind in submission to the Spirit. The body and mind are likely to break down unless such an appointment for healing is kept.

7. <u>Demonic Problems</u>: If a problem is demonic in origin, it must be dealt with as such, not as a physical ailment to be treated by medicine or even by prayers for healing alone. More will be said on this subject in the discussion on the deliverance ministry (pp. 209-11, 217-18, below).

8. <u>Lukewarm Spirituality</u>: The miracle workers of the Bible, those who saw the hand of God moving in mighty ways, and those who saw effective results of their ministries and prayers, were not spiritual weaklings or "do-nothings." They were people who were willing to pay the price for their faith ("unto whom much is given, much is required"). Such people were often ridiculed or persecuted for their faith, but it was a price they were glad to pay. Many people today want all the benefits and blessings of Christianity, but none of the responsibilities or sacri-fices. They try to walk with one foot in the Kingdom and one foot in the world. The Lord's greatest blessings will not rest upon those who are lukewarm, but upon those who are willing to endure the heat of fiery trials, fully realizing that the Lord is a rewarder of "those who dili-gently seek him."

9. <u>Regarding Symptoms More Than Promises</u>: Many people look at their ailments more than they look to the Lord. By

focusing upon their problems, the problems increase. Conversely, placing undivided attention upon the Lord will cause him to increase. Faith must be based upon the promises of Scripture, not upon improvement or changing symptoms. Healing often demands singlemindedness and unswerving dedication. A negative attitude or a constant overconcern about matters of health can often bring the thing that is most feared upon the patient. "As a man thinks in his heart, so is he."

10. Letting Satan Get the Upper Hand: Either a Christian has one foot upon Satan's neck, or it's the other way around. Alert to any advantage a Christian will give him, Satan is swift to move in and steal away a healing even after it is manifested. Christians must learn not to cast away their confidence when testing time comes or if symptoms return. They must not let the ridicule or disbelief of others convince them that they are not or cannot be healed. The only voice one should attend to during a healing process is the voice of the Spirit. Satan will send doubt, discouragement, and confusion to hinder a healing process, but the Lord will provide hope, encouragement, and peace of mind.

11. Grieving or Quenching the Spirit: One of the nine gifts of the Holy Spirit is healing (I Cor. 12:9). Often an opportunity for healing is missed when the Spirit is ready to move but people are fearful, unwilling, or disinterested in moving with him. Paul told Timothy to "stir up the gift within him." Those who have received the Spirit are expected to flow in obedience to the promptings of that Spirit. Sometimes it may mean appearing foolish to others, but it is better than grieving or quenching the Spirit.

12. Failure to Personalize: Often people say they believe in the supernatural power of the Lord to heal, but they don't take it personally. They think the Lord is interested only in other people, that the promises of the Bible are for someone else, and that manifestations of the Spirit such as healing are general conceptions rather than personalized specifics. Sometimes it helps to work through the causes of such a philosophy. If it is because of guilt or feelings of unworthiness ("The Lord would never bother to heal someone as bad as I am"), the person must be led to understand that God's grace is not dependent upon anyone's deserving of it. His love, forgiveness, and healing graces are for the unjust as well as the just. It may also be beneficial to put one's own name into the promises of Scripture in order to personalize God's message to the individual: "By Jesus' stripes, (name) is healed" or "The prayer of faith shall save (name)."

191

13. A Need for Inner Healing: If bondages to the past, unhealed hurts, or unhappy memories are barriers to wholeness, there may be the need for prayer and counseling with someone trained and approved in this ministry. Often problems of the present have roots in the past, and Jesus must be asked to minister to the little child of the past as well as the adult of today. When Jesus is invited into an unhappy scene, past or present, the picture changes as he ministers love and corrective action. (This is dealt with in more detail in the Inner Healing section of this chapter, below.)

14. God Is Using the Ailment for a Purpose: It is risky even to mention this because of the danger of believing that illness is "God's will." Although God wants perfect wholeness for his children (just as earthly parents do for theirs), there are those rare occasions when the Lord uses sickness as an object leasson or "attention-getter." In his infinite wisdom, he knows just the circumstances to use to bring about a change or corrective action in a life. There are times when he must make someone lie down in order for that person to "look up." Perhaps there is a deeper healing of the spirit which could never be attended to if one were well and active or involved in other pursuits. Although in most instances Satan is the destroyer who brings people their ailments and troubles, there are those special times when God is using extreme measures for the perfecting of a person in some area, for a witness to others, or for a purpose the person can never fully understand. Isaiah 45:7 says, "I am the Lord. I form light and create darkness; I make peace and create evil. I the Lord do all these things." It is not incongruous with the teaching that God is love to assume that God will use peculiar circumstances to perfect his children or even break his own laws if necessary in order to bring good from a seemingly evil situation. Do not earthly parents chastise, often with extreme measures when no other way is open, when it is for a child's good in the end? "All things [not some things or just those things we understand clearly] work together for good to them that love God, to them who are the called according to his [not our] purpose" (Rom. 8:28).

15. The Timing Is God's, Not People's: If every prayer were answered immediately and if every circumstance could be controlled by an act of will or a quick prayer request, then people would be in control of the universe, not God. There would be no need for faith. There are times when all the rules seem to be broken. God is not bound to act as people think he usually acts or should act. There are times, for instance, when the Lord miraculously heals someone who is deeply involved in sin, who does not evidence believing faith, who is lukewarm spiritually, who practices improper health habits, and who thinks erroneously or practices false doctrines. These are exceptions, to be sure,

but they nevertheless display the unpredictability of an omnipotent God. If this is true, why bother to pray for healing at all? If God is going to do whatever he wants to do anyway, why should people get involved? Because we have been commanded to do so. The Lord has chosen to make human beings his partners in the work he wants to accomplish. The fact that we cannot figure out God's every motive and action does not prevent us from being used. The important thing is to pray for understanding of what the Lord is doing in the "now" - not what he did yesterday or five minutes ago, but what he is saying at this particular moment. We see only in part; God's ways are not our ways. But there are those glorious moments when the Lord draws back the curtain and allows us to see his divine purposes and to share in them. If someone has followed all the "rules" and prayed all the right prayers and done all the scriptural things and still remains unhealed, what then? Then we must simply hang on by raw faith and trust when everything says give up. We must say with Job, "Shall we receive good at the hand of God, and shall we not receive evil? Though he slay me, yet will I trust in him." In God's perfect timing, all things will become clear. We must be patient to wait for that understanding. Someone who calculated the formula in Scripture "A thousand years to man is as a day to God" determined that our entire lifetime is only about fifteen minutes to God. Those healings and unanswered prayers that we think are coming slowly may be, according to God's clock, very rapid recovery processes.

## Inner Healing

Up to this point, emphasis has been on physical or "outer" healing. But wholeness of the body is not the only concern the Lord has for his children. He wants to minister to the total person - to heal hurt emotions, sick minds, and wounded spirits. This is inner healing.

Inner healing is known by many different names - healing of memories, prayer and counseling, healing of the past, renewing of the mind, and prayers for the subconscious, to name a few. Basically, the ministry involves offering the past to Jesus, so that his cleansing, healing love can restore a life that may have been shattered by traumatic experiences or deep hurts.

It has already been emphasized that a human being, as a trinity, is capable of dis-ease in mind (soul), body, or spirit, and that an ailment in one part of a person's being can affect the other parts as well. The following illustration may make this clearer:

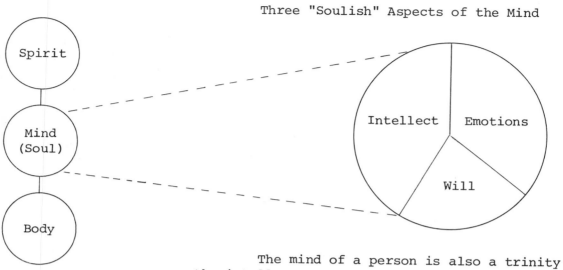

Three "Soulish" Aspects of the Mind

The mind of a person is also a trinity
- the intellect, the will, and the emotions.

These soulish areas of a person's being (emotions, intellect, and will) are what may be called "Satan's Playground." The enemy concentrates on this area because it is to his advantage to do so. If Satan can control one's intellect and make one believe that he or she is too smart to need God or the crutch of religion, or if he can capture the emotions and make a person ruled by anger, lust, jealousy, hatred, evil passions, or other negative emotions, or if he can get a person to refuse to submit to the will of the Lord, then Satan has that person at a decided disadvantage. This is why it is so important to surrender these soulish areas to the control of the Spirit.

The problem here is that much of the human mind is below the awareness level and out of the consciousness of the person. Like an iceberg, which has much more of itself below the surface than the tip that is exposed, the subconscious mind of a person contains many hidden depths where ailments and problems may be lurking undetected by the conscious mind. Psychologists agree that man's memory bank in the subconscious mind is a reservoir of every experience and every emotional feeling from conception to the present. Even those things a person has forgotten with the conscious mind are still stored in the subconscious. Like a computer, the subconscious "tape records" all emotional responses to past stimuli, causing people to react in the present based upon what has happened in the past. If hurtful or traumatic memories have submerged, they may surface unexpectedly, especially when a similar threatening situation occurs and the same emotional responses seem appropriate. People may not even realize why they are reacting as they do or why they feel as they do. The key is buried in memories they cannot remember with the conscious mind.

The subconscious mind also has been compared to a garbage can or a basement where all kinds of clutter collect - all the guilt, pain, and negative feelings associated with unhappy memories. These feelings stay locked up, but they send up signals to the conscious mind that everything is not right. There is uneasiness, depression, or pain, but the person may not know why. There may be uncontrollable actions, compulsions, or strange reactions, which have their reasons for being stored away among this unrevealed collection of clutter.

The cure for this situation is to ask Jesus to "dump the garbage" or to "erase the tape recording" in the subconscious. Jesus can replace old hurts and traumatizing memories with his healing love. He can reveal a hidden sin, long forgotten, and forgive it to set one free from vague, unexplainable feelings of guilt. He can take down the ugly pictures hanging on the walls of the subconscious mind and replace them with peaceful, beautiful scenes. It is rather like doing a thorough housecleaning - getting into forgotten corners of closets and drawers - rather than doing the "general housekeeping" of regular forms of prayer.

The advantages of inner healing over psychotherapy or other psychological methods of dealing with problems in the subconscious are these: (1) Psychiatrists or psychological counselors may discover the source of one's problem, but insight into reasons for behavior is not the same as a cure for it. When the Holy Spirit goes back in time to point out a wound, he not only reveals it, but also brings Jesus there to heal it. (2) Professional counseling methods often take a great deal of time, sometimes years of therapy, and a great deal of money besides. Inner healing counselors find that the Holy Spirit works much more quickly because of the supernatural power being brought to bear upon the need. Also, inner healing should be the freely given ministry offered to the body of Christ as a love gift (usually from one whose own past has been healed by Jesus) and, as such, does not require any payment but that of love. (3) Strictly humanistic methods can do nothing if the problem is spiritual in nature. Inner healing ministers to the total personality, including one's spiritual needs. (4) Some of the teachings of psychology and psychiatry are in opposition to scriptural teachings. When a trained inner healing counselor is operating under the anointing of the Holy Spirit, there is less danger of error or deviation from scriptural teachings.

Who Needs Inner Healing?

Even happy, well-adjusted Christians are often surprised to find that an inner healing session reveals hidden needs and problems requiring attention. Going for inner healing will help anyone who desires to give more of self to the Lord and to be freed from even unconscious sins or hurts of the past. Although everyone should benefit from this prayer and counseling ministry, those who should definitely consider receiving this ministry are people with traumatic pasts or deep-rooted problems; people with unhappy childhoods (especially those with pasts involving rebellion, fears, insecurity or rejection); people in bondage to other people or habits; people with wounded spirits; people who cannot love (parents, others, God, or themselves); people who cannot relate to God as a Heavenly Father because of some past experience; people who cannot forgive (either the problem of forgiving someone else, themselves, or God); people who act and react in strange or unexplainable ways beyond their understanding of them.

Inner healing is not just delving into the mind to dig up sordid details of an unhappy past; it is allowing the healing light of Jesus Christ to shine upon all the dark, hidden areas that Satan wants to keep hidden. When they are brought to light and healed, there is freedom where once there was bondage and peace where once was fear and turmoil.

### Scriptural Allegories to Inner Healing

Perhaps a good way to understand the inner healing process clearly is by examining two Old Testament books which depict allegorical counterparts to this ministry. Describing something as vague as the subconscious mind and the forgotten past may be difficult without some kind of tangible "handle" to connect to the intangibles. Both the book of Haggai and the book of Nehemiah can be used for making such connections. It is suggested that the reader take the time to read over these two, brief Old Testament books for further understanding of the following comparisons.

The book of Haggai opens with the command to rebuild the Lord's house. The former glory of the Temple was lost when the Hebrews were carried away into captivity and everything in the holy city was destroyed. This represents humanity's former glory in its sinless state in Eden, prior to the fall. Satan carried away humankind captive, just as the exiled Hebrews had been carried away. When the command to rebuild the temple was given by the Lord, he rebuked the people for being more concerned about building their own comfortable houses than building a house in which the Spirit of the Lord could dwell. This is analogous to humankind's carnal interests and spiritual neglect. Often people are more concerned about fleshly pleasures than their spiritual well-being. The temple represents the spirit (God-consciousness) of a person, which must not be left in ruins, but carefully and prayerfully rebuilt. The contaminated sacrifices described in Haggai 2:13-14 represent the "uncleanness" that can be passed on from one generation to another. Just as the contaminated priests could pass on the contamination to all they touched, so can people "inherit" the evil practices of their forefathers ("The sins of the fathers visited upon the children"). The contaminations could be passed on by the unclean hands of the priests to innocent bystanders. In the same way, a person is often the victim of other people's sins and may suffer at times for things he or she is not responsible for personally. The temple lay in ruins because of the destructive work of the enemy. Satan, as the enemy of humankind, likewise tries to destroy humanity's spirit and hold people captive to sin. God's judgment rested upon the people who ignored the ruined temple and included problems like drought, famine, and economic crises. Those who neglect their "spiritual temple" (relationship to the Lord) will also find the result is God's judgment - problems in life which come as a result from being out of the will of God. Just as the people were hungry physically because of the drought and famine, people today are hungry spiritually when they are out of a proper relationship with their Creator. The problems of the Hebrews are analogous to the problems people face when they need inner healing.

Notice that the command from God to rebuild the temple was given both to the priest and to the governor, along with the command to go to the mountain for the building materials. This indicates the inter-relatedness of people's spiritual and temporal natures. People must build both "houses"; their spirit cannot help but interact with their mind and their flesh; and all must be constructed according to God's blueprint. The going to the mountain represents looking up to the Lord for the proper "tools" with which to build. In Haggai 2:8-9, the Lord promises that the glory of the new temple, which will be built, will be greater than the former glory of the old temple. The comparison to humanity here indicates that the one who is changed and restructured by Jesus Christ is even greater than Adam in his first state. Adam never experienced the redeeming love and life-changing miracle of adoption into God's family through the atonement of Jesus.

Blessings were bestowed upon the Hebrews as soon as the foundation was laid for the new temple. They did not have to wait until its completion for God to lift the curses upon the land, for the drought and famine ceased immediately. In the same way, the curse upon humankind is canceled immediately and blessings come to Christians as soon as they begin rebuilding their lives according to the specifications in God's plans. People do not have to wait until they are completely rebuilt (perfected) because blessings come when the foundation stone (Jesus Christ) is laid. The rewards that came to the Hebrews for their obedience in rebuilding the temple included the promise that the "Desire of all Nations" would inhabit the temple; the promise that opposing kingdoms and enemies would be destroyed; and the promise that the obedient builder would be rewarded as a "signet ring upon the Lord's finger." These promises have great significance for the analogy's counterpart, obedient Christians. They will have Jesus, the Desire of all Nations, living within them. They will have the power to overthrow all satanic power and influence. They will receive a just reward. A signet ring represented the honor and authority of the king. Believers who build their lives according to God's directions become honored children of the King of kings!

The book of Haggai is like step one for the Christian - getting the foundation laid for the Christian life and starting the "reconstruction" process: clearing away the rubble of the enemy's destruction and starting a new life in Christ. The book of Nehemiah picks up where Haggai leaves off. After the spiritual foundation is laid, there is still more construction work and "clearing away" required. After the Hebrews built the temple, they were commanded to rebuild the walls of the city, which the enemies had also destroyed. These walls represent the soulish areas of people (will, intellect, emotions). The wall around the temple of the Holy Spirit in people is their personality, which must also be constructed according to God's divine plan.

The Hebrews were commanded to rebuild the walls around the city for several reasons. Walls were needed for identity, to draw the borders of the city, to set limits, and to give a sense of belonging to those who dwelt inside. Without walls, the city had no boundaries, no sense of relationship and identity to set it apart from other places. Walls were also needed for protection (to give security to those inside the walls and to keep away the oppressive forces who would assault them from without). Just as the temple represents the human spirit, so the walls represent the human soul or one's total personality. The spiritual temple is built within people when they accept Jesus as their Lord and Saviour, but then begins a full-scale reconstruction process in the personality. If he cannot have humanity's spirit, Satan wants to tear down a person's personality and assault his or her soul. For people to have a sense of identity and security, the walls of the personality must be rebuilt wherever Satan has torn them down in the past. Sometimes the tearing-down process occurs consciously, but at other times the destructive processes occurred in the forgotten past. Perhaps this illustration will focus the analogy more clearly in the mind:

<u>Picture of a Person of God</u>:          <u>Picture of the City of God</u>:

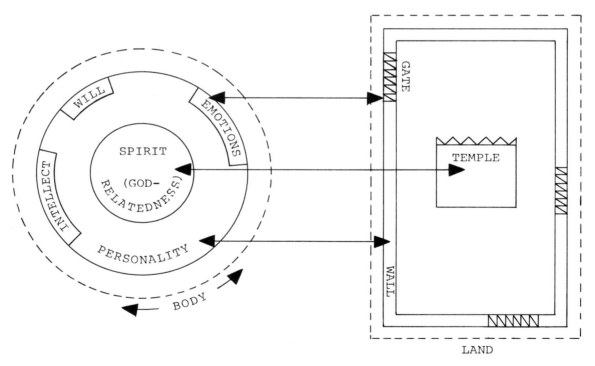

Both the temple and the spirit of the human being are in center positions. People's God-relatedness must be the focal point around which everything else revolves. The personality, as the protective wall around the spirit, must have points of access and egress - just as the Jerusalem wall must have gates through which to enter and exit. Just as the Hebrews were warned to guard the gates of the city wall carefully, so Christians must guard the will, intellect, and emotions. An enemy (a negative emotion) can slip in unless a careful watch is kept. The land upon which the city was situated is analogous to the body of a person. If properly cared for and nurtured, it will be productive and fruitful. If neglected, those dependent upon it (the soul and the spirit) will be adversely affected. The land must be cultivated and cared for properly, but it is subject to those who have rulership over it. Likewise, the body must not be in control but, rather, subject to the control of the Spirit.

There are further similarities to be drawn between the teachings in the book of Nehemiah and inner healing. First of all, the name Nehemiah means "Comforter." It is our Comforter, the Holy Spirit, which helps a Christian to rebuild the personality, just as Nehemiah helped the Hebrews to build their city walls. When the Hebrews came out of Babylonian captivity, they were not slaves, as they had been when they came out of Egypt in the days of Moses. They had a national identity. Although they were exiles, they were returning home to their own place, the holy city, Jerusalem. Christians, likewise, are no longer slaves to the world and sin when they begin their pilgrimage toward their Heavenly Goal. They have the name and identity of Jesus Christ.

It is significant that the Lord commanded that the building of the city walls be accompanied by the reading of the Holy Scriptures. Ezra, the priest, read the Law of God to the workers, who worshiped as they labored. That is a true picture of the life of a Christian. The recovery of Satan's strongholds in a Christian's life must be accompanied by the Word (applying the teachings of Scripture to daily life) and by worshipful praise. It should also be noted that the workers had to stay armed and alert for enemies who wanted to hinder the work they were doing. Christians also have to be alert, armed, and ready for Satan's attacks along the way. Satan does not surrender ground willingly or without a fight. But just as the workers were armed with weapons to drive away those who would hinder them, so Christians can put on the whole armor of God as a protection against the wiles of the devil.

The book of Nehemiah begins in humility and ends in purification and joy. Nehemiah wept, fasted, and prayed when he heard that the walls of Jerusalem were destroyed. The Holy Spirit weeps and intercedes for God's children who are broken and battered by life. He wants to help the spiritual reconstruction process. The purification of the Christian's life comes when the Christian clears away the "rubble" of sin and unhealed hurts that tear down the personality and give ground to the enemy. Just as the rebuilt walls meant identity and protection for the Jews, so a strong, secure personality means self-confidence and stability for a Christian. Although in the spiritual sense, a person becomes a "new creature in Christ" (old things pass away and all things become new) at the moment of conversion to Christianity, there is still much "rebuilding" needed before all the refuse of the old, sinful nature is completely cleared away. To review the proper blueprint for this process of reconstruction, remember these steps to inner healing:*

_____

*The analogy from the book of Nehemiah is an adaptation of a teaching by the Reverend Jack Hayford, Church on the Way, Van Nuys, California.

199

1. First, build the holy place (the spirit must be built first upon Jesus as the only sure foundation).

2. Build the walls of protection (submit the personality to the Holy Spirit who, as a "master builder," will clear away the rubble of the past and reclaim the strongholds conquered by Satan as well as "reconstruct" the personality according to the Lord's divine blueprint).

3. Guard the gates (set a careful watch over the emotions, the intellect, and the will so that Satan cannot gain a stronghold in these crucial areas).

4. Accompany the building process with the reading of God's Word, praise, and worship (establish spiritual disciplines for nurture and growth).

5. Stay armed and alert for the enemy (be ready to counter Satan's attacks).

6. Begin in humility (submission to the plan of God and the leading of the Holy Spirit).

7. Conclude in purification (do all that is necessary to build up a holy self-confidence and stability in a God-centered personality).

### The Scriptural Basis for Inner Healing

Some critics of the inner healing ministry say that it is not valid scripturally, that one cannot find an example of Jesus performing the ministry of inner healing, and that it is dangerous to delve into another's subconscious mind for any reason - even for the purpose of healing. Such people say that the Scriptures record healings of physical illness and exorcism (casting out evil spirits), but where, they ask, did Jesus ever heal the unhappy memories of someone's subconscious mind? Let us deal with each of these charges individually, and then the reader can come to his or her own conclusions about the validity of inner healing.

Although it must be admitted that the term subconscious mind does not appear in the Bible, consider the confrontation between Jesus and the woman of Samaria (John 4:3-30). When, through a word of knowledge about her past ("You have had five husbands and he whom you now have is not your husband"), Jesus put his finger on the unhappy, sordid part of her life, he also delivered her from it. In effect, Jesus healed the woman's memories and set her free from her sinful past. It would not be stretching a point to say that Jesus brought about the healing of her past when the woman proclaimed, "Come see a man which told me <u>all things</u> <u>that</u> <u>ever</u> <u>I</u> <u>did</u>. Is not this the Christ?" This woman could not have become a missionary to her whole town had not her past been offered to Jesus for healing. If one draws the line for valid ministries based upon whether or not a term appears in Scripture, then psychiatry, psychological counseling, surgical operations, administration of sacraments, and many other practices would have to be discontinued. Even though Jesus did not use the term sacrament when he instituted the Last Supper, sacramentalists observe the intent and follow that example.

It must also be conceded that the inner healing ministry can be dangerous, as can the ministry of exorcism, counseling, or even evangelism if not performed under the guidance and direction of the Holy Spirit by those trained and approved for ministry. In every form of ministry there is the chance that the minister will make a mistake or that problems may arise, but these inherent dangers do not prevent the ministry from continuing. The answer lies in training and preparing the ministers and in complete reliance upon the Holy Spirit to both direct and correct as necessary. It also involves having ministries submitted to the church and authorities who can judge and control anyone who may be getting into error. (See chapter 10, "Ministries and Activities," for training resources available.)

As to the argument that procedures in inner healing are not supported by teachings of the Bible, consider the following Scriptures which relate to the various aspects of inner healing: (NOTE:   references have been condensed or paraphrased, for economy of space. They are based on the King James and Living Bible versions.)

1. Enemies in the Mind:  We are sometimes alienated by enemies in the mind, but Jesus reconciles us from them (Col. 1:21). As the serpent beguiled Eve through subtlety, so our minds are corrupted from the simplicity in Christ (II Cor. 11:3). Beware of being spoiled through philosophy and deceitful traditions of men, after the world and not after Christ (Col. 2:8). We must cast down imaginations and bring thoughts into captivity and obedience to Christ (II Cor. 10:5). Purge your conscience from dead works (Heb. 9:14). Let the mind be in you which was in Jesus Christ (Phil. 2:5).

2. Jesus' Power to Heal the Past:  Jesus is the same yesterday, today, and forever (Heb. 13:8). The Spirit of the Lord enables Jesus to heal the brokenhearted, to bring liberty to captives, to set free those that are bound, and to comfort those that mourn (Isa. 61:1-3; Luke 4:17-21). Jesus can show us all things that ever we did (John 4:25-29).

3. The Need for Confession:  Confess your faults one to another and pray one for another (James 5:16). If we confess our sins, the Lord is faithful and just to forgive (I John 1:8-9). The blood of Christ cleanses us from all unrighteousness (I John 1:7). If we judge ourselves, we will not be judged of the Lord (I Cor. 11:31). I said, I will confess my transgressions unto the Lord; and the Lord forgave the iniquity of my sin. For this shall every one that is godly pray (Ps. 32:5-6).

4. Healing of Past Memories:  The Lord will bring to light

the hidden things (I Cor. 4:5). Remember not former things; the Lord will do a new thing, blotting out the past (Isa. 43:18-19). The sins of the fathers are visited upon children to the third and fourth generation (Ex. 20:5). Heal my soul, for I have sinned (Ps. 41:4). The spirit of a man will sustain his infirmity, but a wounded spirit, who can bear? (Prov. 18:14). Jesus heals the broken in heart, and binds up their wounds (Ps. 147:3). Be transforemd by the renewing of your mind (Rom. 12:2). Be renewed in the spirit of your mind (Eph. 4:23). Regeneration and renewing come of the Holy Spirit (Tit. 3:5).

5. Breaking Bondages: Be free from the yoke of bondage (Gal. 5:1). Whatsoever you bind on earth shall be bound in heaven, and whatsoever you loose on earth shall be loosed in heaven (Matt. 18:18). You have not received the spirit of bondage, but you have received the Spirit of adoption (Rom. 8:15). You formerly were the servants of sin, but you have obeyed from the heart that form of doctrine delivered to you, being then made free (Rom. 6:17-18). Deliver them who through fear of death were all their lifetime subject to bondage (Heb. 2:15).

6. Exorcism: Jesus gave his followers power against unclean spirits to cast them out and to heal (Matt. 10:1). Cast out demons (Mark 3:15). Bind the strong man (Satan) before casting him out (Matt. 12:28-29). These signs shall follow them that believe: In my name they shall cast out devils (Mark 16:17). The accuser of the brethren (Satan) is cast down, and they overcame him by the blood of the Lamb (Rev. 12:10-11). Even the devils are subject unto us through Jesus' name. We have power to tread on serpents and scorpions, and over all the power of the enemy; and nothing shall by any means hurt us (Luke 10:17-19). We wrestle not against flesh and blood, but against principalities, against powers, against the rulers of the darkness of this world, against spiritual wickedness in high places. Put on the whole armor of God that you may be able to stand against the wiles of the devil (Eph. 6:11-12). Resist the devil and he will flee from you (James 4:7).

7. A Christian's Powers and Promises: God has not given us the spirit of fear, but of power and love and of a sound mind (II Tim. 1:7). Speak, exhort, rebuke with all authority (Tit. 2:15). The Lord will bring to light the hidden things of darkness and will make manifest the counsels of the heart (I Cor. 4:5). I am radiant with joy because of your mercy, for you have listened to my troubles and have seen the crisis in my soul. You have not handed me over to my enemy, but have given me open ground in which to maneuver (Ps. 31:7-8). God is greater than our heart, and knows all things (I John 3:20). Nothing shall be impossible to you (Matt. 17:20). The works that I (Jesus) do shall you do also, and greater works . . . . And what-

soever you shall ask in my name, that will I do (John 14:12-13).

## Methods of Ministry

There are three basic ways in which inner healing may be ministered: a group healing session, a private inner healing appointment for an individual with a trained and qualified counselor, and self-ministry. Each of these has advantages and limitations.

Group Healing Sessions: In a group session, the procedure is more general than specific. The ministry should be performed by trained counselors who have had experience in conducting such sessions. There should be assistant counselors among the group to assist in the event an emergency arises or in case an individual needs personal counseling with a problem that arises from the group session. The leader may begin by mentioning general areas that frequently cause problems, and members of the group may either write down specific memories or problems that come to mind or offer to the Lord in prayer anything that needs healing. Although the exact procedure will depend upon the direction in which the Holy Spirit leads the one conducting the session, the following is a suggested guide for a group experience of inner healing:

1. Prayers for the unborn child of the past. The leader will pray for all members of the group to be released from any negative influences that touched them in the womb. The Holy Spirit may reveal specific things to mention, such as rejection, fear, insecurity, lack of love, etc. The leader may also mention any message of comfort or healing to an individual that comes by way of prophecy or a word of knowledge.

2. Prayers for the early life. The leader will pray for the group as babies and young children, leaving periods of silence in which the Spirit may bring to mind particular things for each one. In one such session, the leader felt led to pray for someone in the group who was dropped as a baby, asking the Lord's healing of the anxiety the little baby felt, the pain, and the trauma of the experience. After the session, an aged woman confessed that she had never forgiven the midwife who dropped and abandoned her to tend her dying mother. The woman's body still held the scars of the early injury, but the deeper injury was the resentment she had felt so many years. She had finally been able to forgive the midwife and release her resentment in the silence of the healing session. Prayers for the childhood years may include relationships that need healing (bondages to parents or other authority figures that need to be broken), fears, hurts, guilts, or insecurities. First experiences of going to school or leaving home are often traumatizing for a youngster. Punishments, rejection by others, and sibling jealousies are also common problems of childhood. Time should be given for confession of childhood sins and time for Jesus to enter each scene of early years to minister to various needs.

3. <u>Prayers for the teenage years</u>. This is usually a very tumultuous time in the life of every individual. The usual process of giving time for confession, asking the Lord to free one from any unhealthy bondages to people or things, and healing of hurtful memories of the past are suggested. A special emphasis should be given to prevalent problems of teenagers - sexual problems, rebellion, unacceptable habits, feelings of inferiority, fears, secret sins, etc. Another common problem of the teens is a questioning of values and even a questioning of religious beliefs, often bringing feelings of guilt for turning away from God or accepted practices of faith. Leaders should also help the group deal with people who led them into sin or those whom they led into sin, and with anything else that the session brings forth.

4. <u>Prayers for the adult life</u>. Each area of life should be offered to the Lord for ministry: family, business, social relationships, and the individual personality. The leader should allow a time of silence after each new area is introduced and wait for the Holy Spirit to deal individually with each one who is listening in quiet meditation. This process must not be hurried or cut and dried. People need time to reflect upon the names of people they have resented, those they have been envious of or hated, those they need to forgive or who need to forgive them, and those with whom there are unhealed hurts. Areas may include pride, selfishness, temptations, fears, self-condemnation, self-pity, profanity, impurity, deceit, lack of faith, greed, intemperence, irreverence, controlling attitudes, possessiveness, etc. Both general areas and specific problems may come to the leader's mind as he or she moves with the Spirit to cleanse and heal. Whether it is a relationship, an emotional problem, a habit pattern, or a sin, Jesus can provide the corrective action needed in the quiet moments of seeking his healing and restoring power.

It must be remembered that there is no particular formula to follow, for, as always, the Lord will deal with each person as an individual. With or without a leader to direct the thinking of the group, people can sit down with pencil and paper in a quiet place free from distractions and interruptions and write down whatever the Spirit may reveal as a sin, hurt, or unhealed area of life. The person should record any name or image that comes, however inconsequential it may seem. Jesus should be invited into every painful memory and asked to perform the corrective action. The person should visualize actually giving each person, situation, or painful experience to Jesus, stepping back, and becoming released. Then the Holy Spirit can be asked to fill every void and to record in the subconscious mind positive, healthy emotional responses wherever the painful ones were. If the problem is too severe or the hurt too deep for the person to deal with alone, he or she should then seek the Lord's guidance in finding the right counselor for further ministry and assistance.

<u>Private Inner Healing Appointments</u>:  If the ministry is to take the form of a private prayer session for an individual, much is normally required in the way of advance preparation.  In order to protect both the counselor and the counselee, it must be repeated that only trained, qualified, and approved ministers should attempt this ministry. People who wish to become involved in this form of counseling and intercessory prayer should experience the ministry firsthand and before attempting to minister it to others.   They should submit themselves to be prayed for not only to receive firsthand experience, but also to rid themselves of any unhealed areas or unresolved conflicts that might become stumbling blocks to them and to others as they minister.  By going for prayer and counsel (both before starting this ministry and any time thereafter when there is need for it), the minister can offer the Lord as cleansed and usable a prayer channel as possible for others.

A novice should serve as an "apprentice" to someone trained and experienced in inner healing before taking the lead in the ministry. It is always wise to minister by twos.  As one prays and the other ministers, many risks are minimized:  deception, mistakes, and getting sidetracked.  It is also helpful to have a group of individuals in prayer elsewhere during an inner healing session.

Counselors should not perform unless their ministry is submitted to the church, the clergy, or an authorized spiritual authority for approval and judging.  A married person should have the additional approval and support of husband or wife.

Advanced training is essential; it should be more than general knowledge obtained from reading a book.  Further suggestions for training courses and resources are listed under the heading "Inner Healing" in chapter 10.  Such specialized training may be supplemented by discussions with experienced counselors, workshops, books, audio tapes, and courses in professional counseling methods.  Even though academic instruction in counseling and guidance is very helpful in learning techniques of relating to counselees and helping them work through their problems, caution should be taken not to embrace methods or beliefs contrary to Scripture or Christian doctrine.

A general, working knowledge of the Scriptures is a definite benefit to one involved in inner healing.  Ministers should not be speaking their own words or expounding their own advice, but should have the authority of the Word of God behind their counsel.  Often the right verse of Scripture, especially verses related to this ministry, will be the force to change a mind or heart in the right direction.

Inner healing counselors should have both the calling to, and the aptitude for, this kind of ministry.  It will require time, understanding, longsuffering, and dedication.  Love should be the primary motivation for becoming involved in this work.

Inner healing counselors need the gifts of the Holy Spirit in operation for this ministry.  It goes without saying that such counselors should be baptized Christians who have received the infilling of the Holy Spirit and who evidence the spiritual gifts and fruits of a committed follower of Jesus Christ. They must wait upon the Lord to open the doors of ministry and must be submitted to follow the leadings of the Holy Spirit at all times. Because this form of counseling cannot be reduced to a formula or a particular way of functioning, there must be a constant reliance upon the Spirit to guide and direct each appointment for prayer, without preconceived notions or methods in mind.

Every aspect of this ministry must be offered to the Lord for direction - before, during, and after an inner healing appointment. Prior to a prayer session, the Lord may reveal to the counselor "advance information" through a word of knowledge - something which the counselee might not be able to discuss openly but which must be dealt with in order for healing to occur. Not all who ask for ministry may be the ones a specific counselor should pray for; therefore, the Lord, not other people's insistence or the counselor's feelings of compassion or urgency, should determine when and for whom to pray.

Counselors should also pray about their counseling schedule and load, allowing the Lord to pace and space appointments accordingly. Because this ministry often requires a great deal of time (many times an appointment takes several hours and more than one session), the counselor must be willing to commit to the time necessary, especially if the problems are numerous or the hurts are deep. If a counselor cannot continue to meet with a counselee and more healing is needed, the counselor should be able to refer the counselee to other qualified ministers for follow-up. Too many appointments or sessions scheduled when the counselor is busy with other pressing matters will be unfair to the counselee, who deserves a rested, alert, and attentive counselor.

Inner healing counselors must possess attributes of character compatible with this ministry. They can never be judgmental of a counselee's past actions; although they may not condone sinful acts, they must be loving and accepting of the sinner. They must inspire confidence and openness from those they counsel. They must not allow counselees to become overly dependent upon them. They should be aware of their limitations and go only as far as their qualifications and leadings from the Lord allow them to go. They cannot become easily discouraged, but they should offer mistakes as well as victories to the Lord, always willing to learn and improve from every situation. Counselors must stay humble, submissive, and teachable, always on guard against the sin of pride, especially as the Lord uses them effectively and their reputations become known. The glory for this ministry belongs to the Lord alone!

The counselee, as well as the counselor, must be prepared in advance for inner healing to be effective. Counselees must take the ministry seriously and approach it with openness and honesty. They must be willing to release, renounce, forgive, or confess because no one else can do _for_ them whatever is necessary for healing, not even the best of counselors. A counselor may lead and instruct a counselee, but only the counselee can make the decision for change; therefore, the counselee must be willing to do so. Openness includes a willingness to get to the _source_ of a problem rather than dealing only with symptoms or manifestations of the problem. Advance preparation time should be given to prayer, Bible reading, self-examination, and other spiritual disciplines, which will bring the counselee to a point of readiness for ministry.

A counselee must be accepting of the counselor and self. A counselee must also be willing to accept healing, forgiveness, or deliverance. He or she must not allow feelings of guilt or self-condemnation to get in the way, but should approach the inner healing appointment with faith, believing that no matter how sinful, painful, or hopeless the past may seem, the power of God at work in his or her life can bring victory.

In order to understand the depth of commitment and training necessary to become an inner healing counselor, a general picture of that which is involved in a private prayer session may be helpful. People needing inner healing would prayerfully seek out the one they believe the Lord is leading them to for consultation, and then they both would pray about this for confirmation and ask the Lord to arrange the time and preparations for ministry. Usually there is a need for a pre-counseling session in which the counselor and counselee can get acquainted and discuss the problems; however, in some instances, the Holy Spirit may lead the counselor to begin prayers for inner healing immediately. A quiet place, free from distractions, should be sought for such a session. It is always good to pray at a church where clergy and others are available for prayer support and back-up assistance if this becomes necessary. Both the counselor and the assistant in inner healing would want to open the session with prayer - offering the discussions, the questions to be asked and answered, and all that would come forth from prayer or counseling to be guided by the Lord. They would also want to pray for protection, that no hindering influences or demonic forces would thwart the moving of the Holy Spirit during the session.

Inner healing involves offering the past (any traumatizing experience, a fearful or painful memory, or emotional scar that remains from being battered by life) to Jesus to take corrective action. As Jesus is invited into the problem, emotional reactions to the past that may still be causing difficulty in the present can be changed. Because "Jesus is the same yesterday, today, and forever," he is not limited to work in the present; he can go back to the wounded child of the past and offer comfort, healing, and restoration. Psalm 23:3 says, "He restoreth my soul." When the soulish areas are bruised and broken, they can be restored by the Great Physician. As Jesus is invited into a painful experience of the past, the memory of that experience with all its negative reactions can be changed in the subconscious mind. Where there was hatred, jealousy, fear, grief, pain, or bondage, Jesus can minister love, peace, forgiveness, healing, or freedom.

Inner healing often must begin before conception because unhealed memories may be carried with a person from the mother's womb. If the mother suffered fears or strong negative feelings during pregnancy, or if there was even a slight bit of rejection of the unborn child, the child can be influenced by such things. A counselee often needs to know that, even before birth, God knew and loved him or her.

As the counselors move forward from conception to babyhood, early childhood, and teenage years, the Holy Spirit may direct prayers to stop at a certain point in time. Counselors may need to question the counselee about a particular place or experience which may have significance. Counselors may receive a word or a mental picture (a thought or impression) which, when mentioned, will recall in the counselee's mind a problem that needs solving. The mind, especially the mind of a child or even an impressionable adult, cannot always differentiate between that which is real and that which is fantasy. The emotional responses are the same either way. Every painful memory - whether real or imagined - can linger like an unhealed wound, but Jesus can take care of all such hurts - those that are from actual experience and those which Satan tries to influence the imagination to believe falsely.

There are times when a counselee will not or cannot admit true feelings or confess the real reasons for unhappiness because to do so would lessen the image he or she wants to show the world. This is a defense mechanism to push down unpleasant thoughts and attitudes. These submerged feelings, hidden sins, or secret thoughts do not go away just because they are ignored by the conscious mind. They may fester and create strange symptoms until they are, first, allowed to surface; second, confessed; and third, forgiven and healed. This is where the need for confession as a part of inner healing becomes vital. A sin cannot be forgiven and the guilt for it healed unless it is rightly acknowledged.

The process of inner healing also should aid the counselee in becoming free from bondages. People often become bound to other people, as in a dominant-dependent relationship or in a situation where there is possessive love or where someone is bound to another by hatred, unforgiveness, jealousy, or other such negative feeling. People can also be bound to habits, alcohol, drugs, food, compulsive actions, or even religious practices or doctrines. Galatians 5:1 says, "Stand fast in the liberty wherewith Christ has made us free, and be not entangled again with the yoke of bondage." Wherever one draws the line and says, "I'll give the Lord anything except ---," that is the very surrender that must be made for the soul's health and peace of mind. To place anything or anyone before the Lord is a form of idolatry. People can be bound to loved ones or enemies, but they will not be healthy in such bondage. One person should never control or be responsible for the actions of another. That is why those involved in inner healing often must help counselees to become detached from others and the thought projections sent to them from others. The counselees must be willing to be set free before prayers for release can be effective. The problem must be researched back far enough to determine when the bondage began - what caused the counselee to need to depend upon other people or things. Such dependence must be replaced with dependence upon Jesus alone. Often knowing when and under what circumstances the bondage began is helpful. When the true cause of the problem is known and Jesus is allowed to heal it, then and then only can there be release. Otherwise, the counselor and the counselee are dealing with symptoms and not with the causes of the problem.

The Lord does not want anyone bound to anything on earth - not other people, not things, not addictive habits, and certainly not the past. Many people do not realize that they do not have to remain in bondage. It is the joyful purpose of inner healing to bring people the truth that can set them free and "deliver them who through fear . . . were all their lifetime subject to bondage" (Heb. 2:15).

Because evil spirits can enter at a traumatizing time in a person's life, there is sometimes a need for exorcism as well as inner healing in order for the ministry to be complete. Because of the inherent hazards of exorcism, this aspect of inner healing must be approached with caution, understanding, and preparation. Those who feel called to this ministry must have the sanction of their pastor; and in some localities, people are not authorized to practice the ministry of exorcism without being licensed or without having their names registered with church authorities. Exorcism (sometimes called the deliverance ministry) involves the "casting out" of demons that may be possessing or oppressing someone. An evil spirit (or demon) is one of Satan's fallen angels who seeks to control and conquer the minds and bodies of people, drawing them away from the Lord and the paths of righteousness. These harmful influences or demons may manifest themselves as spirits of anger, lust, lying, fear, rebellion, or any other spirit contrary to the Holy Spirit of God. They may also manifest themselves in debilitating illnesses or habits, such as a deaf or dumb spirit, a spirit of drunkenness, a spirit of gluttony, or an epileptic spirit. Not every sin, bad habit, or illness, however, is the result of demon activity. Some sins and habits merely need to be taken to the cross. For instance, it might be desirable to be "delivered" from the sin of gluttony or laziness rather than using self-discipline at mealtime or when there is work to be done. Whether or not one needs deliverance from an evil spirit is determined by the gift of discernment ("the discerning of spirits" of I Cor. 12:10). Discernment is knowing that which is of the Holy Spirit and that which is of an evil spirit. Since Satan often appears as an angel of light (II Cor. 11:14) and often camouflages his evil designs in religious trappings or noble-sounding activities, Christian ministers need this faculty for accurately discriminating in a questionable situation and immediately recognizing that which is of Satan. It is especially important for those involved in the inner healing ministry to be approved for the ministry of exorcism, because traumatizing experiences of the past often become the open door through which demon powers enter. To pray for memories to be healed and bondages to be broken but to leave a demon spirit attached to those memories or bondages is to do half-measures in healing.

Christians are admonished to "test" the spirits: "Every spirit that confesseth not that Jesus Christ is come in the flesh is not of God" but of Antichrist (cf. I John 4:1-3). It is especially advantageous to have the gift of discernment when dealing with the many pseudo-religious groups and cults prevalent today. If these groups proclaim that Jesus was a "good man" or merely a great teacher or prophet but refuse to acknowledge that he is the "Son of God come in the flesh," the Bible says that they are not of God. People who are possessed of an evil spirit often cannot even say the name of Jesus or participate in the worship and praise of him.

A counselor needs the gift of discernment not only to determine whether or not an evil spirit is present, but also to determine exactly which evil spirit it is. Since Satan is such a sly enemy and always deceitful, working together with a prayer partner in inner healing and exorcism is imperative. This provides the opportunity of checking the discernment with another. It is, furthermore, of great benefit to have a prayer group (or other selected prayer supporters) backing up those who are ministering in this delicate area. If someone discerns an evil spirit (or even suspects that there may be the need for deliverance) and has not been called of the Lord, specifically directed by the Holy Spirit to enter this ministry and approved by the church to perform it, that person can bind the spirit in the name of Jesus Christ and then call upon someone with the ministry of exorcism to carry on.

At the time of an exorcism, there may be some kind of physical manifestation when an evil spirit leaves (coughing, wretching, yawning, screaming, trembling, etc.). The exorcist must never become fearful of Satan's antics. He often will put on a show if he thinks it will scare someone away from the deliverance ministry. It should also be remembered that the spirits can be commanded to come out gently and quietly.

It is unhealthy to seek out demons and activities of Satan, but when they are met, they must be opposed. Satan loves attention, so he is delighted if he can get a Christian overly interested in demonology. It is far better to put attention upon the love and praise of Jesus than upon the works of the enemy. Since there is nothing to indicate that evil spirits have ceased desiring to possess and oppress human beings, and since Jesus commanded his ministers to follow his own example of casting out demons and delivering the ones whom Satan has bound, the ministry of exorcism fills a definite need. It is very much a part of inner healing. As it has been pointed out, a hurtful memory of the past may have opened the door for an evil spirit to enter. For instance, the memory of a fear-inducing situation may need healing, but if a spirit of fear has taken over, then that spirit must be cast out also. The ministry of exorcism is not for the fearful, unstable, or unprepared. But, for those whom the Lord has called to it, it can be the most freeing and powerful of ministries.

In order to see how the ministry of exorcism fits into the overall pattern of inner healing, consider the case of a man whose life was falling apart because of his violent temper. His abusive actions toward his wife and children had driven them from him. He wanted to be kind to them, but the old habit pattern of anger/temper outbursts/ violence always resulted in his hitting, threatening, and hurting the ones he loved most. In an inner healing session, it was learned that the man had been abused by a violent father in his own childhood. The father would often come home drunk, beat the boy for no reason, and treat him unmercifully. The man had deep feelings of hatred and rebellion toward his father, and as he grew up, the feelings needed an outlet. He perpetuated the violence visited upon him by becoming violent to others, a carbon copy of his father. In order to be healed, the man had to acknowledge and repent of his hatred of his father and forgive him for every sinful thing he had done. He had to be broken free from the negative bondage to his father (the hatred, resentment, and rebellion bound him to the father with such negativism that the man was not free to be himself). He also needed Jesus to heal all the hurts of the beatings and the undeserved abusive treatment he had received in childhood. And, lastly, he needed deliverance from the evil spirits that had passed from father to son - spirits of anger, violence, resentment, and hatred. There was even a latent spirit of murder, which although it had not manifested itself in the actual act of murder, was discerned as being there, waiting for the right violent outburst in which to take control.

Follow-up to inner healing and/or deliverance is essential. The Bible warns against the folly of leaving a cleansed "house" unattended. Counselees should be attached to a believing body of Christians who will help to nurture them; they should go regularly to church and avail themselves of the opportunities for worship, receiving Communion, instruction and fellowship there; they should commit themselves to daily disciplines of Bible reading and prayer; they should be instructed how to take authority over Satan and old habit patterns; and they should have some spiritual authority to whom they are submitted and upon whom they can call in a time of need.

In helping counselees to assert their believer's authority over Satan and to keep their healing following a prayer session, practical suggestions should be offered, such as putting on the "whole armor of God" each day, claiming the protection of Jesus over all evil, and affirming the promises of the Scriptures. Often just repeating a verse of Scripture is helpful as a follow-up procedure. Suggested Scriptures are: "Resist the devil and he will flee" (Jas. 4:7); "Trust in the Lord with all your heart" (Prov. 3:5); "The Lord has not given us a spirit of fear" (II Tim. 1:7); "I can do all things through Christ which strengthens me" (Phil. 4:13); etc. Counselees should also be encouraged to stay in an attitude of praise and to focus attention upon Jesus, rather than upon sin, demons or their problems.

Another aspect of follow-up is the responsibility of the counselor to keep in touch with the counselee after the prayer session. If there is the need, another appointment should be scheduled.

Even as the inner healing appointment began in prayer, it should end the same way. There should be prayers of thanksgiving for all that has been done; prayers of commitment on the part of counselees, offering themselves more fully in all the newly surrendered areas; prayers for protection and guidance as counselees go about daily life; and a prayer for relinquishment, offering to the Lord everything discussed and prayed about (such a prayer takes from the ministers' minds any remembrance of the sordid details of counselees' pasts, much as a priest is freed from remembrance of a person's sins following confession).

A private prayer session is, by far, the most specific and personal type of ministry in that full attention is focused upon the counselee and his or her particular needs. The counselee does not have to share the stage with others, as in a group healing session. The disadvantage is that this method is very time-consuming and requires trained and qualified ministers who may not be readily available when a prayer session is needed. In such times when a trained inner healing counselor is unavailable (or when the Lord wishes to minister to a person directly and personally without anyone else being involved) there is a third form of inner healing available.

A Prayer Pattern for Self-Ministry: The prayer pattern which follows is offered, not as the only way to pray for oneself or the only words that may be used, but merely as a point of departure and as an aid in understanding what inner healing can mean from an individual viewpoint. Before attempting to do this, the person should spend some time in preparation, spiritually and emotionally and be certain that he or she is approaching this prayer sincerely and expectantly. Select a time that will be free from interruptions and distractions and a place that will be quiet and conducive to meditation, reflection, and prayer. A pencil and paper to write down thoughts or problems that need to be offered up in prayer may be useful.

Prayers before birth: Dear Jesus, go back with me to the moment of my conception and heal anything that was not a part of your divine plan for me. I know that before I was formed in my mother's womb, you knew my name and loved me. I thank you for that. If I was not conceived totally in love and joy, please heal any feelings of rejection, pain, or fear that may have been imparted from any negative projections I may have received before birth. Break any bondages to my parents that may have begun before I was born, and set me free to become the person you destined me to be before the foundation of the world. Protect me now, as I move with your Spirit throughout my past life, and reveal to me anything I should know, anything I should confess, and anything I should release to you. May your guardian angels be in attendance watching over me as I open myself to you. I know, Lord, that you had a plan for my life and a perfected image of me long, long before I knew anything about your will for my life. Help me to become conformed to that image, that perfect picture of what you want me to be. Release me from any false image I have of myself or any image that others have tried to force upon me. Free me, Lord, to be your perfect creation. And thank you, Lord, for loving me and protecting me before I was even capable of understanding or responding to such compassion.

Early childhood: Thank you, Lord, that your hand of protection was upon me all through my formative years. Thank you for being there when my needs were greatest and when I wasn't even aware of your presence. Set me free from anything in my early childhood that may be a barrier to my wholeness. Break all bondages to my ancestors - family, relatives, and close associations which may have influenced my life in ways contrary to your will for me. Protect me from and set me free from any curse of the enemy or satanic influence that may have filtered through others to touch my life. Bring back to my memory now any painful or sinful experience that may need your healing touch. Heal the memories of times when my parents or others were unkind or hurtful to me . . . when I felt unacceptable or insecure . . . when I was lonely . . . when I was afraid . . . when I felt pain or caused pain to others . . . when I became angry or rebellious . . . and any other negative emotional response that has been recorded deep in my subconscious mind. As I pause now and give your Spirit time to bring things to my remembrance, I ask you to do a thorough house-cleaning of every dark corner of my past. (Pause.) Take away the old, negative feelings and give me positive ones in their place. Heal relationships of my childhood that need the redeeming power of reconciliation brought to bear upon them. Bring to my mind anyone I need to forgive . . . or anyone who needs to forgive me. (Pause.) Make up for the lack of mothering or fathering I may have missed, and give me anointed eyes with which to see those who have wounded me. Let me understand that those who mistreated me were also mistreated by others, and those who abused me were likewise abused. Give me, Lord, your eyes of love with which to see clearly every situation and relationship of my past. Break me free of any bondages to anyone or anything that I became bound to in childhood. Bring to my mind right now any experiences at home . . . at school . . . at play . . . or in any other place . . . . Heal anything that needs your love or forgiveness or correction. Set me completely free from all aspects of my childhood that have left scars upon my life or that have influenced my thinking in twisted ways. As I offer my childhood to you, bring in your healing light to every dark, secret corner of my mind, and release me from all trauma . . . pain . . . fear . . . or sin of the past.

Teenage years: Go back with me now, Lord, to my teenage years. Ease the anxiety and confusion I felt as my body changed from child to adult . . . calm the fears I had about myself, others, and the world . . . heal the pain of growing up and feeling misunderstood. Lord, I give to you right now the problems I had with my parents and other authority figures. Take away the rebellion and resentments that developed at this time in my life. Bring to my mind those I need to forgive . . . those who hurt me in any way at this period of my physical and emotional development . . . remind me of those I need to ask forgiveness from . . . show me the secret sins of my youth that I've never confessed openly before. Lord, unlock that secret door where I've hidden thoughts and deeds too ugly to mention. Let me be rid of them here and now as I offer them to you and ask your forgiveness for them. (Pause.) Lord, break any bondages that developed between myself and others at this time of my life, and set me free from any unholy attachments I may have had to others - any dependent or dominant tendencies, any resentments I may have had, any possessive or controlling attitudes. Lord, I especially lift up to you my relationship with my parents. Thank you for those who gave me life and enabled me to come to know you. I give them to you right now with any negative feelings that have ever developed between us. Make our relationship what you want it to be, and minister your divine love to every area of hurt or dissatisfaction. Forgive me, Lord, for judging them and criticizing them. Let me see them through your eyes of love and acceptance. Open my eyes to my own failures in being the kind of obedient child I should have been. (Pause.) Lord, walk back now into every trauma of my past that has left a mark upon my life, and heal my wounded spirit. I give you the sins of yesterday: all the pride and selfishness, unacceptable habits or attitudes, any self-pity or complaints, and especially the temptations that I was unable to handle. Heal the feelings of insecurity and inferiority I often had when I compared myself to others. Let me see myself as you see me: loved, forgiven, accepted, and approved. Give me a healed and restored self-concept, that I may glorify you with my total being. (Pause.) Lord, I give to you my sexuality and ask you to release me from any guilt of the past. I know how vulnerable everyone is in this area, and how Satan works to abuse and misuse the blessed gift of sex you bestow. Re-create me right now, and make me the sexual being you would have me be, and sanctify this area of my life from anything that was not of you. Break me free from any past sins, habits, or attitudes that may be spiritually impure. (Pause.) Lord, renew any wrong attitude I have had about you or the church. Forgive me for my doubts or rebellion against holy things. Walk back through every problem of my youth right now and change the images in my subconscious mind, remove the ugly, distorted pictures, and let me see my past in truth and light. Sweep away the cobwebs of sin and distortion, and shine your holy light into every dark or hidden corner of my past. Release me from any barriers that stand between me and an open, personal, and healed relationship with you. Finally, Lord, bring to my recollection anything else from my teen years that may need correction or healing.

Adulthood: Lord, I give you myself. I also lay before your altar any mistakes or wrong decisions I have made, knowing that you can take the broken pieces of my life and create a beautiful mosaic. Release me from any guilt or self-condemnation for wrongdoing. Help me to see that Satan is the accuser who wants me to be tormented with false guilt, but that you are the one who forgives, heals, and even remembers my sins against me no more. Bring me out of the shadows of dark despair, regret, and wasted time. Re-create in me right now a new heart. I give to you my loved ones. Break any negative bondages I may have to spouse, children, relatives, or other loved ones. Let me love all those you have given me with a holy detachment, allowing them the freedom to be themselves - even the freedom to be wrong. Pour your love into me and then out to those I find it difficult to love unconditionally. Teach me how to turn over to you every area of my life - my relationships, my social life, my home situation, my work, and my play. Remind me that you want to be Lord of all my life each and every day, in every moment, in every decision, in every emotion and attitude. Forgive me for not realizing that everything that has happened to me has been for a reason - to teach me, to change me. Help me to cooperate with you and to learn my lessons quickly. Bring to my mind anything that needs your healing touch . . . any relationship . . . any personal sin . . . any wrong attitude . . . any habit . . . any negative feelings toward others . . . any temptation . . . any compulsion . . . any sin of omission . . . any idolatry for putting other people or things in first place above you in my life . . . any of your commandments I have broken . . . whatever you want to show me. In the

silence, Lord, open me up completely and allow me to see myself as you
see me. (Pause.) Thank you, Lord, that you are healing my past and
giving me a renewed mind, a fresh start. As I confess my sins and ask
you to set me free from anyone or anything I may be bound to, I thank
you that you will not leave me here at this point, but that you will
continue to heal and cleanse and sanctify me by bringing to my mind,
day by day, those things I need to release to you. Protect me and
deliver me from any evil spirit or demonic influence that has had any
kind of control in my life. Reveal to me how such influences have
gained access - show me what the spirit feeds upon, the open door
through which it came into my life, and heal that fleshly part of me
that gives ground to the enemy to stand upon. (Pause.) Show me anything further that I need to look at honestly; bring up from my past
those things I must acknowledge, repent of, make restitution for, or
lay aside from my life. Then set me free from it all. Make me what
you want me to be, Lord, as I yield myself - my body, my mind, and my
spirit - to the control of your Holy Spirit. Help me to give myself
more completely to you each day, that I may grow as Jesus grew: "in
wisdom...and in favor with God and man." I praise you and thank you
for the freedom and joy that are mine through my Lord and Saviour,
Jesus Christ! I worship, praise, and adore you both now and forever-
more. Amen.


Hindrances to Ministry

There are four major hindrances to the (inner) healing ministry
that have been mentioned previously, namely, unforgiveness, sexual
sins, occult involvement, and abortion (see pp. 186-87). Inner healing
counselors should be aware that if a counselee has been involved in any
of these four areas, there is likelihood of the need for deliverance
and the possibility of difficulty in further healing until these things
are dealt with first.


Questions and Answers on Outer Healing and Inner Healing

1. What can be said to people who do not believe in God's power
   to heal or whose prayers for healing appear unanswered?

There are many possibilities as to why this may be. The Bible
says, "The prayer of faith shall save the sick." The gift of healing
may be offered by the Lord, but one who is unwilling to accept the gift
cannot possess it. Jesus asked the man at the pool of Bethsaida
(who had been seeking healing for thirty-eight years), "Do you want to
be made whole?" That may sound like a ridiculous question, but many
people subconsciously do not want healing because of the demands that
wholeness would place upon them or because they enjoy the attention
and pity their physical or emotional problems bring. The Lord always hears and answers prayers, but his answer is not always Yes.
Sometimes he works in a situation different from what a person expects.
Sometimes his timing is different from humankind's. Sometimes barriers
to healing must be removed before wholeness comes. But the Lord always
desires wholeness as the highest good for a human being.

2. Why do Christians get sick?

There was no illness - physical, emotional, mental or spiritual -
in God's original plan for creation until Satan initiated the fall of
humanity. Sickness is to the body and mind what sin is to the spirit.
God does not will for us to be sick any more than he wills for us to
be sinful. We have to combat all kinds of evil because "in the world
[the fallen world of sin] ye shall have tribulation." There is, however, victory in Jesus, who said, "I have overcome the world."

3. If the ministry of inner healing is controversial and not
   accepted universally, what is the value of it?

The value of this ministry is evidenced in the countless lives
that have been changed and freed from specters of their pasts. The
only real danger is that of operating outside the will and guidance
of the Holy Spirit. The Lord will never lead a counselor to do anything harmful to another, so a total commitment and reliance upon the
Lord is the primary concern. Naturally, Satan tries to destroy the
works of the Spirit. He will try to get people into error or discredit
the good that is done. This is true in any ministry. Perhaps the
greatest value of inner healing is that it does what no single type of
prayer can do. It combines introspection, intercession, deliverance,
confession, counseling, healing, and cleansing all in one. It should
be remembered, however, that all ministry is to be submitted ministry.
If one's pastor or spiritual authority forbids this ministry, it should
not be practiced outside the approval and oversight of that authority.
Where the door is closed to inner healing, prayers should be offered
for the Lord to open it. The door should not be "pushed" open by
zealous people who run ahead of the Lord.

4. Why is there such emphasis upon the dangers of the occult?
   Must one confess "innocent" dabbling that is not accompanied
   by real belief in it?

There is no such thing as "innocent" dabbling in the occult.
All occult practices are an "abomination unto the Lord" (Cf. Deut.
18:1-13). To participate even casually or unknowingly must be confessed and renounced. Even though there is widespread acceptance of
astrology, psychic phenomena, and other occult practices, the Word of
God points to the dangers of such idolatry (looking to any source
other than the Lord for aid, strength, power, or guidance). The medical profession has come out with warnings about the physical and
psychological dangers to one's health in such practices; so, even if
the occult were not spiritually wrong, there are inherent problems
from other standpoints. There is nothing to recommend the occult
from the standpoints of a person's mental, emotional or spiritual
health. There are often demonic influences associated with such
practices. All such involvement is to be avoided, including games,
reading materials, occult movies, charms, and images. It also includes
relationships with those so involved: "There shall not be found among
you those which do such things." Anyone involved in the healing ministry (or even those interested in their own health and well-being) should
be aware of these dangers.

5. Why is the ministry of exorcism such a specialized field? What are the dangers of this ministry?

Those involved in exorcism are not fighting against flesh and blood, but against supernatural powers of darkness (Eph. 6:12). To take on such a battle without the calling, proper training, and approval from spiritual authorities is foolish. Evil spirits have been known to leave one person and enter another; therefore, everyone present during an exorcism should be "covered" with the protection of Jesus Christ. Those who practice exorcism must have adequate training and preparation in order to know how Satan operates and how to combat him. There may be, for instance, a curse (upon an entire family or an individual), which can be perpetuated from generation to generation. Evil spirits may also attack the exorcist with great violence (see Acts 19:13-16 for a scriptural example of this). This possibility is especially true if the exorcist is fearful or uncertain, or is ministering outside the guidance of the Holy Spirit. This means that the exorcist must, at times, have physical as well as spiritual strength. An evil spirit cannot take over territory controlled by the Holy Spirit, but if someone chooses to open self up to sin and the powers of evil (or if the person has "inherited" an evil spirit because of the sins of others), demons are most happy to take over. Fear of demons is from the demons themselves, so an exorcist must not allow demon powers to deceive or mislead. This is not a ministry for the cowardly or unstable, but it is a powerful and necessary ministry when one is called to perform it.

6. What is the difference between "possession" and "oppression" (influence) by demons?

Possession is from the inside, while oppression or demonic influences are outside forces coming against someone. Demon possession indicates that a person has no control of his or her own thoughts and actions but is manipulated by the powers of evil. Those who are oppressed by evil spirits have not been invaded by demonic forces to the intense degree of those "possessed." It is difficult for demonic forces totally to possess a Christian, for whatever part of the person is surrendered to Jesus cannot be controlled by the enemy. Satan can, however, oppress Christians in areas that have not been given over to the control of the Holy Spirit. It is difficult to discern between these two types of demon activity, but the method of deliverance is the same: combating the enemy through the name and blood of Jesus, through faith, and through the authority to command demon powers to depart. In some cases, fasting and sacrifice over an extended period of time are also needed (cf. Mark 9:17-29).

7. Why is it necessary to pray in the name of Jesus?

The Bible teaches that a person's name indicated that person's nature. People's names were often changed when their natures changed (Saul to Paul, Jacob to Israel, etc.). Those who pray in the name of Jesus Christ are praying in the nature of Jesus, standing in his authority. Jesus conquered all the powers of darkness and evil upon

the cross.  Devils know who Jesus is, and at his name "they tremble."
At the name of Jesus, "every knee shall bow and every tongue confess
that He is Lord."  There is, therefore, great power and authority in
the precious name of Jesus.  It is only through the power and authority
of Jesus Christ that any prayer should be offered, any exorcism practiced, any ministry performed.

8. How does discernment work?

There is an inner witness from the Holy Spirit to the Christian
which can detect the presence of evil, demon spirits, or things contrary
to the teachings and purposes of Jesus Christ.  Often, without having
had instruction or without knowing appropriate Scriptures, a Christian
will just "know" something is or is not of the Lord.  It is like an
inner alarm clock that goes off at the appropriate time.  Such discernment should, however, be "tested."  The test is to offer the discernment to the Lord in prayer for confirmation.  Every notion that
comes to a person is not divine discernment.  Some ideas may be from
the flesh or may be Satan's counterfeit guidance.  But that which is
true and right not only will witness in one's own spirit, but also will
find agreement in the spirits of other Christians to whom the discernment is submitted for confirmation.

9. Why is after-care (spiritual disciplines and Christian practices for growth and further maturity) stressed so much?
   Isn't the healing power of Jesus sufficient for complete
   release from problems and ills?

Until Christians reach heaven and perfection, there will always
be further to go with Jesus.  No one has "arrived" and no one is ever
completely whole in mind, body, or spirit in this life.  Christians
must constantly be growing, maturing, and keeping on their guard
against the enemy who would like to rob them of their victories every
time.  Even after a miraculous healing or a very thorough prayer and
counseling session, there may still be more healing needed.  It may be
compared to a diver going into the depths of the ocean.  The diver must
learn to function at one depth before being able to adjust to the
pressure of going deeper.  Yes, the power of Jesus is sufficient for
every need, but there are always more needs.  Christians must keep on
progressing.  Attention to after-care helps to keep the doors closed
to more problems that will need healing.  Frequent confession is one
of the best after-care methods available.  Inner healing counselors
should suggest this as a follow-up to a prayer and counseling session
and as a regular habit to all who wish to keep spiritually "healthy."

10. How does supernatural guidance such as a "word of knowledge"
    work?

Among the gifts of the Holy Spirit are wisdom, knowledge, prophecy, faith, healing, miracles, and discernment.  Any or all of these
may be manifested during a time of inner or outer healing.  The Lord
may supernaturally impart wisdom (counselors may hear themselves giving
advice or speaking words direct from the Holy Spirit or obviously not

from their own intellect). The Lord may give a word of knowledge (the counselor will "know" something about the counselee and his or her problem or past without having been told previously). The Lord may also impart discernment (a recognition of that which is not of the Lord) or prophecy (a message from the Lord to another person). Such supernatural gifts are not thought up or "conjured up" by the counselor. They come from the Spirit - initiated by him and given for his purposes. The counselor becomes merely a "delivery boy" to bring the gifts to another. When a supernatural message or guidance comes, the counselor must be careful to check it out or, as the Bible puts it, to "test the spirits." Satan is a good counterfeiter and will often give guidance that "sounds" like the voice of the Lord. Counselors should not assume that revelations are from God just because they popped into their minds. They should not only pray about such a revelation but also command it to leave if it is not from the Holy Spirit. It should be remembered that the Holy Spirit will never give guidance that is in opposition to Scripture and that the Holy Spirit gently leads (he doesn't push or compel forcefully). Although Satan can counterfeit the gifts of the Spirit, he cannot duplicate the fruits. If any supernatural guidance disturbs inner peace or seems unloving, check it out some more!

## Conclusion

Despite this lengthy discussion about healing of body, mind (soul), and spirit, the subject has barely been broached. There is always more to learn - more ways, different ways, better ways. The words offered here are not final words of authority or absolutes, but merely suggestions and gleanings from experience to be considered, judged, and applied only as they are confirmed by the Holy Spirit. The Lord will lead each individual in the special path he has chosen for that individual as the gifts and ministries of healing are performed to his honor and glory.

# 9 · Ministries of Group Leadership

Every person who becomes involved in lay ministry will not necessarily become a leader. There are numerous opportunities for service that require fellowship as well as leadership. But there are situations where even followers have places of leadership thrust upon them. It is important, therefore, for everyone to know something about the dynamics of leadership and how to fulfill such a role should the occasion occur. It is also important to understand the various types of groups that exist and how leadership responsibilities will vary from one type of group to another.

## Leadership Dynamics

### What Is a Leader Like?

Leaders come in all shapes, sizes, and colors. Although there is no one criterion to fit every leadership position, the following attributes are relevant:

1. Committed: Christian leaders must be committed leaders - committed to the Lord, to others, and to their responsibilities.

2. Submitted: Those having authority must be under authority. Leaders should have someone to whom their ministry of leadership is submitted and judged.

3. Assertive: Even the gentlest of people can, under the inspiration of the Holy Spirit, put themselves forward to fulfill an obligation. Leaders must not draw back from taking charge or hesitate once authority is asserted.

4. Courageous: Because it is impossible to please everyone and to be right at all times, leaders must have the courage to stand for their convictions and the courage to admit their mistakes.

5. Dependable: People in positions of leadership must be depended upon to fulfill their responsibilities, to keep their word, and to be genuine (no mask-wearing or pretense).

6. Accepting: Leaders must accept and love those they lead, even the difficult and unloving ones.

7. Mature: Leadership is not a role for those who are spiritually or emotionally immature. Leaders must take an adult approach to their functions.

8. <u>Inspiring</u>:  Leaders should inspire the confidence of others and inspire others to have confidence in themselves (leaders should delegate responsibility and encourage their followers to assume leadership themselves rather than one person trying to handle the leadership single-handedly).

## What Does a Leader Do?

1. <u>Initiates</u>:  Leaders get things moving and get people going.

2. <u>Plans</u>:  Leaders organize ideas into workable operations and take time to discover the best ways to proceed.

3. <u>Orients</u>:  Leaders help people become acclimated to the group, project, or study, and set the tone for the meeting or event.

4. <u>Stimulates</u>: Leaders stimulate thinking and action, helping others to reach beyond their grasp, to question, to learn, and to grow.

5. <u>Clarifies</u>:  Leaders help others to see relationships, to learn from instruction or experience, and to work through confusion to clarification.

6. <u>Exemplifies</u>:  Leaders set examples for others to follow and never require of others what they are unwilling to do themselves.

7. <u>Listens</u>:  Leaders do not think they already have all the answers; they listen to the Lord for guidance  to others for suggestions, to authorities for correction, and to their own creative thought processes for self-confident determination.

8. <u>Guides</u>:  Leaders keep people and things on the right track, bring people back from tangents, and give direction and instruction, offering correction and support whenever necessary.

9. <u>Controls</u>:  Leaders do not let others take the ball away or usurp their authority; they do not let projects "run themselves."

10. <u>Concludes</u>: Leaders help others to make sense out of a meeting or a study by drawing ideas together, tying up loose ends, making concluding remarks, or suggesting follow-up and evaluation.

## What Types of Groups Need Leadership?

Any number of organizations, committees, guilds, clubs, and classes need leadership.  The leadership role may be as simple as holding an office in a church or community organization or as complex as organizing and conducting an extensive training course.  Before assuming leadership roles in any capacity, there are some questions that should be asked.

1. What is the purpose of this group?

2. How will this purpose be implemented?

3. What structure will the group take?

4. Who is qualified and willing to lead the group?

5. How will the group's efficiency and productivity be evaluated?

Exploring these questions before initiating group activity will help to guard against unrealized expectations and goals. Unless everyone in the group knows what to expect from the group and what the group expects from each, there is apt to be frustration.

There are five basic types of groups, which may best be remembered by the acrostic S-W-I-F-T. It will be a "swift" accomplishment to determine the purpose of a group by placing it under one of the following catagories:

Service: A group performing a service or an outreach ministry, such as a church guild, a visitation committee, an evangelism task group, or a community improvement organization.

Worship: A group whose main purpose is to praise and worship together, such as the choir or a prayer-and-praise group.

Interest: A group sharing a mutual interest or talent, such as a sewing circle, a drama guild, or an arts and crafts group.

Fellowship: A group whose main function is to socialize and enjoy each other's company, such as a youth group, or a regular meeting of people for potluck suppers, card parties, or other recreational experiences.

Training: A group which meets for instruction, such as a Bible study group or discipleship training class.

Sometimes a group may have more than one basic purpose or sometimes purposes overlap. For instance, a training group may also participate in worship, outreach, or fellowship from time to time. But it is important to determine the central purpose for which the group is to come together and to make all activity and direction center upon this main thrust. Unless goals are established, no one can know when or if they are realized.

Obviously, the leader of a training group has the most difficult and specialized job. Those who are involved in leading interest or fellowship groups do not need as much structure and regimentation as an instructional program leader. The leader chosen for a particular group should be suited not only to a leadership role in general (being able to take charge of people and/or things) but also to the particular type of group he or she will be leading. It takes different skills, for instance, to inspire a group to effective worship and praise than it does to organize a group service project for a local orphanage. Leaders should evaluate their interests, personalities, and aptitudes before taking charge of a group, and they should determine whether or not their abilities fit the purposes of the particular group they are asked to lead. In other words, is this leadership role a particular person's "calling"?

## Leading a Service Group

A service group is a task-oriented group. The most important aspect of the group function will be the project or task to be performed. It is imperative that the work projects be suited to the group members who will be performing them; therefore, a two-part survey (formal or informal) of needs and talents should be the first step in implementation. The next steps involve organizing the work and the people, the administrative function of overseeing and checking on performance, and, finally, following up and evaluating. In a nutshell, the program would look like this:

Survey needs:     What should be done? Where are the greatest needs?

Survey talent:     Who can do that? What kind of people and resources are available?

Organize work:     What must be done in what order?

Organize people:     What assignments and responsibilities should be given and to whom?

Administrate:     What goals and deadlines should be set? What materials and finances must be provided? Where are the loose ends and the "holes" that need to be plugged?

Follow-up:     What criteria will determine success? How can the program be improved, expanded, or modified?

(NOTE: Steps 1 and 2 may be reversed.)

Sometimes the needs of the church or community will determine the type of group to be organized. For instance, a crisis may exist, such as children from underprivileged homes needing shoes and clothing. This will cause people to band together to meet that need. At other times, the desires or talents of a group of people will be the starting point. People sharing the mutual desire to be of service may ask themselves, "What can we do?" and "Where can we do it?" Suggestions for typical service projects and activities follow:

1. Outreach Projects: People reaching out to people may occur in any number of ways. There are visitation programs that may include visiting new or lapsed members, hospital calling, or ministries to shut-ins, orphanages, prisons, nursing homes, or other community institutions. There are also home-based progams that may involve bringing people into the church for mininstry, such as planning a supper or special program for senior citizens or for youth. Such programs may include making gifts, sending cards or letters, or providing food or financial assistance to those on the receiving end of the outreach ministry.

2. Programs: People who share talents and interests can organize programs to entertain, inspire, or motivate others. This may take the form of a musical group or a dramatic guild to give performances for the church or the community. It may also include skills programs, such as demonstrations for child care, grooming, family relationships, crafts, or other vocational or avocational talents which may be provided in an ongoing service program. In this instance, the group has a marketable product and looks for a place in which to "sell" it.

3. Work Projects: There are always innumerable fix-up, clean-up jobs that need doing. Work parties can be planned to include social functions as well as painting or repairing the church buildings, lawn care or gardening, making or building furnishings, babysitting or preparing meals for the ill or needy. Youth are especially suited for such work projects, which they can perform either "on call" or at a regularly scheduled time. Sending work teams into the community or to small or understaffed churches in surrounding areas is beneficial both to those performing the service (giving them an outlet for their talents and desire to be of service) and to those on the receiving end who need assistance.

4. Collections: Collecting food, clothing, or other necessities can take many different avenues. Members of the group may provide or purchase needed items for some charity, or they may sponsor fund raisers or drives to collect whatever may be needed. Some churches have a food pantry or clothes closet, which is maintained on a regular basis for those who may need them.

5. Sponsorships: Some groups decide upon one or more sponsorships to be supported regularly. This may be aid to the retarded, sponsorship of a Scout troop or youth organization, support of a ministry in the community, financial assistance to a seminary student or a missionary, or the adoption of a war orphan or other needy person. It often personalizes the ministry when the place where the money, time, or gifts are going is not just a vague "cause" but a particular place or a particular person with a name. People can identify with real names

and specifics better than with those things wherein they have no direct communication or knowledge.

6. Volunteers: Members of a group may volunteer their time to the church library, nursery, office, kitchen, or "hot line" telephone for crisis aid.  Or they can donate time to a local clinic, welfare agency, or other places where their efforts are needed.

7. Instructional Services:  A group with skills (either spiritual know-how or temporal aptitudes)  may sponsor workshops or classes as a service to the church or community.  Leadership training programs, lay ministry training, and guidance programs can be provided through such a group effort.  Or a group may elect to bring in speakers or educators to put on special programs or workshops.

8. Witnessing:  Groups may distribute Bibles or tracts or circulate Christian literature or tapes.  They may also go out in teams to bring programs of an evangelistic nature (sharing testimonies or sacred music) where such a ministy has not yet been provided. They may choose to offer prayer and financial support to evangelistic efforts.  Starting Sunday schools or Vacation Bible School programs in neglected areas or surveying a community to determine where the unchurched are located are also important related functions.

9. Money Raising:  It takes financial assistance for almost any service to be performed.  Some people are especially skilled in organizing fund raisers of various kinds or in soliciting donations.  A group may wish to devote its main emphasis to raising money for various worthy charities - either for the church, the community, or relief of hunger, ignorance, or oppression throughout the needy world. (It is best for such a group to start out on  a small scale before expanding into projects of gigantic proportions.)

10. Hospitality:  Some service groups may best spend their time in greeting and expressing love to others, making them feel welcomed and appreciated both as individuals and as members of the church or community.  They may form themselves into official church greeters or they may sponsor receptions, fellowship functions, home get-togethers, or socials to include newcomers, the lonely, the neglected, or those in need of being loved.  (For additional suggestions on services, see chapter 3, "Ministries of Helps.")

In whatever ways the group may decide to use its time, talent, or resources, the leader must keep a firm hand on all aspects of the program.  To assume that a project will successfully run itself once it has been started is a false assumption.  To assume that people will perform without supervision and  encouragement is also faulty.  Many excellent services and projects have started off with great enthusiasm only to die because no one assumed responsibility for oversight and administration. Although the leader must rule with a gentle hand, there must be accountability and responsibility. When dealing with volunteers who are not bound by any personal motive other than a desire to serve, there is often a tendency to let down one's efforts or to pass the buck to another when it may suit a whim. One of the leader's most important responsibilities is to keep the workers' eyes focused upon the real reason for all the activity and effort: ministry to and glory for the Lord. If the service is given but is seen only as a toilsome job or burden, it will not be joyfully or faithfully performed. If it is viewed as just humanistic involvement with other people or as "good works," it may lack the impetus for bringing forth best efforts. Only as people see their involvement as obedience to Christ's command to "feed my sheep" will people respond willingly and faithfully. When they realize that as they do for others, they are doing for the Lord, and that when they neglect responsibilities to others they are neglecting responsibilities to Jesus Christ, then they are more likely to perform in an attitude best suited for bringing forth fruits of righteousness.

## Leading a Worship Group

Guidelines for starting a prayer group with an emphasis on praise and worship have already been given in chapter 4. Suggestions for group leadership have also been given in the Prayer Groups section of that chapter. Following are suggestions for leading such a group, whose emphasis is upon worship.

1. Select a place that is conducive to worship. If the group does not meet in the church, be certain that the surroundings are quiet and free from distractions.

2. Create an atmosphere of worship. The mood and tone for the gathering should already be set before people begin to arrive. Quiet music, a period of silence before the meeting, or such items as religious pictures, candles, an altar, or an interest center relative to the topic or mood of the meeting all help to focus attention away from the earthly and toward the heavenly.

3. Have a theme or dominant emphasis for the gathering. Some worship is quiet, reverent, and meditative. Other forms of worship are joyful, exuberant, and demonstrative. Seek to know the Lord's divine purpose for each gathering and to lead the group to flow in the moving of the Holy Spirit. The mood may change as the Spirit moves, but all activity and purposes should be anointed and initiated by the Spirit, not prefabricated from past ideas or human expectations.

4. Have a plan but make it flexible. There is a delicate balance between coming to a meeting with absolutely no idea of what will take place and having such a rigid schedule that

the Holy Spirit could not change the plan were he to try.
Every leader will experience a last-minute leading to switch
gears at times or to adjust to an unexpected circumstance
that points in a new direction, but generally, there should
be thoughtful and prayerful preparation and some idea of the
Lord's direction and purpose in advance.  There should be,
therefore, advance planning, but it should remain flexible.

5. Be open to new or different methods.  Forms of worship may
   include anything from reading or reciting a liturgy, giving
   a talk, singing, listening to music, reading Scriptures,
   meditating in silence, offering prayers, to listening to
   others in an attitude of reverent adoration for the Lord.
   In a highly structured meeting, printed services may be used
   as a guide or a prepared liturgy may be utilized.  In more
   open meetings, participants may bring forth and share songs,
   Scriptures, testimonies of praise and thanksgiving, or prophecy as the Spirit leads.  However, in either form of worship - directed or open - there must be leadership to guide,
   judge, correct, and encourage as the meeting flows from one
   aspect of worship to another.  Some prayer-and-praise groups
   have found it especially meaningful to write their own liturgies of worship.  Using a flip chart or blackboard, the leader
   writes down the responses to an outline for worship; then
   everyone reads the created group liturgy together when it is
   finished.  Although the form of  this may be elaborate and
   poetic or very simple, depending upon the creativity and inspiration of the group members and the mood, it may be helpful to follow a structured guide or model the first few times
   this is tried.  As members become comfortable with creating
   a free-flowing liturgy, the model may be eliminated.  A very
   simple form for such an original liturgy might be:

        God, the Father, means to me . . .

        Jesus, the Son, means to me . . .

        The Holy Spirit means to me . . .

        The church means to me . . .

        Worship means to me . . .

As members give one-word or short-phrase responses (such as "love,
forgiveness, power, unity, freedom to be myself, constant and unchanging grace," etc.) the various contributions are recorded on the chart
or board for reciting together.  The addition of special music or the
singing of choruses after each topic in the liturgy may be included.

Members may also enjoy rewriting or personalizing a psalm or other
portion of Scripture as a meditative exercise or as a liturgy.  If,
for instance, a verse of a psalm is read aloud, members could give short
responses (what the passage or verse means personally) to form a liturgy.  If a longer Scripture passage is given, members may create para-

phrased versions as a meditative exercise. An example of a paraphrased and personalized version of Psalm 23 might go like this:

> The Lord is always with me; I'll never lack for
> anything or be afraid. He provides all that I need.
> He gives me guidance and peace. He gives me rest
> and assurance. He helps me grow in grace. He re-
> stores me when I am weary and gives me comfort when
> I face unknown trails. The Almighty controls both
> life and death, comforting my soul in both. Every
> good gift I possess and every victory I achieve are
> from him alone. My heart is overwhelmed with thanks-
> giving for his blessings. Because I am his child, my
> cup of blessings runs over. I will enjoy good things
> here on earth, and I can look forward to even greater
> joys in heaven with him forevermore.

There are also creative ways to worship with the use of drama,
musical instruments, vocal music, and dancing. The group may be
divided and each section asked to prepare a visual, written, or
dramatic interpretation of a Scripture passage or some aspect of
church worship or doctrine (baptism, Communion, confession, thanksgiving, etc.) Pantomime or liturgical dance can often focus ideas
that cannot be expressed in spoken words. Sometimes such group
projects may be worked on for an extended period of time, and then
everyone may come together to share the offerings and to rejoice
together in celebration. Worship group presentations may be given
for the entire church congregation on holy days or at special services. If a group prefers to work on an artistic project, members
may make paintings, collages or banners depicting aspects of worship, rather than performing dance or drama. Such offerings can
likewise be shared with the entire congregation.

Folk masses, song fests, home Communions (when clergy are
available), and other such aids to the regular church worship experiences will enhance and personalize the traditional modes of worship.
There are always new, different, and unexplored ways to offer praise
and adoration to the Lord. In leading worship, the leader must be
an open and flexible person, free from rigid and "only one way to do
it" philosophies, yet be committed to following approved church practices of worship.

6. Emphasize prayer. Chapter 4 of this manual also suggests several
   modes of prayer that can be adapted for use in a worship-oriented
   prayer-and-praise group. To achieve variety and creativity in worship, the format should be changed and new approaches explored from
   time to time. A good leader is open to experiment and improvisation,
   as long as that which is done is in good taste and glorifying to
   the Father. Whether the prayers are offered in unison (such as reciting the Lord's Prayer or selections from a prayer book), read together from other sources, offered in silence, or given conversationally, focus on prayer should have a prominent place in the
   regular format of the worship experiences of the group.

7. Seek to draw everyone in the group into the worship program in some meaningful way. Some people are more vocal and expressive than others, but even the shy, retiring individuals should be given time and opportunities to share something with the rest. It may be nothing more than being asked to read a passage of Scripture or to select the next song to be sung, but everyone should take some active part.

8. Be certain that everyone present understands what is going on. If a visitor or newcomer is unaccustomed to the form or practices of worship, allow time for explanations and clarifications. People can be very uncomfortable if they do not see the meaning or significance of things.

9. Use silence creatively. Do not be afraid of silence, for periods of quiet can be therapeutic and fruitful in the ministry of worship. Help members of the group to learn to get in touch with God and their inner beings in times of meditation, introspection, and silent worship.

10. Be free to use the entire body in worship. The more of one's senses and physical characteristics involved in an activity, the more personalized and meaningful it will be. Allow members of the group to experiment in worship through sight (pictures, visual aids, interest centers); through hearing (music, listening to devotional messages, meditations, and Scriptures); through touch (holding hands in a prayer circle, the laying on of hands for prayer, embracing); through speech (discussing, responding to questions, reading, reciting); and through physical responses (clapping, singing, lifting hands, kneeling, dancing). There should be a freedom and an acceptance of other people and their differing responses to the Lord. Although care should be given to be certain that people will not be offended by a particular form of worship and to be certain that all things are done "decently and in order," there should be an openness and a relaxed atmosphere where people are free to respond without fear of criticism or ostracism.

11. Draw conclusions. Before the group disbands, there should be some time in which the leader or another designated person summarizes the focus of the experience. If it was a time of learning, the leader may want to go over the main points emphasized from the Scripture lesson; if it was a joyful time of praise, the leader may want to conclude everything on a note of joy; if it was a quiet, introspective time together, it may be necessary to draw thoughts inward for further meditative experiences at home; if it was an especially inspiring or stimulating experience, the leader may be led to commission everyone to "go thou and do likewise." The session should end on a note of reverent conclusion, summary, or challenge to continue that which was begun through worship.

12. Be certain to check out all procedures and experiences with the clergy in advance. Allow nothing to be done that is not accepted practice in the church.

## Leading an Interest Group

People are naturally drawn together by mutual interests and shared concerns. There are any number of approaches to organizing and implementing an interest group. An announcement in the church bulletin or just passing the word to a few friends is often enough to get things going. Depending upon the type and the formality (or informality) of the group, the structure will be loose or tightly organized and the program may be spontaneous or well planned in advance. Since this is probably the easiest type of group to start and maintain (owing to the common bond that draws the people together to start with), it can be a relaxed and uncomplicated event, the gathering of people together to give and receive in an unthreatening way. Some examples of interest groups that bring people together follow:

1. Activity Groups: People in the group enjoy or want to learn to perform the same activity, such as tennis, golf, swimming, hiking (outdoor activities) or card games, gourmet cooking, sewing (indoor activities).

2. Age Groups: People at the same stage of life are drawn together to share interests and concerns or to solve mutual problems - teen-agers' groups, young mothers' groups, senior citizens' groups, etc.

3. Self-improvement Groups: Amateurs who want to learn from others and to improve their own self-images or talents may form a group to explore such activities as creative homemaking, arts and crafts, music appreciation, foreign language improvement, creative writing programs, exercise or weight reduction activities, or dance classes. Such a group may also explore spiritual disciplines or psychological approaches to more fulfilling lives.

4. Problem-solving Groups: There are established professional and re-cognized nonprofessional groups that often meet (at a church or elsewhere) to help people with their problems - Overeaters Anony-mous, Alcoholics Anonymous, Gamblers Anonymous, and family or in-dividual counseling services. Such a group might also include mem-bers of similar professions with problems of mutual concern.

5. Community Concerns Groups: People come together to discuss problems in government, civic problems, social issues, and other mutual in-terests that touch and affect their lives. Such a group may include praying for leaders and programs or becoming involved in changing things about which there is concern or opposition.

6. Educational Groups: Information is exchanged either through the membership or from invited guest speakers. Such a group may view educational films, give book reviews, take field trips, or attend lectures or exhibits in the educational field of their choice.

A leader for such groups should act as coordinator to get in touch with where the group is and where it wants to go. Duties that may need to be performed are these: (*a*) contact the people involved or delegate someone else to notify others of activities and meetings; (*b*) determine

the best time and place for meetings and programs; (*c*) arrange for programs - speaker, demonstration, sharing time, refreshments, or whatever;
(*d*) arrange for or delegate housekeeping chores, such as room arrangement and comfort, seeing that materials and supplies are available and
where they should be at the proper time, etc.; and (*e*) encourage the
efforts of the membership.  There also may be a need for evaluation of
the program or projects from time to time to be certain that everyone
is receiving the most possible from the effort.

There is something very scriptural about giving the body time to
rest amid the hectic routine of daily activities.  Rest often means
merely a change, not necessarily inactivity.  Interest groups that provide Christian activities and uplifting recreational opportunities
(something interesting, educational, or worthwhile to do in one's spare
time) are helping to edify ("build up") the body of Christ.


## Leading a Fellowship Group

A fellowship group can be anything from an informal, unstructured
get-together to a well-planned and organized recreational program.
Fellowship groups meet in the church parish hall, outdoors, or in someone's home.  Chapter 5 of this manual details various types of fellowship
groups with suggestions for providing them (see Fellowship section of
chapter 5).

The four main ingredients in any fellowship program are refreshments; conversation and sharing; activity (something for the members of
the fellowship group to "do" or become involved with); and entertainment
(music, programs, etc.)  Not all fellowships will have activities and
entertainment, but the first two ingredients - refreshments and conversation - are almost always included.

One such fellowship, popular among youth and young adults, is the
coffeehouse fellowship.  The purpose is to provide a wholesome environment in which people can relax and enjoy Christ-centered entertainment
and a friendly, social atmosphere. Leadership for such a program should be
in the hands of spiritually and emotionally mature people who relate well
with young people and who understand their needs and problems.  Although
the leaders should "speak the language" of the youth and be in touch
with their feelings and values, they should not try to become artificial
replicas of the youth they are leading. There should always remain a
healthy respect for the leader as a recognized authority figure.  In
other words, the leader should not try to become "one of the kids" to
the extent that the leadership role is undermined or completely lost.

Although the exact format for each fellowship group will be determined by the desires and interests (or needs) of those involved, some
general guidelines for a coffeehouse or similar place of fellowship are
as follows:

1. Relaxed Environment:  Large pillows for sitting on the floor, or
   card tables and comfortable chairs, are better than a formal arrangement.  Soft furnishings are preferable to formal or uncomfortable

appointments. There should be enough room to avoid overcrowding, and yet an intimate closeness is better than large, open spaces where people cannot find such intimacy.

2. Lighting: Soft lighting is preferred to harsh lights. Candles or lanterns can be used instead of electric lighting. If there is a stage area, a spotlight may be used for the entertainment programs or to feature something.

3. Music: The music can be either recorded or live, usually taking the form of religious, folk, or popular selections in good taste (no acid rock or loud music that interferes with the quiet atmosphere needed for conversations). Often the record player can be supplemented by entertainers with guitars or other instruments conducive to the atmosphere.

4. Refreshments: These should remain simple unless there is someone responsible for food preparation and clean-up and unless financing is not a problem. Usually soft drinks and finger snacks are adequate.

5. Decorations: Frequently, young people like to decorate "their" place with their own kind of motif. Posters, art work, murals, and "junk" furnishings may be less than formal, but they should be in good taste. Nothing morally or spiritually questionable should appear on the walls or on the premises. Often young people will make their posters, banners or furnishings to typify their own personalities and feelings.

6. Entertainment: If more entertainment than listening to music and informal conversation is desired, it may take the form of a talent program (planned or spontaneous) or dramatizations. People in the audience may participate by reciting poems, singing, playing instruments, dancing, or putting on skits. Sometimes it is good to have discussion drama (also called socio-drama) in which problems are enacted and the audience discusses the situation afterward, evaluating what was observed, and drawing conclusions as to proper actions and reactions in similar life situations. Although an occasional speaker or program with a "message" may be included, these should not come across as sermonizing or dictatorial. It is better to have the participants themselves perform than to bring in authority figures who may seem a threat.

7. Activities: Although no planned activity is necessary, it is good to have some prepared things to "plug in" if the evening seems to be dragging or if stimulation seems in order. It is good to have a balance of the familiar and comfortable along with the variety of the unexpected from time to time. Although humans are creatures of habit, they can become easily bored and need new stimulations. The easiest type of activity involves structuring the conversations around suggested topics of interest. This may be accomplished by giving out questions for discussion or problems to be worked through to a solution. Topics may be spiritual, social, or world issues,

but they should be of interest and concern to those in the group. Participants can be surveyed to determine topics of interest for such discussion. Some form of reporting conclusions or sharing insights from small groups to the entire audience should be implemented. Activities may also include working on a project together, playing games (preferably leading to self-discovery or group building, such as those suggested in Serendipity books), or reacting to a film, speaker, or other stimuli. Activities should be on the spiritual and emotional levels of maturity of those involved as well as at their level of interest.

8. Feedback: Some method of evaluating the ongoing program and getting in touch with the reactions of participants should be followed from time to time. This may be accomplished easily by having a suggestion box available for reactions or by providing questionnaires for rating various aspects of the program (either a 1-2-3 for good, fair, poor for various aspects, or a continuum upon which to place a rating mark). Vocal reactions may also be given before the followship concludes if there is time. Caution is needed, however, not to allow the whims or immature evaluations of the youth supersede the approved plans or guidelines set forth by those in charge.

In addition to leadership responsibilities already mentioned, there are a few other requirements for a leader of such a fellowship program. The leader should be a good organizer, coordinator, and delegator. It is good to have youth committees (such as refreshment committee, decoration committee, housekeeping committee, entertainment committee, etc.) so that the participants become actively involved rather than just being spectators. Leaders also need to know how to tailor the experiences so that they are both meaningful and relevant to those who will be involved and, at the same time, spiritually uplifting and growth-inducing. It goes without saying that such leaders need to be stable and not easily thrown off balance when things go wrong. Anything can and often does happen in such fellowship groups, and it is important to have a steady hand at the helm during a crisis. It is also advantageous to have the leadership well trained in counseling. Although this is not an absolute requirement, it will certainly be an asset when dealing with youth. Often those drawn into the fellowship will need guidance and help with problems. Those who come should be able to find a model in the leadership, a worthy example to follow. Leaders not capable of counseling should be in touch with people who are willing to be called in to provide such assistance.

Another type of fellowship group that requires organization and leadership is the social for visitors or new members at the church. Such a social should be a regular part of the ongoing chuch program in order to acclimate newcomers to what may be a strange environment among unknown people. The reason many people become disinterested in the church and its activities is because they do not become personally involved and do not feel in touch with what is going on or feel a part of the "system." As soon as a newcomer visits a church, there should be immediate follow-up to get the person in touch with other people. The "new members' social" idea is an excellent method to accomplish this.

The social for newcomers may be a covered-dish supper, a reception, or a simple coffee-and-dessert party. Workers and leaders in various church organizations and activities should be present to acquaint the new people with what is going on and to help newcomers find their own particular niche. If representatives from various church groups cannot attend, then the leader for the new members' social should be well versed in the total church program and able to answer questions about the various activities of different groups.

A program for such a new members' social could highlight the history of the church and its various programs and organizations (a slide show or visual presentation from a flip chart or posters or overhead projector to accompany a short and interesting lecture) and be incorporated into the initial meeting of the group. In addition to serving refreshments and informal "get-acquainted" chatter, there should be a formalized introduction time in which participants and host tell about themselves. Church leaders should be identified to the newcomers. The newcomers can be assisted in their introductions of themselves by giving them a list of questions in advance. In addition to asking for the newcomer's name, occupation, family status, residence, and how he or she became interested in this particular church, it is good to get some feedback from new people on these questions: (1) How is the church meeting your needs? (2) What needs do you have that have not been met? (3) How would you best fit into one or more of the activities or ministries of this church?

If the newcomers have not had enough time to become acquainted with the church in order to answer these last three questions at the first social, they can be asked to be thinking about the answers to give at the next meeting of the group (or some further form of follow-up with the newcomers can be instituted). If there is to be another gathering of the group (and there should be) a definite time and place for the next get-together should be determined and announced. Possibly the clergy could arange to be at these socials from time to time to answer questions which the new people want to ask.

Such a social can be combined with confirmation groups or new members classes, but should not be restricted to just those people. Visitors and those who transfer into a new congregation do not always attend special classes, but they should definitely not be overlooked. Every effort to extend a welcome and to foster friendly, accepting vibrations should be put forth so that visitors and new members do not feel that they are on the outside looking in. Such a program ensures that the old-timers get to know the new faces and that the new faces become one with the old-timers very quickly. The old-timers should continue to come to such functions on a regular basis and the newcomers should "graduate" to some other kind of group after the get-acquainted period is over.

This kind of fellowship can be incorporated into the regular coffee hour after Sunday morning services, for churches that have an after-service social hour, but at least an occasional evening get-together should supplement such a program. There needs to be enough time to visit, explore, and react without the pressure of a rigid schedule interrupting the bonding of the newcomers to the established fellowship. Usually clergy and leaders have too many other duties on Sunday morning to be relaxed and uninvolved with other things to give the newcomers their undivided attention.

Those involved in leading such a group must be friendly and out-going, and they must be willing to organize, plan, implement, delegate, and follow-up. As the newcomers respond to the questions and their needs become known, someone must pass such information along to others who can help the new people find their places of acceptance and involvement. The leader will also want to integrate the new people into the fellow-ship group by giving them responsibilities (bringing refreshments, help-ing to fill out name tags, participating in a panel discussion about church activities, calling another new member about coming, participating in a role play depicting problems of new church members, etc.). The leader will most likely need a team effort to coordinate all the aspects of such a fellowship program: contacting and inviting the newcomers, planning the refreshments, arranging for name tags and other materials, getting hostesses and a clean-up crew, planning the program (getting speakers or coordinating the discussion, etc.), introducing people to one another, getting feedback, and doing follow-up (seeing that newcomers get established in some group or activity that will continue to nurture them and support their spiritual growth). Such leadership requires the ability to coordinate many aspects of a total program and the ability to work well with many different kinds of people - both those on the giving and those on the receiving ends of such a ministry.

In addition to these two examples of a structured and planned social, there are many informal get-togethers which occur in church life and for which some kind of leadership must be assumed. Some churches have a family recreation night or a regular parish supper, which involves little more than alerting people to come with or without food in hand. Whether the fellowship is formally structured or not, the essentials of showing love and acceptance must be supplemented with the goal of draw-ing everyone into the inner circle of involvement. Everyone should be encouraged to have some input or some contribution to make. Those who lead fellowship groups need to remember this above all else. Involve-ment is the key to feeling worthwhile and fulfilled as a person. A lead-er who tries to do everything alone will not only become overworked but also deny someone else the opportunity to be of service.

The church and the home are the two places where fellowship and recreation should be focused. With the world of X-rated movies, unaccep-table television programs, and demoralizing forms of entertainment put-ting such improper choices before Christian youth and adults, it becomes increasingly necessary for church and home to provide acceptable alter-natives and to teach church members how to fellowship effectively. Families used to be closer and more involved with one another before the advent of "instant everything" - including rapid transportation and immediate gratification of desires. The home should be an ever available center for Christian recreational activity for both family members and guests, but often parents and children know little of how to go about

involvement in the ministry of Christian fellowship on a personal
level. The responsibility for instructing and giving models to follow
falls, then, to the church. Church leaders are needed who can help
families and individuals plan wise use of free time and who can plan
programs which are so uplifting and appealing that unacceptable alter-
natives are rejected in favor of Christian fellowship activities.
Needed are leaders to plan and coordinate family night programs, recreational activities, youth club models, and other spiritually uplifting social functions that will refresh and renew rather than degenerate.
Such a task requires leadership from dedicated Christians who will devote themselves to the prayerful performance of their duties in order
that recreation may become re-creation.

## Leading a Training Group

Some people are under the mistaken impression that only professionally trained teachers can provide leadership in instructional programs. The gift of teaching is often bestowed supernaturally by the
Lord upon unlikely candidates, and often untrained teachers become successful in imparting God's message to others. The Lord is not as interested in a person's academic credentials as he is in a person's
willingness to submit to the leadership of the Holy Spirit. The most
important requirement for someone who is in charge of a training group
is the willingness to listen to and obey the promptings of God's Spirit.

A person who lacks self-confidence is in a good position to have
God-confidence. Doubt looks to self (inadequacies, mistakes, weaknesses),
while faith looks to the Lord (who is all-knowing, all-powerful, and
completely able to bring his purposes to pass and his truth to a person's mind). Once this complete dependence upon the Lord becomes the
foundation, all other aspects of preparation for leading a training
group will fall into place more easily.

It must be admitted, however, that training groups require more
from their leadership than any other groups. This is because a training-group leader must take the leadership qualities required of one in
charge of any kind of group and combine them with the ministry of teaching. Such a ministry will require extra time for preparation and a
special dedication that may take one beyond the usual leadership responsibilities of organizing, coordinating, delegating, administrating, and
correcting. Those who train others must give the extra time and energy
needed to learn the lessons first before trying to impart them to others.

There are four types of training groups that will interest church
leaders: Bible study groups, discipleship training groups, self-discovery groups, and community-building groups. Under these broad head-
ings, there are various subgroups of differing kinds in each category.
Before exploring these training-group categories one by one, however,
there are some general principles (which apply to all people involved
in leading training programs) that need consideration.

# Ingredients for Any Training Program

## Discovery - Understanding - Application

These are the three keys to any kind of learning. In terms of better understanding, they may be translated into the following questions: (1) What is the message? (2) What does it mean? (3) How does it apply to me (or, What do I do about it?). If a leader can bring any training group to find the answers to these questions, it will be a meaningful time of instruction.

## Training Techniques

Often a training leader tries to put in "too much" to be absorbed in the time allotted for the study. It is advantageous to have a key-word outline giving the basics to be covered in clear, uncomplicated language. If a copy of the outline can be distributed to the participants, that is even better. The outline not only will keep the lesson on the right track, but will also lead everyone logically from point to point coherently, making the lesson easy to follow and understand.

The leader's role is that of stimulator and guide. Leaders should never consider themselves to be oral readers or lecturers. Of all the methods of oral communication, reading and lecturing are the least effective methods. The goal is to get participants as actively involved in the lesson as possible. When only their hearing is involved (as in listening to the instructor read or lecture), there is no more than a 10 percent chance of retention of what is communicated. As other senses of the students are stimulated, the percentage of retention increases. For instance, there is more pupil involvement if the visual senses are included, as in observing animated story-telling, viewing visual aids, or seeing gestures and physical involvement (facial expresson, emotiveness, etc.) in a conversational delivery. Although this is much better than merely sitting and listening, there is still limited pupil involvement because only the eyes and ears are involved. When students are allowed to participate vocally, there are both higher ratios of pupil involvement and higher percentages of information retained. This involvement may take the form of questions and answers, class discussions, or verbal games or contests. The highest pupil retention is achieved when their is total pupil involvement (90 percent retention). This is when pupils are discovering for themselves through research, interviews, committee work, or creative projects where their total personalities and all their senses are absorbed in the learning process. Obviously there cannot be constant involvement at this level in each learning session. There must be some time for explanations from the instructor, some instruction time, and some discussion time. But trainers should try to visualize their instructional periods and include demonstrations as well as discussions that will draw in pupils to participate actively as fully as possible. For instance, during an instructional period, the trainer would not read or lecture, but would conversationally explain the information to be given, perhaps using visual aids (flip chart, board, pictures, objects, slides, films, etc.). The trainer might also have an involvement sheet for the pupils, which would both outline the lesson and provide blanks at important points for students to fill in. Having students take notes or fill in information will not be just "busy work." It puts the brain power, touch power, and eye power in combination with the ear power, and helps to achieve high pupil involvement for optimum retention of information.

There will most certainly be times when a passage must be read aloud to the group (e.g., a Bible passage or a quotation that must not be paraphrased). The leader should not skip over this part of the lesson merely because reading is the poorest teaching method, but should, instead, try all the harder to make the passage to be read as stimulating as possible with vocal and facial expression and eye contact. The reading should be followed up with questions or other stimulators to ensure that understanding has been achieved. Also the reading time should be limited to brief passages rather than lengthy readings, which would increase the possibility of losing the audience.

A good teacher keeps asking three questions: (1) Are my lessons enjoyable? (There is nothing that says fun and laughter will inhibit learning.) (2) Are my lessons relevant? (Do the students really need to know this information?) (3) Are my lessons involving my students in varied ways? (Each lesson should not be given in the same old way every time. New experiences and interesting methods of delivery will keep students on their toes, expectant and ready to learn. This variety should, of course, include as many of the pupils' senses as possible in as many different ways as possible.)

## Cognitive and Affective Learning

Leaders of training groups should be familiar with the two kinds of learning that exist and seek to include them in various ways throughout the training program. Cognitive learning is what is commonly thought of as "head knowledge" - facts and informational data. Affective learning is emotional and personal response to what is learned - opinions and judgments. Both kinds of learning have their place and should be incorporated in instruction. To make this clearer, listed below are these two aspects of learning, further broken down into subcategories.

Cognitive Learning: Cognitive-learning applications are listed from easiest to hardest (or simplest kinds of learning operations to the more complex). The further down the list one goes, the more involved the learning process and the more the pupil's personal involvement is required in terms of "think power."

Knowledge - Information given back, parrot fashion: "Recite the Ten Commandments."

Comprehension - Understanding information: "What does it mean to bear false witness?"

Application - Using information:  "In what specific ways
            can you honor your father and your mother in
            this coming week?"

Analysis - Breaking down information into its component
            parts:  "Which commandments refer to one's
            relationship to God, and which refer to one's
            relationship with one's fellows?"

Synthesis - Bringing parts together into a meaningful
            whole:  "Each student will research one
            commandment and prepare a visual or sym-
            bolic interpretation of it for inclusion
            in a program on the Ten Commandments."

Evaluation - Drawing conclusions:  "Evaluate the Ten
            Commandments, one by one, in terms of rele-
            vancy for life in the twentieth century."


Affective Learning:  Since there are no right or wrong responses in
affective learning, it is often less threatening than being put on the
spot for one particular right answer.  Trainers should be sensitive to
the attitudes and insecurities of the training group and should use the
affective-learning approach whenever it best suits the situation.

Opinions and Responses - No right or wrong answer, just
            personal response:  "What color do you think
            of for each of the Ten Commandments and why?"

Value Judgments and Choices (preferences) - "Which com-
            mandment is most important to you?  Which is
            hardest to keep?"

Feelings (emotional responses) - "How do you feel inside
            when you know you have broken one of God's
            commandments?"

Personal Interpretations (meaning in an individual's
            life) - "What do you consider to be 'other
            gods' that modern people put before the Lord?
            What 'gods' do you have?"


## Leading Discussions Effectively

Oftentimes a leader will open the floor for a discussion and
either nothing happens or what does happen is not significant.  Discussions do not occur spontaneously; they must be designed and guided to
a fruitful conclusion.  The following guidelines are suggested:

1. Introduce the topic:  The leader has the responsibility of
    setting the boundaries for the discussion and of giving the

239

participants some idea of the direction in which the discussion is to flow. Leaders should never just let people talk on unrelated or inappropriate topics.

2. <u>Know in advance what kind of discussion it is to be</u>:  There are two basic kinds of discussions - problem-solving and informational.  The leader should know the components of both kinds and how to direct conversations along the pattern for each.

   Problem-solving discussions involve the following:

   What is the problem?  (Define terms and state clearly.)

   What is the history of the problem?  (Background information.)

   What are the possible causes of the problem?  (Contributing factors.)

   Suggested solutions?  (Possible methods of coping with the problem.)

   Evaluations of each solution suggested?  (Strengths and weaknesses of suggested solutions.)

   What is the <u>best</u> solution?  (Determing the best course of action.)

   Informational discussion involve the following:

   What is the topic?  (Terms defined and stated clearly.)

   What are the aspects of the topic to which the discussion is to be limited?  (Points to be covered.)

   What information is available on each point?  (Examples, facts, illustrations, and respected opinions concerning each point.)

   What conclusions can be drawn?  (What is learned from this information?)

3. <u>Launch questions</u>:  The leader should have some questions prepared with which to open the topic to discussion and lead it in the proper direction.  Questions may be factual (cognitive) or opinion-oriented (affective), but they should be chosen carefully for relevancy and interest value.

4. <u>Keep on target</u>:  Discussions can easily ramble from the subject, so a discussion leader must stay alert to observe when this starts.  The leader should courteously but firmly

bring the discussion back to the topic. This may be done by directing a related question to another person or by breaking in to say, "I think we're going afield of what we're after here. The point we are discussing (question we are asking) is . . . ."

5. Give everyone a chance: Because of the differences in personalities, there may be verbose individuals who will want to dominate the discussion or quiet ones who are content to sit back and listen while offering no opinions. A very important part of the leader's job is to draw in the shy and to control the dominators. The leader must be alert to keep everyone involved equitably. This may take some doing. Drawing in the shy may be accomplished by directing questions to them by name ("Mary, we haven't heard from you on the subject. What do you think about . . . ."). Passing over the loud-mouths requires more finesse: ("Thank you, Bob, for sharing your thoughts. Now let's hear from . . ." or "There are some others who haven't had a chance to express themselves yet. Let's find out what they have to say."). If such approaches are not enough to control the talkative ones, a more direct measure may be in order. The leader may have to break in to set further guidelines for the discussion, such as limiting the number of times a person may take the floor or limiting the length of time for any one opinion. Although it is contrived and less spontaneous and natural, it may be necessary as a last resort to go around the room one by one in order to get balanced contributions from each participant.

6. Summarize occasionally: Even with an outline to guide the discussion from point to point, participants often lose sight of the direction of the discussion. From time to time the leader should make clarifying statements and sum-marize conclusions drawn from the group. This is especially appropriate before moving from one main idea to the next.

7. Keep the discussion moving: A leader should not let a discussion get "bogged down" at one point. When enough time to explore a particular aspect of the topic has been given, the leader should introduce the next question or point.

8. Draw the discussion to a conclusion: Every discussion should have some outcome. The leader needs to clarify and state this outcome so that participants will know exactly what was learned from the encounter. If there is agreement as to the conclusions (or solutions) reached, the leader might say something like, "The consensus is that . . . ." If, however, there is difference of opinion at the end of the discussion, the leader may describe the views of each side and make an appropriate summation: "Although there are differing viewpoints on the topic [give a brief review of each viewpoint], the conclusions we have reached are . . . ."

241

## Preparing and Asking Questions

Every leader will need to involve the participants in responding to questions (asked by the leader). Some advance planning should go into determining the kinds of questions to ask.

1. Questions should be worth knowing the answer to (important questions).

2. Questions should be relevant (related-to-the-topic questions).

3. Questions should be stated simply and briefly (uncomplicated questions).

4. Questions should be stated clearly (nonambiguous questions).

5. Questions should cause people to think and grow (challenging and inspirational questions).

6. Questions should summarize and highlight the lesson (insightful questions).

7. Questions should spark more interest and further study (stimulating questions).

Before a training session, leaders should test out the questions they plan to ask either orally or in some other form (written responses, research projects, group analysis, etc.). If a question does not meet the criteria, it should be discarded or rephrased.

## Preparing to Lead or Teach Training Groups

Chapter 2 of this manual, under the section titled "The Teacher," contains suggestions for teachers, which may have bearing upon this section on leaders of training groups. Although written more from the viewpoint of a Sunday school teacher, some of the guidelines there apply to the leader of any instructional group, and may therefore be an appropriate supplement to this section.

The most important question trainers need to answer is, "What will the participants know or be able to do after instruction that they will not know or be able to do before instruction?" Too often leaders think of a lesson only in terms of what they will be saying and doing. It is most needful that such thinking be turned around to the viewpoint of those on the receiving end. Lessons should always be prepared from the standpoint of the students' needs, abilities, and potential toward growth and understanding. The best lesson in the world is no good if a student cannot grasp it, relate to it, or become involved with it.

After a trainer has considered the course in general and the next lesson in particular from the students' viewpoint, the actual design of a lesson plan is the next step. Preparation of a lesson plan will most likely include the following steps:

1. Prayer and meditation: Each lesson should be lifted to the Lord in prayer for guidance. Often the Lord will have a different approach in mind from that in a lesson guide or in the leader's mind. It is essential that a time of meditative listening be given before beginning to prepare a lesson. The Lord knows who will be at the meeting with what needs and what expectations. Allow the Holy Spirit to design and direct every session. Learning to trust inner guidance rather than printed guidebooks or predetermined formulas is sometimes scary at first. But it is something the Lord will help leaders learn to do as they "hang loose" and learn to walk by faith.

2. Reading and research: Leaders should know a great deal more about the lesson than they plan to bring out. They may need to look to several sources for the right information, to underline, to take notes, and to assimilate. Training-group leaders should enjoy such reflective study times rather than viewing them as instrusive or burdensome chores. Often, in such times of preparation, the Lord will reveal secrets and jewels of wisdom never discovered before. A regular time should be set aside for this study and preparation - and it should be adequate time (not a last-minute rush to get it done). Choose a time free from interruptions and a time when freedom from other responsibilities will allow for undivided attention.

3. Synthesis of materials: Leaders must be discriminating and must use good judgment in the selection of what to teach or choose for participants to do. Everything offered in a guidebook may not be relevant or necessary. Often leaders may need to take things from several sources and put them together in a lesson. At other times they may eliminate whole portions of suggested information or throw out the guide materials altogether and use an entirely different approach. Leaders should not fear to experiment and be creative in their training program. The outcome of the final lesson should be the result of considering many different approaches and the prayerful selection of the best one.

4. Outlining the lesson: Leaders should not attempt to guide others without a guide for themselves. Although many leaders seem to be successful without benefit of an outline to go by, it is better to have one and not need it than to need it and not have it. Outlining the lesson in advance gives a step-by-step preview of the program and will keep things moving logically and coherently to a meaningful conclusion.

5. Reviewing and reflecting: After the lesson has been prayed about, thought about, read about, researched, synthesized, and outlined, it should be reflected upon.

Look back at the lesson as a whole to see if there is too
much emphasis here or not enough emphasis there. Ask,
"What nonessentials need to be eliminated?" and "What has
been forgotten?" Does the content of the entire lesson
assist in moving the class toward the educational goal
for the learning experience? Review should also include
some mental and oral practice. Try the lesson out on someone in the family to determine if explanations are clear
and if understanding takes place. Or record the lesson on
a cassette tape and play it back for self-evaluation. Give
enough time to ensure that a meaningful learning experience
will take place at the proper time.

6. Asking evaluative questions: Questions leaders should ask
before giving a lesson include: (1) What information
should be used? (2) What should be omitted? (3) What is
my educational purpose? (4) Where will emphasis be placed
in this lesson? (5) How will I know if I achieve my purpose or reach my goals for this lesson? (Criteria for
evaluation should be determined in advance.)

Sample Lesson Plan

Some elements are common to all lesson plans, regardless of the
type of training program for which they are prepared. The following
is a sample plan:

Lesson Title: _____    Lesson Date: _____

Lesson Goal:  (concepts of the lesson; objectives to
              be accomplished)

Materials Needed:  (teaching aids - books, Bible
                   references, supplies)

Teaching Methods:  (what teacher will do - lecture?
                   show film?  demonstrate?  lead discus-
                   sion?  give a chalk talk?)

Learning Activities: (what pupils will do - read?
                     listen?  write?  dramatize?  research?
                     construct?  discuss?)

Evaluation:   (what criteria will be used to determine
              success - quiz?  class participation?
              completion of a project?)

Now that some principles common to all types of training programs
have been discussed, attention may be turned to specific types of
training groups.

# Leading a Bible Study Group

People who lead Bible study groups do not have to be "Bible scholars," but they should be willing to learn along with the group and to keep discussions and lessons to the point. They should also be sensitive and responsive to the leadings of the Holy Spirit.

Some general suggestions for a beginning Bible teacher follow:

1. Because the majority of the participants will not be well versed in a systematic knowledge of the Bible, do not try to cover too much too fast. One main idea each lesson is preferable to many ideas which end in confusion.

2. Begin preparing a week in advance, working on a lesson a little at a time rather than trying to do it all at once. New ideas will come, details can be worked out gradually, and the Holy Spirit can bring circumstances and examples to include throughout the week.

3. Do as much reading as possible in the book or passages of Scripture to be covered. Read the entire section to get an overview; then go back and reread it more slowly to look for themes, patterns, main ideas, etc. Finally, read it a third time to determine its message, meaning, and application to life. Study guides and commentaries may be helpful, but do not forget to rely upon the Holy Spirit to show the "message" he wants delivered to the students each lesson.

4. Determine the main or dominant theme for each lesson. Try to relate this message to the needs and personalities of the students so that they can see the Bible as more than just a story or history book, as a guidebook for life with relevant applications for themselves.

5. Remember to teach rather than give a devotional. Other types of inspirational groups and meetings can move people and stir their emotions, but the purpose of a Bible study group is to give knowledge and direction to lives based upon what the Bible has to say. A touching story may move people to tears, but unless there is a life application of a solid biblical truth behind the story it will have little lasting effect.

6. Decide in advance what points to emphasize. Everything in a passage will not be of equal importance, so determine what to stress and what to go over quickly or lightly.

7. Review frequently to refresh memories of past lessons and to relate former lessons with present ones. Do not to into great detail on reviewing, but keep the lessons flowing in continuity and coherence.

8. Determine the type of Bible study it is to be. There are three basic patterns that may be followed: lecture method, class discussion method, and student preparation method. The lecture method is used for large groups where student participation is difficult to handle. Even if the teacher does all the talking, it should not be a rigid, formal presentation, but should include as much visualization and stimulation as possible and should also include a question period. Class discussion methods include the participants in analyzing, questioning, debating, and discussing the lesson material. Topics for discussion can be handed out in advance for preparation and preconsideration, or the discussion can be spontaneous. Students may also hand in questions they would like to have discussed, if this method is preferred. The student preparation method of Bible study requires the most work from the pupils because they help to teach the lessons. This may be done either by assigning different sections of a lesson to various students or by letting students take turns presenting the lesson from week to week. The advantage of student-involvement studies is obvious - interest and enthusiasm is greatly increased. The drawbacks are there also, however. If students are not dependable (frequently absent or unprepared or poorly prepared) the whole lesson can fall through. For this reason, the leader should always have a substitute lesson ready even when others have been assigned the responsibility for it.

By whatever method a Bible lesson is presented, high pupil involvement is important. Even if one uses the lecture method, everyone in the group should know what the assigned Scripture lesson will be the coming week and should study it in advance. This not only fosters the all-important aspect of pupil involvement, but also saves time when the lesson begins. Each person already is oriented to the passage under consideration and has some idea of the content and possible interpretations of meanings, rather than starting "cold."

The three keys to meaningful study have been mentioned already: discovery, understanding, and application. The biggest responsibility of the leader is to guide the group members into their own personal discovery of the message of the Scriptures and then to help them to comprehend the implications of these discoveries, and finally, from this to encourage each one to make the appropriate personal applications that will help foster spiritual growth. The leader keeps asking, and encouraging others to ask, "What does the passage say? . . . What does it mean? . . . How does it apply to my life?" The answers to these three questions may be different for various people, but there will be a thread of unity binding together those who are seeking to read, understand, and apply truth for their lives.

The leader sets the pace for the entire group. A leader who moves lessons along too fast will leave the group behind, whereas the one who moves too slowly will have a bored and restless group. The leader must determine "where the group is" spiritually and how much they can absorb at one time - and then adjust the lessons to that particular pace. It is best to keep sessions to about an hour in duration (unless there is a reason for a prolonged session: the maturity and desire of the group might demand longer sessions; or preservation of continuity for a particular lesson might mandate on extended session to complete a particular segment).

Leaders must also remember the importance of their individual preparation. Even if the lesson is a familiar Bible passage and even if they have led a training group through the study previously, each session should be viewed as a fresh and unique experience to which their best efforts must be applied. Praying for the members of the group by name and asking for discernment about their needs prior to the lesson; praying for the Bible study, that the Lord will anoint the teaching and the learning that goes on and will bless and harvest the seeds of truth to be sown; and praying for themselves as teachers that they may be cleansed and usable vessels, fit for the Master's use - these are essential parts of spiritual preparation before attempting to teach. Prayer must be predominant, not only before the time of the teaching session, but also during it. Open and close with prayer and rely upon it anytime between when it is appropriate to do so.

After the main points of a Bible lesson are determined and written down, leaders will want to give some time to preparing questions and discussion outlines for lesson follow-up. Suggestions for this follow:

## Questions to Ask

1. <u>Clarifying questions</u>. These questions guide the participants' thoughts and keep the lesson in focus.

2. <u>Summarizing questions</u>. These questions consolidate what has been learned previously with new information.

3. <u>Discussion questions</u>. These questions open discussion and provide an opportunity for group input.

## Discussion Directions

Following the guidelines given previously (section on Leading Discussions Effectively, this chapter), will provide the group with the opportunity to comment upon the lesson content, to report on applications of the previous lessons, and to suggest applications for the present lesson. Applications should be realistic (obtainable goals, not unreachable expectations). During discussion, leaders should keep their own talking to a minimum. They will have the opportunity to have their say during the lesson portion, but during discussion their function is to launch the questions, to keep the discussion flowing without rambling or getting off onto tangents, to provide everyone with an opportunity to be heard, and to summarize the thoughts and conclusions of others.

The leader should also remember that the Bible is the most relevant and exciting book one could read; therefore, it is wrong to bore people with it by dreary plodding and slowly moving through every single verse of a lengthy chapter. The leader should have determined in advance how much ground to cover and should have selected the most important passages to emphasize, eliminating the rest from the discussion. If a member of the group finds that a particular important verse or aspect of the Bible lesson has been overlooked, he or she will usually bring it out anyway, so a leader should not worry if every verse is not covered line by line.

## Approaches to Take

Bible study groups may follow a printed curriculum guide or a "home-grown" pattern of study. Before determining the approach to take, the needs, maturity, and desires of the group should be taken into consideration. It is best for a beginning group to have some printed guidebook or course of study (even if this is modified or supplemented according to preferences). The Navigators (P.O. Box 1659, Colorado Springs, Colorado 80901) have courses of study at different levels of interest and maturity which might be considered. The Bible Reading Fellowship (P.O. Box M, Winter Park, Florida 32790) is another source of information on curriculum. Book and Bible stores are usually full of curriculum materials and aids for Bible study classes. One particularly good reference source is Henrietta C. Mears, What the Bible Is All About (Gospel Light Publications, Glendale, California). This volume is an easy-to-understand survey of the entire Bible, book by book. It contains information on content of each book, explanations, commentaries, and teaching aids. Companion volumes, which may be used as students' books, are entitled A Look at the Old Testament and A Look at the New Testament.

Whether Bible study leaders choose a printed curriculum or develop their own (or whether it is a group project of the class to determine what and how to study), the final determination should be submitted to the clergy in charge for approval before the instruction begins. This is an important safeguard that should not be overlooked.

Once the curriculum has been determined, the next step is determining which of the many appropriate approaches would be best to follow. Here again, the age level, spiritual maturity, and needs of the group to be instructed must be considered, because the leader is not teaching a curriculum but people! For instance, Bible quizzes and games may appeal to one group and be considered an immature approach to another. One group may want to follow prepared outlines with printed discussion questions to guide their study, while another group may prefer freely to discuss questions of their own making that originate out of the study itself. It may be necessary to try out several approaches before the one best suited to a particular group becomes evident. If everyone enters the study with an adventurous spirit, ready to listen to the leading of the Holy Spirit and ready to explore and learn together (and if there is a free and open atmosphere where objections and personal reactions are accepted), it will not take long to determine what works best.

One approach is a topical study. The group members may be asked to prepare a list of topics they are interested in studying (prayer, the Holy Spirit, forgiveness, witnessing, faith, etc.). Scriptures related to these topics are then researched in a concordance and through other Bible reference sources for reading, comparison, and discussion.

Another approach is a character study. The group selects characters of the Old or New Testament about whom they want to know more. Bible passages about the lives of these people are then read, researched, and reported on. Each person in the group may be given a name to research and tell about, if the leadership is to be shared. The characters may be the patriarchs, the prophets, the disciples, women of the Bible, children of the Bible, or an in-depth study of a particular character, such as Jesus (early life, miracles, teachings, ministries) or St. Paul (early life, conversion, missionary career, final days, letters and teachings). A character study should be accompanied by some underlying lesson for life that the person's life exemplifies.

Thematic studies are still another approach. In such a study, a theme is selected ("Promises to the Believer" . . . "Convenants in the Bible" . . . "Parables of Jesus" . . . "History of the Church" . . . "Methods of God's Revelations to Man" . . . "The Writings of St. John," etc.). Each week's lesson is a segment of the overall theme until the unit is completed.

Doctrines of the church may also be researched in Scripture and studied from week to week. A unit of study can be prepared on the sacraments, for instance (baptism, Communion, marriage, holy orders, penance, etc.) or on holy days and celebrations of the church (Advent, Lent, Pentecost, etc.). When studying doctrines or church practices it is often interesting to determine when present traditions were first mentioned in Scripture. Where, for instance, is the first reference to baptism or speaking in tongues or sanctification? Tracing the development of such traditions, practices, or beliefs to see how they have changed and developed and comparing them with modern interpretations can be both educational and meaningful to one's individual participation in accepted practices. Often one does things or believes things without fully realizing the scriptural teaching or reasons behind them.

The most common approach to Bible study is to take the Bible, one book at a time, and read it, discuss it, and determine its personal applications. When a passage is long or complicated it is a good idea to advise the students to read it over three times. The first time, read it through ocmpletely and generally to get the feel of the passage as a whole. The second reading should be approached specifically to look for details, key verses, key words, particular themes and insights into purposes and meanings. The third time, read it personally, looking for what it says to you as an indiviudal. A notebook and pen should be readily available to jot down these three responses: (1) general impression of the reading as a whole; (2) key message or theme; and (3) personal application. Often sharing these notes will make for a lively and meaningful discussion.

It is also helpful to one's understanding to determine background information on particular passages, such as the author, where it was written and under what circumstances, and the history of the time (what the people and the country were like then, etc.). Someone may be appointed to give background information for each lesson if the leader does not assume this responsibility. The emphasis should be placed upon the theme or "message" of the lesson, however, not upon background data.

For advanced Bible students or for those who enjoy digging in for extensive research, a comparative Bible study may be launched. In such a study, one book or passage is compared with another for similarities, differences, and insights. Such a study might be finding Jesus and New Testament teachings in the Old Testament, prophecies of the Old Testament fulfilled in the New Testament, or a comparative study of the four Gospels or the Epistles.

By whatever method a Bible study is approached, it may be wise to begin with a lesson on "Why Study the Bible?" There are many reasons for becoming involved in Bible study, but often people approach it without a full understanding of why they are doing so. It may just seem the thing to do or maybe people are coming from improper motives. Participants need to be made aware of the advantages, blessings, and promises that are their legacy as they start the adventure of Bible exploration. The following is a sample list of research questions which can be used for an introductory lesson to aid students in an appreciation for the Bible and to heighten their feelings of responsibility toward reading and living by biblical precepts. The questions may be put on a flip chart or duplicated and passed out to the group members. Each person may look up one of the Scripture references and report, in turn, about the benefits of Bible study.

## Why Study the Bible?

1. What relationship does Scripture reading have to faith? (Rom. 10:17)

2. What relationship does Scripture reading have to conversion or being "born again"? (I Pet. 1:23-25)

3. What profitable correction comes from Bible reading? (II Tim. 3:15-16)

4. What profitable purposes are derived from Bible reading? (James 1:21; I John 2:5)

5. How is the Word of God like a mirror of life? (Heb. 4:12)

6. How does the Bible keep us from stumbling in the dark of sin and uncertainty? (Ps. 119:105)

7. What promises are given those who obey God's Word? (Deut. 11:8-9; Josh. 1:7-8)

8. What help is the Bible in preparing for life? (Ps. 119:9-11)

9. How has God promised to bless when his word is used in ministry? (Isa. 55:8-11)

10. What did Jesus say about the importance of the Scriptures? (Matt. 4:4; 22:29)

11. What did Jesus say about himself in relation to Old Testament Scriptures? (Luke 4:16-21; 24:44-47)

12. What warnings are given to us about adding to or subtracting from the Scriptures? (Rev. 22:18-19)

13. What did Jesus say concerning the fulfillment of all things written in Scripture? (Matt. 5:17-18)

14. What promise is given teachers of the Word? (Matt. 5:19)

15. How long will the Scriptures endure? (Isa. 40:8; Matt. 24:35)

16. Name five additional things Scripture reading will do. (John 15:3; 17:17; 8:31; Ps. 19:7; 119:50-51)

## Follow-Up Activities

Once the lesson has been introduced and the Scriptures read, explained, and discussed, there may still be a need for further pupil involvement prior to making applications. If an activity is needed to stimulate interest or to get students motivated to participate more fully, the leader may need some gimmicks in addition to discussion questions. Activities may be as simple as asking participants to find the key word or key idea in a passage or to underline the most meaningful part of a selection. They may also involve sensory responses such as writing or describing the color, sound, texture, or smell that a particular passage brings to mind. "What Happened Next" explorations are also creative idea-starters. For instance, the leader might ask, "What happened the next day after Adam and Eve were sent away from Eden?" or "What happened the next day after the Prodigal Son returned home and confronted his elder brother?"

Students may also be asked to react to Scripture passages vocally, nonverbally, or in written form. For instance, if a passage is controversial in its acceptance or interpretation by the group, those who agree with someone's actions in the Bible story or who disagree with an interpretation may gesture thumbs up, thumbs down, or raise a designated number of fingers. From this may follow a discussion of why each voted as he did. A written reaction may take the form of symbols to place alongside verses. Although each group may originate its own symbols, some suggested ones are these: a question mark by passages one does not understand; a check by those understood; an "x" by verses one disagrees with; a star by those in agreement with; an arrow pointing upward for passages that inspire or lift faith; and an arrow pointing downward for those that convict or make the reader uncomfortable.

Another activity may involve the drawing of a graph or picture to represent the Scripture passage. By placing oneself in the story pictorially, a personalization occurs. For instance, in a graph, how would Jesus' life or his response to others at a particular time compare with a graph of your own life or reactions? (The situation may involve forgiveness, time spent in prayer, concern for others, submission to unjust authorities, and other such experiences in life.) Another graphic activity involves sketching a picture or line drawing of a particular Bible story or excerpt and placing oneself somewhere in the picture. For example, in a drawing of the cross at the time of Jesus' crucifixion, where would you be? At the time of the early Christian church when followers of Jesus were imprisoned for their faithfulness, where would you be and what would you be doing?

Review quizzes to determine understanding may also be incorporated at the conclusion of each lesson or from time to time (say, at the conclusion of a unit of study). These may be given in game form or as a contest (teams working together for the most right answers), or individuals may write their answers to check out their comprehension of the lesson.

The curriculum chosen, approaches used, and method of follow-up may vary from group to group or from time to time within the same group. Those things, after all, are secondary to the real purpose of Bible study: opening hearts to receive the nourishment and strengthening power of God's Word.

## Leading a Discipleship Training Group

While closely related to Bible study groups, discipleship training groups have a different emphasis. The use of the Scriptures is a supplemental part of a wider-based program that concentrates upon discovering what it means to be a disciple of Jesus Christ in general and how individuals can do it in particular. A disciple is a "learner" (one who receives instruction and follows the practices of the instructions received). The making of a disciple involves discipline. It requires study and application. Sometimes a group involved in such a study is called by other names such as "Spiritual Growth Group" or "Being a Christian in Today's World" or some other similar title. The purpose is to discover answers to questions such as the following:

What is a disciple? How does a disciple act and react?

How does one become a disciple?

How can one be a disciple in daily life - at church, at home, at work, etc.

How does a disciple behave when no one is looking?

What problems are confronted by disciples - temptations, sacrifices, persecutions, difficult choices in home life, social life, business, etc.

What help is available to disciples to enable them to keep progressing?

Obviously, the leadership for such a group should rest in the hands of someone who is at least moderately successful at being a disciple. Such potential leaders do not have to have all the questions answered completely or all their own problems solved, but they should be sincere about becoming a committed disciple. They should be able to inspire others to join them in the quest of "becoming."

The type of curriculum or program depends upon the needs and interests of the group, as always. For some, a published curriculum guide or workbook is followed. The Churches Alive series (Box 3800, San Bernardino, California 92413) offers a good program at various levels to help Christians attain effectiveness in discipleship and evangelism. The program offers "Discovery Classes" for the brand-new Christian or those who wish a review of basic biblical principles, such as assurance of salvation, forgiveness for sin, overcoming temptation, and answers to prayers. After completing the basic course, members of a Discovery Group "graduate" to a "Growth Group." Growth groups are for the church members who are committed to continued spiritual growth through programs of Bible study, sharing of experiences and insights, prayer, and methods of outreach (performing specific acts of love and concern for others in the church or community). There are also courses offered in evangelism (intensive training in witnessing) which include class and field experiences. These types of programs are designed to help Christians see their devotion to the Lord through both taking in (going to church, receiving Communion, fellowshiping) and giving out (committing themselves to study and spiritual disciplines, performing apostolic actions of outreach and service). This particular training program offers suggestions for developing leadership and for clergy involvement in the ongoing program.

The starting place for the development of these kinds of groups is in an evaluative survey. Questions that need to be asked are these:

How well are present programs working in terms of church growth and spiritual development of the membership?

How are present programs organized, funded and controlled for quality?

What are the weaknesses in present programs?

What improvements need to be implemented?

What opportunities exist for changing lives, adding to church vitality, strengthening leadership capabilities, causing growth, and creating enthusiastic interest among the membership?

Are responsibilites clearly defined?

Do participants work in mutual love and respect in unity?

How clearly are objectives and goals outlined?

What method of appraisal and evaluation of progress exists for future improvements?

Where are the potential leaders and how can they best be trained to help carry out the missions of growth and outreach?

For those desiring a less structured format and a more flexible program in a discipleship group, the study may grow out of the problems and concerns of the group members themselves. Some groups invite guest speakers to share insights in Christian living. Other groups select Christian books as well as Scriptures to study together and discuss. Still others look to the leader to design the content of each session, or various leaders take turns presenting lessons. The format is not as important as the outcomes. By whatever means, it is the end result (strengthening the commitment and furthering the growth of Christians) that should be the point of concentration.

Some method of screening and training discipleship group leaders should be instituted. This may include interviews with the clery and attending special training sessions. At other times, leaders emerge from one discipleship training class to form new ones. Certainly such leaders should be dedicated Christians who support the services and programs of the church regularly and faithfully and whose leadership potential has been evidenced in definite ways. The spouse of such a leader should be in sympathy with the program and should support and encourage the leader's dedication of time and effort to fulfilling responsibilities.

Leaders of discipleship groups should seek to be enablers. They must encourage and support others who are struggling with Christian concepts in a pagan world, those who face daily the conflicts of warfare between flesh and spirit, between the desire to serve the Lord wholeheartedly and the pull of worldly cares upon time and attention. Through the open sharing of these struggles and hopes, victories and failures, others gain support and strength in understanding that they are not alone on the path toward Christian growth and commitment. The group becomes the place where one can be trained and armed for battle, healed and restored after a defeat, and encouraged and supported in each new conquest. Through the inspiration and testimonies of those who have walked the path before, through Bible study and prayer, through sharing of mutual problems and concerns, and through the encouragement and outreach of the group, disciples begin to emerge.

If a time is set aside during the discipleship group for formal instruction of some kind, it should take place first, at the beginning of the session. Following the instructional period (no more than an hour or so) should come a time of sharing experiences and discussing mutual problems. Praying for one another and encouraging one another should climax the program. Some groups also include a time to plan for and implement some kind of outreach ministry - a special activity planned for the youth of the church, a supper for the elderly, a program to take to a local institution, or some other kind of missionary or evangelistic effort that will involve the discipleship group in giving of themselves to others. It is sometimes good to take a Bible lesson to emulate or an example from the life of a Bible character being studied to follow in some practical application. Either as a group or individually, the members experiment with putting into practice the lessons studied in class. Life becomes the "laboratory" in which spiritual experiments are tested. The results are then compared and discussed by the group when it meets again. In this way, biblical truths and lessons taught by speakers or through other sources become the springboards to thrust members into apostolic living day by day.

Discipleship groups may meet at the church, in homes, or in another designated place. The advantage of meeting at the church is that it has a built-in atmosphere conducive to spiritual things - an altar for prayer and commitment is close by, the reverence of the church setting is in keeping with the purposes and goals of the group, etc. Also, the church is usually centrally located and easy for group members to come to each week. The advantage of meeting in homes rather than at the church is the relaxed and informal atmosphere, which often allows people to be less self-conscious and freer to explore their true feelings and thoughts. It is a further advantage to see church people out of the church setting. Everyone is expected to "play church" (put on spiritual attitudes and actions) when they are on the church grounds, but it is quite another thing to take the commitment into one's home and into one's personal relationships. People are usually more open in a home setting. It may be a good idea to try out different meeting places until the right one speaks to the group, or alternate between regular meetings in homes and an occasional Commitment or Communion service at the church. The opposite of this can also be tried - meeting regularly at the church with an occasional home service or social. One such group, which usually met at the church, decided to have a series of covered-dish suppers in homes of various members during Lent. The host for the evening provided the main dish and drink while others in the group brought side dishes. Their pastor was invited to come and conduct a home Communion service in which the members participated freely and ministered to one another.  A time of Bible study, devotion, singing, and worship thus supplemented the regular routine of sharing problems and praying for one another.  It is good to keep any group, no matter what its main emphasis, balanced and varied so that the main emphasis does not become all-consuming and commonplace, causing members to lose sight of other important aspects of spiritual growth.

## Leading a Self-Discovery Group

The purpose of a self-discovery group is growth as a person.  In today's unbalanced world, many people are broken and wounded by others to the extent that they feel no sense of worth or purpose in life.  A group such as this provides an opportunity to discover the self (the beloved person for whom Jesus Christ died, the child of God who is a worthwhile person with special gifts and a special place in God's divine plan).  The group helps individuals explore their unique gifts, their dreams and their potentials.

There is a definite tension between the biblical teachings about humanity's old nature and new nature.  While "all have sinned and come short of the glory of God," there is the glad news that the human being is a "new creature in Christ; old things are passed away; behold, all things are become new."  The tension that exists is between the "already" and the "not yet."  People get caught in the struggle of becoming. Sanctification (or becoming holy as God is holy) is complex.  It is, at the same time, past and present and future.  It is past because at the moment one accepts Jesus as Saviour, the person is made holy in the eyes of God.  It is present because as one grows in grace and over-comes the temptations and sins of the world, one is "becoming" sanctified. It is future because final perfection will not be attained until one receives a glorified body at the second coming of Jesus: "The God of peace shall sanctify you wholly, and I pray God, your whole spirit and soul and body will be preserved blameless unto the coming of our Lord Jesus Christ" (I Thess. 5:23).  At present, human beings are not blame-less and they know it.  That knowledge often leads to guilt that hurts one's self-concept and weakens one's effectiveness as a person.  Research has proven that people with low self-esteem tend to be less creative, more anxious, and less likely to have successful experiences than ones with high self-esteem.  What can the church, clergy, counselors, parents, and teachers do to help a person with a poor self-concept?  Teach and encourage the application of the truth in the lives of God's children. Self-discovery groups provide one means of attaining such an end.  Among the concepts to be taught in such a program are the following:

1. A Christian self-image is rooted in divine grace.  People cannot take credit for what they are or what they will become. As St. Paul put it, "By the grace of God I am what I am" (I Cor. 15:10).

2. There is a connection between a negative self-concept and a critical, unaccepting attitude toward others.  Conversely, there is a connection between a positive self-concept and an openness to accept and be accepted by others.

3. The Bible's view of people is that they are sinners, unworthy, and headed for defeat apart from Jesus Christ, but through Christ they are cleansed from sin, made acceptable, and headed for victory.

4. There must be a balance in one's thinking concerning sin. It is unhealthy to have either a worm's-eye view of oneself as a wretched sinner who can never improve or a view of oneself as completely whole with no need for further improvement. Christians know they can <u>fall</u> into sin, but they will not want to <u>live</u> in sin. Christians must maintain a satisfactory standard of behavior in order to accept themselves as worthwhile persons. Therefore, confession of sin and restitution for wrongdoing must be a part of one's life in order to have a positive self-concept.

5. Christians must accept themselves before they can accept others. A realistic self-concept will allow one to see Christ in others, to deal compassionately with those who fall into sin, to forgive, to thank God for all people (even for difficult people who may be unkind) and for all circumstances of life, and to maintain unity and peace among the brethren.

6. Christians will seek through Bible study and prayer to discover God's will for their lives; they will set realistic goals; and they will work toward attainment of high standards of moral conduct and spiritual growth. Such action will make them like themselves and will cause them to increase in "favor with God and man."

7. Christians will remember that they can change for the better. They must never give up hope of becoming but, at the same time, they must accept themselves (as God does) as they are right now.

8. Christians will keep in balance - trusting in God's grace to make them what they should be and still doing their part: surrendering themselves, giving their sins and guilty feelings to the Lord, and setting high standards for themselves. They will work to overcome irresponsible behavior and at the same time be patient with themselves while the "reconstruction" process is going on.

In summary, the three "keys" to unlock the door to a negative self-concept and to bring one out into the sunshine of self-acceptance are these concepts: God loves you; you are accepted; you can do worthwhile things.

There are several ways of going about self-discovery and building a healthy self-concept. One approach is to use a Bible lesson as a springboard into a personal application. For instance, Jesus called uneducated and unpopular people (even hated sinners!) into his service. The Lord always looked beyond the outward appearance or the present condition to see something valuable, which he took the time to go after, refine, and transform. Such lessons suggest that the Lord can still do that kind of thing for people today. Follow-up activities after a devotional message or Bible teaching along these lines can encourage others to follow the biblical patterns set forth.

Another approach is to prepare group exercises and activities that foster self-understanding. Participants may be asked to draw a picture, prepare a symbolic visual, or complete a project that indicates their feelings or problems. By sharing and explaining the symbols or pictures, each person in the group begins to get in touch with self and with others. An example of this kind of exercise would be to have everyone look through a magazine for pictures or slogans that tell something about the person, to cut these out and paste them onto a poster collage. Each person would then tell what each part of the collage represented. Or participants might be asked to draw a symbol or write down a word to describe four major interests or attitudes (dreams, secret wishes, hobbies, ambitions, goals, etc.) and then color the background around them in shades which reflect how the person feels about each one. By sharing and explaining these symbolic representations, people are allowed to open up to others in areas that are often kept hidden - sometimes even from themselves.

Another method of encouraging self-awareness is to have participants look at themselves from several viewpoints - how they see themselves, how they appear to their families, how they appear to close friends, and how they seem to strangers. There are different approaches to accomplish this. One is to have participants draw four masks which reflect these different views. For instance, a person might see himself as worthless and leave the face on the mask blank; parents might see the individual as perfect and so an angel's mask might be created; strangers might think an individual to be bright and well educated, so a mask with graduation cap might be designed; close friends might think one silly (a clown or cross-eyed mask) or loud-mouthed (one large mouth in the center of the face) or bad-natured (a devil's horns). It is sometimes interesting to let members of the group try to guess which mask is the viewpoint of the person, of the family, of friends, and of strangers.

Art work and creative projects do not always have to be a part of this type of self-discovery. People may be given a mirror and asked to describe "what they see." Insightful leaders and others in the group will be able to pick up on negative attitudes or areas where the self-concept is in need of healing.

Another suggestion is to give out a printed (or written) list of adjectives (outgoing, friendly, loving, unloving, cold, warm, shy, sincere, dishonest, thrifty, greedy, insecure, self-confident, temperamental, easygoing, etc.) and ask the members of the group to check those which describe how they see themselves and to star those which describe how they think others see them. Or people may be asked to fill out lists for each other. The gimmick, after all, is not the important part of the discovery session.  The important part is what happens afterward.  The goal is to help people to look at themselves honestly and to be unafraid to reveal this true self to others.  From there, the group strengthens and affirms the best qualities and tries to help individuals free themselves from destructive ones.

Another helpful exercise, one which encourages participants to see their value as worthwhile persons, is to take turns, going around in a circle, giving one-word adjectives or brief phrases which describe their positive attributes.  For instance, the first person may say, "I'm intelligent" while the next says, "I'm unselfish" and the next, "I like to make others happy."  Often, when people are very insecure or shy, this will be difficult at first.  But by patience and encouragement, thinking positively about oneself can become easier.  Continue the  process around the circle several times to reinforce the positive self-concept.

An important part of self-discovery is goal setting.  People should continually be encouraged to reach beyond their grasp, to try new things, to overcome obstacles, and to fulfill their potentials. The leader will need to help the members set realistic goals, those which are neither at standards below their capabilities nor too far beyond obtainable heights.  A self-inventory to discover one's gifts and aptitudes may be the starting place, or perhaps a time of sharing among the group where people state or write down what they believe to be the greatest strengths and gifts of others in the group.  From this base, members of the group are encouraged to build.  By concentrating upon one gift or aptitude, the individual "invests" it in some project or place of service, like the faithful stewards in the parable of the Talents.  This investment is nurtured by prayer and encouragement from the group until it brings a return, and all rejoice in the Lord's commendation, "Well done, good and faithful servant!"

The writing of a contract is sometimes an effective way of setting goals.  The person promises to do certain things to work toward a particular end (to overcome shyness, to forgive someone, to pray and study daily, to try for a promotion at work, etc.) for a particular period of time.  After determining the best means to the end and working toward them for the designated period, the group evaluates their progress in terms of the contracts.  If the goals have not been reached, the persons concerned may renew or change their contracts.

Before people can understand themselves and set realistic goals for self-improvement, time may need to be given for defenses to be laid down and an attitude of trust to be built among group members. The leader will need to be sensitive to the individual needs in the group and move only as fast as members can go without becoming uncomfortable or threatened.  Helpful ways of getting ready include (1) being certain the group knows one another and trusts one another before launching into self-improvement campaigns; and (2) doing self-discovery activities and nonthreatening interaction activities until the time is right to suggest the personal-growth programs.

Questionnaires are useful tools in this readiness program. The following format is suggested, but it may be modified to meet particular group needs.

## Self-Discovery Questionnaire

1. Who are you?

2. What are your values?

3. Where are you emotionally . . . physically . . . mentally . . . spiritually?

4. If you could live your life over, what would you change?

5. What three wishes would you make if you knew they could be granted?

6. What would you like to have done with your life that you haven't?

7. What makes you feel most guilty?

8. What makes you feel most self-satisfied?

9. What has been your greatest accomplishment in life?

10. What are your greatest strengths? How can these be increased?

11. What are your greatest weaknesses? How can these be minimized?

12. What goals are you willing to set for your life?

13. What do you visualize for yourself five years from now? How would you like to change or improve that picture?

14. What does it take to get you moving?

15. What commitments have you made in the past? Did you keep them?

16. What commitments are you willing to make for the future?

17. What do you feel is God's will for your life? What "calling" have you heard?

18. Is God able to bring about his highest will for your life? Why or why not?

19. What spiritual disciplines do you keep daily? Weekly?

20. Write the words agree, disagree, or unsure beside the following:
    _____ God loves me.
    _____ I am a worthy and accepted human being.
    _____ I can do worthwhile things.

Sometimes original questionnaires filled out at the start of a self-discovery program can be filed away and then brought out later on in the year, after commitments and goals have been worked on, for evaluation and renewing. People can see from their earlier responses that they are growing as persons.

Discussion drama and role playing are also useful tools in aiding self-discovery. Discussion drama involves acting out a scene from a script and then discussing the way the characters in the scene solved a problem or reacted to one another. (Scenes may be read aloud if members do not want to enact them.) In role play, people choose their own problem situations to act out for group evaluation. Often people express their true feelings in the "safety" of role playing because they feel separated enough from reality to be themselves, to reveal hidden attitudes, or to give honest reactions. Often, when suppressed feelings come out through such dramatizations, they may be dealt with afterward. Participants decide upon a problem (an actual life situation, preferably a problem someone in the group has actually had or is having) and then work through it in improvised drama to try to reach a solution or compromise. After the enactment of the problem situation, the audience evaluates what has been dramatized as follows:

1. What was the problem?

2. How was the problem solved?

3. How well was it solved? (What other solutions are possible?)

4. What is best to do about such a problem?

Sometimes, following the discussion after role play, the scene will be reenacted using alternative solutions suggested. Or roles may be reversed (parent plays the child and child takes the parent's role, someone on one side of a confrontation takes the other side to argue from a different viewpoint, etc.). This role reversal allows people to see a problem from more than one viewpoint and to get "into another person's shoes" for more insight.

In addition to role play, where group members assume the roles of people involved in problems, there is another exercise which can be used to promote self-awareness and insight. It is called "transference roles." An empty chair or other inanimate object represents someone with whom a group member has difficulty relating or it represents a problem (temper, jealousy, insecurity, rejection, etc.). A person then talks to the chair or object as one would to the person or problem. In this way, the person's inner feelings come to the surface where they can be understood, worked through, and offered to the Lord in prayer. Care must be taken here, however, that in transferring hostility or other negative feelings that may be bottled up inside, participants are not encouraged to take unchristian approaches to dealing with these problems. The leader must be able to assist the members in finding scriptural answers to any problems which may surface.

Most likely, the leader for this kind of group will need some
experience in counseling in addition to the other leadership qualifications expected.  For that reason, chapter 7, "Ministries of Counseling," should be a companion study to this chapter.  The leader
must also be loving and accepting of people in the group, able to
affirm them as worthwhile individuals, and able to help them set and
achieve realistic goals.  Perhaps the leader's greatest responsibility is to help others apply to their lives the biblical teachings of
selfhood - to help them see themselves as forgiven sinners in the process of becoming conformed into the image of Jesus Christ.

Although any age group will benefit from participation in a self-
discovery group, this kind of program is especially beneficial to
youth.  Teenagers and young adults are struggling to find an identity
and a place of usefulness in the world.  To assist them in this quest
by helping them develop a healthy concept of themselves will certainly
make the task easier.  In addition to the suggestions offered in this
manual, one may find more exercises in programs which are adaptable to
self-discovery in the Lyman Coleman "Groups in Action" series and
other Serendipity materials (Serendipity Books, Word, Inc.).

## Leading a Community-Building Group

It has been said that the only thing harder than living with
people is living without them.  Because human beings are sinners, they
hurt one another.  Because they are basically (in fleshly or unsancti-
fied parts of their beings) selfish, they are often thoughtless and
unconcerned about others.  It becomes the task of community-building
groups to work through such attitudes of selfishness to attitudes of
relationship.  The thing that set the early Christians apart from the
world and called attention to their newfound faith was "how they
loved each other."  Such love does not just "happen."  It grows, first,
from the supernatural love of Jesus Christ permeating the individual
to the extent that it spills over into the lives of others, and second,
the desire to follow the example of Jesus, who said, "Deny yourself . . . ."

The goals of a community-building group include:

1.  Accepting others - loving people "as they are"

2.  Forgiving others - releasing grudges and resentments

3.  Cooperating with others - working together to build
    the Kingdom

4.  Finding unity with others - widening the circle of
    acceptance to all

5.  Encouraging others - enabling others to be their best
    selves

Whereas in self-discovery groups the goal is to learn to accept oneself, the goal in community-building groups is to learn to accept others. The group becomes a family of concerned individuals working for the good of the entire body rather than selfish individuals interested in their own concerns.

Any of the previously mentioned methods and approaches may be used to work toward these goals. There should certainly be some form of Bible instruction, for in the Bible the patterns of behavior are set forth that this kind of group will want to follow. There will also be prayer - mostly intercessory prayer for the members of the group, their needs, and their petitions. Additional activities will vary according to the particular group but may include such things as worshiping together, sharing testimonies and mutual concerns, group interaction activities, and outreach. Although the outreach ministry may be expanded in time, at first it will be limited to those in the group "family." It will take time really to know one another (with masks off and with weaknesses bared) and it will take time to begin really to love one another (not a surface love or a casual love, but a genuine agape kind of love).

It may seem, at first glance, that such a group as this is exclusive and too limited. While it is granted that the danger of cliquishness and snobbery does exist and must be countered with instruction, prayer, and openness to others in different ways, the goal is to belong to a caring, supportive body which will provide the kind of love (unconditional love) so desperately needed in the world today. People must learn to live together in unity for the health and safety of the world. How can there be world peace when there is no peace in the home or in the church or even within the minds of people? When people begin to learn how to get to know other people as they "really are" and love them anyway, a step in the right direction has been taken.

In such a group as this, the members must commit to meet together for a definite period of time. The whole purpose breaks down if people are infrequent in attendance or disinterested in working continually with the other members. No community is built if membership is constantly changing. Although new community-building groups may be started (as spinoffs of the original group or as an entirely different group of people in another place), the membership must be stable and unchanging once the commitment is made to work and fellowship together.

The idea is to become a family - a loving, caring, disagreeing, problem-confronting family, which must learn to (1) be real with each other; (2) contribute to each other; and (3) receive from each other.

In order to do these things, there must be interaction. It may be from the mouth (conversing, discussing, confessing, sharing, joking, praying); from the head (ideas, intellectual responses, problem solving, thought projections); or from the heart (feelings, concerns, needs, support, encouragement). Naturally, it is the heart interactions that really count in building community. When someone lets another person inside to see the heart, there is communing; communing is communion; and communion is the stuff of which community is made. Necessary ingredients for such a community are as follows:

1. Covenant:  The covenant is a promise of commitment to be at the appointed place when the group meets; to contribute to the group in an active and supportive way; to be open to receive ministry, correction, and direction from the group; and to pray for the group individually and collectively.

2. Contact:  The contact must be more than a polite but distant recognition of others in the group.  It must be a close and warm diffusing of oneself into the lives of others.  There should be touching - hand clasping, embracing, and greeting each other with a holy kiss in the name of the Lord.

3. Submission:  This does not mean a blind acceptance of any group decision or action.  It is, rather, an appreciation and respect for the personhood of others to the extent that one will put one's own selfish desires aside to "honor and prefer one another."

Because such a group as this can raise many problems as well as solve them, leadership and membership must be carefully considered in advance.  Everyone is not ready to make such commitments.  No effort to coerce or "talk someone into" this kind of relationship should be made, for this must be a voluntary and enthusiastic experiment in living.  Leadership must be in the hands of committed, capable, and spiritually mature Christians who can train, counsel, and enable others.

The format for meetings may be structured or informal, as the Lord may lead.  If gimmicks or ice-breakers are needed at first, any of the activities suggested in the Self-Discovery Group section (group exercises, role play, questionnaires, etc.) may be applicable.  In addition, group members may be assigned prayer partners (from the same group) who commit to each other for daily intercessions, or secret pals who will send letters of encouragement, cards or gifts on special occasions, and other loving expressions of concern in different ways. Sometimes a group activity such as making posters or banners or preparing a meal together will help to teach cooperation and working together in unity.

Building community is like building a marriage; it is often a commitment which must be for better or for worse, in good times and bad.  Regardless of what kinds of training programs, Bible lessons, group activities, fellowships, or outreach missions such a group may participate in together, the focal point around which everything must revolve is love.  If the group cannot love one another, there can be no community.  The building of the Kingdom rests, in great measure, upon Christians' ability to build community.

## Interrelatedness of Training Groups

Many of the purposes and activities of one instructional group will overlap and interrelate with those in another type of group. There can be no rigid rules which say any particular group must or must not do a particular thing. There may be, in fact, some training groups that will embrace all of the goals and functions of each kind. Others may embrace none of them and still have effective Christian training programs. It is a matter of emphasis and need. Perhaps the following look at the training groups discussed will give, in a nutshell, a better visualization of this:

| Name of Training Group | Purpose of Group | Method of Discipline |
| --- | --- | --- |
| Bible Study Group | To learn | Through study |
| Discipleship Training Group | To commit | Through obedient action |
| Self-Discovery Group | To grow | Through awareness |
| Community-Building Group | To relate | Through love |

Every Christian needs all of these purposes and disciplines at work in his or her life. However, some Christians need to be helped in developing the skills to fulfill some of these purposes and disciplines. This is where association with a group - or the banding together with others who are learning, committing, growing, and relating - will give the support and strength we need in order to become all that Jesus wants all of us to be.

## Leading a Youth Group

Some churches do not have a specialized ministry to youth. This is regrettable. Young people have the same needs as adults, but these needs must be met in youth-oriented, not adult, ways. Some churches, on the other hand, have extensive youth programs, often under the direction of paid youth directors, which offer such diverse activities as Sunday school, youth organizations or other youth fellowship programs, sports, coffeehouse or recreation night activities, youth prayer-and-share groups, youth choir, Scouts, Youth Club, and so on. Although every church may not be staffed or financially able to provide an extensive range of sophisticated youth services, every church should seek to have a well-rounded and balanced program in which youth may become involved. Those with the responsibility for leading youth groups should strive for a program which includes the following essentials:

1. An Opportunity to Worship: Young people need to supplement the Sunday-in-the-pew worship with expressions of themselves to God

in their own language and in their own ways. Prayer-and-praise services, folk masses, retreats, lock-ins, and other such opportunities for youth worship services should be provided.

2. An Opportunity for Instruction: Bible study through Sunday school and midweek programs should put the Scriptures on a level of understanding and application to which youth can relate. The use of a modern-language translation of the Scriptures (such as Good News for Modern Man) will make understanding easier for young people. Teachers should be personable and able to communicate on the level of youth while still maintaining authority and respect. Discipleship training, evangelistic training (witnessing to friends, visitation programs, etc.), self-discovery groups, and community-building programs should also be offered as needs and interests dictate.

3. An Opportunity for Service: Too often the church tries to entertain or babysit youth rather than involving them in ministry. The enthusiasm and vitality of young people should be put to use in outreach, leadership roles, and missions of loving service to others. It is in giving (not in receiving) that youth will be fulfilled as human beings and prepared to assume their church leadership roles in the future. That is not to say that they do not need to take in as well as give out, but there definitely should be an opportunity for offering time, talents, and resources to the church, the community, and the youth group membership (caring and sharing with one another).

4. An Opportunity for Fellowship: Wholesome Christian recreational activities and regular programs of fellowship should make the church the center of a young person's social life. Parties, beach trips, picnics, wholesome movies, indoor and outdoor sports, church teams, and other fellowship opportunities should provide acceptable alternatives to worldly forms of entertainment.

5. An Opportunity for Counseling: Group interaction sessions, rap groups, and informal get-togethers with trained leaders should be provided for offering guidance and direction and for problem solving. Private appointments with approved counselors should also be available when needed.

6. An Opportunity for Personal Commitment: The most important ministry to youth is to introduce them personally to Jesus Christ. Leaders should know every young person individually by name, and they should make special efforts to determine where each one is in relationship to the Lord. Private interviews with individuals or in small groups will be helpful. Another useful tool in determining where young people are in relationship to Jesus is a questionnaire, such as the following.

266

# Youth Questionnaire

Name:_____Address:_____Phone:_____

Grade:_____Age:_____School:_____

Church attending:_____Member? _____Yes _____No

Have you a personal relationship
with Jesus Christ? _____Yes _____No _____Unsure

Do you pray regularly?_____ Do you read the Bible regularly?_____

Do you attend Sunday worship regularly?_____ Sunday school member?____

Other activities and/or leadership roles taken in church:_____

_____

What, in your opinion is sin? _____

What, in your opinion, is "eternal life"? _____

Is Jesus Christ alive today?_____ Explain your answer:_____

_____

Has the church youth program ministered to you?_____ If so, explain
in what ways:_____

_____

What do you enjoy most about the church and its programs?_____

_____

What do you enjoy least and why?_____

_____

What suggestions for improvement of the youth ministry can you offer?

_____

What is your greatest need?_____

What is your greatest strength (talent, aptitude, or ability)?_____

_____

What is your greatest weakness?_____

Describe what God is like to you:_____

If you were to die tonight, where would you be tomorrow?_____

Explain your answer or tell how you know:_____

What spiritual things do you find hard to understand?_____

Would you like to know more about the Bible?_____ Do you have problems
you'd like a minister or counselor to help you solve?_____

_____

Suggested Duties for Youth Director or Youth Leader

I. Planning Responsibilities

A. Plan total program for all church youth to include opportunities for worship, instruction, service, fellowship, counseling, and commitment

B. Schedule special events and regular offerings on the church calendar; arrange for such events (bring in guest speakers, plan retreats, etc.)

II. Liaison Responsibilities

A. Act as liaison among other youth leaders (Sunday school, choir director, Scout and Youth Club leaders, etc.)

B. Act as liaison between clergy and the youth and their programs

III. Implementation Responsibilities

A. Provide worship experiences - church attendance, rejoice or folk masses, private and corporate devotional experiences

B. Provide instruction programs - retreats, seminars, Bible studies, speakers

C. Provide service opportunities - projects for church and community outreach (witnessing, visiting, working, helping)

D. Provide fellowship times - socials, fun nights, recreation, team sports, coffeehouse gatherings, music, crafts, etc.

E. Provide counseling - rap sessions, group counseling, private sessions

IV. Leadership Training Responsibilities

A. Offer leadership training programs for adults involved with youth

B. Offer leadership training programs for youth to assist them in assuming responsibilities in church and community activities

V.   Visitation Responsibilities

A.   Visit homes of the youth of the church and surrounding area

B.   Visit prospects for inclusion in youth activities

C.   Get to know parents, home situations, backgrounds of youth in order to give input to clergy and to offer assistance where needed

VI.  Counseling Responsibilities

A.   Be available for private or group counseling sessions with youth and for counseling sessions with parents and others involved with youth.

B.   Become a friend to whom any youth may turn in times of problems.

VII. Commitment and Growth Responsibilities

Determine where youth are in relation to Jesus Christ; seek to bring youth into personal commitment; help youth to grow and mature in mind, body, and spirit.

## Planning a Youth Retreat

One of the responsibilities that often falls to youth leaders is that of planning special weekends or special emphasis programs. The youth retreat is a popular vehicle for combining instruction, worship, recreation, and commitment. The following outline may be of value in planning such a program.

1. Determine an objective or goal for the weekend (example: "To prepare youth for spiritual warfare").

2. Select a theme or emphasis for the weekend ("The Whole Armor of God").

3. Choose a theme song and a Bible verse that emphasize the theme and which can be used throughout the weekend to capsulize the dominant message:

   Song: "Onward, Christian Soldiers."
   Bible verse: "Put on the whole armor of God" (Eph. 6:11).

4. Select a time and place for the retreat that will be convenient (not during vacation time when youth will be away or during a time when other special activities are planned). The cost of the retreat should not be prohibitive. Parents and other interested adults may be asked to donate food and supplies or underwrite the cost of scholarships for youth

who cannot afford to go.  Publicize the event well in advance
with posters, bulletin announcements, announcements in Sunday
school, at youth organizations, and from the pulpit.  Give
specific information, such as the following:  "Friday supper
at 6:30 P.M. until Saturday supper at 6:30 P.M.  The bus will
leave the church at 4:30 P.M. on Friday and return to the
church by Saturday at 8:30 P.M.  Items to bring include:
sports clothes, Bibles, linens," etc.

5. Determine leadership:  Who will the main speaker or leader
   be?  (It is good to ask someone from outside the church to
   come in.  Be certain it is someone who speaks well and who
   relates well with youth.)  Also determine who the assistant
   counselors, workshop leaders, kitchen helpers, and recreation leaders will be.

6. Arrange for music:  Have someone to play guitar or piano to
   accompany group singing and to assist with music for worship.
   Select music appropriate to the weekend themes and purposes.
   Bring song sheets for the youth if possible.

7. Provide worship opportunities:  A suggested schedule might
   be as follows:

   Morning watch - early morning devotional before breakfast.

   Vespers - evening campfire services.

   Cabin worship - Scripture reading and prayer before retir-
                   ing.

   Communion service - may be folk mass type.

   Prayer and praise - music, liturgy, intercessions, and
                       group responses.

   Quiet time - private devotions, silence, listening, and
                meditating with pen and paper.

   Prayer partners - time for sharing and praying with
                     another.

   Conversational prayer - opportunities for intercessions
                           and petitions.

8. Teaching-learning sessions:  The instructional program should
   relate to the overall theme.  For example:

   Friday evening:  "The Girdle of Truth and the Breastplate
                    of Righteousness."

   Saturday morning:  "The Sandals of Peace and the Shield
                      of Faith."

Saturday afternoon: "The Helmet of Salvation and the
Sword of the Spirit."

Saturday evening: Review, celebration, and commitment
service.

9. Group learning activities: Choose one or more appropriate follow-up experiences to include after each teaching session -
buzz groups, Scripture search games, question-answer periods,
handouts or involvement sheets, study guides to complete, opin-
ionnaires, small-group interaction activities, etc.

10. Recreation-fellowship activities: Have a variety of offerings
such as the following: outside - swimming, team sports, relays,
nature walks, etc.; inside - table games, stunts, talent shows,
crafts, etc.; music - fun songs, rhythmic activities, musical
games, etc.

11. Personal response opportunities: Time should be made available
with leaders for prayer, counseling, confessions, commitments,
etc. Sometimes a young person just needs someone to talk to
privately.

12. Concluding service: The entire weekend should build toward
the climax, some sort of a dedication service, celebration,
or altar-call service. Youth should not be coerced into decisions, but gently encouraged when they want to make them.
Sometimes such a dedication service is enhanced by the making
of symbolic "offerings" to present at the altar as representations of themselves. These may be posters, decorated boxes,
flowers, drawings, or handcrafts. There should also be some
way of receiving feedback from the youth as to the meaning of
the weekend in their lives. Written or oral evaluations should
be solicited.

13. A final evaluation from the leadership (filling out post-
meeting reports or getting together to discuss the weekend)
should be held to make recommendations for future programs
and to follow up on any problems or needs. This final evaluation should be written up as a report and filed away for
future reference.


A Final Word to Youth Leaders

Youth leaders have perhaps the greatest challenge and the most
rewarding, yet demanding, responsibility of all those called to minister in group-leadership capacities. Like parenthood, youth leadership
is not without its frustrations as one seeks to mold and direct young
lives in the proper ways. There will be successes and defeats, smiles
and tears, steps ahead and steps backward. Because of the demands of
working with youth (especially teenagers), many lay leaders back away
from such involvement. But for those dedicated souls who are willing

to accept the challenge, there is satisfaction in knowing that they are
doing what Jesus did - disciplining, teaching, guiding, and loving
those of whom Jesus said, "Of such is the kingdom of heaven." A few
final guidelines should be remembered when working with youth:

1. Find out where the youth are and start there.

2. Plan activities (special events, spiritual experiences,
   and recreation) on the level of the youth's maturity and
   interest.

3. Keep challenging, by seeking to lead the youth beyond
   where they are (no resting on laurels). Go on to new
   experiences and growth.

4. Get youth actively included and involved (participants,
   not spectators).

5. Find worthwhile things for them to do (get them praying,
   sharing, giving, helping, and loving) rather than insig-
   nificant "busy work."

6. Be friendly, loving, and concerned for each one, but remain the leader in charge (don't let the "tail wag the
   dog").

## Conclusion

Ministries of group leadership are many and varied. There are
small groups and large groups, beginning groups and mature groups,
groups brought together by age or mutual interests, concerns, or needs.
Leadership for any group, no matter what kind, is too heavy a responsibility for one to carry alone. The burden must be shared with Jesus.
His strength and direction must prepare the way; his love and power
must dominate each session; and his purposes and the glorification of
his name must be the motivation for everything said and done. Jesus'
example is the only safe guide through the maze of group leadership,
for "he who would be greatest among you must be servant of all."

# 10 · Ministries and Activities:
## An Alphabetical List, with Definitions and Resource Suggestions

Accounting - interpreting and preparing financial records for the church or for Christian ministries, support services, or community outreach programs. Accounting courses are available through local high school extension departments and community colleges.

Acolytes - assistants to the clergy at the altar (in sacramental churches) who light candles, receive the alms basin, and bring the elements to the celebrant for Communion. Acolytes are usually trained by the clergy or their designated assistants. Books offering information on this subject are The Complete Acolyte by Ellwood Post (Morehouse-Barlow) and Server's Manual by Charles E. Danner, Jr. (Foward Movement Publications).

Administrators - those with the responsibility for oversight of business, finances, and other secular matters of churches or ministries. Business courses relating to administrative functions are available through local educational facilities.. A book on this subject is New Hope for Congregations by Loren B. Mead (Seabury Press).

Alcoholic Rehabilitators - people who work with those who have a drinking problem by use of counseling, encouragement, group therapy, or self-help programs such as Alcoholics Anonymous. Extensive training is needed for this ministry and is usually available through colleges and community alcoholic rehabilitation centers. A book on this subject is Alcoholism: The Hidden Addiction by Ebbe Curtis Holt (Seabury Press).

Altar Guild - those responsible for preparing the altar, vestments, and elements for Communion services (in sacramental churches). Local parishes provide training for this and usually have a training guide available. Books on this subject are A Working Manual for Altar Guilds by Dorothy Diggs (Morehouse-Barlow) and An Altar Guild Manual by Edith W. Perry (Morehouse-Barlow).

Altar Ministries - laypersons who assist at the altar in some capacity, as those who pray with others who come to the altar for prayer or ministry. In some churches, only clergy perform this ministry, but as laypersons become trained and approved by their clergy to assist, they can be available during or after regular services on Sundays or at midweek services to intercede in prayer or to offer counsel to those who request their aid.

273

**Apostles -** those sent forth beyond the church boundaries to proclaim the gospel of Jesus Christ or to perform Christian service in some form of outreach. For specific apostolic emphases, see also Evangelism; Missionary Work; Outreach.

**Artistic Ministries** - drawing, painting, sculpting, banner-making, or other forms of artistic expression used in Christian work, decorating, or church-related enterprises such as publicity, promotion, or advertising. Art courses and workshops are generally available through local educational institutions and community cultural groups. See also Banner-Making; Symbolism.

**Babysitters** - those who take care of children in the church nursery or elsewhere to free parents to attend services or to do ministry. Child-care courses are available through many social-service organizations.

**Banner Making** - preparing flaglike wall hangings or standards for religious processions or display. Such banners usually feature or symbolize some aspect of the Christian faith. A book on this subject is The Banner Book by Betty Wolfe (Morehouse-Barlow).

**Bible Teachers** - instructors in the Scriptures and related Bible topics. Courses to assist in qualifying lay ministers in Bible knowledge and instruction are offered through various denominational headquarters, local churches, and religious publishing houses. Books on this subject include What the Bible Is All About by Henrietta C. Mears (Gospel Light Publications); How to Teach the Bible by Joseph M. Gettys (John Knox Press); The Successful Sunday School and Teachers' Guidebook by Elmer Towns (Creation House, Carol Stream, Ill.); and "The BRF Approach to Group Bible Study," Bible Reading Fellowship, Winter Park, Florida 32790. For additional information consult International Centers for Learning Workshops and Seminars, P.O. Box 1650, Glendale, Calif. 92109; Teaching and Training Conferences, The Navigators, P.O. Box 1659, Colorado Springs, Colo. 80901; The Bethel Series, Adult Christian Education Foundation, Box 5350, Madison, Wis. 53705; Conferences in Christian Education, Liberty Baptist College, Lynchburg, Va.; Theological Education by Extension, The School of Theology, University of the South, Sewanee, Tenn. 37375. See also Christian Education.

**Bookkeeping** - the keeping of records of income, debits, and accounts payable. Training courses are available through local educational institutions.

**Bulletin Preparation** - writing, editing, typing, and preparing graphics for the church newsletter or other publications (such as the weekly order of service sheets for Sunday worship,

274

special events publicity, etc.). Workshops on bulletin preparation may be requested of church headquarters personnel or of local printing or journalism experts. Write for "Publicity Handbook," Consumer Services, The Sperry and Hutchison Company, P.O. Box 935, Fort Worth, Tex. 76101. See also Publicity.

Business Management - the oversight of the church office or administrative functions of Christian business enterprises. Business courses are available through local educational institutions. See also Administrators.

Calling - visiting in the homes of church visitors, new members, lapsed members, prospects, or the bereaved to bring the ministry of the church to individuals or families in a personal and loving way. Guidelines for church callers and training seminars are available through Evangelism Explosion, Coral Ridge Presbyterian Church, P.O. Box 23820, Ft. Lauderdale, Fla. 33307. Books on the subject include "Guidelines for Visiting Newcomers and Lapsed Members," Episcopal Diocese of Central Florida, P.O. Box 790, Winter Park, Fla. 32790; The Apathetic and Bored Church Member by John S. Savage (with regard to lapsed members), L.E.A.D. Consultants, P.O. Box 311, Pittsford, N.Y. 14534; and Visitation by C. S. Lovett (Personal Christianity, Baldwin Park, Calif.)

Calling Committee - a specially selected group, usually representative of various organizations and interests in the church, who assist in the selection of clergy when positions become open. Church headquarters may have guidelines available to assist a calling committee. Resources available include "On the Calling and Care of Pastors" by Richard J. Kirk; The Minister Is Leaving by Celia A. Hahn; and "Religious Authenticity in the Clergy" by John C. Fletcher; all are available from The Alban Institute, Mount St. Alban, Washington, D.C. 20016.

Campus Ministries - outreach to students on school and college campuses offering evangelistic information and spiritual growth programs. Literature and training assistance may be obtained through Campus Crusade for Christ, Arrowhead Springs, San Bernardino, Calif. 92414. Various denominational headquarters will also provide information about such programs. See also Youth Ministries.

Children's Ministries - various services to youth, which may include Sunday school, children's prayer groups, child evangelism, Youth Club, young people's church organizations, Scouting, choir, instructional programs, and recreational activities. For additional information, write Child Evangelism Fellowship, Box 348, Warrenton, Mo. 63383; Youth Club, 700 Dewberry Rd., Monroeville, Pa. 15146; or Youth Specialities (Idea Books available) 861 6th Ave., Suite 411, San Diego, Calif.

92101. See also <u>Bible Teachers</u>; <u>Christian Education</u>;
<u>Youth Ministries</u>.

<u>Christian Education</u> - all aspects of instruction in the total church
program including youth and adult instruction, confirmation
classes, Sunday school, midweek training programs, special
workshops, seminars, etc. Consultant assistance in design-
ing Christian education curricula and teacher training
programs may be obtained by contacting Barbara Kuhn,
20-22 Moree Loop, Winter Springs, Fla. 32707. Resources
available are <u>AWARE: A Religious Education Resource</u>
(Seabury Press); <u>Adventure in Renewal</u> by A. Donald Davies
(Morehouse-Barlow); <u>Will Our Children Have Faith?</u> by John
H. Westerhoff III (Seabury Press); <u>The DRE Book</u> by Maria
Harris (Paulist Press). Universities and seminaries offer
courses in Christian Education. Resource people include
The Rev. William Baxter, Drawer 2127, Charleston, S.C.
29403; Mrs. Lynn Young, 1551 10th Ave. E., Seattle,
Wash. 98102; and Joseph C. Neiman, St. Mary's College
Press, Winona, Minn. 55987. See also <u>Bible Teachers</u>.

<u>Choir</u> - singers who assist with leadership in the worship of the
church, either by leading congregational singing and offering
special music or by performing in concerts. Training for
adults and children is usually provided by the church choir
director.

<u>Church Governing Board</u> - elected officials responsible for the admin-
istrative functions of the church, variously called
Official Board, Parish Council, Session, Vestry, etc.
Laypersons who conduct the church business and who assist
the clergy in decisions concerning the general welfare
are usually selected on the basis of past dedication and
faithfulness in service to the various organizations and
functions of the church program. Contact denominational
church headquarters for information on guidelines and
suggestions for efficient church government. Resources
include books such as <u>Your Vestry and You</u> by John R.
Sherwood (Forward Movement Publications) and <u>Confessions
of a Board Member</u> by Karl Mathiasen (Alban Institute).
See also <u>Administrators</u>.

<u>Civic Ministries</u> - projects in the community which extend the ministry
of the church to the needy or which promote civic improvements and welfare. Contact area information, referral,
or resource centers (such as Chamber of Commerce, civic
clubs, or social service organizations) to determine needs
and possible ministries.

<u>Cleaning</u> - keeping the church buildings and grounds free of dirt and
litter, or offering to clean someone's home as a support
service or charitable ministry.

Clerical Work - secretarial functions such as addressing envelopes,
typing letters, producing church communiqués, answering
the telephone, filing, etc. Churches are always in need
of this type of volunteer effort and usually provide the
special training necessary for particular operations.
Secretarial skills are taught through local educational
institutions and business schools.

Coffeehouses - social and recreational places for youth looking for
fellowship, relaxation, entertainment, and direction as
a Christian alternative to questionable forms of entertainment. Assistance and suggestions for starting a
coffeehouse program may be obtained through Teen Challenge
Center, 444 Clinton Ave., Brooklyn, N.Y. 11238. See also
Youth Ministries.

Communications - keeping the church membership and the community
apprised of news, important dates, events, and responsibilities through church communiqués or the local media.
It may also include Christian broadcasting. Contact
denominational church headquarters concerning information,
volunteer aid needed, and training opportunities in
Christian communications. See also Publicity.

Committee Workers - those who serve on various church groups (such as
the Christian Education Committee, Memorials Committee,
Finance Committee, etc.) under the leadership of a committee head. Volunteers may serve on standing committees (those of continuing duration) or temporary committees (those who function only so long as the need for
them exists - Rummage Sale Committee, Pancake Supper Committee, Christmas Pageant Committee, etc.). See also
Volunteers.

Conference, Diocesan, District, Provincial, or Synodical Work - assisting with efforts of committees, individuals, or churches
in the district presided over by an ecclesiastical head
or governing body. Contact denominational headquarters
for information concerning volunteer help needed in such
work.

Confirmation Class Instructors - those who indoctrinate prospective
church members or new converts prior to confirmation and
acceptance into church membership. Training for this
ministry is usually given by the local clergy and exercised under their general supervision. Skills in communication and teaching as well as knowledge of church
doctrines and practices should be prerequisite to this
ministry. Books on the subject are Belonging: An Introduction to the Christian Church by Sherman E. Johnson
(Forward Movement Publications); Confirmation: Celebration of Maturity in Christ by Urban T. Holmes (Seabury
Press); and Christian Faith by Donald Coggin (Forward
Movement Publications).

**Consultants** - those who advise or conduct workshops or training sessions in a particular field (as a financial consultant, an educational consultant, lay ministry consultant, etc.). Contact denominational church headquarters for names of people available in various categories of expertise or to volunteer to assist with such a program.

**Counselors** - those who assist others in personal growth, problem solving, and human relationships or who aid others in overcoming blockages to physical, emotional, mental, or spiritual health. Professional counselors require academic training in methods of psychology or psychiatry. While a degree in counseling is not necessary for all forms of counseling, some form of training and approval is neccessary for all Christian counselors. Local colleges may offer courses in formal counseling techniques. Those interested in informal counseling should contact their clergy to recommend training opportunities. Books available include Competent to Counsel and The Use of the Scriptures in Counseling by Jay Adams (Baker Book House) and The Kink and I by James Mallory (Victor Books). For information on additional training, contact the American Association of Marriage and Family Counselors, 225 Yale Avenue, Claremont, Calif. 91711; The Narramore Christian Foundation, Rosemead, Calif. 91770; Jay Adams, Westminster Theological Seminary (Presbyterian), Philadelphia, Pa. 19118. The Clyde Narramore Christian Foundation also has a center at 104 N. 26th St., Camp Hill, Pa. 17011. See also Inner Healing; Pastoral Care.

**Crafts-** creating manual arts or handwork to decorate the church or for some charitable fund-raising project or other utilitarian purpose. Books on this subject include Christian Family Craft Book by Burton Everist (Morehouse-Barlow) and Eyes to See God by Anne Elliott (Morehouse-Barlow). See also Banner-Making.

**Crisis Comfort** - assisting and encouraging others who are undergoing a tragedy, loss, or difficulty in life; this may take the form of counseling, sending cards or letters, bringing food, providing financial assistance, giving emotional support, or merely listening and consoling. Check with local Human Relations Referral Service (or equivalent) for information on "Hot Line" or "Fish" (or other crisis ministries available in the local area). See also Pastoral Care.

**Dancing** - performing rhythmic patterns of body movement set to music or executed in pantomime; often used as a form of worship in interpreting Scripture or dramatic forms of inspiration. Dancing may also be used as a form of exercise or entertainment for recreational, health, or self-improvement programs.

**Decorating** - making surroundings more attractive, as to decorate the minister's home, to decorate the church altar for a special service, or to decorate the parish hall or church recreational room for a banquet. Information on interior design, color coordination, and themes (for a party or special occasion) may be obtained from a local library or in community adult education courses.

**Deliverance** - the ministry of exorcism or the casting out of evil spirits performed by trained and approved exorcists. Lay people who feel called to this ministry should discuss it in detail with the clergy for specific guidance on training methods and resources. Books on this subject include <u>Defeated Enemies</u> by Corrie Ten Boom (Christian Literature Crusade, Fort Washington, Pa. 19034); <u>Demons and How to Deal With Them</u> by Kenneth Hagin (P.O. Box 50126, Tulsa, Okla.); <u>Pigs in the Parlor</u> by Frank and Ida Mae Hammond (Impact Books, Kirkwood, Mo.); <u>Deliver Us From Evil</u> by Don Basham (Fleming H. Revell Co.).

**Design** - to fashion according to a plan, pattern, or model, as to design robes for the choir, to design a cover for a church bulletin, to design a motif for the minister's office, or to design articles used in worship (banners, vestments, etc.). See also <u>Banner-Making</u> and <u>Symbolism</u>.

**Directing** - conducting people or taking charge of responsibilities, as in directing the choir, directing a church play, or directing an organized church or task group. See also <u>Administrators</u>.

**Discipleship** - the process of becoming a disciple or follower of Jesus Christ, which may include attending training sessions and making commitments to perform discipleship tasks such as prayer, study, witnessing, and outreach. One way for a layperson to begin a program of discipleship is to participate in a Cursillo. Write for information to National Episcopal Cursillo Information Center, P.O. Box 213, Cedar Falls, Iowa 50613, or to the Roman Catholic Cursillo Information Center, U.S. Catholic Conference, 1312 Massachusetts Ave., N.W., Washington, D.C. 20005.

**Discernment** - the gift of the Holy Spirit for rightly determining that which is of God and that which is evil; this gift is included in various ministries, such as inner healing, deliverance, and group-leadership responsibilities.

**Drama** - the enactment of plays, pantomime, role play, or other interpretations of dramatic works for the purpose of entertainment, instruction, or inspiration. Chancel drama is performed in the church as a part of worship, while other forms of drama are usually performed in the social hall or educational buildings. Church drama provides a variety of people of numerous talents an opportunity to be of service -

anyone from a director, actor, technical crewman, musician, set designer, properties assistant, costumer, prompter, or stagehand. Books on this subject include Creative Drama in Religious Education by Isabel B. Burger (Morehouse-Barlow) and Two Plays about God and Man by Dorothy L. Sayers (Seabury Press).

Drug-Abuse Rehabilitation - assisting those addicted to narcotic substances in overcoming the habit; methods include prayer, counseling, providing professional services, and mental health programs. Those interested in this ministry should contact the closest college or drug-abuse center for courses or information.

Edification - the building up or strengthening of oneself or others, as to edify a pastor or leader following their ministries, to edify one who is troubled with words of comfort and encouragement, or to edify oneself through prayer or study.

Elderly, Ministry to - providing services and ministries to senior citizens, for instance, to visit nursing homes or to provide meals, socials, or programs for older people of the church or community. Laypersons interested in such ministry can contact local nursing-home directors for suggestions or assistance needed. A book on this subject is Living in a Nursing Home by Sarah Greene Burger and Martha D'Erasmo (Seabury Press). Contact the local chapter of the American Association of Retired People or the state ACTION office for volunteer programs involving the elderly.

Entertaining - to provide hospitality, amusement, or diversion for guests. The art of entertaining may be performed at church, as in arranging receptions, banquets, socials, or special functions; or in homes, as in providing for needs of guests or extending the entertainment services of the church into members' homes. It may also include taking socials or fellowships to institutions or to the needy.

Evangelism - sharing the message of the gospel of Jesus Christ; evangelistic ministries may be performed directly through personal confrontations, or indirectly through bringing others to church, sharing a book or audio tape with an evangelistic theme, introducing others to those involved in evangelism ministries, or support services to evangelism (financial assistance or other aid). Helpful resources in evangelistic work include Evangelism Explosion, Coral Ridge Presbyterian Church, P.O. Box 23820, Fort Lauderdale, Fla. 33307 (seminar and training programs available); Evangelism and Renewal Office, Episcopal Church Center, 815 Second Avenue, New York, N.Y. 10017; MORE (Mission for Outreach, Renewal and Evangelism), P.O. Box 550, Eureka Springs, Ark. 72632; and Churches Alive,

Box 3800, San Bernardino, Calif. 92413 (a total church program for evangelism, discipleship, and growth).  Books on this subject include <u>Sharing</u> <u>God's</u> <u>Love</u> by Rosalind Rinker and Harry Griffith (Zondervan Publishing Co.); <u>You</u> <u>Can</u> <u>Witness</u> <u>with</u> <u>Confidence</u>, by Rosalind Rinker (Zondervan Publishing Co.); <u>The</u> <u>Master</u> <u>Plan</u> <u>of</u> <u>Evangelism</u> by Robert E. Coleman (Fleming H. Revell Co.); <u>How</u> <u>to</u> <u>Give</u> <u>Away</u> <u>Your</u> <u>Faith</u> by Paul E. Little (Inter-Varsity Press); <u>A</u> <u>Coward's</u> <u>Guide</u> <u>to</u> <u>Witnessing</u> by Ken Anderson (Creation House); <u>Evangelism</u> <u>Explosion</u> by James D. Kennedy (Tyndale House); and <u>Your</u> <u>Church</u> <u>Can</u> <u>Grow</u> by Peter Wagner (Regal Books).  See also <u>Lay</u> <u>Witnesses</u>; <u>Renewal</u>.

<u>Exhortation</u> – to incite enthusiasm and action from others, as to exhort someone to a worthy course of action.  Exhortation may take the form of preaching, teaching, or simple encouragement or advice.

<u>Faith Ministries</u> – to launch upon a service or program in which total dependence for its spiritual and financial direction rests upon the Lord.  Examples of faith ministries are healing or miracle services or activities supported by free-will offerings.

<u>Family Counseling</u> – providing instruction and assistance to families to aid in relating to each other more effectively and working through family problems.  Such problem solving may be provided through workshops, seminars, home visitations, or private counseling appointments.  Assistance for those interested in this ministry is available through community organizations dealing with family services.  A helpful book on this subject is <u>The</u> <u>Christian</u> <u>Family</u> by Larry Christenson (Bethany Fellowship, Inc.).

<u>Family Ministries</u> – family groups or "clusters" performing a service for others or for each other as a community project.  Sometimes these joint family ventures include completing projects, preparing a program, or making something together for the church or community.  The term may also encompass family members helping one another spiritually such as in home worship projects, sharing together in spiritual growth programs, or convenanting to pray for each other.

<u>Fellowships</u> – Christ-centered activity designed to draw people close to each other and the Lord.  Ministries may include planning or serving on various committees for fellowship activities or "fellowshiping" with others, as in being friendly to visitors at church or hosting social functions.

<u>Financial Management</u> – planning and directing the wise use of money, as in budget planning, purchasing wisely, or making good investments.  This may include Every Member Canvass work and stewardship programs at the church or offering finan-

cial counseling to those in need of such assistance. For seminars or books on the subject by Raymond B. Knudsen, contact National Consultation on Financial Development, 475 Riverside Drive, Suite 456, New York, N.Y. 10027.

Flower Arranging - creating centerpieces or attractive floral designs for decorating the altar or other areas around the church (as for receptions, head tables at banquets, or special designs like an Easter floral cross or Thanksgiving arrangement). Also, this ministry may include taking such flower arrangements to hospitals, shut-ins, or the bereaved.

Food Preparation - serving as hostess, cook, baker, server, dishwasher, or clean-up crew for church suppers and socials. This may also involve preparing food at home to bring to the church for special functions or to others who may be needy or bereaved.

Furnishing - providing equipment, furniture, or other necessities as needed, as to furnish the church nursery with cribs and toys, to furnish the pantry with foodstuffs, or to furnish the church library with tables or books.

Gardening - raising and tending of flowers, plants, and shrubs as a ministry. Gardeners may give time to the beautification of the church grounds, bring decorative plants from home to be used at church or charitable functions, take plants or flowers to the sick, or sell plants or cuttings as a fund raiser for charity projects.

Giving - a ministry that should involve everyone because everyone has something to contribute - either the offering of money, time, talent, or prayerful concern to some worthy cause. See also Stewardship.

Greeting - the offering of cheerful words of welcome or messages of salutation to others. Although every Christian should be involved in this ministry in an informal way, formal greeters at church are those who have the responsibility for identifying and welcoming new people, getting information about them, and showing them around the church or introducing them to others. See also Calling and Evangelism.

Group Leadership - assuming responsibility for conducting gatherings of people who meet on a regular basis for some specified purpose. Groups may be prayer groups, service groups, worship groups, interest groups, fellowship groups, or training groups (for Bible study, discipleship, self-discovery, or community building). The Bible Reading Fellowship (P.O. Box M, Winter Park, Fla. 32790) publishes for $1 "Guidelines for Group Bible Study," which contains information helpful in almost any type of group leadership, but particularly in leading Bible study programs. To develop group leadership in the congregation, Churches Alive (P.O. Box 3800, San Bernardino, Calif. 92404) is a useful resource. Other books include Lyman Coleman's "Groups in Action" series (Serendipity Books, Word, Inc.) and Encyclopedia For Church Group Leaders edited by Lee J. Gable (Associated Press).

Guilds - an association of people in the church with a common purpose. A guild is another name for a group, and may have the same specified purposes as those mentioned above. Usually, a guild performs some charitable service for others.

Healing - the ministry of promoting wholeness in mind, body, and spirit through various means. Those involved in the healing ministry may attend healing services and assist with such programs, belong to an organization that emphasizes healing, such as the Order of St. Luke, pray with others for healing, act as an intercessor for those in need of wholeness, participate in prayer chains or prayer groups whose emphasis is upon healing, do hospital calling or related ministries to the sick, or offer support (financial or prayer support) for various ministries involved in healing. For additional information, contact the International Order of St. Luke the Physician, Office of the Secretary, 1161 E. Jersey St., Elizabeth, N.J. 07205. Books on the subject include Healing and The Power to Heal by the Reverend Francis MacNutt (Ave Maria Press); The Healing Power of Christ by Emily Gardiner Neal (Hawthorn); and The Healing Light by Agnes Sanford (Macalester Park Publishing Co.).

Health Services - providing assistance in the promotion of good nutrition, soundness of body, mind, and spirit with regard to proper habits and care, and attention to avoidance of things detrimental to well-being and wholeness. Those involved in health services may be youth leaders, counselors, teachers, nurses, first-aid directors, or simply interested laypersons. Such people may provide educational programs or demonstrations as ministries. For information and assistance with volunteer efforts, contact local hospitals, Red Cross Headquarters, or community health-service facilities. See also Volunteers.

Helps - a vast spectrum of ministry services which may be rendered to the church or to other individuals in the name of the Lord. Any vocational or avocational activity or talent can find a place of usefulness in some volunteer effort. One's occupational training, hobby and area of special interest are potential "helps." Helps may also include support services to those who are involved in ministry.

Organizations such as "Fish" and "Meals on Wheels" offer opportunities of involvement for those called to this form of service. Contact a local Human Relations Referral Service, Volunteer Service Bureau or their equivalent for information about such organizations and programs. See also Volunteers.

Home Ministries - counseling or assisting with implementation of Christian concepts of home life or services brought into and performed for the benefit of strengthening the home. See also Family Ministries.

Hospitality - welcoming, entertaining, or offering services to visitors or guests. See also Entertaining.

Hospital Calling - visitation of those confined in hospitals or nursing homes to minister in various ways, such as offering prayers, chatting, or bringing flowers or remembrances. The ministry may also be expanded to include offering to run errands or doing tasks confined individuals cannot do for themselves. See also Healing.

Hot Line - the name given to a special telephone number to call in case of an emergency, a need for prayer, or a request for special services. Often prayer groups or other organizations sponsor such a telephone service and take turns answering requests. For additional information, call local crisis intervention services (such as "We Care" or state department of social services in the state capital) for names of local organizations involved in emergency services.

Housekeeping - attending to the work required in a home, church, or other building in order to keep it neat, clean, orderly, and attractive. There are many housekeeping duties at church or for the needy which provide opportunities for ministries.

Inner Healing - one of several names given to a ministry that involves offering of the past to the Lord for healing of subconscious hurts or hidden sins. Also known by such terms as Healing of Memories, Renewing of the Mind, and Prayer Counseling, this ministry consists of one or more of the following: confession, breaking away from negative bondages, prayers for healing of subconscious wounds, and deliverance. Those interested in this ministry should begin by discussing it with their clergy for specific guidance. Training programs are available through Victorious Ministry through Christ, P.O. Box 1804, Winter Park, Fla. 32790 (Schools of Prayer Counseling). Books associated with this ministry are Trial by Fire (Victorious Ministry through Christ) and Healing Adventure (Logos International) both by Anne S. White.

Training in other inner healing programs is available through Schools of Pastoral Care, P.O. Box 164, Chicopee, Mass. 01014. Books on the subject include The Gift of Inner Healing by Ruth Carter Stapleton (Word Books); Healing by Francis MacNutt (Ave Maria Press); The Healing Gifts of the Spirit by Agnes Sanford (J.B. Lippincott Co.). See also Counseling; Pastoral Care.

Intercessory Prayer - the offering of prayers of petition on behalf of others. Intercession is a priestly ministry in that the intercessor stands in the gap between God and another person or persons to plead for the Lord's favor and blessings upon such individuals. Intercessory ministries may be performed by a single person or with prayer partners or groups who are also involved in praying for the health, guidance, or welfare of others. Resources include the Anglican Fellowship of Prayer, 529 E. King St., Lancaster, Pa. 17602 and Prayer Ministries, The Upper Room, 1908 Grand Ave., Nashville, Tenn. 37203. Books on the subject include Rees Howells - Intercessor by Norman P. Grubb (Christian Literature Crusade, Inc.); A Time for Intercession by Erwin Prange (Creation House, Inc.); Prayer, Living with God by Simon Tugwell (Templegate Publications); Beginning to Pray by Anthony Bloom (Paulist Press); Prayer - Conversing with God by Rosalind Rinker (Zondervan); We Dare to Say Our Father by Louis Evely (Doubleday); The Praying Church by Donald M. Hultstrand (Seabury Press); The Exploding Mystery of Prayer)by Helen S. Shoemaker (Seabury Press); and Creative Prayer by E. Herman (Forward Movement Publications).

Janitorial Duties - caretaking or custodial services for the church, offices, building, or grounds. Included also may be maintenance and repair work. Training is usually available at local churches for specific duties.

Junior Wardens - Vestry members responsible for oversight of the church property and the smooth operation of machinery, the repair of all property or equipment and the responsibility for other temporal functions. See also Church Governing Board.

Kitchen Ministries - assisting with food purchasing and preparation and the maintenance of kitchen equipment and supplies for the church or for charitable ministries. The ministry may also involve organizing of volunteers to bring or prepare food to serve at special functions. See also Food Preparation.

Landscaping - planning and arranging the natural scenery surrounding buildings or grounds for the best aesthetic effects. This ministry may include landscaping the minister's home as well as the church property and providing for care and maintenance of the yard, flowers, trees, plants, and shrubs. See also Gardening.

Lay Readers - nonordained members of a congregation who have been trained and approved to assist in public worship by reading the assigned Scriptures for services and to lead the congregation in appropriate prayers and responses of the liturgy. A lay reader may also be asked to perform additional functions at the discretion of the clergy in charge. Training courses are often offered through denominational church headquarters. Books on the subject include Lay Readers Guide to the Proposed Book of Common Prayer by Clifford W. Atkinson (Morehouse-Barlow); Laity and Liturgy by William S. Pregnall (Seabury Press); "Selected Sermons" (for Lay Readers) published by Seabury Press. See also Preaching.

Lay Witnesses - members of a team which goes into churches for weekend renewal emphasis and who give testimonies of their personal relationship with Jesus Christ in daily life. Such lay witness teams are usually associated with Faith Alive Weekends or Lay Witness Missions or similar organizations. The Cursillo movement is another which offers laypersons an opportunity to witness to their personal faith through an organized program. The term "lay witness" also may refer to anyone who shares the message of God's love with another, either individually or through a group project at church. Contact Faith Alive, P.O. Box 21, York, Pa. 17405 and Faith at Work, 11065 Little Patuxent Parkway, Columbia, Md. 21044. See also Discipleship; Evangelism; Renewal.

Leadership - the role of taking charge of people or responsibilities to direct them toward a desired end. Leadership is needed in all forms of church and community activities from chairing committees, holding offices, and directing functions or events, to assuming responsibility for expanded ministries of leading groups or broad programs of outreach. See also Group Leadership.

Letter Writing - the ministry of conveying messages in written form. This may include sending words of cheer, condolence, encouragement, or prophecy (a message inspired from the Lord). Sending cards or letters may be a regular function of volunteers in the church office or those assigned such a duty in an organization, or they may be unassigned and volunteer ministries of those who feel called to do them.

Librarians - those who take charge of the books, magazines, cassette tapes or other materials in the church library, in homes, or in community service organizations. Such a ministry may be expanded to the selling of books, ordering of

supplies, and assisting as reference persons to those
needing information.  Other library ministries include
bookmobiles or library services to out-of-the-way areas.
Information on church libraries and the lay ministry
of church librarian may be obtained through the Church
and Synagogue Library Association, P.O. Box 1130, Bryn
Mawr, Pa. 19010.

Machine Operators - any people who work with the assistance of some
mechanical apparatus, such as typists, mimeograph machine
operators, address-o-graph workers, computer operators,
or adding machine operators.  Such skills are always
needed in church offices, church organizations, and
community service organizations.

Maintenance - upkeep of property, buildings, or materials.  The maintenance at the church may include repair work, caretaking,
and keeping of supplies.

Management - skillful executive control over other people or matters
of business, as office management or management of a
church team.  See also Administrators.

Media - involvement in communications networks such as radio,
television, newspapers and advertising methods.  The use
of the media in ministry may involve public relations,
publicity for church events, or programming Christian
broadcasts or inspirational journalistic messages.  For
a valuable resource,contact The Religious Public Relations
Council, Inc., 1031 Interchurch Center, 475 Riverside
Drive, N.Y., N.Y. 10027.

Men, Ministries to - Men's club activities at church, men's prayer
breakfasts and meetings, and organizations for men in
the church and community (such as service organizations)
are all examples of ministries especially designed for
and involved with the needs of men.  Contact local chapters of the Full Gospel Business Men's Fellowship, the
local church, or civic organizations.

Miracle Ministries - services and activities in which the supernatural
moving of the Holy Spirit is manifested.  See also
Faith Ministries; Healing.

Missionary Work - activities involved in taking the gospel or Christian
services to other areas.  Such work may include the
financial support of missions to home fields or foreign
countries.  It may also include assistance to underprivileged areas of the community or the actual sending
out of church members to assist with programs, services,
and welfare to the hungry in mind, body, or spirit.  The
work may further involve the starting of new prospective

churches (or "missions") in areas where none exist.  For additional information, contact the Episcopal Church Missionary Community, 1567 E. Elizabeth Street, Pasadena, Calif. 91104 or the Mission Department, Moody Bible Institute, Chicago, Ill.  60610, or local church mission boards.

Money-Raising - the sponsoring of fund drives or projects for the purpose of making a financial profit for some worthy cause.  Money raisers for church projects include rummage sales, bazaars, suppers, talent shows, dramatic productions, auctions, raffles, bingo parties and the like.  See also Stewardship.


Needlecraft - see Sewing.

Nursery Work - attending the babies and small children during church services and special activities.  See also Babysitters.


Organizing - arranging various parts into a meaningful whole, as to organize different committees for a bazaar or to organize various office responsibilities for a smooth business operation.

Outreach - various types of ministries involving interaction with other people or performing services for other people, such as hospital calling, visiting prospects, performing missionary work, or ministering to physical, emotional, or spiritual needs of those both in and outside the church.  Usually, outreach connotes going beyond usual boundaries (home and church) to broaden the circle of concern to include strangers, underprivileged, neglected, etc.  See also Evangelism; Missionary Work; Social Action.


Pastoral Care - assuming spiritual oversight for others.  Although the term usually refers to the duties of the pastor, minister, or priest who has charge of the spiritual welfare of a congregation, a broader definition includes anyone appointed by the clergy to assist in duties of counseling, praying for others, encouraging others spiritually, visiting, and assisting with leadership or spiritual growth development.  Sometimes laypersons will be given responsibility for a certain number of families in the church and will provide for them guidance and assistance whenever necessary. Those interested in such a ministry should contact their pastor.  Because this ministry is so broad, the various aspects of pastoral care should be examined individually by categories.  Books on this subject include Depth Perspectives in Pastoral Work by Thomas Klink (Fortress Press) and Principles and Practices of Pastoral Care by Russel L. Dicks (Fortress

Press). See also <u>Calling</u>; <u>Counselors</u>; <u>Evangelism</u>; <u>Group Leadership</u>; <u>Hospital Calling</u>; <u>Inner Healing</u>; <u>Spiritual Direction</u>; <u>Teaching</u>.

<u>Personnel Work</u> - duties assigned to people involved in training, directing, hiring, or overseeing the work of others engaged in some job or service. Such work may become the responsibility of a paid business manager with staff in larger churches, or the church secretary or volunteers in smaller congregations.

<u>Phoning</u> - making telephone calls as a ministry, as to conduct a prayer chain, to call volunteers to assist with charitable work, to conduct church business over the phone, to assist with telephone surveys, and the like.

<u>Photography</u> - the taking of pictures or slides as a ministry, as to photograph special events for a church scrapbook, directory, or display (such as a pictorial panorama of the church's history) or a slide show of Vacation Bible School, retreats, etc.

<u>Playing Instruments</u> - performing musically with guitars, pianos, organs, or other musical instruments for worship instruction, or entertainment, as in playing for Sunday school, folk masses, special programs, talent shows, etc.

<u>Planning</u> - the responsibility for setting goals and outlining procedures to attain these goals, as the planning of a fund-raising function or the planning of a Christian education program.

<u>Prayer Ministries</u> - work among any one of many involvements in offering of intercessions, petitions, praises, thanksgivings, confessions, or meditative listening exercises, etc. Ministries of prayer may include such things as prayer groups; prayer chains; preparing of prayer lists; serving as an intercessor, prayer leader, or Christian counselor; and making oneself available as a prayer channel in any capacity to which one may be called. Resources include Helen Shoemaker's book, <u>Schools of Prayer for Leaders and Learners</u>, available through The Anglican Fellowship of Prayer, 529 E. King Street, Lancaster, Pa. 17602. See also <u>Inner Healing</u>; <u>Intercessory Prayer</u>.

<u>Preaching</u> - to deliver sermons or homilies to a congregation or audience. Generally, preaching is the responsibility of the clergy, evangelist, or full-time minister, but volunteer laypersons may find opportunities to become involved in bringing the gospel message or a Bible teaching sermon at such places as a funeral (eulogizing the deceased), a prayer group, a prison or other institution, a lay ministry retreat or conference, a training group, or other special program. Contact local clergy for training helps or write to the nearest seminary for further information.

Printing -     the art of typography to publish or duplicate written ma-
               terials, as in printing the church bulletin, church direc-
               tories, annual reports, educational booklets, or other com-
               munications pamphlets, or materials. See also Publicity.

Prison Ministries - work among those confined to correctional institu-
               tions after committing a crime - as witnessing teams, coun-
               selors, or those who take inspirational programs or enter-
               taining socials to prisons, jails or detention halls for
               youth.  Contact local church headquarters for information
               about denominational programs of this kind of outreach or
               contact local institutions for information on services needed.

Prophet -      one who speaks God's messages.  Prophecy may include bringing
               forth supernatural revelations of the Holy Spirit or speak-
               ing a word of Scripture - any word from the Lord via a human
               being. Although prophecy sometimes includes predictions of
               coming events, the broader definition includes not only
               "foretelling" but also "forth-telling."  Bob Mumford's Take
               Another Look at Guidance and its study guide, Practical Prin-
               ciples of Guidance and accompanying  cassette tapes provide
               teaching on listening and proclaiming messages from divine
               revelations.  For information on this series and other in-
               structional programs, write Christian Growth Ministries,
               P.O. Box 22888, Fort Lauderdale, Fla. 33315. Another book on
               the subject is Anyone Can Prophesy by Robert B. Hall
               (Seabury Press).

Public Speaking - giving speeches or addresses before audiences, as to
               speak on behalf of the church or some Christian program either
               before a live audience or over the media.  Public speaking skills
               are needed by teachers and group leaders of all kinds and can be
               obtained through educational institutions in local communities.

Publicity -    putting before the public any newsworthy information for dis-
               semination, as to publicize a fund-raising event, speaker, or
               special program. Denominational church headquarters should be
               able to furnish information as to usual methods of disseminating
               publicity information effectively. See also Bulletin Preparation.

Public Relations - maintaining sound and productive relationships between
               the church (clergy or special organizations) and the communi-
               ty at large. Such work may involve meetings among different
               groups, journalistic publications to keep the public informed,
               or engaging in activities which promote well-being and mutual
               acceptance. A valuable resource is the 64-page Religious Pub-
               lic Relations Handbook (for local congregations of all
               faiths), published by Religious Public Relations Council, Inc.,
               1031 Interchurch Center, 475 Riverside, N.Y., N.Y. 10027.
               See also Bulletin Preparation.

Quality Control - work to maintain standards of production or efficiency,
               as to determine minimum requirements for office work, educa-
               tional standards, or church programs.  Good quality control
               includes evaluation and follow-up to correct that which
               falls below the quality standards.

Reading -        the ministry of relating information from printed
                 matter vocally to another, as one who reads to the
                 elderly, blind, or incapacitated, or those who peruse
                 mail or literature and give summations to others (as
                 assisting the clergy by reviewing large volumes of
                 reading material). This ministry may also include
                 giving book reviews, as reviewing an inspirational book
                 at a gathering or as a teaching ministry for youth or
                 adults. Local public libraries sometimes give training
                 in book reviewing.

Recreation -     programs or activities to promote wholesome, Christian
                 activities which will build up, rather than tear down,
                 the mind, body, and/or spirit. Recreation programs may
                 include church socials, family night gatherings, fellow-
                 ship activities, team sports, suppers, coffeehouses, and
                 the like. Leadership is needed in various aspects of re-
                 creation from organizing games to preparing refreshments
                 to directing total programs. Some denominations, such
                 as the Southern Baptists, have Recreation Departments at
                 church headquarters which can furnish information on this
                 ministry. See also Coffeehouses and Youth Ministries.

Renewal -        the term given to several aspects of a movement of the
                 Holy Spirit among church people, calling them to a re-
                 dedication of themselves to the Lord and a renewed spiri-
                 tual experience which manifests itself in many forms (in-
                 cluding witnessing, assuming lay ministries or leader-
                 ship roles, and personal involvement in spiritual things
                 beyond Sunday church attendance). Many services and
                 ministries are the resulting outgrowth of involvement in
                 such programs of renewal: participation in witness teams,
                 conducting renewal programs in churches, involvement in
                 prayer groups, evangelistic work, serving on renewal
                 committees, etc. Resources and training helps are available
                 through such organizations as the following: Institute of
                 Church Renewal, 1610 La Vista Rd., N.E., Atlanta, Ga. 30329;
                 Episcopal Charismatic Fellowship, 769 Wye Rd., Bath, Ohio
                 44210; Episcopal Center for Evangelism, 127 N.W. 7, Okla-
                 homa City, Okla. 73102; Invitation to Live Crusades, 7716
                 Yonge St., Ont., Canada L4JI W2; and Marriage Fulfillment
                 Episcopal Expression, 240 First Ave., Malvern, Pa. 19353.
                 Additional resources and addresses are available under
                 the following listings: Discipleship; Evangelism; Lay
                 Witness; and Healing.

Repairing -      restoring that which has been damaged or broken, as to
                 repair the church roof or office machinery or kitchen
                 equipment.

Research -       investigation or experimentation in order to reach con-
                 clusions, as to research better methods of church school
                 organization, or to research a financial problem for the
                 church board. Research may include critical reading, in-

terviewing, or empirical study. Local public libraries
will usually assist with research projects.

Retreat Ministries - any one of a number of services needed in the
conducting of a program in which participants go away
for a period of time together for study, worship, and
recreation. Leadership is needed in organizing such programs: acting as leaders, counselors, or teachers, and
serving on such committees as food or transportation.
Church headquarters should provide additional information.
See also Youth Ministries.

Scripture Ministries - the sharing or imparting of Bible messages to
others. The ministry of the Word may include lay reading
functions, teaching, Bible study or Sunday school classes,
preaching, prophecy, or sharing (in written or oral form)
appropriate verses with those who are in need of the comfort or edification of the Scriptures.

Secretarial Work - any one of a number of stenographic and office functions needed for the church office or for church or charitable organizations, such as typing, taking of minutes,
taking dictation, letter writing, filing, answering the
telephone, recording of messages, making of reports, etc.
Volunteers are usually needed to assist with these functions in the church office.

Serving - performing the ministry of a servant of the Lord or of
others. This term is broad enough to encompass all forms
of ministry from volunteering to serve on a committee to
offering a cup of cool water to one who is thirsty. Jesus
said all his followers should become involved in the role
of servant (the ministry of "serving"). See also Helps;
Volunteers.

Sewing - any one of a number of needlecraft activities to prepare
garments, decorations, or useful articles. Sewing circles
or classes may be conducted for teaching needlecrafts,
making vestments or choir robes, or preparing decorative
or useful articles for the church or the needy.

Sharing - the giving of oneself and one's possessions, as the sharing
of a testimony, the sharing of one's talents, the sharing
of the gospel message, or the sharing of food, money,
possessions, or love. See also Evangelism; Helps.

Shut-ins, Ministry to - the offering of loving service to those confined at home or those who are bedridden. Such ministries
may include visiting; sending cards, letters, food, or
gifts; or doing additional services or ministrations of
love. Contact local welfare office, nursing homes, or
community service organizations for suggested ministries.

See also <u>Volunteers</u> or write to the state department of
social services (Health and Rehabilitative Services) in
the state capital for further information.

Singing -   vocal music used in the service of the Lord, as to sing
in the choir, to provide special music for a worship service or program, to lead others in offering songs of
praise, or to use singing to teach children or adults.
Singing talents may be used in worship, instruction (Sunday
school, Vacation Bible School, etc.), entertainment (talent
programs, recreation nights, etc.), or service (taking
musical programs to shut-ins, institutions, or the needy).

<u>Social Action</u> - meeting needs by becoming engaged in informed action
to alleviate social ills or to espouse the cause of the
impoverished and disadvantaged.  This can involve anything from political action (supporting candidates for
office or educational programs) to engaging in nonviolent
demonstrations in support of a cause for social justice.
To become informed of issues, contact various organizations with which there may be individual interest.  One
such organization is the National IMPACT Network, 110
Maryland Ave., N.E., Washington, D.C. 20002.

<u>Social Work</u> - ministries to promote welfare in areas of the under-
privileged, in minority groups, or in areas of undereduca-
tion.  Social work may include providing for needs, educating, or raising the level of living standards in and
among the poor or those discriminated against.  Contact
local welfare agencies for suggested social ministries.

<u>Spiritual Direction</u> - the responsibility of guiding another in dis-
covering a spiritual rule of life and living according to
that rule.  It includes Christian growth and development
along a predetermined plan of action on an ongoing basis,
and may include a plan for various techniques of meditation, prayer, Bible study, Christian disciplines, church
participation, and service.  Resources include The Center
for Spirituality, General Theological Seminary, 175 Ninth
Ave., New York, N.Y. 10011.  Books on the subject include
<u>Western</u> <u>Mysticism</u> by C. Butler (Constable Publishers, Lon-
don); <u>The</u> <u>Prayers</u> <u>of</u> <u>Jesus</u> by C. Jermias (Allenson); <u>The</u>
<u>Living</u> <u>Reminder</u> by Henri J. M. Nouwen (Seabury Press);
and books by Evelyn Underhill, Thomas Merton, Louis Evely,
Karl Rahner, Douglas Steere, and Martin Thornton.  See
also <u>Discipleship</u>.

Sports -   games or diversions, usually those engaged in the out-of-
doors.  Individual sports such as fishing, swimming, golf,
etc., and team sports such as baseball, football, basketball,
tennis, etc., can all be worked into a recreational program of
the church or community. Such programs require Christian
leadership and example for optimum results. Christians
who volunteer to coach a Little League or to sponsor a

church team or community recreation program can use such opportunities as service and ministry if they are prayerfully performed.

Stewardship - faithful management of accounts or responsibilities. Stewardship includes fulfilling obligations to provide responsible investments of that which has been committed to an individual, as to be a good steward of one's money by tithing, of one's talents by using them in the Lord's service, or of one's time by establishing priorities for balanced living (enough time for work, play, spiritual devotion, rest, education, and ministry to others). It also may include helping others to establish such involvement in stewardship. Books on the subject include Stewardship: Myth and Methods by John MacNaughton (Seabury Press); Jesus, Dollars and Sense edited by Oscar C. Carr, Jr. (Seabury Press); Beyond Pledging by C. Supin (Seabury Press); and "A Guide for Visitors" by W. Ebert Hobbs, Development Office, Episcopal Church Center, 815 Second Ave., New York, N.Y. 10017.  See also Financial Management.

Sunday School Workers - those involved in the church program of Christian education as Sunday school teachers, adult educators, helpers, arts and crafts leaders, nursery workers, musicians, and coordinators for programs of Bible study and spiritual growth. Church denominational headquarters and publishers of Sunday school curriculum materials will have suggested helps for those involved in Sunday school work. See also Bible Teachers; Christian Education.

Support Services - any one of a number of assisting activities which, while not in the mainstream of ministry, uphold such ministry in useful, backup ways.  Examples include praying for others who minister, keeping records for those who do visitations or other services, taping and distributing messages of those who teach, or giving aid (financial or otherwise) to the clergy or others who minister.

Symbolism - several ministries mentioned can involve the use of Christian symbolism, including arts and crafts, banner-making, Christian education, and teaching. Some books on symbolism are Saints, Signs and Symbols by Ellwood Post (Morehouse-Barlow); Symbols of Church Seasons and Days by John Bradner (Morehouse-Barlow) and The Symbolism of the Biblical World by Othmar Keel (Seabury Press).

Tape and Cassette Ministries - activities involved in recording on audio tape special speakers, musicians, or programs. A lending library of tapes and the actual mechanical activities of recording provide opportunity for various ministries of this kind.  Some churches or homes maintain tape lending libraries as a community service. One such library service is Tongues of Fire Tape Ministry, 6327 Jennings Rd., Orlando, Fla.  32808.

Task Groups - special committees set apart to concentrate on a particular aspect of ministry, to promote such ministry, and
to engage in activities which will educate and involve
the church or community in such ministry.  It may be a
task group for Christian education, stewardship, spiritual development, evangelism, prison ministry, senior
church people, etc.  Such groups may distribute educational materials or promote workshops to train people in aspects of ministry.  Contact denominational church headquarters for names of task groups that already exist or
to get recommendations for starting a group where a need
is apparent.

Teaching - the art of instructing or training others.  Teaching opportunities include both spiritual aspects (as in teaching
a Bible class) and temporal aspects (as in teaching cooking or auto mechanics).  Additional information on improving teaching skills may be obtained from local educational
institutions or from resources listed under Bible Teachers
and Christian Education.

Teenagers, Ministries to - involvement with youth between twelve and
seventeen in various church and community functions.
Leadership may include conducting church organizations
for youth, leading rap sessions, teaching, leading fellowship or recreational programs, leading retreats, conducting youth prayer-and-share groups, or counseling.
For a listing of resources, see Campus Ministries; Children's Ministries; Youth Ministries.

Training - involvement in educational programs, either as a trainer
or a trainee.  Training groups include Bible studies,
discipleship or growth groups, self-discovery or personal development groups, and community-building groups.
Training programs may be conducted as a regular part of
ongoing church programs or as special events, such as
workshops or seminars.  See also Group Leadership;
Teaching.

Treasurer - one responsible for collecting monies and disbursements,
as the church treasurer or the treasurer of a guild or
other organization.  Also, often the one responsible for
preparing a budget and signing checks.  Professional bookkeepers can be of assistance in setting up financial
books correctly, and those well versed in parliamentary
procedure can offer suggestions for performing responsibilities of treasurer if the local church or organization
does not have standard procedures outlined for this office.  See also Financial Management; Stewardship.

Ushering - those responsible for greeting people as they enter the
church, for assisting them to their seats, for providing
them with the order-of-service bulletins, for attending
295

to the housekeeping functions for the comfort and convenience of the congregation, and for assisting with
other functions of the worship service (collecting offerings, assisting with a head-count tally, etc.). Usually,
there is a head usher responsible for training and sched-
uling ushers to be on duty for various services or else
the clergy provide training for this ministry.

Vestry -      see Church Governing Board.

Visitation -  the process of going into the homes of the congregation;
              calling upon visitors, prospects, or lapsed members; or
              extending the ministry of the church into the homes of
              the surrounding community. This personalized form of
              ministry may be for the purpose of evangelism, crisis
              comfort, parish calling, or involvement of the ones visi-
              ted in some aspect of church life (attendance, steward-
              ship, assistance with a program or project, etc.). For
              resources, see also Calling; Evangelism.

Volunteers -  people who respond willingly to a need without being con-
              strained; anyone who acts intentionally from free will to
              do a work or service. Volunteers are needed in every as-
              pect of church and community work. Also needed are lead-
              ers to organize and assign volunteers to various minis-
              tries and to train them for service. Information on vol-
              unteer services may be obtained from the Association of
              Volunteer Bureaus, Inc., 801 N. Fairfax St., Alexandria,
              Va. 22314 (directories available listing local Volunteer
              Action Centers); National Center for Voluntary Action,
              1214 16th St., N.W., Washington, D.C. 20036; and state
              departments of social services in the state capital (in-
              formation available on health and rehabilitative services
              and ACTION - the organization which sponsors such groups
              as VISTA, the Peace Corps, Senior Companion Program, Fos-
              ter Grandparents, and Retired Senior Volunteer Program).
              A book on the subject is Volunteer Training and Develop-
              ment by Anne K. Stenzel and Helen M. Feeney (Seabury
              Press). Contact also Volunteer Corps, Episcopal Church
              Center, 815 2nd Ave., New York, N.Y. 10017. See also
              Helps.

Witnessing -  the sharing of the love of God with others through words,
              deeds, or attitudes. Direct witnessing involves con-
              fronting someone about his or her relationship to Jesus
              Christ. Indirect witnessing includes such ministries as
              distributing literature, taking people to church or pray-
              er groups, introducing others to people involved in evan-
              gelism, or living before others in such a way as to be a
              silent witness to the loving concern of the Lord. For
              resources, see also Evangelism; Lay Witness; Social Ac-
              tion.

296

Women's Organizations and Ministries - various groups composed of
          women in the church or community, such as guilds or mis-
          sionary organizations or community service groups. Such
          groups promote opportunities for Christian growth or
          service. Contact local churches or community service or-
          ganizations for specific information. See also Volun-
          teers.

Worship -     reverence, devotion, praise, and acts of adoration in-
          volved in honoring the Lord. Ministries of worship in-
          clude attending and participating in both regular Sunday
          morning services and special services, receiving Commu-
          nion, participating in small group worship experiences,
          and keeping personal disciplines (family and private
          devotions, personal Bible study, prayer, reading of de-
          votional books, etc.). Ministries may include assisting
          others in worshiping more fully - serving on the church
          worship committee, leading a worship service, and assist-
          ing in ways that enhance and foster worship experiences
          for oneself and others.

Youth Ministries - any one of several activities involving one in
          leading or serving children and teenagers. Youth Club
          activities, family night programs, leading youth organi-
          zations, or starting a youth prayer group are all pos-
          sible aspects of a broad program which should be devel-
          oped for helping youth become more involved in personal
          growth (mind, body, and spirit) through worship, educa-
          tion, service, and wholesome recreation. Consult denom-
          inational headquarters for information about special
          youth ministries and training opportunities. Resources
          include Youth Club, 700 Dewberry Rd., Monroeville, Pa.
          15146; Youth Specialties (Idea Books and Workshops),
          861 6th Ave., Suite 411, San Diego, Calif. 92101;
          Young Life Campaign, 720 W. Monument St., Colorado
          Springs, Colo. 80901; Teen Challenge Center and Teenage
          Evangelism, Inc., 444 Clinton Ave., Brooklyn, N.Y. 11238;
          and Elizabeth L. Crawford, Youth and College Ministries
          Coordinator, 815 Second Ave., New York, N.Y. 10017 (Epis-
          copal). Books and printed resources available are Making
          Youth Programs Go by Terry Powel (Victor Books); Organ-
          izing for Youth Ministry by Charles Courtoy and Clifford
          E. Kolb, Jr., Service Dept., United Methodist Church,
          P. O. Box 871, Nashville, Tenn. 37202; Program Planners
          Manual by John Forliti (Ave Maria Press); Successful Bibli-
          cal Youth Work by Elmer L. Townes (Impact Books); Youth
          Ministry with Senior Highs by Sheila Campbell (Service
          Dept., United Methodist Church); Youth Ministry Resources
          by Division of the Local Church (United Methodist Church);
          Youth Ministry Subscription Service edited by Lowell Ander-
          son, (Lutheran Church in America, Philadelphia, Pa.); Youth
          Ministry Training Kit by Robert R. Hansel (Seabury Press);
          Youth Ministry Workbook by Kenneth Mitchell (Board of Edu-
          cation of United Methodist Church); Parish Youth Ministry

by Bill and Patty Coleman (Twenty-Third Publications);
<u>Youth Ministry: Sunday, Monday and Everyday</u> by John
Carroll and Keith Ignatius (Judson Press); <u>The Exuberant
Years: A Guide for Junior High Leaders</u> by Ginny Ward
Holderness (John Knox Press); <u>Creative Youth Leadership</u>
by Janice M. Corbett (Judson Press); and <u>Eight Special
Studies for Senior Highs</u> by Lois Kilgore (National
Teacher Education Project, Scottsdale, Ariz.). See also
<u>Bible Teacher; Children's Ministries; Christian Educa-
tion.</u>

## Additional Resources for Lay Ministry

Further information on the broad subject of lay ministry is
available by contacting The National Institute for Lay Training,
815 Second Ave., New York, N.Y. 10017; The Alban Institute, Inc.,
Mount St. Alban, Washington, D.C. 20016; and Coordinator for Lay
Ministries, Episcopal Church Center, 815 Second Ave., New York, N.Y.
10017. Books and similar resources on lay ministry include <u>Mutual
Ministry</u> and <u>More Than Wanderers</u>, both by James C. Fenhagen (Seabury
Press); "The 99 Percenter" packet distributed twice yearly by the Co-
ordinator for Lay Ministries, Episcopal Church Center, 815 Second
Ave., New York, N.Y. 10017; and the following which are available
through the Alban Institute, Inc. (Mount St. Albans, Washington,
D.C. 20016): "Action Information on Lay Ministry"; "Lay Ministry:
A Tool Kit"; "Christian Pilgrimage";"Learning to Share the Ministry;
and <u>Stress, Power</u>, and <u>Ministry.</u>


<u>NOTE FROM THE AUTHOR</u>: Unless accompanied by evaluative wording,
books and resources included in the alphabetical listings of this chapter may not have been read nor are they necessarily endorsed. Numerous
resources have come as recommendations from reliable sources other than
the author's personal knowledge.